Learning Trajectories, Innovation and Identity for Professional Development

Innovation and Change in Professional Education

VOLUME 7

SCOPE OF THE SERIES

The primary aim of this book series is to provide a platform for exchanging experiences and knowledge about educational innovation and change in professional education and post-secondary education (engineering, law, medicine, management, health sciences, etc.). The series provides an opportunity to publish reviews, issues of general significance to theory development and research in professional education, and critical analysis of professional practice to the enhancement of educational innovation in the professions.

The series promotes publications that deal with pedagogical issues that arise in the context of innovation and change of professional education. It publishes work from leading practitioners in the field, and cutting edge researchers. Each volume is dedicated to a specific theme in professional education, providing a convenient resource of publications dedicated to further development of professional education.

For further volumes:
http://www.springer.com/series/6087

Anne Mc Kee · Michael Eraut
Editors

Learning Trajectories, Innovation and Identity for Professional Development

Springer

Editors
Dr. Anne Mc Kee
Anglia Ruskin University
Faculty of Education
Chelmsford Campus
Bishops Hall Lane
CM1 1SQ Chelmsford
United Kingdom
anne.mckee@anglia.ac.uk

Prof. Michael Eraut
Sussex University
Sussex School of Education
Sussex House
BN1 9RH Brighton
United Kingdom
m.eraut@sussex.ac.uk

ISBN 978-94-007-3725-9 ISBN 978-94-007-1724-4 (eBook)
DOI 10.1007/978-94-007-1724-4
Springer Dordrecht Heidelberg London New York

Printed on acid-free paper

Springer is part of Springer Science+Business Media (www.springer.com)

Preface

Education in the professions includes deep knowing and reflective practice that are gradually integrated within learning contexts—those settings where formal and informal, individual and collaborative learning visibly occur. Similarly, educational researchers learn together in their professional associations. This book is an example. It is an outcome of a day-long symposium that I convened in April 2006 at the American Educational Research Association's annual meeting, with formal support from its executive director, Felice Levine. As head of AERA's division, *Education in the Professions*, I invited division members to envision a range of themes and relevant studies by authors within and outside the division. Each of the four book concepts was formally presented to the larger membership with requests for member involvement.

Subsequently, book editors and authors—including Anne Mc Kee and Michael Eraut, who are members of the British Educational Research Association as well as AERA—opened these themes and contributions to rigorous critique. Symposium proposals were blind-reviewed in the division's exemplary program review process. Colleagues from within and outside the division who attended the symposia provided extensive constructive feedback. This volume will be joined by *Extraordinary Learning in the Workplace*, edited by Janet Hafler (2011).

In this book, Mc Kee and Eraut argue that individual and collaborative learning need to be joined by *organizational learning* for optimal institutional growth. For me, this implies continual cycles of transformative learning by administrators, faculty, and academic staff at each level of departmental and institutional practice. As these professionals attend to conceptual frameworks, create opportunities for deep reflection, engage in rigorous self-assessment, and project actions and consequences, they are likely to create innovations that result in organizational improvement. Organizational learning is a requirement when members of professions and their associations intend to meet future demands for expertise, leadership, and service.

The scholars in this book are studying how professionals reason, practice, reflect, and develop in complex settings. They collaborate not only with students or individual professionals but also with departments and institutions where seasoned professionals work. In turn, mature professionals are responding by opening what, how, when, and where they learn by creating sustained partnerships with the field of education research.

Consider, in chapter sequence, the *range of professions* that have collaborated with the authors. They include early-career and mid-career engineers, nurses, and accountants; secondary care specialists and primary care providers; teams of physicians, nurses, pharmacists, and risk-managers; military company commanders; managers and their employees; dentistry students and practitioners, practitioners sanctioned by professional bodies, and those identified by peers as exemplars; novice and expert physicians; community nurses and advanced nurse practitioners; students transitioning from law and psychology programs to practicing professionals; community surgeons from established practices and their industry providers; and professors and teachers in higher education who serve in a range of roles, including management of centers.

The authors represented here have conducted studies in a wide *range of authentic contexts* of professional practice in three states in the United States, across the UK, in Brazil, and in Iraq, the Netherlands, and Norway. For example, one study involved community health professionals in 21 partner clinics across health departments, prisons, community health, and rural environments with a widely diverse patient population. Another study included education professionals across 81 government-initiated centers of learning and teaching across disciplines that served a broad range of faculty/staff and their students. Still another study involved military commanders who were engaging in war with enemies and peace-keeping with civilians, sometimes during the same day.

These inquiries in authentic settings have been equally matched by the authors' focus on *life span professional development.* Studies include professional school students who made the transition to practitioners. Mid-career professionals, who were successful in the eyes of their peers, were studied alongside others who were sanctioned by peers. Still others were judged by their peers as moral exemplars, often toward the end of their formal professional contributions. In these cases, educators as researchers are expected both to affect professional development and to study it at the same time.

Such collaborative inquiries can lead to understanding learning in diverse ways across the disciplines and institutions in which professionals work, and across the professional life span. Along with new insight, innovation is an outcome of inquiry. Together, these studies set the stage for mutual learning that can advance both schooling and practice because each partner is primed for *creating innovations in theory, research, practice, or policy.*

Several authors strive toward a substantive and meaningful effort to better unite theory, research, practice, and policy in a continual search for innovation at multiple levels in education and work. Often, these researchers deal with contradictions inherent in conflicting identities (e.g., researcher as critic on the one hand and educator as advocate on the other); complex roles (e.g., researcher grounded in a discipline yet astute in issues that cross professions); and multiple methods (e.g., survey and interview, grounded ethnography, and theory-based observation).

These scholars often experience a need to include their participants' policy perspectives as well, which adds to the complexity of conducting studies in a changing organization. Study teams might also need to engage the contradictions that may arise when university or scientific values are in conflict with the purposes and values of other organizations. For example, developing and then honoring appropriate informed consent at the individual, department, and institutional levels are essential, but become awkward when a researcher is expected to be a participating team member as well as a research manager.

Readers will appreciate the complications that accrue when study teams seek to connect theory and research with practice and policy as a condition for conducting educational research in an organization. Often, a study team may be initiating and responding to emerging topics with innovations in questions and methods. Or a study team may be developing organizational structures not only to collect data in authentic settings, but also to enhance student and/or professional learning. In this case, educational researchers may intentionally partner with educators to create innovative curricular structures so they can study the effects of innovative teaching practices together.

In these studies, educational researchers often cross boundaries. For example, a professional who meets rigorous criteria in one discipline may also benefit individuals and organizations in another discipline. Thus, professional development for researchers is not only about what an educational researcher needs to know in order to make innovative contributions. Researchers also need to become members of interdisciplinary groups who are gifted at dealing with the complexity of studies and settings that cross professions, but do not overstep their expertise or role.

How an educational researcher deals responsibly with such critical issues depends in part on strengthening one's own *identity* and *role*—without presuming that of others. This makes some chapters in this volume a guide for the kinds of educational research now practiced in education in the professions. These scholars show research integrity—the search for meaning and value through ethical inquiry in a discipline, supported by peer review.

This somewhat ideal picture of complex, multidimensional, scholarly practice is more nearly met by the most experienced authors in this book who document a program of research that has taken years of iterative studies. These authors articulate how they have discovered the questions, developed the theory and method, and made meaning of findings for diverse audiences and organizations. Some authors have worked across professions—others within a single profession—each with increasing depth, clarity, and interconnection at each level of professional expertise.

Other authors have studied a broad set of contexts where theory–research–practice–policy interconnections are most visible because they are situated in policy and practice communities. As a result, their findings lead to innovative practices that contribute to responsible and responsive educational policy. In the process, scholars and professionals assist each other in creating learning organizations in both universities and other institutions where both scholars and professionals practice.

For a decade or more, members of the American Educational Research Association's division, *Education in the Professions,* have committed their time and energy to extend the range of disciplines and professions that contribute to the literature in education research and inquiry.

As scholars in the professions, the authors of this book continue in this tradition, and also set new standards for educational research. They cross boundaries across disciplines and professions in a continual search for diverse sources of ideas, evidence, and contexts of practice. They take up the most difficult problems in professional work and do not shy away from the complexity of situations by using simpler and safer methods.

In this way, the authors join educational research in the professions as a field of inquiry. As the authors explain an aim of the book is to share knowledge and practice across disciplines, particularly how methodologies are deployed within and across professional groups and the institutions in which they work. These authors clearly demonstrate that breadth and depth of methods are the *de rigueur* of educational research in the professions and their institutions. They illustrate the value of the division's efforts to broaden its reach across the professions, a necessary condition for future interdisciplinary work.

This integrative effort toward coherence within the diversity of professions and the wide range of institutions where they contribute is noteworthy. Together, the editors and authors of this book set high expectations for the continuing contributions of educational researchers. I trust that readers will notice what I did: that education research is itself becoming a well-respected profession.

Alverno College
February 10, 2011

Marcia Mentkowski

Contents

The Editors and Contributors

Michael Eraut did a Doctorate in Chemistry from Cambridge, and then spent two years in Chicago studying and developing new teaching methods in the University of Illinois. He returned to the University of Sussex, where he developed new master's programs for teachers in FE and HE, and worked with several departments on new teaching curricula and learning methods. He became Professor of Education at the University of Sussex in 1986. For the past 20 years, his work has been focused on professional education, where his strong interest in the tacit dimension of professional practice and the nature of practical knowledge led him to explore the discourses of knowledge, competence, and expertise across a range of professions. These ideas were first brought together in his 1994 book, *Developing Professional Knowledge and Competence*, and have now been extended by further research and theoretical work. He was the founder editor of Blackwell's international journal, *Learning in Health and Social Care*, from 2002 to 2006.

He has developed master's programs in Higher Education, Public Sector Management, and Management of Change, and supervised 50 doctoral students. He has led several research projects focused on learning in a wide range of workplace settings: students on placements, early-career learning, mid-career learning, and management learning. These produced considerable evidence about the preponderance of informal learning in the workplace and the factors affecting it. Michael's theoretical work has also addressed the problem of finding ways of representing the complexity of professional practices through developing an epistemology of practice to assist our understanding of practical knowledge, rethink the process of transfer, and complement the formalized propositional knowledge that dominates the discourse of universities.

Anne Mc Kee, after an honors degree in history and experience teaching school, received her master's degree and PhD in applied research and education from the University of East Anglia with a specialty in primary health care. Currently, she is a Principal Lecturer in Anglia Ruskin University. Dr. Mc Kee has held administrative, research, teaching, and educational advisory positions at the Open University, Milton Keynes; London University; King's College London; and University of East Anglia.

The recipient of several grant awards, Anne Mc Kee researches the complexities of learning and learning contexts in the professions, particularly the health sciences and education, at the local, national, and international levels. She examines both formal and workplace learning, creates curricula for on-site professional development, and evaluates curricular outcomes. Dr. Mc Kee consults regularly with individuals and groups in applied research within and across the disciplines and professions. She facilitates participants' creation of reflective and investigative approaches in a workplace challenged by changing professional roles and organizational structures that must be responsive to intensifying public scrutiny.

Mc Kee studies interrelationships among policy, research, and practice, and draws implications for higher education in the professions, professional bodies, and diverse practitioners. Recent publications include *Making Evaluation Democratic in a Climate of Control* (2002, with Robert Stake), *Linking Research and Teaching: Evidence Based Practice in Health Sciences* (2002), and *Conversations Within Conversations: An Ethnographic Approach to Working Across Disciplines* (2004, with R. Pinder). She has served on committees for the American Educational Research Association's Education in the Professions and has been an external examiner for medical education at Cambridge University. Currently, she chairs a national network on pedagogic learning and teaching and serves on the European Evaluation Society's Board of Directors. In addition to this volume, Dr. Mc Kee has been an editor and author for the Radcliffe Medical Press and the journal *Learning in Health and Social Care.*

About the Contributors

Nate Allen, PhD George Washington University, is a LTC in the U.S. Army and is currently on faculty at National Defense University's Information Resources Management College. Prior to joining the National Defense University, Nate was a professor at the United States Military Academy at West Point, where he taught leadership and most recently served as the director of the U.S. Army's Center for the Advancement of Leader Development and Organizational Learning. He is co-founder of CompanyCommand.army.mil and PlatoonLeader.army.mil (distributed communities of practice for U.S. Army company commanders and platoon leaders). As a result of his experiences, he co-authored two books, *Taking the Guidon: A Practical Guide to Leadership at the Company Level* and *Company Command: Unleashing the Power of the Army Profession*, focused around the development of distributed communities of practice. And, as representatives of the Company Command and Platoon Leader founding team, Nate and project co-founder, Tony Burgess, were recognized among *Fast Company Magazine*'s Top 50 Innovators Internationally in 2002 for their work in connecting leaders laterally across the Army in an ongoing conversation about lessons learned and exceptional leadership. Nate has published and presented about this experience in numerous venues.

Jan Armstrong, a first-generation college student, grew up in Edina, Minnesota, and completed her undergraduate degree at the University of California, Berkeley. She earned her doctorate at the University of Minnesota, specializing in the anthropology of education and educational foundations. Her dissertation research investigated Jamaican children's perspectives on West Indian life in the past, present, and anticipated future, comparing the views of children growing up in communities that had varying degrees of contact with the tourism industry. In 1990, she joined the faculty of the College of Education at the University of New Mexico. Her current research examines how social and psychological theories can inform our understanding of human life span development, offering new ways to conceptualize our experiences at work, school, and home. Jan is especially interested in the interpretive study of professional groups as cultural communities, professional education, and visual research, and the role of the university and its faculty as mediators of societal change.

Muriel J. Bebeau, PhD, is Professor, School of Dentistry; Affiliate Faculty in the Center for Bioethics; and Director Emerita of the Center for the Study of Ethical Development at the University of Minnesota. Bebeau pioneered the evidence-based teaching of ethics in dentistry. Her numerous research and publication awards include: Honorary Fellowship in the American College of Dentists, the Lifetime Achievement award for contributions to the psychology of morality from the International Association for Moral Education; an Outstanding Book Award for contributions to moral theory described in *Postconventional Moral Thinking: A Neo-Kohlbergian Approach* (Rest, Narvaez, Bebeau, & Thoma, 1999) from the American Educational Research Association; and a Civilian Meritorious Service Award for her curriculum work on character and leadership development while a Visiting Scholar at the United States Military Academy. The long-term involvement of Minnesota dentists in the design and validation of outcome measures, as well as their 25 years of service as expert assessors for the curriculum, was nationally recognized by the American College of Dentists in 2007, the year she presented the inaugural Daniel Laskin Lectures in Professional Ethics at Indiana University.

Dr. Bebeau's research on teaching and assessing ethical development are summarized in the Institute of Medicine's *Integrity in Scientific Research (*National Academies Press, 2002), and her work on professional identity formation is described in *Dentists Who Care: Inspiring Stories of Professional Commitment* (Quintessence Books, 2005), co-authored with James Rule. Recent chapters in Volume 10 of *Advances in Bioethics* (Elsevier Ltd., 2006), the *Handbook on Moral and Character Education* (Routledge, 2008), and an article in the *University of St. Thomas Law Journal* summarize what has become known as the "Minnesota approach" to professional ethical development. Four recent co-authored articles in *Professional Psychology: Research and Practice* reflect the broadening concern for inclusion of ethical development in professional competence assessment.

Summers Kalishman, PhD, is an Assistant Professor in the department of Family and Community Medicine at the University of New Mexico School of Medicine. She directs the Office of Program Evaluation, Education and Research (PEAR), and is Assistant Dean, Medical Education Scholarship. After graduating in English from Stanford University, she worked in a community health clinic in California for several years. She earned an MPA in administration and a PhD in education from the University of New Mexico. Her current work includes curriculum evaluation, faculty and professional development, assessment of reflective practices, and workplace learning.

D. Christopher Kayes, PhD Case Western Reserve University, is Dean's Research Scholar and Associate Professor of Management at George Washington University. He has won awards for his unique approach to learning including best paper awards and nominations from Academy of Management Learning and Education, Human Relations, the Organizational Behavior Teaching Society, and was awarded the first ever "most significant contribution to the practice of management" award by the

Organizational Behavior division of the Academy of Management. He is author of over 30 peer-reviewed articles and chapters and two books.

Sílvia Mamede is a physician, who worked for several years in continuing education and postgraduate programs for family health professionals and health managers in the School of Public Health of the State of Ceará, in Brazil. She was the dean of the School of Public Health from 1995 to 2002, when her institution was one of the first Brazilian adopters of problem-based learning and other educational innovations. In collaboration with other colleagues, she published her first book on problem-based learning in Brazil, in Portuguese the native language, in 2001. For the past 10 years, she has worked with several Brazilian universities and health institutions on faculty development and the design of innovative curricula in both undergraduate and postgraduate medical education. Her strong interest in learning from reflection upon experience led her to explore new approaches for the continuing education of family doctors. She has a doctorate in medical education from the Erasmus University, Rotterdam. For the past few years in her current role in research on the development of medical expertise and clinical reasoning. In collaboration with Henk Schmidt and Remy Rikers, she has studied the nature of reflective practice in medicine, the characteristics of reflective physicians, and the effect of reflection on clinical performance. Their more recent studies have explored the origins of diagnostic errors and the role of reflection in minimizing mistakes and improving performance throughout professional life. She became an Associate Professor at the Erasmus University in 2008 and is currently a scientific researcher in the Department of Psychology at Erasmus University, Rotterdam.

Verna E. Monson is an educational psychologist specializing in ethics in the professions. Currently, Verna is a Research Fellow with the Holloran Center for Ethical Leadership in the Professions at the University of St. Thomas School of Law. Her research investigates how lawyers understand professionalism and the formation of professional ethical identity.

Monson's doctoral thesis examined the relationship between morality, clinical interaction, and clinical outcomes in case simulations in dental education. Together with Professor Mickey Bebeau, Monson co-authored "Guided by Theory, Grounded in Evidence: A Way Forward for Professional Ethics Education," in the *Handbook for Moral and Character Education.*

Previously as a research assistant with the Center for the Study of Ethical Development at the University of Minnesota, Monson investigated moral identity, motivation, and empathy in the professions and in graduate business education. She has presented her research at national and international conferences.

She serves as an ethics education consultant to professional schools and organizations, including the Henry Latimer Center for Professionalism at the Florida Bar and the University of Notre Dame Mendoza School of Business. Monson volunteers with the Phyllis Wheatley Community Center's community-school initiative, aimed at improving academic performance of children in a high-poverty area of Minneapolis, where she resides.

Remy Rikers is a professor of Educational and Developmental Psychology at the Institute of Psychology and holder of the Tinbergen chair at the Erasmus University Rotterdam, the Netherlands. He was formerly trained in the cognitive sciences and philosophy at the Radboud University in Nijmegen, the Netherlands. His research focuses on topics such as expertise development (in medicine and chess), instructional design, and problem-based learning, and he has published widely in refereed journals and book chapters. He is a member of the Psychonomic Society and the European Association for Research on Learning and Instruction, and he was section chair Division C of the American Educational Research Association. Prof. Dr. Rikers has been an invited scholar in Canada and the United States (University of Maryland) and has been the featured speaker at various international research conferences.

Lynne Robins, PhD, is a Professor at the University of Washington School of Medicine in the Department of Medical Education & Biomedical Informatics, with adjunct appointments in the Departments of Family Medicine and Pediatric Dentistry. She holds a PhD in anthropology from the University of Michigan, where she analyzed medical discourse and described how pronoun usage reflects and reproduces the asymmetrical power relations between physicians and patients. She taught linguistics and anthropology before entering the field of medical education as director of curriculum evaluation at the University of Michigan's Medical School.

Dr. Robins currently directs the University of Washington's Teaching Scholars Program, a leadership and professional development program for clinicians and basic scientists who have a passion for teaching and a desire to become academic leaders. She has mentored over 100 teaching scholars, many of whom have become leaders locally nationally. Dr. Robins is engaged in a variety of funded research projects looking at the effects of physician communication behaviors on patient health outcomes; the impact of interprofessional education on learners' knowledge, skills, attitudes, and team competence; and the value of simulation as a training modality to improve error disclosure and increase patient safety.

Robert E. Saggers is a certified management consultant who since 1989 has headed up his own consulting practice in organizational learning and leadership development. Over this period of time he has assisted a wide variety of clients: to assess their organizational capability; to design and facilitate leadership and management competency development programs; and to coach their managers and in-house facilitators to lead change and team-building efforts. Previously he worked in both operational and corporate human resource management roles within the manufacturing and financial sectors, and subsequently was a principal with a major international consultancy.

Bob has been associated with McGill University for over the past 20 years as a graduate studies instructor, first teaching human resource management (1988–1994). He then helped McGill's School of Continuing Studies to develop a graduate diploma and certificate leadership program, in which he continues to teach courses in leadership skills development. He was recently named an adjunct professor in the Department of Integrated Studies in the Faculty of Education, where he teaches resource management to Masters in Educational Leadership students. He also works with the University on a joint venture basis to develop/deliver corporate training programs. He received his Master's in Education in 2001 and completed his doctorate in instructional psychology and adult education in 2009, with a thesis investigating the relationship between teaching, learning, leading, and managing.

Alenoush Saroyan is a full Professor and Chair of the Department of Educational and Counselling Psychology at McGill University in Montreal, Canada. Her area of expertise and research is quality of teaching and learning with specific focus on the pedagogical development of academics, academic leadership, and quality assurance. She teaches in the Learning Sciences program and supervises doctoral and masters students.

After receiving her doctoral degree in Educational Psychology from McGill University and working briefly in industry, she returned to her alma mater as an Assistant Professor in 1991. Until 2005, she was cross appointed to the McGill Centre for University Teaching and Learning and very actively involved in faculty development initiatives in the University. Research on the processes involved in the pedagogical development of professors and the effectiveness of various teaching development initiatives led to two books: *Rethinking Teaching in Higher Education* (2004, co-edited with Cheryl Amundsen) and in collaboration with international colleagues *Building Teaching Capacity in Universities: From Faculty Development to Educational Development* (2009, co-edited with Mariane Frenay).

As a consultant to the World Bank and UNESCO, she has contributed to reform projects of higher education systems in Egypt, Jordan, Georgia, and Iran. She has been an invited speaker in international ministerial conferences in the Middle and Far East. Currently, she serves as a member of the Steering Committee on Quality Teaching under the auspices of OECD's project on the International Management of Higher Education.

The opportunity to apply her research findings to enhancing university teaching has enabled her to retain a dynamic link between theory building and practice, and in this way she has been able to contribute to the development of both.

Henk G. Schmidt is a professor of psychology at Erasmus University, Rotterdam, The Netherlands, and founding dean of its problem-based psychology curriculum. Presently, he is the rector magnificus of the university. Previously, Schmidt held academic positions as professor of cognitive psychology, Faculty of Psychology, Maastricht University, and as professor of health professions education at the same university. His administrative positions include the deanship of the Faculty of Health Sciences of Maastricht University and the deanship of the Faculty of Social Sciences of Erasmus University. In addition, he has been the president of the Dutch Psychological Association (NIP), the chairman of the Dutch Society for Research into Higher Education (CRWO), and the associate secretary general of the Network of Community-Oriented Educational Institutions for Health Sciences, a World Health Organization–supported NGO.

He was R. Samuel McLaughlin Professor at McMaster University, Canada, and Prof. L. Verhaegen Professor at the Limburg University Centre, Belgium.

His research areas of interest are learning and memory, and he has published on problem-based learning, long-term memory, and the development of expertise in medicine. He has published more than 250 articles in refereed journals, chapters in books, and books, alone or together with his 30+ PhD students. In addition, he is the founding editor of two journals.

In 1996 the Université de Sherbrooke in Canada awarded him an honorary degree. In 2004, the Karolinska Institutet, Stockholm, Sweden, gave him its international medical education research prize for his work in medical expertise and problem-based learning. In 2006, he received the Distinguished Career Award of the American Educational Research Association, Division I.

Dr. Debra Sharu, DPhil, ANP, is an academic and author with over 30 years' experience as a practicing clinician and educator in the USA and the UK. She is a fully qualified Advanced Family Nurse Practitioner and founding director of Practitioner Development UK, a provider of short CPD courses for health-care professionals. Her work as an education consultant and company director keeps her in touch with the everyday needs of health-care providers. This is reinforced by her work as a clinician in a walk in center.

Debra first became active in promoting the role of the British Advanced Nurse Practitioner (ANP) when she became a senior lecturer at the Royal College of Nursing in London. After working at the RCN, she became involved in the first distance learning program for ANPs at the University of Cumbria, where she currently holds a senior lecturer post.

Debra has a special interest in continuing professional development for health-care providers. This includes formal and informal learning in the workplace. Her DPhil thesis completed at the University of Sussex focused on Advanced Nurse Practitioner learning in the clinical environment. Results from this study have produced findings that are unique to ANPs, highlighting the pioneering quality of the role along with key components that foster professional learning and development.

Tone Dyrdal Solbrekke is Associate Professor and Researcher at the Faculty of Medicine, Institute of Nursing and Health Sciences, and the Faculty of Education Institute for Educational Research University of Oslo and Editor of the *Norwegian Journal of Pedagogical Research.* Prior to entering academe, she worked as a teacher and principal in primary education. Her research interests are wide ranging and include school development, leadership and professional identities, issues of professional responsibility, qualification for professional life, the normative dimension of higher education, and the consequences of international trends and increased integration of European Higher Education (Bologna process) with regard to normative issues and practices in higher education. She is co-author of Scandinavian books on School Leadership, and her recent publications in English include "Professional Responsibility as Legitimate Compromise—From Communities of Education to Communities of Work" in Studies in *Higher Education* and "Educating for Professional Responsibility—A Normative Dimension of Higher Education" in *Education and Democracy*. She is co-author of *Students as Journeymen between*

Communities of Higher Education and Work, HPSE CT-2001-00068, Final report. European Commission, Fifth Framework Programme 1998–2002 (2005).

Ciaran Sugrue is Reader in School Leadership and School Improvement at the Faculty of Education, University of Cambridge. Previously, he was Director of Postgraduate Education at St. Patrick's College, Dublin City University, and worked as a primary teacher, schools inspector, teacher educator, and researcher in the Irish system for several years. His research interests are wide ranging but primarily focused on School Leadership and Educational Change, as well as connecting these with continuing professional learning within the teaching profession, and on qualitative research methods—their cultural conjunctures and disjunctures across national borders and in the international arena. He was General Editor of *Irish Educational Studies* from 1998 to 2008 and is a member of the editorial boards of several international journals. He has published widely on his research interests. His most recent book is *The Future of Educational Change: International Perspectives* (London: Routledge), while the following journal article is forthcoming: "From Heroes and Heroines to Hermaphrodites: Emancipation or Emasculation of School Leaders and Leadership?" In *Leadership & Management*, 29 (4).

Chapter 1
Introduction

Anne Mc Kee and Michael Eraut

Education in the professions has acquired increasing expectations from the public that include:

- Keeping pace with rapidly evolving knowledge bases
- Developing skills and attitudes appropriate for good practice
- Fostering learning, in the workplace
- Sustaining public confidence

Over the past 20 years, new demands have created new educational imperatives. Public accountability has become more intensive as its scope has extended. The climate in which practitioners practice and learn is more subject to scrutiny and less forgiving of error. The contexts in which professionals practice and learn have changed and will continue to change. Three questions central to professional learning are as follows:

- What is it that professionals need to know?
- What must they be able to do?
- How best can they acquire the relevant expertise?

These questions have now spread beyond the professional bodies to become major concerns for policy makers, senior and middle managers, clients and their families, employers, voters, tax payers and the media. One consequence of this is that professional competence, learning and expertise have become subject to stakeholder perspectives. How these different perspectives are accommodated and with what effects on learning and practice is an emergent issue for many professions. The landscape of professional education is changing, and the consequences are only just beginning to emerge, as professional bodies are engaging in discussions with stakeholders about professional practice and the priorities for professional education.

A. Mc Kee (✉)
Faculty of Education, Anglia Ruskin University, Chelmsford CM1 1SQ, UK
e-mail: anne.mckee@anglia.ac.uk

A. Mc Kee, M. Eraut (eds.), *Learning Trajectories, Innovation and Identity for Professional Development*, Innovation and Change in Professional Education 7,
DOI 10.1007/978-94-007-1724-4_1,

In this book we explore the emergent issues by examining contemporary challenges facing professional education and their implications for professional development. In particular, we aim to widen the lens of professional development beyond its current emphasis on what it is that individual practitioners should learn and do, to include and explore the systemic and contextual dimensions of change in professional education. These challenges have stimulated new areas in professional learning and innovations in scholarship, pedagogic research, and learning and teaching practice, and these new directions will provide the central focus of this book.

Some of those new directions are the result of disciplinary boundary crossing. This occurs when a profession engages with another discipline in the pursuit of learning from different approaches to researching and developing professional practice. One common feature of the book is that although some of the examples and narratives in each chapter may come from one profession, they also address problems that are relevant to other professions.

The main purpose of this book is to support those who are engaged in or have responsibility for the education of professional workers. In particular, we aim:

1. To identify key contemporary challenges in professional learning, assessment support and provision *and how these may be addressed*
2. To understand the complexities of professional practice, particularly how policy makers, managers, professional bodies, practitioners and clients have different views about what practice could and should be *and the implications of this for professional development and professional practice*
3. To learn from the experience and contexts of a range of professions *about how educational challenges are interpreted, what solutions have been applied and what lessons have been learned*
4. To learn about the empirical educational research employed in professional education and emergent methodologies

The chapters in this book differ across the professional lifespan of their participants. Some start in higher education, some are followed from higher education into their early careers, some go in and out of formal education during the course of their professional lives, some become academic members of their professions and some make large and difficult transitions in the second half of their projected career. The strength of this book is that, while only a few authors have conducted research projects that together covered a whole professional lifespan, our collection of chapters does meet that overall coverage. The book is focussed around three critical aspects of professional work in the first decade of the 21st century, and our title suggests a particular approach to understanding the changing nature of professional work over time.

Innovation is recognized as an essential feature of work, whose purpose tries to respond to its changing needs. Some needs arise from new discoveries within professions developed for a particular purpose. Some arise from changes in their external or internal environments. In either case, a few professional workers will be involved with new practices from the beginning, while others will try to follow them sooner or later. This does not mean that early adopters of an innovation will be doing the same thing. Differences in clients and their contexts may require different variations, and discussions between interested professionals pursuing different variations may lead to improved practices. These changes can range from small initiatives to radical changes in practice. Both can be useful, but the amount of change required is a critical component in the learning process. This will probably include both scepticism about the claim for improvement and concerns about one's capability to handle it. This is where it is very useful for professional workers to become more aware of how best to introduce new practices. Many of the chapters in this book describe examples of innovations, often using approaches that are novel and effective.

The concept of a *learning trajectory*, introduced by Eraut (2004), provides several advantages. Learning trajectories describe what learners develop over time through a series of jobs and roles, thus bringing more purpose and clarity to the concept of *lifelong learning*. This allows learners to plan and evaluate learning experiences from different contexts, both formal and informal, and to create new practices with the help of significant others. They also offer alternative approaches to describing both theoretical and practical knowledge and their interactions.

Another advantage of the *learning trajectory* approach is the extraordinary confusion over the concept of *competences*. This word began as a description of 'good' practices at work, but was then taken up by formal education to describe student outcomes from elementary schools to master's degrees. There are two major confusions in its usage. McClelland (1976) and his co-worker psychologists defined a competence as 'an *underlying characteristic* of an individual that is *causally related to criterion-referenced effective and/or superior performance* in a job or situation' (Spencer & Spencer, 1993). Most educators, however, used the term competence as a direct description of a person's performance, thus losing focus on the development and application of professional judgement in complex and unpredictable contexts. Some educators referred informally to underlying characteristics, but this was more likely to occur in casual conversation or occasional comments that they would not expect to defend.

The other confusion highlights the difference between *socio-cultural* and *personal perspectives*. Eraut (1998) argued that the socio-cultural definition of competence as *meeting other people's expectations* has the longer provenance. It also plays an important role in professional climates of accountability.

In English, the meaning of *competent* encompasses the following:

- Being properly qualified
- Being able to perform on your own
- Being capable
- Being adequate but not expert

The scope of such competence is rarely specified but is often implicit in the context. Our own definition of competence is *being able to perform the tasks and roles required to the expected standard*. This expectation, being socially defined, will either be part of professional regulation or be determined by the micro-politics of the particular context. In either case, unlike terms like 'knowledge', 'learning' and 'capability', the word *competent* entails a social judgement, which may vary across contexts and over time and also, sometimes, with the experience, responsibility and reputation of the person concerned.

Another advantage of this definition is that it enables us to explore the important links between individuals' capability and their competence. All their competence will be within their capability, but not all their capability will be needed for any specific job. So they will also have *additional capability*, which provides a useful resource for changes in the job or changes of job. Such additional capability may be helpful both in enhancing one's competence through further learning (this could use prior knowledge or acquired modes of learning in a new context) and in helping to transform one's job through *innovation* (which requires confidence, imagination and appropriate interpersonal skills).

Eraut's (2004) versions of *learning trajectories* were based on research into the early career learning of chartered accountants, engineers and nurses. The problem of describing what was being learned across these professions and age groups led us to a set of 54 types of knowledge under eight main headings (see Chapter 9 for a full list):

Task performance	Awareness and Understanding
Role performance	Personal Development
Working with Others	Knowledge of the Field
Decision-making and Problem Solving	Judgement

These were refined by both researchers and participants, and were compatible with the data from an earlier mid-career project on the learning of business, engineers and nurses (Eraut et al., 2000). Other people might choose different sets of words, but they would still need to make some difficult choices. At this point we decided that, given the changes in participant performance over three years, our list was best described as a set of *learning trajectories.* Since it was rare for a learner to use only one trajectory in any one performance, we decided to focus on the linkages between learners' portfolios and their overall performances, which could be achieved only if the information about each performance included the following:

- The setting in which it took place and features of that setting that affected or might have affected the performance
- The conditions under which the performance took place, e.g. degree of supervision, pressure of time, crowdedness, conflicting priorities and availability of resources
- The antecedents to the performance and the situation that gave rise to the performance
- The other categories of expertise involved
- Any differences from previously recorded episodes
- Indicators of expertise in the domain of the trajectory having been maintained, widened or enhanced

This last point draws attention to the complexity of learning and performance in most professional, technical and managerial jobs. It is unusual for a performance to use knowledge from only one trajectory, and the seamless integration of personal knowledge from several trajectories may itself be an important learning challenge that goes beyond progress in several separate trajectories. The holistic nature of any complex performance should never be neglected. Within this overall framework, it is still possible, indeed desirable, for different types of representation to be used for different trajectories and at different career stages. There is no one best way for describing complex knowledge in use.

Sharu's research in Chapter 9 provides an interesting example of *learning trajectories* in action, because her research was based on mid-career nurses who were making a big step in their work capabilities by a combination of a purpose-designed degree course and on-the-job learning support from their current employers in primary care organizations. This group also showed themselves to carry a very strong sense of *identity*. Their journey to become nurse practitioners, who were allowed to take on much greater responsibility than before, could be very difficult without appropriate support from community doctors. Most of the nurses needed a *strong sense of agency* to reach this level without having to move to another organization. Their transition to more complex, responsible work began during their formal courses, but even those who received more support than others found that most of it occurred in the year after they qualified as nurse practitioners. Some of them had to change their jobs to find the kind of work that they had always wanted to achieve.

The work of Bebeau and Monson (Chapter 7) presents evidence from multiple sources that support constructivists' theoretical understanding of a developmental continuum of identity that proceeds from self-interest and concreteness of thought to more other-oriented and abstract ways of making sense of the self (Kegan, 1982; Blasi, 1984). At more advanced levels of professional identity formation, the exemplary professional's personal and moral values are both fully integrated and consistent across context and situation. They are able to articulate the public duties of the profession, integrate them with personal value frameworks, and regularly and consistently engage in socially responsible actions. The identity of such exemplary professionals is contrasted with the identities of (1) entering students, (2) entering professionals and (3) professionals who have been disciplined by a licensing board. Methods are suggested for supporting learning and improving commitment to professional values.

They describe five strategies for raising student consciousness about what people fundamentally believe they should be able to expect from persons in society that are accorded the power and privileges granted to the most essential professions. These are as follows:

1. Eliciting understanding of professional expectations
2. Using moral exemplars to help students set aspirational standards for the formation of a professional moral identity
3. Engaging students in self-assessment, reflection and development of a learning plan to achieve their professional moral identity

4. Providing feedback on self-assessment and the learning plan
5. Engaging students and professionals in periodic reflection on professional and societal expectations

The discussion of the second strategy is particularly relevant to the concept of learning trajectories. Students were assigned (in groups of three) to read one of 10 stories of dental exemplars (Rule & Bebeau, 2005) and to present (to the class) (1) how the exemplar they read about lived up to each of six expectations and (2) how the individual came to see professional expectations as he or she developed across the lifespan of professional practice. Presentations from small groups have given the class an opportunity to learn about each of the exemplars in the text. Students have been encouraged to set aspirational goals for themselves, while faculty help them to view professional identity formation as a lifelong developmental process. This experience has been followed by a panel discussion with professionals who have been disciplined by the licensing board for violations of the state dental practice act.[1] These dentists are asked to discuss their personal experience in living up to the six expectations where they fell short and how they have modified their activities to address personal shortcomings.

Chapter 3 describes a remarkable change in healthcare arrangements in New Mexico, the poorest US state, that brought a wide range of low-level workers into key roles in supporting a new approach to Hepatitis C and brought them into much greater responsibility than they had ever expected. Armstrong's Chapter 11 described her anthropological approach to community doctors training each other in laparoscopy[2] before it began in hospitals, revealing both their early concerns and their positive feelings about developing new identities. However, not all identity issues are supportive of their clients' needs. Chapter 10 goes beyond this work-based pattern of identity to include family, friends and other interests, and engagements with colleagues often cross over from work to leisure and vice versa.

We chose eight themes for editorial discussion across the chapters of the book. Then we decided that four themes would probably be more useful to readers before reading the chapters, while the other four themes would be more useful after the chapters have been read. The first four themes are *accountability, stakeholders, engagement* and *contexts for learning*, while the final groups of themes at the end of the book will be: *formal* and *informal learning; errors, mistakes and reflective practices*; the *emotional dimension*; and finally *identity, transition and the management of change*.

[1] Arranging for students to interact with disciplined professionals may not be as difficult as it may appear. In the United States, every state board of medical or dental practice publishes the disciplinary cases and many states require that disciplined individuals engage in some kind of community service. It merely takes a creative ethics educator to initiate it. Our colleagues in legal education regularly invite lawyers who have been convicted of 'white collar crime' to hold discussions with law students. Such learning opportunities are very powerful, especially when accompanied with a programme that also uses positive mentors.

[2] Keyhole surgery of the abdomen.

1.1 Responsibility, Complexity and Integrity

Responsibility, complexity and integrity feature highly in discussions of the ethical basis of professional work and provide the main theme of Chapter 7. All workers are expected to be responsible, but professionals are responsible to their professional bodies as well as their clients. The justification for this is that much professional expertise is not easily evaluated by non-experts. So it would be wrong to suggest that professionals are more ethical than other workers, although some clients might have greater expectations from them. Another feature, again not only for professional work, is the huge increase in formal learning for degrees in the second half of the 20th century, which has led to concerns that practice-based learning has been given too little attention. The proportion of professionals that are self-employed or partners in professional practices is quite small. Much larger numbers are employed in the public sector, industry and commerce, where concepts of professional service and economy may differ from those promoted by the professional bodies. For most professional workers, the pursuit of 'autonomy' is primarily a strategy to secure some freedom in their daily practice and a significant role in determining those organizational policies which most affect them.

Several issues concerning professional workers are well described by Solbrekke and Sugrue (Chapter 10). They cover general issues, law and psychology, and a few extracts provide a useful introduction to the theme above.

> It seems quite evident that professionals in the public sphere are increasingly exposed to dilemmas between being accountable to the 'demands of efficiency' and to what they perceive to be the best standards of good work. . . . Even the clinical psychologists responsible for the treatment of seriously ill patients highlight such conflicts between responsible treatment and the demands for increased . . . efficiency. (p. 205)

> Without doubt, all professionals, and particularly novice workers (Fishman et al., 2004), have to concentrate on the tasks that are most pressing. As May reminds us, it may represent a 'legitimate compromise' and a way of 'surviving' in the complexity of challenging daily tasks at work. (May, 1996, p. 207)

Many of the participants in the study are at the stage of having children. Hence, they have to balance the interests of family and work. Defining 'boundaries between their work and private spheres appears to be as important to them as the immediate pursuit of ongoing professional development. The possibility to work regular hours and not be compelled to study in the evenings propels them towards what they see as a legitimate negotiated compromise of the "quality" of work' (p. 207). 'Such priorities do not necessarily mean that these novice professionals do not take their professional responsibilities seriously. Rather, it suggests that it is necessary to understand professional responsibility in the light of all the relationships that exist for a person' (p. 208).

> Although they do not see their future work as a self-sacrificial calling, they want to dedicate their expertise to the needs of others, and the service of society. However, it appears that the shift from the context of education to contexts of work, where the subjects encounter the realities of 'multiple responsibilities' and conflicts of interest in daily situations at work can cause them to renegotiate their (pre)conceptions of professional responsibility. While such

> re-negotiations might be anticipated, deemed necessary and apposite, the evidence suggests a tendency at this career stage to lurch from a broader notion of professional responsibility to a professional horizon that is overly narrowed to the local and the confining contours of the actual community of practice. (p. 208)

> Nevertheless, it is important to acknowledge that the participants in this study were at a delicate stage of negotiating community membership of a particular professional group and, in so doing, they had to re-negotiate newly created understandings of professional responsibility, all of which simultaneously shape the creation of a professional identity – a tall order and a steep learning curve. (p. 208)

> Compromises are often necessary in the context of plurality, insecurity and the need for flexibility, because making *legitimate* compromises implies taking into consideration the multiple conflicts of interest a professional is obliged to handle. They deal with complexity, rather than a more reductionist approach that ignores too many factors. (p. 209)

> We are also aware of the significance of language in relation to seeking a more satisfactory resolution to the tensions and dilemmas in the rhetoric and practice of professional responsibility and accountability. Professionally responsible behaviour is contingent on the professional's integrity and a profound understanding of the moral implications of professional work. Thus there is a critical limit to how far personal stances, professional values and commitments may be (re)negotiated before they 'tip' towards 'illegitimate' compromises. Without a moral awareness of the normative professional mandate there is a risk that what remains is 'compromised' compromises – and not what results from *legitimate negotiations.* (p. 209)

Mamede, Rikers and Schmidt (Chapter 8) define *complexity* in terms of going beyond algorithmic learning, and this requires some exploration of the nature of *reflective reasoning in medicine*. This is important for minimizing diagnostic errors and needs (1) discussions with a range of experienced physicians and (2) pursuit of several lines of inquiry at once. They argue that reflective practice in medicine has a multidimensional structure that draws on at least five approaches to the complex problems found in professional practice, and these have to be explored together as dimensions of the same problem. These approaches are (1) *deliberate induction* and (2) *deliberate deduction*, both searching for alternative explanations and their consequences; (3) a willingness to *test predictions* against the data and *synthesize new understandings* about the problem; (4) an attitude of openness towards *reflection during problem solving* and (5) *meta-reasoning*, reflecting on one's own conclusions, assumptions and beliefs about a problem. However, experience is not enough. *Deliberate practice* is also needed, because it is oriented towards the recognition and overcoming of weaknesses in one's own performance.

Mc Kee (Chapter 12) draws our attention to the teaching aspects of academics' learning trajectories, through the evaluation of a five-year programme of 81 Centres of Excellence in Teaching and Learning (CETLs) funded by the UK government. A key shift in learning and teaching practice was the widespread encouragement and promotion of pedagogic research and small-scale development projects as a means of enhancing learning and teaching. However, despite a growing acceptance for and uptake in the use of pedagogic research, there was an enduring unease with this form of practice. Underpinning this unease was a tension between pedagogic research and established views about what academic practice should involve, particularly around the relationship between research and teaching and how these activities met in the learning and teaching process. Continuing unease regarding pedagogic research centred round concerns that academics engaged with it might reduce their engagement with research in their own subject discipline.

> The national CETL evaluation examined the tensions around three aspects of academic practice. These were discipline-based research, disseminating that research through teaching, and pedagogic knowledge (research-based or student focussed). These elements of academic practice have fuzzy boundaries. Thus Scott, the Vice-Chancellor of a new university and well known scholar of Higher Education argued that:
>
> (The) boundary between 'teaching' and 'research' is getting fuzzier rather than clearer. Indeed there are some forms of teaching which have less in common with other forms of teaching than they have with some types of research. (Scott, 2004)
>
> What are the implications of the tensions and overlaps between teaching and research practices; and how do they relate to this paper's assumption that the role of universities and academic practices are related?" (p. 250)

Extracts from 71 CETL self-evaluations showed a very wide diversity of activities (Table 1.1):

Table 1.1 Academic practice and links between research and teaching

Dimension of academic practice	Pedagogical approach, or form of scholarship	Link between research and teaching
(1) Active research within a discipline or cluster of disciplines (traditional research based practice)	(1) Pedagogy of knowledge transmission	(1) The link between teaching and research is the dissemination of research through 'telling'
(2) Research-based knowledge is reproduced through teaching and learning programmes	(2) Pedagogy of knowledge construction	(2) The link between teaching and research is embedded in the design and practice of the course. Teaching becomes inquiry oriented. Examples of this would be problem based learning approaches and evidence based project work
(3) Pedagogic knowledge (produced through research or experientially), which may have a disciplinary boundary	(3) Research-based pedagogy. The fundamental integration of knowledge and inquiry	(3) Teaching involves the conduct of research. This may involve practitioners, such as higher education teachers, examining their own practice within particular courses or modules. There are overlaps between 2 and 3

1.2 Accountability

Accountability has become a difficult issue to discuss, not because it is a central feature of professional responsibility and integrity, but because many professionals find that some requirements introduced to 'strengthen' accountability benefit neither their clients nor themselves. Accountability is a major issue at the centre of professional identity, but in Chapter 10, what counts as accountability is highly contested. Much of what is often called 'the accountability movement' is seen as replacing professional responsibility by a series of rules and accounting mechanisms which reduce professional discretion and judgement. How did this arise? One of the early research projects on accountability in UK primary schools, which involved teachers, principals, parents and officers (Becher et al., 1981), discerned three complementary approaches to accountability: contractual, moral and professional. The problem was to get the right balance between them.

The *contractual approach* concerns the relationship between teachers and their school district, which appoints them and pays their wages. The district will expect their teachers to be professional teachers who can be relied upon to teach their classes appropriately, both for current learning and for helping their students to become good citizens over a period of time. In practice, teachers work under the leadership of their head teachers/principals, unless there are major problems causing concerns from either party.

The curriculum, however, is determined at district, province or national level, and this is the key issue in Chapter 10. Major changes in many countries and states have greatly increased the detail expected of teachers, and many teachers find it very difficult to reconcile this level of prescription with the daily needs of their students. Given the variations between schools, this is not surprising, but there is also a danger of under-rating the potential of some students. Problems of this kind can be found in a large number of professions and are often seen as restricting innovation.

The *professional approach* is mainly concerned with training: initial training, higher level awards and continuing professional education/development. There is a very wide range of post-initial training, and most professions now require regular CPE. Some professions, such as medicine and architecture, have well-developed on-the-job training throughout their members' lifetimes; others offer formal training after graduation, but very little practice training. Chapter 2 discusses the role of informal learning at work, which is sometimes linked with professional requirements, but often quite separate from it. The other role of professional bodies concerns misconduct and/or incompetence. Many threatened professionals retire before they are formally reprimanded or struck off the register, and this can result in dubious bullying, the nasty side of accountability.

The *moral approach* is rigorously discussed in Chapter 7, which focuses on how the personal and moral values of exemplary professionals are both fully integrated and consistent across context and situation. This requires them to articulate the public duties of their professions, integrate them with personal value frameworks and regularly and consistently engage in socially responsible actions. The professions' goal should be to develop a professional identity consistent with such expectations. There are no contradictions because they are talking about different contexts and purposes. The main examples come from dentistry and the military. Chapter 7 finds that prospective army leaders with little combat experience progress very slowly in their ethical development, whereas in Chapter 5 we find an overwhelming emotional response from company commanders when their soldiers are at risk. Many professionals receive neither combat experience nor the kind of ethical support developed by the authors of Chapter 7, so ethical behaviour is most likely to depend on a professional's personal development before, during and after their first few jobs. Chapter 7 reports that this is insufficient for most dentists, and probably for several other professions. The authors also provide a great deal of useful research for enhancing the ethical awareness of professionals.

1.3 Stakeholders

The basic principle of *moral accountability* is that people are accountable for the effects of their actions insofar as those effects are reasonably foreseeable. The same principle can be applied to the moral accountability of organizations, so that all those people likely to be affected by the actions of an organization can be properly described as stakeholders. The term *stakeholder* is broader than that of client or service user and enables a wider set of accountability relationships to be considered, including special-interest groups, the local community and the environment. It should also be noted that many stakeholders have multiple roles; e.g. they may be both clients and taxpayers. The concept of stakeholders can be traced from two main sources, responsive evaluation and the ethics of organizations.

Responsive evaluation can be summarized by two questions: Who has a *stake* in the findings of an evaluation, and what are their *concerns*? (Stake, 1975). 'Evaluation can perform a service and be useful to specific persons. For an evaluation to be useful, the evaluation should know the interests and the languages of his audiences' (p. 13). '... An educational evaluation is a responsive evaluation if it orients more directly to program activities than to program intents; responds to audience requirements for information; and if the different value perspectives present are referred to in reporting the success and failure of the program' (p. 14).

Guba and Lincoln (1981) go on to provide a set of key definitions:

> A *stakeholding audience* is a group of persons having some common characteristics ... that has some stake in the performance (or outcome or impact) of the evaluand, that is somehow involved in or affected by the entity being evaluated. An audience has a right to be consulted about its concerns and issues, to have those concerns and issues honored by the evaluator as he goes about his tasks, and to receive reports (or communication or feedback) from their evaluator that are responsive to those concerns and issues. (p. 304)

> A *concern* is any matter of interest to one or more parties about which they feel threatened, that they think will lead to an undesirable consequence, or that they are anxious to substantiate (a claim requiring empirical verification). (p. 304)

> An *issue* is any statement, proposition or focus that allows for different, often conflicting, points of view; any point of contention. ... The task of the evaluator is to develop information that will aid in understanding two or more sides of an issue and perhaps help to resolve or reduce the conflict that will almost surely attend the different value positions represented by the sides of the issue. (p. 304)

> A *contextual factor* is any force or constraint that compels or inhibits some action and that is beyond the power of the persons dealing with the evaluand to control. Such factors may be concerns and issues that could be dealt with at some other level or in some other context but that are outside the scope of the context in which the evaluand is found. (p. 305)

Bryson's (1995) approach to stakeholders is equally strong, but is focused primarily on public and non-profit organizations. His stakeholders are 'defined as any person, group or organisation that can place a claim on an organisation's attention, resources or output or is affected by that output. Examples of a government's stakeholders include citizens, taxpayers, service recipients, the governing body, employees, unions, interest groups, political parties, the financial community, businesses and other governments. Examples of non-profit organisation's stakeholders include clients or customers, third-party payers or funders, employees, the board of directors, volunteers, other non-profit organisations that provide complementary services or are involved as coventurers in projects, banks holding the organisation's mortgages or notes, and suppliers' (p. 27).

Bryson argues that a *stakeholder analysis* provides a way for an organization's decision makers and planning team to familiarize themselves in the politics surrounding the organization. Only by understanding stakeholder interests and concerns can an organization take truly ethical action. The first few steps require a strategic team 'to identify who the organisation's stakeholders are, what are their criteria for judging the organisation's performance ... and how well the organisation performs according to those criteria from the stakeholders' point of view' (p. 28).

Chapter 3 describes the growing awareness in the University of New Mexico Medical School (UNM) of *potential stakeholders whom they never met.* In spite of being the only medical school in the state, they felt accountable for reaching out into areas beyond their normal reach, both financially and geographically. So they created a partnership project with the 15 poorest counties to develop non-medical healthcare workers to care for patients with Hepatitis C. This was a major educational challenge for both the university and the local healthcare workers, which encompassed UNM staff in very innovatory work and asked for local healthcare workers to commit to new training and work with patients with Hepatitis C in addition to most of their normal workload. This involved working with new sites through local visits and distance learning, and a remarkable build-up of expertise from both groups of health workers.

The evaluation of the CETL approach in Chapter 12 required objective evidence on the overall effectiveness of (1) the programme at the different levels of sector, institution, teacher, student and external stakeholders and (2) the strategy as viewed from particular perspectives, including those in senior management within the institutions, academics, students and communities of practice. This is wider in scope than most evaluations, even those that range over a large number of organizations.

1.4 Engagement with Colleagues and Other Stakeholders

Treating stakeholders appropriately is often a challenging problem, particularly when they involve people who meet only in crowded settings. Discussions among stakeholders depend on their opportunities to exchange information about their mutual activities, hopes and concerns. Where and when can they support each other? Although there may be many differences between them, there can also be areas of common needs and interests. The greatest difficulty is usually the lack of any significant mutual engagement.

One of the most important assets of this book is the large number of approaches to engagement between different types of stakeholders.

Project ECHO in Chapter 3 works through outreach to community-based clinics, followed by weekly case-based, consultative education clinics focused on a complex disease and conducted via technology (web or telemedicine or cell phone access). This enables primary care providers to access the best practice standards of care and support for screening, managing and treating patients whom they might diagnose but generally do not treat. Sub-specialists share knowledge about best practice protocols using a case-based learning approach and co-manage patients with primary caregivers in rural communities and prisons. Telemedicine and Internet connections enable specialists and primary care providers to co-manage patients with HCV infection, thus increasing the capacity of rural clinicians to provide treatment for HCV. Project ECHO network partner organizations are recruited through state-wide healthcare conferences, presentations and partner contacts.

Once a provider organization joins the Project ECHO network, members of the UNM team visit the site to conduct a one-day training workshop. After that network, clinicians present and discuss their HCV patients during weekly 2-h telemedicine clinics. These clinics use a standardized, case-based format that includes discussion of treatment complications and psychiatric, medical and substance use issues. Seventy-five providers (pharmacists, nurse practitioners, primary care physicians and physician assistants) have presented patients in these clinics, where network clinicians also collaborate with specialists in gastroenterology, infectious disease, psychiatry, substance use and pharmacology. These case-based educational experiences, called *learning loops,* provide learning through (1) longitudinal co-management of patients with specialists, (2) other primary care providers on the network via shared case-based decision-making and (3) short didactic presentations on relevant topics, such as vaccination for Hepatitis A and B and diagnosis of depression.

Chapter 4 is pioneering a new method of training for disclosing medical errors. The authors had to find appropriate forms of engagement for healthcare workers to learn how they could disclose errors to patients soon after the event, instead of trying to brush them away until they created a scandal. These events are unusual, so the first decisions were to train younger groups with no record of errors and to treat all those involved with the patient as a team. The next decision was to add reality and emotional feelings by selecting models of real cases, with actors as patients. In order to handle any future *real cases*, they trained risk managers to be coaches, so they were also involved with the actor-patients. One important finding was the growth of teamwork between doctors and nurses; they all recognized how important it was to liaise more closely and that most accidents occurred when mistakes were not noticed or reported to others. The doctors also recognized that most nurses were more proficient in talking to patients than were most doctors. Hence this 'very real' experience engaged three groups: doctors, nurses and risk managers.

Chapter 6 developed a research project to decide whether the *development of others* was an effective strategy for leaders/managers to use. Their results showed that both employees' satisfaction with their managers and their perceptions of their managers' relative productivity were positively correlated with the time managers devoted to teaching. Moreover, those managers whose employees said they had been 'taught' the lessons of the leadership workshop by their managers were seen by their employees to be more effective. This confirms the previous claim that *transformative leaders and managers* are likely to devote more time to *employee development,* and among them the most effective are likely to be those who take an *employee-centred approach* when they engage in teaching those whom they lead.

Most advanced nurse practitioners (ANPs) in primary care (Chapter 9) had both to get their degrees and to learn a great deal on the job in their current organization. Much of this learning depended on their engagement with the doctors and their willingness to support their learning needs. Their problem was getting access to the right patients and helpful doctors who were willing to help and *good at explaining things.* One doctor could be keen to have an ANP who could *work with me and support the practice and patient load is very important,* while another avoided them. Another problem was the reception area, where they tended to send only minor things to ANPs. A year later, many ANPs were seeking out more specialist practitioners. Some had firmly established themselves in their role and were independently referring to a wide range of link health providers, while others were still finding resistance from colleagues in accepting their new role. There was, however, some degree of increased acceptance by colleagues and patients for all the ANPs.

1.5 Contexts for Learning

Our first context comes from Allen and Kayes's research on *company commanders in Iraq* (Chapter 5). Like Kouzes and Posner (1995), who indicated that challenging experiences are essential to leader development in executives, this study revealed several characteristics of the nature of experiences that lead to learning in combat. Allen and Kayes called these experiences 'molten' in nature, as they share, metaphorically, characteristics of molten lava.

'Molten experiences are chaotic, complex, volatile and ambiguous. They are unpredictable, with threads from multiple, simultaneous, and overlapping experiences woven together. Moreover, they may demand that the leader wear multiple hats, requiring him or her to agilely shift from one role to another – roles which, in some situations, may require the leader to hold opposing viewpoints simultaneously. And finally, within each of these experiences and multiple potential roles, there is ongoing information oscillation – which consists of either too much, not enough, or conflicting information. There is something about leading through experiences like these that is highly developmental'.

Furthermore, they were characterized by a profound sense of responsibility for the lives and actions of those in their care, as well as for non-combatants and the wounded.

'Experience often triggers an emotional response; but in the case of combat, the emotional response is more complex, more deeply felt, and of stronger intensity. Intense affect describes how the experiences identified as developmental by participants in this study were charged with emotion – emotion ranging from sheer rage, anger, and fear to relief, joy, and love – emotion experienced both by the leaders and by those around them'.

'Embodied feedback describes feedback that manifests itself in such a way that it is experienced by all the senses and leaves a lasting impression. Such feedback holds a mirror up for the leader, enabling sight of issues the leader might otherwise miss. While embodied feedback might include verbal and written forms, it goes beyond this conceptually to provide deeper meaning and sustained impact. This might include tangible failure, success, loss of a soldier, loss of a critical piece of equipment, or a personal crisis of limitations. There's no way for the leader to avoid the impression that embodied feedback delivers. It is in the moment, it is raw, it is in your face, it is not couched in politically correct terms, it is uncompromising. The experience of embodied feedback leads us to consider the learning process of reflective observation in the broadest possible terms. During reflective observation, the leader in combat must continue to gather information from the environment, even after the initial experience evaporates'.

> This study suggests that company commanders in combat are developing important competencies related to effective leadership. While the context of combat requires specific skills related to time-critical and highly consequential decisions, many of the competencies leaders learn in combat are generalizable. Four of the most critical outcomes include judgment, innovation, resilience, and compassion.

Our second context comes from Armstrong's study (Chapter 11) of how surgeons were enabled to pioneer *minimally invasive abdominal surgery* in the United States in the early 1990s. The majority of workshop participants started with two- or three-day surgical training workshops, offered across six independent training programme sites in various regions of the United States. These were directed by community surgeons in mid-adult life (aged 40–60) with established practices. The structure of the surgical training workshops served cultural (transformational) as well as technical ends. Surgeons were forced by circumstances to acquire new skills, while their 'identities' were modified through the ritual process created by the workshop developers. Finally, the early development of minimally invasive abdominal surgery took place in decentralized centres of knowledge production and transmission. The widespread adoption of new surgical techniques in the 1990s required ongoing, dynamic assessment of changing risks, roles, responsibilities and routines. To understand this change process, researchers must investigate why, where and how professionals acquire not only explicit but also *tacit* understandings of their craft. This significant change (transformative learning) is best understood in context, which means shifting scholarly focus to the broader societal and cultural domain within which professionals develop and change over time. Significant, transformative professional learning occurs when contextual demands impel the learner to acquire both new skills and schemas, and the dispositions or attitudes associated with them. Thus, professional identities change in response to forces beyond the individual.

Our third example of a context for learning is a *by-product of working.* Chapter 2 starts with a list of work processes which engender learning but are often taken for granted. Eraut (2007) found that the majority of learning events at work were described as working but not as learning, because formal learning activities were not involved. We found four processes that always involved working with other people: *working alongside other people, consultations within or without the working group, participation in group processes* and *working with clients.* Four other processes could involve other people, but did not necessarily need it: *tackling challenging tasks and roles, problem solving, trying things out* and *consolidating, extending and refining skills.* The chapter continues by (1) looking at activities within these processes, (2) reporting research on the contextual factors affecting this kind of workplace learning and (3) Hirsh et al.'s (2004) report on managers as developers of others.

Our fourth context for learning, cross-functional groups, also from Chapter 2, describes three substantial studies.

'West and Slater (1996) found that less than a quarter of primary health care groups were successful in building effective teamwork, and cite organisational contexts as a major hindrance. In particular, there are diverse lines of management, anomalous reward systems, poor training for teamwork, and a lack of ongoing support for teams. There are examples of successful teams in the literature, but they are not common and do not often last for long' (p. 10).

'Miller et al. (2001) studied six cross-professional teams in detail, only one of which could be described as fully integrated. Some had a central core of members and a rarely consulted group of outliers, the others could only be described as fragmented' (p. 10). When government policies in the late 1990s made changes in the healthcare environment, allegiance to professional rather than team groups was reinforced, and the outcomes for patients were detrimental. Many 'professionals were expected to work with patients outside of the designated population defined by the team; . . . and teams of professionals were brought together who had very different patient foci and did not know who was contributing in what way to a particular patient's care' (p. 11). 'Where communication structures remained within one professional group, the effectiveness of inter-professional communication was often reduced through professionals neglecting or misjudging others' contributions, thus further weakening team allegiance. . . . Where people were located together in order to practice, then there were opportunities for learning about each other's contribution. But working separately made this more difficult, and the lack of any central location where they could meet to discuss team practice and patient issues made it even more difficult. In addition, professionals who did not work closely were denied the opportunity to engage in on-going . . . discussions or . . . form social bonds that strengthened their teams' (p. 11).

A more positive approach was 'Pissarro et al.'s (1991) comparative study of 16 US cardiac surgery departments implementing the same innovation, a new technology for minimally invasive cardiac surgery, was remarkable for its inclusion of key outcome measures for an identical project in different organisations' (p. 11). 'By the 40th case, the fastest team's adjusted procedure time was 143 min and the slowest team took 305 min, the average was 220 min. The faster times both improved patient safety and saved money. What factors accounted for this variation? The fastest team was handpicked by the adopting surgeon on the basis of their demonstrated ability to work well together, seniority was not considered. . . . The entire cardiology department was invited to a presentation at which the new system was explained and indications for referral were discussed, both in general and for the early cases in particular. Weekly meetings to discuss upcoming cases still take place. The perfusionists and operating-room nurses met to agree on the standard terminology they would use during the operation. The surgical procedure strictly followed the training model for the first 30 cases, and there were team debriefings after each of the first 20 cases. They started much more slowly than the average and reached the average speed on their 8th case. There were no changes of team members for the first 15 cases, and after that new members had to observe 4 cases and be mentored through 2 cases before being fully admitted to the group. The surgeon encouraged input and feedback from other team members in the operating room, and was described as "willing to empower the team." Both the ongoing attention to the learning of the team and the coordination with the other relevant departments that enabled organisational learning were rarely found in the cross-professional teams that participated in the other studies' (p. 12).

Finally, we return to the academic context in Chapter 12. Mc Kee examines the contemporary policy and economic context of British universities which are increasingly expected to broaden their range of applicants and their curricula provision to support the need for a knowledge-based society. The UK government decided that learning and teaching practices should become sites for innovation and change. Implementing changes proved to be problematic and required shifts in individual and organizational practices and identities. Underpinning these challenges were differing views about the purposes of higher education and the nature of scholarship, particularly the relationship between teaching and research.

In 'the more research-intensive universities, CETLs appeared to enable a shift towards developing teaching and learning practice and valuing teaching with reward and recognition at individual and institutional level. In post 1992 universities (new universities, usually without many established research profiles), CETLs seemed to enable a shift towards pedagogical research through providing opportunities to engage with it. How much re-balancing could be achieved depended upon resources supporting engagement in new activities. For example, not all teaching staff were given time by their departments to engage in "extra" CETL commitments; so efforts to move in new directions were sometimes additional to established workloads. Survey and interview data both indicate that the relationship with the host institution was key to how CETLs could function. 42% of CETL directors considered they had little or no support from senior managers', and this limited 'the extent to which CETLs could engage people both within institutions and beyond that to the sector' (p. 11).

Encouragement to improve the quality and status of teaching within higher education has created new practices and identities at individual and institutional levels. In common with other chapters, the sustainability of these new forms of practice is intricately linked with how they will continue to be valued and recognized institutionally, within the profession and among stakeholders and the client base of higher education.

References

1. Becher, R. A., Eraut, M. R., & Knight, J. (1981). *Policies for educational accountability*. London: Heinemann Educational Books.
2. Blasi, A. (1984). Moral identity: Its role in moral functioning. In W. M. Kurtines & J. L. Gewirtz (Eds.), *Morality, moral behavior, and moral development* (pp. 129–139). New York: Wiley.
3. Bryson, J. (1995). *Strategic planning for public and nonprofit organizations*. San Francisco: Jossey-Bass.
4. Eraut, M. (1998). Concepts of competence. *Journal of Interprofessional Care*, *12*(2), 127–139.
5. Eraut, M. (2004). Informal learning in the workplace. *Studies in Continuing Education*, *26*(2), 247–274.
6. Eraut, M. (2007). Learning from other people in the workplace. *Oxford Review of Education*, *33*(4), 403–422.
7. Eraut, M., Alderton, J., Cole, G., & Senker, P. (2000). Development of knowledge and skills at work. In F. Coffield (Ed.), *Differing visions of a learning society, Vol. 1* (pp. 231–262). Bristol: The Policy Press.
8. Fishman, W., Solomon, B., Greenspan, D., & Gardner, H. (2004). *Making good: How young people cope with moral dilemmas at work*. Cambridge, MA: Harvard University Press.
9. Guba, E., & Lincoln, Y. (1981). *Effective evaluation: Improving the usefulness of education results through responsive and naturalistic approaches*. San Francisco: Jossey-Bass.
10. Hirsh, W., Silverman, M., Tamkin, P., & Jackson, C. (2004). *Managers as developers of others*. IES Report 407. Brighton: Institute for Employment Studies.
11. Kegan, R. (1982). *The evolving self*. Cambridge, MA: Harvard University Press.
12. Kouzes, J. M., & Posner, B. Z. (1995). *The leadership challenge*. San Francisco: Jossey-Bass.
13. May, L. (1996). *The socially responsive self. Social theory and professional ethics*. Chicago: The University of Chicago Press.
14. McClelland, D. C. (1976). *A guide to job competency assessment*. Boston: McBer.

15. Miller, C., Freeman, M., & Ross, N. (2001). *Interprofessional practice in health and social care: Challenging the shared learning agenda*. London: Arnold.
16. Pissarro, G. P., Bohmer, M. J., & Henderson, A. C. (2001). Organizatonal differences in rates of learning: Evidence from the adoption of minimally invasive cardiac surgery. *Management Science*, *47*(6), 752–768.
17. Rule, J. T., & Bebeau, M. J. (2005). *Dentists who care: Inspiring stories of professional commitment*. Chicago, IL: Quintessence Publishing Co, Inc.
18. Scott, P. (2004, July). *Knowledge work in a knowledge society: Rethinking the links between university teaching and research*. Unpublished manuscript. The Higher Education Academy Learning and Teaching Conference, University of Hertfordshire.
19. Spencer, L. M., & Spencer, S. M. (1993). *Competence at work: Models for superior performance*. New York: Wiley.
20. Stake, R. E. (Ed.). (1975). *Evaluating the arts in education: A responsive approach*. Columbus, OH: Merrill.
21. West, M. A., & Slater, J. (1996). *The effectiveness of teamworking in primary health care*. Report for Health Education Authority, UK.

Chapter 2
Developing a Broader Approach to Professional Learning

Michael Eraut

Our own research (Eraut et al., 1995; Eraut, Alderton, Cole, & Senker, 2000; Eraut, 2007b, 2007c) demonstrated that the majority of learning events in workplace contexts are not formally taught, but become embedded in normal work. This may result from socialisation processes that are only partly recognised or from aspects of common practices that are forgotten after they became routinised. The key factors affecting such informal learning are the appropriate levels of challenge and support, confidence and commitment, and personal agency. These factors, in turn, are influenced by the allocation, structuring and perceived value of the work and the quality of relationships at work. Hence, the work processes and activities that lead to learning are strongly influenced by the immediate supervisors' and/or managers' own interpretations of appropriate working practices. Cross-functional teamwork, in particular, requires more than just good communication, good will and good support.

The success of this approach also depends on the quality of higher level professionals and managers. The need for both specialist expertise and organisational learning raises strategic issues on future work, and how to select and/or develop others for unknown organisational changes and areas of expertise yet to be developed. This brings us back to the two major influences affecting formal learning: continuing professional education (CPE) and human resources development (HRD). However, additional practical learning in the workplace is often neglected, and courses have to be just in time to be effective. Many organisations find it very difficult to develop strategic, coherent foci and effective communications that connect CPE with HRD, working practices, organisational practices and senior management. Thus, the chapter ends with a summary of what helps, or hinders, workplace learning.

M. Eraut (✉)
Sussex School of Education, University of Sussex, Brighton BN1 9RH, UK
e-mail: m.eraut@sussex.ac.uk

A. Mc Kee, M. Eraut (eds.), *Learning Trajectories, Innovation and Identity for Professional Development*, Innovation and Change in Professional Education 7,
DOI 10.1007/978-94-007-1724-4_2, © Springer Science+Business Media B.V. 2012

2.1 Informal Learning and the Factors That Affect It

The past two decades have given rise to very different approaches to the development of practices, capabilities, expertise, management and organisations. Learning is no longer treated mainly as a separate activity, but as an ongoing dimension of normal work in all but the most static organisations. Thus the first section of this chapter presents evidence on *the role of informal learning in the workplace and the factors that affect it*. The common reluctance to recognise the significance of informal learning stems from the dominant academic epistemology of formal knowledge and learning. Most working practices cannot be adequately described by codified knowledge alone, and self-accounts of learning usually focus on formally recognised outcomes that can easily be described and justified. Failure to appreciate these problems leads to the exclusion of knowledge that is not easily explained or discussed, and the exclusion of informal learning that is not noticed by learners because (a) it is a normal taken-for-granted part of work and (b) it is not noticed when it occurs within formal education or training contexts.

This creates important methodological problems. How can researchers detect and describe learning that is neither known to them nor recognised by the learners concerned? The answer we found was to start with observations and the discourse of description, not by asking questions which lead to a discourse of justification. We then extended the discourse of description to ask what we might have seen on other recent occasions, if we had been present. Finally, going back for a few months, and looking forward to expected changes at work, enabled us to ask about how they had coped, or were coping, with changes in individual or collective working practices. Only then did we feel it safe to ask questions about learning.

Eraut et al.'s (2000) research on the mid-career learning of 120 managers and professionals in the *engineering*, *business* and *health-care* sectors found that most of the learning that occurred was informal, neither clearly specified nor planned in advance. It arose naturally out of the demands and challenges of work, solving problems, improving quality and/or productivity or coping with change, and out of social interactions in the workplace with colleagues, customers or clients. Responding to such challenges entailed both working and learning, because one could not be separated from the other. Sometimes, however, people recognised a need for some additional knowledge or skill to improve the quality of their work or expand its range, and pursued their goal by a combination of self-directed learning and taking advantage of relevant learning opportunities as and when they appeared.

In normal working groups, we found three main types of learning situation: collaborative teamwork, ongoing mutual consultation and support, and observing others in action. In *collaborative teamwork*, mutual learning tended to be assumed, but with other types of working group, there was often more overt discussion about learning from each other. Typical consultations could entail a request for quick advice, seeking another perspective on a problem, help with a technical procedure or information on whom to ask for help on a particular issue. In a *start-up activity*, knowledge and skills are being acquired in a multitude of ways and can flow from person to person in several directions at once, whereas in an *established activity*, newcomers may acquire the skills and knowledge needed from those already proficient.

When Eraut et al. embarked on a larger longitudinal study of the first three years in employment of chartered accountants, engineers and hospital nurses[1] in 2001, we found that our previous distinction between informal and formal learning was difficult to sustain because although most recruits were clearly recognised as 'learners', they were more likely to be given informal advice and feedback from those around them than by those formally designated as their mentors. Hence we decided to classify learning processes according to whether their principal object was working or learning (Eraut et al., 2005a; Eraut, 2007c). Processes in the left column of Table 2.1 were judged to be *working processes*, of which *learning* was a *by-product*, while those in the right column were clearly recognisable as *learning processes*. We also chose to distinguish these ongoing processes from *short activities*, such as asking questions, observing or reflecting. These activities could occur many times in a single process and were found within almost every type of process, often several at a time. Hence we located them in a central column in Table 2.1. The right column is discussed with CPE in Section 2.4.

Work processes with learning as a by-product accounted for a very high proportion of the learning events reported by those we interviewed during both mid-career and early career projects. Their success depended on both the available opportunities and the quality of relationships in the workplace. Hence the amount of learning reported varied significantly with person and context.

Participation in group processes covers *team-working* towards a common outcome and *groups* set up for a special purpose such as discussing a client, problem solving, reviewing some practices, planning ahead or responding to external changes.

Table 2.1 A typology of early career learning

Work processes with learning as a by-product	Learning activities located within work or learning processes	Learning processes at or near the workplace
Participation in group processes	Asking questions	Being supervised
Working alongside others	Getting information	Being coached
Consultation	Locating resource people	Being mentored
Tackling challenging tasks and roles	Listening and observing	Shadowing
Problem solving	Reflecting	Visiting other sites
Trying things out	Learning from mistakes	Conferences
Consolidating, extending and refining skills	Giving and receiving feedback	Short courses
Working with clients	Use of mediating artefacts	Working for a qualification
		Independent study

[1] This began with 40 nurses, 38 engineers and 14 accountants, and 72% continued for all 3 years.

Working alongside others allows people to observe and listen to others at work and to participate in joint activities, and hence to learn new practices and new perspectives, to become aware of different kinds of knowledge and expertise, and to gain some sense of other people's tacit knowledge. When people see what is being said and done, explanations can be much shorter while the fine detail of incidents is still in people's minds. Hence, multi-sensory engagement over some time enables the gradual development of tacit as well as explicit situational understanding.

Consultations within or outside the working group or even outside the organisation are used to coordinate activities or to get advice. The act of initiating a consultation, however, depends on the relationships between the parties, the extent of a worker's network and the culture of the workplace. For *newcomers* the distinction between a consultation and being mentored or supervised is not always clear, as part of a mentor's or supervisor's role is making oneself available for consultation.

Tackling challenging tasks and roles requires on-the-job learning and, if successful, leads to increased motivation and confidence. However, people are less likely to take on challenges until they feel confident in their ability to succeed as a result of previous experience and/or in the support of their manager and/or colleagues. Without such previous experience and support, challenges pose too high a risk.

Problem solving, individually or in groups, necessarily entails learning; otherwise there would be no problem. Such problems are not only technical, but may also involve acquiring new knowledge before one can start, searching for relevant expertise, imagination, persistence and interpersonal negotiation.

Trying things out is distinguished from less purposeful behaviour by the intention to learn from the experience. It requires some prior assessment of risk, especially where other people might be affected, and it may also require special arrangements for getting feedback, as well as time for subsequent reflection and evaluation.

Consolidating, extending and refining skills are particularly important when entering new jobs or taking on new roles, when it is sometimes supported by episodes of supervision, coaching or feedback. It is greatly helped by informal personal support and some sense of an onward learning trajectory.

Working with clients entails learning (1) about the client, (2) from any novel aspects of the client's problem or request and (3) from any new ideas that arise from the encounter. Some professionals have daily experiences of working with clients, which may or may not be recognised as learning opportunities. Some progress from less to more important clients or from those with simple needs to those with more complex needs. There can also be a strong *emotional dimension*, for example when a client arrives in a distressed state or expects to receive bad news. This is a context where sharing experiences with colleagues can be helpful. Client contacts often give the work meaning and value, and thus enhance a worker's sense of collective purpose.

Four of the eight learning modes in the left column of Table 2.1 *always involve* communication with other people, and the other four modes may *often involve it.* Although the *overt learning processes* in the right column of Table 2.1 are associated with acknowledged modes of formal learning, many of them may also occur informally and spontaneously without being visible to those outside the working group.

This brings us to the central *activities* column, which is less well defined and could be described in terms of opportunities for *personal agency* within the contexts listed in the two outer columns. The *giving and receiving of feedback* is probably the most difficult, the most important and the most sensitive of all activities. Our research found it in four very different settings. Working alongside people provides opportunities for *immediate comment* on aspects of a task or role given *on the spot,* or soon after the event, by a co-participant or witness. The focus is usually very clear, and the immediacy allows straight talk without giving offence, whereas *informal conversations away from the job* often convey indirect and/or unintended messages as well as the intended advice. Managers normally have some responsibility for a person's *short- to medium-term progress* and an obligation to provide formative feedback on a regular basis. The greatest difficulty, however, seems to be the process of *appraisal* where designated appraisers are expected, but often do not succeed, when giving normative feedback on personal strengths and weaknesses and meeting expectations (see below).

Mediating artefacts play a very important role in structuring work and sharing information. Patient records in a hospital cover temperature, fluid intake and output, drugs administration, biochemical data and various types of image. These refer both to the immediate past and to plans for the immediate future, and salient features considered important are prioritised for the incoming shift at every handover. Engineers and architects create and discuss virtual design 'drawings' and photographs with colleagues, contractors and clients on an almost daily basis. Chartered accountants learn how to interpret audit files and how their clients' business processes are represented in their accounts. Both accountants and engineers learn to use large software packages for organising parts of their work processes.

These two research projects also enabled Eraut et al. (2005b) to develop a model (Fig. 2.1) of the factors affecting workplace learning and their mutual interactions.

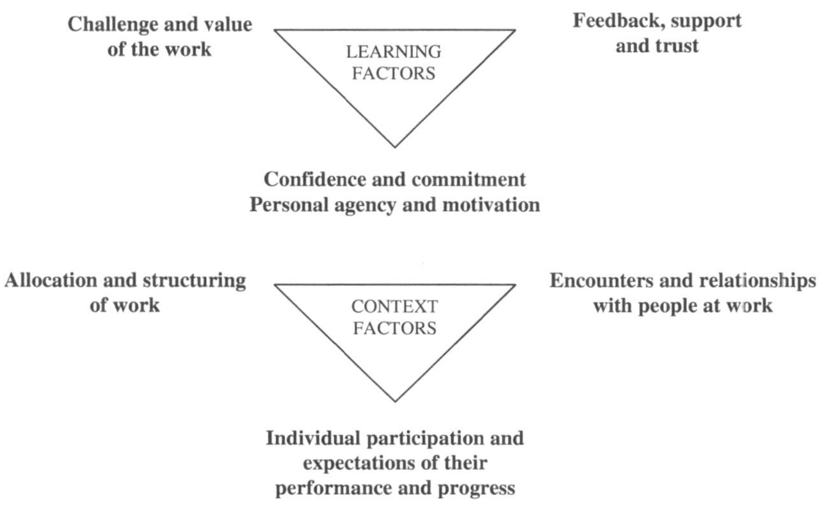

Fig. 2.1 Factors affecting learning at work: the Two-Triangle Model

The similarities between these two triangles are important. The top left corners are concerned with the work being done, the top right corners are concerned with the people encountered at work and the bottom corners are concerned with individual workers. The most frequently cited factor was *confidence*: this was seen both as a major outcome of a significant learning experience and as a critical determinant of good performance at work. This applied to off-the-job learning, especially in mid-career, as well as to learning in the workplace. Sometimes it derived from the achievement of a good result or the solution of a problem, and sometimes from the recognition that others were no less fallible than themselves; usually it was fairly specific, relating to the ability to execute a task or successfully perform a role. Such job-specific confidence is believed to be a major determinant of the goals an individual will set and their motivation to achieve those goals. Other sources of *motivation* reported in our interviews were self-development through learning, changing and proving oneself, career progression, an orientation towards outcomes for clients or the work group and professionalism in the sense of pride in a job well done. All these other outcomes, however, helped to sustain confidence rather than create it. People tend to learn more in those areas where they are already fairly confident. Learning in areas where one's confidence is low often requires support in the form of confirming the value of the learning goals, general facilitation and encouragement, and sensitive but honest and well-directed feedback.

Offering support to an individual, particularly at critical junctures, leads to them developing confidence in their capabilities. Increasing confidence enables them to better manage more challenging work, which, if successfully achieved, increases confidence further. A virtuous circle of positive development is established, in which the interactions between *challenge*, *support* and *confidence* are reciprocal, each reinforcing and being conditional upon the other. The contextual significance of the word 'confidence' depended on which aspects of this triangular relationship were most significant at any particular time. Often, it came close to Bandura's (1995) concept of self-efficacy, relating to their self-perceived ability to execute a particular task or successfully perform a role. But, especially in the early stages, it could also refer to their confidence in their colleagues' support. In accordance with our recognition of the importance of learning from work colleagues and the need for a positive learning climate in every work setting, challenge and support need to be seen as *distributed roles* to which all members of a working group contribute. *Personal agency* was also added to recognise participants' own sense of choice, meaningfulness, competence and progress (Thomas, 2000), which is not necessarily aligned with their employer's priorities.

The second triangle draws attention to the context of learning. *Allocation and structuring of work* was central to our participants' progress, because it affected (1) the difficulty or challenge of the work, (2) the extent to which it was individual or collaborative and (3) the opportunities for meeting, observing and working alongside people who had more or different expertise. We found that decisions affecting the *allocation and structuring of work* for novices (Eraut, 2007b) could be determined by any combination of the following factors:

(1) The *nature of the work*, the way in which the organisation handled it and the discretion given to local managers in decisions of this kind. In all three of our professions, local managers had significant opportunities to facilitate learning through their allocation of work and support of novice workers.
(2) The *quantity and urgency of the work* in hand at the time. This was a major issue in hospitals where work overload almost overwhelmed novice nurses, while at the same time reducing the amount of support they could get from more experienced colleagues. On the other hand, if an engineering company was undergoing a fallow period, it could be forced to limit the supply of challenging work.
(3) *Periodic decisions made by managers* in which learning needs might or might not have been considered. This was relevant when allocating novices to audit teams, nursing shifts or medium-term engineering tasks.
(4) *Decisions made by more experienced colleagues* with delegated authority, who were currently working with a novice and able to judge the appropriate level of challenge, provided they gave it sufficient priority.

Whether these decisions benefited the learning of the novice professional depended on the disposition, imagination, competence (in making these kinds of decisions) and available thinking time of those who made them.

The second triangle also focused on *encounters and relationships* with people at work and their effect on the learning of mid-career professionals. Thus, Eraut (2000) suggested that more attention be given to the micro-climates of workplaces, whose most desirable attributes might include

- A blame-free culture which provides mutual support
- Learning from experiences, positive and negative, at both group and individual levels
- Encouraging and talking about learning
- Trying to make full use of the knowledge resources of its members
- Locating and using relevant knowledge from outside the group
- Enhancing and extending understandings and capabilities of both the group as a whole and its individual members

Factors working against the development of such climates include the increasing instability of working groups, many individuals' lack of experience of positive working groups and the tendency of many groups to develop an introspective protectionism that resists change. Our analysis suggests that a group climate for learning has to be created, sustained and recreated at regular intervals, and this has to be a management responsibility. The learning of individuals and work groups has to be high on managers' agendas, and managers have to be educated and supported in this role.

2.2 The Role of Managers in Supporting Learning

This section follows up the implications of the previous two sections, and then moves on to consider the role of line managers in the longer term development of those they manage. These roles are complementary, and the optimal balance between them will vary with the context. When organisations focus on learning which takes place on or very near to the job, they need to concentrate on the role of managers and supervisors as facilitators of learning. Whether or not improvements start with off-the-job learning, the relevant managers have to provide and follow through the development and support of improved or novel activities. Hence, managers are expected to use their own initiative to identify and respond to learning needs at team or unit level.

Our typology of learning modes in Section 2.1 indicates how learning opportunities in the workplace depend on both the organisation of work and good relationships. This is an area where managers and supervisors can play an important role in promoting and enhancing the learning of those whom they manage, both individually and collectively. One major obstacle is that knowledge of workplace learning is conspicuously absent from most workplaces, yet most of the required behaviours are within most workers' capability and simple common sense. Moreover, much of what is needed can be done by people other than managers. The manager's role is not to provide most of the learning support themselves, but to set the climate, encourage their staff to take on this role as an integral part of their working responsibility and include the facilitation of learning in their management of performance. They also need to receive some feedback from their peers and those they manage, a practice now formalised in some organisations as 360-degree feedback.

In order to fulfill this role, managers need to know that being *over-challenged* or *under-challenged* is bad for learning and morale. So providing an appropriate level of challenge is important for developing confidence and making good progress. Hence, this needs to be given attention when *allocating and structuring the work of individuals and groups*. When this is not under the control of the managers concerned, they should discuss it with their immediate peers and draw it to the attention of their own managers, because of the following reasons:

(1) The quantity and quality of *informal learning* can be enhanced by increasing opportunities for workers to *consult* with and *work alongside* others in teams or temporary groups. Hence, good opportunities are needed for meeting and working with others to develop mutual trust and cooperative relationships.
(2) They may need skills in *conflict resolution* and addressing bad relationships that threaten the group climate and/or achievement, and may need to consult others for a second opinion or mediation if they themselves are directly involved.
(3) Support and feedback are critically important for learning, retention and commitment. *Feedback* is most effective within the context of good working relationships, and the rapid feedback essential for short-term learning is best provided by people on the spot. Hence, it is important for managers to develop

a positive learning culture of mutual support both among individuals and within and across work groups.

(4) More feedback on *progress*, *strengths and weaknesses*, and *meeting organisational expectations* is also needed, and appraisal needs to be carefully prepared both for these performance issues and for discussing future learning trajectories and aspirations. We often found that good short-term feedback on performance was accompanied by an almost total absence of strategic feedback, giving even the most confident workers an unnecessary sense of uncertainty and lowering their commitment to their current employers (Eraut, 2007a).

(5) Upsetting feedback, anxiety about one's status or performance, client behaviour, relationships or events outside the workplace can all influence the *emotional dimension* of a person's working life, and this may require ongoing attention for a period. The manager needs to signal their awareness and to check that they are receiving appropriate support (Eraut & Hirsh, 2007).

The role of line managers in supporting learning is quite complex. It includes identifying skill and learning needs at both individual and group levels against their understanding of what performance should look like. It also embraces discussions with individuals about their *own work* and *career aspirations* and the extent to which the organisation can support these through learning opportunities inside or outside the organisation. Where the individual or team needs learning support, it is up to the manager to think about whether this should be in the form of a *course* or through *on-the-job support*. For the former, the setting of training objectives and decisions about how to procure training would also often rest with the manager, ideally in discussion with a training professional. For the latter, the manager will have to either do the on-the-job coaching themselves or find someone else to do it. Managers are also expected to make an input into learning evaluation and to assess the *impact* which learning has on job *performance*. The deceptively simple phrase '*manager as coach*' does not really unpack either the complexity or the scale of learning which is often needed in a team.

Workplaces are complex interpersonal environments, where managers need to be well informed about relationships and personal or collective concerns without being unduly intrusive. They also need to delegate and to work through other people as well as by direct action. Otherwise, they will never have enough time to realise their good intentions and those they manage will have less opportunity for self-development. It is increasingly recognised that frequent informal conversations with individuals and small groups create good settings for preparing people for coming issues, listening to their problems and concerns, seeking their advice, asking them to consult others about a problem and come back with suggestions, etc. In this context, managers' personal interests need as much attention as the collective interest, if they are not to feel exploited. This means being supportive both when they have personal problems and in developing their future careers.

The Institute of Employment Studies Report on *managers as developers of others* (Hirsh, Silverman, Tamkin, & Jackson, 2004) studied managers' roles in developing their workers in four organisations, two private and two public. They found that *good development* was delivered through a supportive relationship, sometimes short lived but often over a period of months or years, and was typically characterised by the following features:

- Managers set a *climate* in which they are easy to approach, and where development is an important part of working life.
- They build *developmental relationships* with individuals in their teams and more widely. These relationships are often fostered by frequent, informal conversations about work, listening to concerns and offering positive support.
- Good development support is quite *focused* through a clear, shared analysis of development needs, frequent review and honest but constructive *feedback.*
- The delivery of development is through a wide range of learning methods tailored to individual needs. They often engage in *informal coaching*, make good use of formal training offered by the organisation and focus heavily on finding the *right kinds of experience* both within the job (often through delegating developmental tasks) and outside the job (through projects, etc.).
- They offer *active career development* and work to help individuals have a realistic sense of their own potential and readiness for possible job moves. They see the individual in the context of their previous work experiences and their interests and obligations outside work.

These individuals reported increases in motivation and behaviour at work resulting from the increased sense of interest in work they obtained from the first two or three steps above. So it seems that attention to development can improve both the *capability* of individuals and their *motivation* and *engagement.*

We conclude that *managers have a major influence on workplace learning and culture that extends far beyond most job descriptions.* Doing nothing about learning and development will have a strong negative effect. Thus managers need (1) to have greater awareness of the modes through which people may learn in the workplace, (2) to recognise and attend to the factors which enhance or hinder individual or group learning and (3) to take the initiative in the longer term development of their staff. Preparation for this role should be given much greater priority in management development programmes, incorporated into qualifications for managers and supervisors, and included in the appraisal of all managers. The justification for giving this such high priority is that what is good for learning is also good for retention, quality improvement and developing the skills and people that will be needed in the future (Eraut & Hirsh, 2007).

2.3 Teamwork, Organisational Learning and Knowledge Management

Some of the most useful research on groups and teams goes back to the post-war period. Hackman's (1987) review is still one of the most useful sources. Developments since then have included both cross-functional teams and research into learning at the organisational level.

Kettley and Hirsh's (2000) report on Learning from Cross-Functional Teamwork found that the teams in their study were created for one of the following reasons:

- Innovation and new product/service development
- Problem solving across traditional organisational/functional boundaries
- Integration of systems typically via process re-design/re-engineering
- Coordination into a 'one-stop shop' or a single point of contact or delivery

Two important distinctions were the team's purpose and its mode of organisation. Their purpose was either to 'shape the future of the organisational strategy and development of the business', i.e. to generate new knowledge or synergistic learning, or to take responsibility for largely operational business processes, with an emphasis on the application and delivery of shared knowledge. They could either be integrated into the organisation as a semi-permanent structure or be organised as a largely separate project. However, there seemed to be no expectations about *how* or *what* group members might learn, nor did group members find it easy to answer questions about learning without some prompting. When asked which of four alternatives enabled them to learn the most, 43% answered 'direct transfer from experts' and about 20% chose each of the alternatives: 'picking things up from observing diverse others in action, collective problem-solving and experimentation' and 'consolidating prior experience and re-framing new insights'.

The health sector is full of cross-functional groups, but most of the research reveals that few function well. There seems to be an assumption that professional services can be developed without developing effective teams. West and Slater (1996) found that less than a quarter of primary health-care groups were successful in building effective teamwork, and cite organisational contexts as a major hindrance. In particular, there are diverse lines of management, anomalous reward systems, poor training for teamwork and a lack of ongoing support for teams. There are examples of successful teams in the literature, but they are not common and do not often last for long. Miller, Freeman, and Ross (2001) studied six cross-professional teams in detail, only one of which could be described as fully integrated. Some had a central core of members and a rarely consulted group of outliers; the others could only be described as fragmented. They also identified four organisational factors hindering team development, which can also be found in other contexts:

(1) *When government policies in the late 1990s* reduced the levels of stability and predictability in the health-care environment, both communication and understanding of others' roles were compromised, allegiance to professional groups rather than team groups was reinforced and the outcomes for patients were detrimental.
(2) *The diversity of the patient population* with which teams had to work related to two issues. The first was the extent to which professionals were expected to work with patients outside of the designated population defined by the team. This caused professionals to prioritise their work in ways that were sometimes detrimental to work with patients within the team, thus creating frustration for

themselves and other team members. The second issue was when teams of professionals were brought together who had very different patient foci and did not know who was contributing in what way to a particular patient's care.

(3) *Team-oriented structures and processes* related to two aspects: the degree of collaboration across professional management and the development of collaborative communication structures. Lack of collaboration across management structures was seen to inhibit the development of team practices and to create, through arbitrary decision making, unpredictable situations for team members, which resulted in frustration and professional defensiveness. Where communication structures remained within one professional group, the effectiveness of inter-professional communication was often reduced through professionals neglecting or misjudging others' contributions, thus further weakening team allegiance.

(4) *Opportunities for working closely* were important in two ways. Where people were located together in order to practice, there were opportunities for learning about each other's contribution. Working separately made this more difficult, and the lack of any central location where they could meet to discuss team practice and patient issues made it even more difficult. In addition, professionals who did not work closely were denied the opportunity to engage in ongoing ad hoc communication around particular issues and to form social bonds that strengthened their teams. These structural issues and their associated processes had implications for the way in which teams were able to function and, as a consequence, affected patient care.

Pissarro, Bohmer, and Henderson's (2001) comparative study of 16 US cardiac surgery departments implementing the same innovation, a new technology for minimally invasive cardiac surgery, was remarkable for its inclusion of key outcome measures for an identical project in different organisations. In comparison with conventional surgery, the new procedure was 'a far more integral process in which task boundaries are more blurred and tasks are more interdependent. Thus, the technology disrupted the smooth flow of the [conventional] operating routine and required the development of new communication behaviours to enable the execution of a more interdependent set of processes'. The main outcome criterion was the net adjusted procedure time, for which the period of aortic occlusion was subtracted because the only significant variation was the doctor's speed, rather than that of the team as a whole. All teams attended a three-day training programme before starting their first case. By the 40th case, the fastest team's adjusted procedure time was 143 min and the slowest team took 305 min; the average was 220 min. The faster times both improved patient safety and saved money.

What factors accounted for this variation? The fastest team was handpicked by the adopting surgeon on the basis of their demonstrated ability to work well together; seniority was not considered. There had been previous cross-department cooperation, and this was increased. The entire cardiology department was invited to a presentation at which the new system was explained and indications for referral were discussed, both in general and for the early cases in particular. Weekly meetings to discuss upcoming cases still take place. The perfusionists and operating-room nurses met to agree on the standard terminology they would use during the operation. The surgical procedure strictly followed the training model for the first 30 cases, and there were team debriefings after each of the first 20 cases. They started much more slowly than the average and reached the average speed in their eighth case. There were no changes of team members for the first 15 cases, and after that new members had to observe four cases and be mentored through two cases before being fully admitted to the group. The surgeon encouraged input and feedback from other team members in the operating room and was described as 'willing to empower the team'. Both the ongoing attention to the learning of the team and the coordination with the other relevant departments that enabled organisational learning were rarely found in the cross-professional teams that participated in the other studies.

The term '*organisational learning*' was introduced in the 1970s to describe the development of, and continuing changes in, organisational behaviour. Argyris and Schon (1978) described it as both an agency with a task system and a cognitive enterprise with a complex system of norms, strategies and assumptions which constitutes its *theory of action*, the way we do things here. In theory, appropriate changes are made if the intended outcomes are not achieved, but their effect will depend on the accuracy and timing of the information received and how that information is interpreted. Hence, Duncan and Weiss (1979) defined *organisational learning* as the process by which knowledge is developed about action–outcome relationships between the organisation and its environment. Argyris and Schon (1978) would also add *double loop learning*, the second-order development of knowledge about previous organisational learning and the factors that helped or hindered it.

Daft and Weick (1984) took this problem still further in their explanation of the diverse ways in which organisations obtained knowledge about their environment in terms of (1) management's beliefs about the analysability of the external environment and (2) the extent to which the organisation intruded into the environment to understand it. When the environment is deemed to be analysable, the organisation seeks for formal data, either passively from available sources or actively by surveys and data gathering in the field. When the environment is deemed to be unanalysable, the passive organisation resorts to hunches and seeks for informal data, while the active organisation uses experiments or pilot testing.

When considering the knowledge needed to inform decision making at different levels and in different parts of an organisation, there is a balance to be found between the technical knowledge acquired through training, the practical knowledge acquired through experience and the interpersonal skills in acquiring relevant knowledge from customers, suppliers or other relevant organisations. At the strategic level, judgements about marketing, technical innovations, organisational capability and financial implications have to be considered in relation to each other by people who can respect each other and work together. Organisational learning depends on the organisation's ability to handle its existing knowledge, its acquisition and use of external knowledge and its priorities for developing new knowledge through learning and recruitment.

In the UK, the idea of the *learning organisation* has been developing since the mid-1970s, especially through the work of Pedler, Burgoyne and Boydell. In *The Learning Company* (Pedler, Burgoyne, & Boydell, 1991), they define the learning company as *'an organization that facilitates the learning of all its members and continuously transforms itself'*. So the first central idea is that increasing the amount and frequency of individual learning in organisations can somehow lead to positive change in the organisation as a whole. Pedler et al. provided no particular model of how this might happen, but preferred to give what they called 'glimpses' which illustrate how reflecting learning throughout the activity of an organisation might appear. Many of these glimpses are taken from real organisations.

Meanwhile, Senge (1990), who had become the best-known US proponent of the 'learning organisation', explored a third important idea – how you move beyond an organisation in which people learn a lot all the time to an organisation in which individual learning is shared and taken up in the way things are done generally. Only in this sense can we see organisational learning as something additional to individual learning. Senge argues that the team forms the most critical link between individual and organisational learning. Team learning is 'where the rubber meets the road; unless teams can learn, the organization cannot learn'.

The process of what came to be called *knowledge management* started with the conservation of documents for future use, and this led to the possible creation of new documents to describe aspects of the experience of the organisation which might be useful in the future. This was often referred to as its organisational memory. It included notes and memoirs written by senior managers for their successors, and often not publicly available; advice from workers, especially those with specialist knowledge; and helping others act sensibly when they were away or not available for consultation. With improved communication technology and more flexible and distributed working, electronic access to this and other knowledge became increasingly important. Distance courses and an increasing number of library resources also became available electronically.

The next stage was to try and codify workers' practices in order to make it possible for others to learn them independently, and this raised many problems. Printed accounts and audiotapes posed considerable difficulty to both practitioners and potential users, because of their significant tacit dimension (see below). In particular, three crucial questions were conveniently forgotten:

(1) What knowledge do people need in order to be able to use the knowledge management system?
(2) What does a person need to know in order to perform a skilled action in the right way, in the right place, at the right time and appropriately fine-tuned to the particular situation?
(3) How much of any particular performance is potentially transferable and how much is person specific, or situation specific or both?

Thus even when the instructions did provide some of the required advice, people were often unable to use them. For example, Eraut et al.'s (2000) research into the mid-career learning of professionals and technicians in engineering, business and health care found that only 20% had succeeded in learning from a manual.

Elmholt (2004) found similar results in a Danish software company, when it introduced a knowledge centre based on the assumption that knowledge could be conceptualised as a resource that could be stored and retrieved from databases. He concluded:

> (1) The company's practice of knowledge sharing seems better conceived from a situated and embodied perspective, seeing knowledge as an enactment inseparable from action, and learning as social participation.
> (2) The management's occupation with implementing technological solutions for codifying, archiving and creating global access to information is conflicting with the practitioners' focus on seeking context-rich information through collegial networks.
> (3) The strategy of exercising knowledge management through control and ownership invokes a discourse that threatens to ... [treat] ... the employees as replaceable resources in a lifelong learning imperative.

Given these difficulties, many people have recognised that it is more appropriate to treat knowledge management as a process for sharing knowledge rather than codifying it. This process is more promising, although some of the micro-political concerns and communication difficulties are still there. Reducing the concern about revealing one's personal knowledge needs both initial trust in the other members of the group and anticipation of benefiting from other people's knowledge. These will be easier to develop if the groups are small and someone with training in knowledge elicitation is present. Good relationships enable people to develop their learning by using mediating artefacts as foci for conversations. The knowledge to be shared is not in the text and/or pictures but in the conversations around them, and that is where a facilitator, familiar with the artefacts, can be most helpful. The artefacts themselves can be narrative accounts of cases, customers and critical incidents or prototype diagrams or knowledge maps that invite detailed additions from practical experience and adaptation to fit them.

For example, Eraut et al. (2005b) observed huge differences in the learning climate between wards in the same hospital, which could be attributed to their ward managers. The most positive managers had often developed senior nurses with the same vision for learning, who were ideal candidates for promotion to management jobs where they could begin to share their vision and gradually transform their ward. The social nature of workplace learning suggests that problem wards might be more effectively improved by importing a manager and two or three senior people with the same vision than by any change in policy. Although this change would take two or three years, the idea of 'growing' a new climate might be more acceptable than that of 'transforming' an old climate. Building new groups by introducing an effective core group of people with experience of developing learning is probably more effective than making grand, universal interventions.

New knowledge is likely to arise from these knowledge-sharing groups and networks, so they can also be viewed as being engaged in knowledge construction. The recognition and wider distribution of their work will enhance the morale of the groups and their willingness to continue to learn from and work with others. Wenger (1998) is now using the term *community of practice* to describe such groups, and it is posited that communities of practice may cut across the power structure of organisations by being relatively self-defined (i.e. you choose which communities you belong to) and self-governing (i.e. the community runs itself). However, the use of ICT alone could still be a limited option if tacit knowledge plays a prominent role. The term 'community of practice' was originally defined to describe communities where people learned by working alongside each other rather than exchange codified knowledge at a distance. The possibilities and limitations of learning practices in new forms of distributed networks are now beginning to be researched (Hakkarainen, Palonen, Paavola, & Lehtinen, 2004) but have yet to be fully explored.

Another source of new practice is the *transfer of new knowledge* from one context to another. This may either come with a newcomer or be imported as an innovation. In either case, being accepted and resituated in a new context will be greatly helped by the support of a team or network, which can bring several minds to bear on the transition problem as well as providing those involved with emotional support during the more difficult problem-solving activities. There are many groups where it is almost forbidden to talk about one's previous job and potential new knowledge is wasted. To adopt an innovation is not just a decision but a significant learning process for all concerned, in which the mutual interaction of the knowledge accompanying and embedded in the innovation and the explicit and tacit knowledge embedded in the context of adoption creates yet newer knowledge (Eraut, 2005). The failure to recognise the need for innovations to be resituated by creating new local knowledge, and the learning and time this requires, is responsible for the failure of the majority of potentially beneficial innovations and the late detection of inappropriate innovations (Eraut, 2004c).

Although organisational learning sounds like something the organisation controls, it has become increasingly clear that organisations truly learn only when they give much of that power back to individuals and self-selected groups. If managers will not allow employees to challenge and question accepted practices, or if they block employees from talking to people in other functions or departments, then the organisation will not learn.

2.4 Continuing Professional Education and Human Relations Development

Most CPE activities are initiated by higher education or professional associations. Some more generic activities are developed by education or adult education departments, and many specialist concerns are covered by relevant charities, particularly in education and health and social care. HRD units originated from a merger between *training* departments for technical and administrative workers, *personnel* departments and a burgeoning interest in *management development*. In general, HRD units support a wider range of learning activities than CPE, because they usually have responsibility for the learning of several professions, non-professional workers, managers and other groups of employees. However, in most organisations, managers, professional workers and safety workers get the most ongoing support. CPE is still dominated by short events with a strong emphasis on updating and university-based courses linked to potential career advancement. Its major problems are as follows:

1. The difficulty in coordinating the wide variety of potential providers
2. The cost of supporting CPE, both directly and by providing sufficient time for it to be effective
3. The limited awareness of the potential role of more informal patterns of learning

HRD has a better chance of providing a more coherent service, but is crucially dependent on management understanding of its potential. In general it focuses its attention on management, skill gaps, recruitment and retention, and legal requirements.

Both CPE and HRD practices vary widely, and some organisations have very narrow perspectives. One problem for those with a broader view is that training is more visible and familiar to most managers, while other practices require more interaction with managers and take longer to develop and evaluate. My three foci for this comparative discussion of HRD and CPE are *learning*, *performance* and *strategy* (Bierema & Eraut, 2004).

2.4.1 Learning Focus

Watkins (2000) identifies the process of fostering learning and change in organisations as a key challenge of HRD. Learning is viewed as occurring across organisation levels (individual, group, organisation), and also as impacting performance and possibly values. This emphasis on learning is shared within CPE, but it is often given less priority than knowledge. Moreover, CPE gives far less attention to learning at group and organisational levels. One reason for this may be the ambiguous position of those who have the dual role of professional practitioner and manager. The prevailing tendency is for practitioner learning to be the main focus of CPE, whereas management learning is more likely to be prioritised and provided by employers under the auspices of their HRD function. However, there are a number of processes which can be used to encourage managers and employees to attend to learning. For example, managers can and should be partly assessed on whether they develop their subordinates. Other individuals can have personal development objectives built into their job objectives, and teams can also be given performance targets that include a learning dimension.

Perhaps the most critical issues at any level are those which determine and prioritise learning needs, with what kind of consultation and at what level of detail. CPE tends to favour a market model in which providers advertise conferences, courses and workshops, and interested professionals either seek financial support and/or time off from their employers or pay their own expenses and claim tax relief. HRD has tended to use a training needs model focussed on performance, in which the contribution of employees to the learning needs analysis varies widely according to the organisational culture and the area of concern. CPE provides opportunities for sharing practitioners' experiences across organisations. HRD concentrates on sharing experiences within a single organisation, but this could include people from different sites or even different countries.

The most neglected aspect of both HRD and CPE is the problem of transfer. This covers four distinct processes with some important common aspects:

- Transfer of formal knowledge into performance in a specific context
- Transfer of performance from one context to another
- Transfer of practices from one person to another person
- Transfer of practices from one group to another group

Eraut (2004a) argues that this fundamental difficulty can be attributed to two problems: the narrow conception of practical knowledge used in most formal education and the lack of any significance or ownership of the transfer process itself. The transfer process can be deconstructed into five inter-related stages:

(1) The extraction of potentially relevant knowledge from the context(s) of its acquisition and previous use
(2) Understanding the new situation, a process that often depends on informal social learning
(3) Recognising what knowledge and skills are relevant
(4) Transforming them to fit the new situation
(5) Integrating them with other knowledge and skills in order to think, act or communicate in the new situation (Eraut, 2004a)

Salomon and Perkins (1998) made a distinction between forward-reaching and backward-reaching kinds of transfer. The forward-reaching approach anticipates that certain kinds of knowledge will be useful in the future and is most likely to occur in education and training contexts. Nearly all the taught components of professional and vocational education are intended for future use at work, but the evidence that this happens as intended is usually disappointing. Backward-reaching transfer is required when one faces a new situation and deliberately searches for relevant knowledge already acquired. This is very likely to occur with knowledge previously used in fairly similar contexts, when its relevance is quickly recognised, but committing time to searching for previously taught knowledge is rare unless someone has a memory trace that they can follow up quickly. The discourse and culture of the workplace are so different from most education and training environments that persistent searching for what is perceived as 'past knowledge' is very unusual.

When transfer is from initial qualification programmes in higher or further education, the learning problem is exacerbated by the difference between the forward transfer discourse of higher education and the backward transfer approach expected in the workplace. Higher education tends to assume that simple recognition of what it teaches is all that is needed. So it attends mainly to stage 1, even though many students fail to transfer knowledge from one higher education course to another, and occasionally to stage 3. Employers take stage 2 for granted and often argue that knowledge from higher education should be 'ready to use', but may give some attention to stage 3 when students come on placement. Stages 4 and 5 are off both their radars.

The problem that remains is that of how best to help those who have learned knowledge appropriate for their field of work to use that knowledge in a range of potentially relevant situations. Before they start, they need first to establish which areas of knowledge are relevant to a particular case or situation, second to focus more precisely on what knowledge is needed for a particular investigation, decision or action, and then finally to ascertain how that knowledge is interpreted in a manner appropriate to each particular situation and context. This process can be greatly accelerated if another person with relevant expertise can share it and offer appropriate advice. This brings us to the third type of transfer, the sharing of knowledge between people.

The difficulty here is that proficient workers cannot easily communicate their taken-for-granted local practices and may not even be aware of their more tacit aspects. Those with recent experience of using relevant knowledge in two or more contexts (the second transfer category) will be better prepared to help newcomers. For others, approaches to sharing tacit knowledge that we have used or encountered in the literature (Eraut, 2004b) include the following:

- Demonstrating skills with a voice-over commentary – this may not be an authentic account of normal thinking in action but can still communicate much useful tacit knowledge
- Discussing common episodes at which the participants were co-present
- Recordings of episodes, with the possible addition of a voice-over commentary (Holmstrom & Rosenqvist, 2004)
- Describing incidents or telling stories, followed by discussion (Fairbairn, 2002)
- Discussing cases and/or problems, real or fictional
- Use of mediating artefacts, as suggested in Section 2.1

Over time, it also becomes possible to develop new vocabulary and practices for discussing expertise, and gradually to introduce concepts and theories that may help people to make more sense of their experience. Then proficient workers will also expand their repertoire of knowledge. If the expertise is available only elsewhere, then a short secondment would almost certainly give value for money. If CPE is the only available source of expertise, then sending two or three people together and supporting their mutual learning after they return will enhance the pace and quality of their progress. The challenge of transferring group practices is even more complex and very dependent on whether or not the receiving group was already established. One important feature would have to be shadowing people with different roles in the group.

2.4.2 Performance Focus

HRD is most often judged by its impact on the performance of individuals, groups and organisations. The main criteria for judging such impacts are normally efficiency (productivity), effectiveness (which may or may not include quality) and economy (unit costs). Giving serious attention to the evaluation of these issues requires that HRD practitioners have a deep understanding of the organisational system in which they work. Thus, Stolovitch and Keeps (1999) argued that HRD practitioners must identify and analyse factors within the organisational system that might affect an employee's performance and/or its consequences (rewards and punishments) in order to uncover root causes of inadequacies and construct a performance solution to address them. However, this interpretation of performance focus is far too narrow.

A survey by the Career Innovation Group (Winter & Jackson, 2004) asked over 700 high performers in a small sample of large, mostly global, organisations to comment on the conversations they had had at work which had a high impact on them. Although these high-performing employees got a lot of attention, and had quite a lot of conversations about their work with their managers, they were not getting the conversations they needed:

- They had far more high-impact conversations about their performance than about their development.
- The lack of development conversations was a major source of dissatisfaction which correlated with the intention to leave. They wanted conversations about career development (especially future career opportunities and development planning for the future) rather than skills and training for the current job.
- 40% of respondents had an issue about work which they had not had an opportunity to discuss, and this group were nearly three times more likely than other respondents to be planning to leave the organisation in the next 12 months.

The study concluded that *conversations about performance which do not also address development for the future do not engage high-performing employees*. In other words, 'the best leaders are those who address performance and development together'.

The normal response to this kind of information is to assign this function to an annual appraisal. However, a British study of the views of employees in large UK organisations (Kidd, Hirsh, & Jackson, 2004) found that only 7% of the discussions which employees found useful in their career development took place in the formal setting of appraisal. At least half were informal and not part of any HR or management process. The key to an effective career discussion was combining a high level of mutual trust with challenge and information giving. This gave employees a better sense of direction, increased self-awareness and more confidence, and led to concrete actions by both parties.

Closely related to this issue are the organisation's career options. There are two possible career trajectories above a certain level, management and specialist expertise. The importance of a smooth boundary between management and professional expertise is exemplified by Hoag's (2001) account of skills development in an engine company. They had constructed a set of five proficiency levels (a paragraph for each level) for each of the 15 areas of engineering, and could rely on self-assessment because discrepancies would soon become apparent. These could then be used for assigning people to projects and reviewing the match between the company's anticipated skill mix and its anticipated future demands. This covered the following:

- Providing a clear snapshot of department deficiencies
- Succession planning for retirements, transfers or resignations
- Rapid and intelligent staffing of new projects
- Ensuring that the best choices are made in internal staffing selections (employer transfers)
- Ensuring that staff selections fully consider employee diversity

Another HRD intervention is personal support through coaching, mentoring and enriched feedback. Carter's (2001) report on executive coaching sees this as responding to three problems: the isolation of many managers, the increasing demand for 'soft skills' which are not amenable to formal teaching and the failure of organisations to give managers enough feedback. Both coaching and mentoring have proved exceptionally popular with employees, as well as being perceived as effective by HR professionals. Eighty-eight percent of respondents to the CIPD 2005 survey of training and development reported using internal coaching, 72% mentoring, and 64% external coaching: a pattern extending well into the smaller firms in the sample. But normally coaching is offered only to managers.

Historically, CPE has given less attention to performance issues, partly because CPE providers have little knowledge of the factors within the organisational system that may affect an individual's performance in any particular workplace. Nevertheless, CPE is now beginning to be asked to measure their ultimate impact on service users. This is an absurd idea because, although a well-conceived course can be an excellent learning event, it cannot be a complete learning package that delivers the desired outcomes. That normally requires a considerable further amount of on-the-job learning, and this will happen only if the learning is treated as high priority by the participants' work group. That is why research has consistently reported that courses are effective only when delivered 'just in time' (Eraut et al., 2000).

2.4.3 Strategic Focus

This focus involves moving HRD away from a support role to one that plays a pivotal role in shaping business strategy. Traditional HRD managed by a separate HRD office is almost bound to cause business plans and HRD plans to drift apart. However, strategic HRD is integrated into an organisation's mission or purpose and incorporated into all major planning initiatives. Case study–based research by the

Institute of Employment Studies (Hirsh & Tamkin, 2005) found that many large organisations do not have a single formal training plan, but a range of plans and budgets at varied locations. The study identified five main mechanisms which influence training plans and priorities:

(1) *Formal business planning both at top level and more locally*, leading to training priorities. Either a training plan or a set of priorities can be produced on the basis of business plans or targets, or the two processes of business planning and workforce development planning are wrapped together.
(2) *Links from HR strategy to training implications*. The IES study did not find many cases in which HR strategies gave clear indications of training needs. Competence frameworks were often used in training and development, but there was little evidence that they mapped onto real skill gaps.
(3) *Plans for key workforce groups*. Organisations often have a specific plan and budget for management and leadership development, partly because this aspect of learning tends to be coordinated by a centralised corporate team. Some have specific early career entry and training schemes at graduate level.
(4) *Major business issues or changes* often lead directly to major training interventions, usually with extra funds from the corporate centre. Typical of these would be re-organisations, mergers or acquisitions, or major changes in technology or products. In a similar way, specific changes in work at local level can lead to the identification of learning needs which may not have been foreseen on the normal annual planning cycle. But responding to such needs may depend upon the local unit being able to set aside specific funding.
(5) *Take-up of training provision* is a strong influence on future plans. Training courses or other interventions which are well used and receive positive feedback through evaluation are often repeated. Learning provision which is not well used tends to be dropped. This effect is particularly strong where local managers have to pay for the training, whether provided in-house or by external suppliers.

As the workforce becomes more highly skilled, managers do not always come from the same disciplines as those who work for them. Hence it can be helpful to have someone, often called a Head of Profession, who acts as a spokesperson for the specific skill needs of functional or professional groups. Their intimate understanding of the work and of internal and external trends can make them better placed than business unit heads to identify the learning needs of their community, especially with regard to technical knowledge and skills.

CPE has given much less attention to strategic issues, and this causes many problems for professional workers. In particular it needs to address the issues of specifying and providing a quality service and giving greater priority to user perspectives. This will require both close alignment with strategic HRD and a greater focus on learning at group and organisational levels. This is especially important in health-care organisations because of their multi-professional character. Not only is there lack of alignment with HRD, but also there are separate CPE policies and practices for each professional group.

2.5 Summary (From Eraut & Hirsh, 2007)

What helps workplace learning?	What hinders workplace learning?
Individual-level factors Appropriate degree of challenge in work Frequent and constructive feedback on job performance Time to learn at work, especially through talking to others	**Individual-level factors** Unnecessarily restrictive job design Excessive work pressure and stress
Team-level factors Supportive relationships with others, based on mutual respect Frequent informal discussions of work with colleagues Formal team processes (e.g. team meetings, project reviews) which include discussion of skills and learning Attention to learning opportunities when allocating and designing work processes	**Team-level factors** Work issues not discussed with others Unsupportive or threatening relationships, or social isolation at work
Line management Clear role for managers and experienced workers in supporting learning of others, and time built into their jobs to do this Attention by managers to emotional aspects of work Tolerance of diversity and willingness to consider alternative suggestions Supporting managers by giving them tools and opportunities to practice the skills of coaching, giving feedback, delegation, negotiation, etc. Selecting line managers with an interest in, and aptitude for, developing others	**Line management** Line managers who are defensive or unwilling to resolve work issues in a constructive way Lack of time and attention on giving employees meta-skills and confidence in learning Line managers unwilling to delegate Leaving managers to develop their staff even if they lack the skills or motivation to do it
Approach to learning and development Employees motivated and supported to take responsibility for their own learning Accessible learning advisers for both managers and employees and a flexible capacity to design bespoke learning interventions and work with teams Learning interventions linked closely to the work context, with careful consideration of learning transfer to the job	**Approach to learning and development** Seeing on-the-job learning as not needing any resource or time 'Courses' seen as the main or only means of learning Learning interventions unrelated to current or future work needs The learning and development function seen as about 'delivery' of courses and not able to advise/work with line managers or understand business needs Overly mechanistic or bureaucratic approaches to competence, assessment and documentation of learning

What helps workplace learning?	What hinders workplace learning?
Organisational context, processes and leadership behaviour	**Organisational context, processes and leadership behaviour**
Performance and reward systems which pay attention to knowledge sharing	Promotion and reward mechanisms which emphasise the short-term and individual performance at the expense of investing in medium-term or collective performance
Clear organisational values underpinning work and personal behaviour	Political and senior management context in which people avoid change to protect their job security and/or power
Behaviour at the top which discusses problems and issues and develops other people	
Encouragement of networking and development of social capital outside the immediate workplace	
Cooperative employee relations climate	

References

Argyris, C., & Schon, D. (1978). *Organisational learning*. Reading MA: Addison Wesley.

Bandura, A. (1995). *Self-efficacy in changing societies*. Cambridge: Cambridge University Press.

Bierema, L. L., & Eraut, M. (2004). Workplace-focused learning: perspective on continuing professional education and human resources development. *Advances in Developing Human Resources, 6*(1), 52–68.

Carter, A. (2001). *Executive coaching: inspiring performance at work*. IES Report 379, Brighton: Institute of Employment Studies.

Daft, R. L., & Weick, K. E. (1984). Toward a model of organizations as interpretation systems. *Academy of Management Review, 9*(2), 294–295.

Duncan, R., & Weiss, D. (1979). Organizational learning: Implications for organizational design. *Research in Organizational Behavior, 1*(4), 75–125.

Elmholt, C. (2004). Knowledge Management and the practice of knowledge sharing and learning at work: a case study. *Studies in Continuing Education, 26*(2), 327–339.

Eraut, M. (2000). *Teachers' learning in the workplace*. Symposium Proceedings, Continuing Teacher Education and School Development, Aristotle University of Thessaloniki, 54–68.

Eraut, M. (2004a). Transfer of knowledge between education and workplace settings. In H. Rainbird, A. Fuller, & H. Munro (Eds.), *Workplace learning in context* (pp. 201–221). London: Routledge.

Eraut, M. (2004b). Learning to change and/or changing to learn. *Learning in Health and Social Care, 3*(3), 111–117.

Eraut, M. (2004c). Sharing Practice: Problems and Possibilities, *Learning in Health and Social Care, 3*(4), 171–177.

Eraut, M. (2005). Factors affecting the transfer or sharing of practice in schools. In W. J. Nijhof & F. M. Nieuwenhuis (Eds.), *The learning potential of the workplace* (pp. 113–127). The Netherlands: University of Twente.

Eraut, M. (2007a). *Feedback and formative assessment in the workplace*. Presentation to TLRP seminar series on Assessment of Significant Learning Outcomes.

Eraut, M. (2007b). Early career learning at work and its implications for Higher Education. In N. Entwistle & P. Tomlinson (Eds.), Student learning and University Teaching. *British Journal of Educational Psychology, Monograph Series II, 4*, 113–133.

Eraut, M. (2007c). Learning from other people in the workplace, *Oxford Review of Education, 33*(4), 403–422.

Eraut, M., Alderton, J., Cole, G., & Senker, P. (2000). Development of Knowledge and Skills at Work. In F. Coffield (Ed.), *Differing visions of a learning society, vol 1* (pp. 231–252). Bristol: The Policy Press.

Eraut, M., & Hirsh, W. (2007). *The significance of workplace learning for individuals, groups and organisations*. SKOPE, Department of Economics, University of Oxford.

Eraut, M., Maillardet, F., Miller, C., Steadman, S., Ali, A., Blackman, C., et al. (2005a). *What is learned in the workplace and how? Typologies and results from a cross-professional longitudinal study*. Nicosia: EARLI Biannual Conference.

Eraut, M., Maillardet, F., Miller, C., Steadman, S., Ali, A., Blackman, C., et al. (2005b). *An analytical tool for characterising and comparing professional workplace learning environments*. Pontypridd: BERA Conference.

Fairbairn, G. J. (2002). Ethics, empathy and storytelling in professional development, *Learning in Health and Social Care, 1*, 22–32.

Hackman, J. R. (1987). The design of work teams. In J. Lorsch (Ed.), *Handbook of organizational behavior* (pp. 315–342). Englewood Cliffs NJ: Prentice-Hall.

Hakkarainen, K., Palonen, T., Paavola, S., & Lehtinen, E. (2004). *Communities of networked expertise: professional and educational perspectives*. Amsterdam: Elsevier/EARLI.

Hirsh, W., Silverman, M., Tamkin, P., & Jackson, C. (2004). *Managers as developers of others*. IES Report 407, Brighton, Institute for Employment Studies.

Hirsh, W., & Tamkin, P. (2005). *Planning training for your business*. IES Report 422, Brighton, Institute for Employment Studies.

Hoag, K. (2001). *Skills development for engineers; an innovative model for advanced learning in the workplace*. London: The Institution of Electrical Engineers.

Holmstrom, I., & Rosenqvist, U. (2004). Interventions to support reflection and learning. *Learning in Health and Social Care, 3*(4), 203–212.

Kettley, P., & Hirsh, W. (2000). *Learning from cross-functional teamwork*. IES Report 356, Brighton, Institute for Employment Studies.

Kidd, J. M., Hirsh, W., & Jackson, C. (2004). Straight Talking: the nature of effective career discussion at work. *Journal of Career Development, 30*(4), 231–245.

Miller, C., Freeman, M., & Ross, N. (2001). *interprofessional practice in health and social care: challenging the shared learning agenda*. London: Arnold.

Pedler, M., Burgoyne, J., & Boydell, T. (1991). *The learning company*. London: McGraw Hill.

Pissarro, G. P., Bohmer, M. J., & Henderson, A. C. (2001). Organizational differences in rates of learning: evidence from the adoption of minimally invasive cardiac surgery, *Management Science, 47*(6), 752–768.

Salomon, G., & Perkins, D. N. (1998). Individual and social aspects of learning. *Review of Research in Education, 23*, 1–24.

Senge, P. (1990). *The fifth discipline: the art and practice of the learning organization*. New York: Doubleday.

Stolovitch, H., & Keeps, E. K. (Eds.) (1999). *Handbook of human performance technology: a comprenensive guide for analysing and solving performance problems in organizations*. San Francisco: Jossey-Bass.

Thomas, K. W. (2000). *Intrinsic innovation at work: building energy and commitment*. San Francisco: Berrett-Koehler.

Watkins, K. E. (2000). Aims, roles and structures for human resource development. *Advances in Developing Human Resources, 7*, 54–59.

Wenger, E. (1998). *Communities of practice: learning, meaning and identity*. Cambridge: Cambridge University Press.

West, M. A., & Slater, J. (1996). *The effectiveness of teamworking in primary health care*. Report for Health Education Authority.

Winter, J., & Jackson, C. (2004). *The conversation gap*. Oxford: Career Innovation Group.

Chapter 3
Knowledge Networks for Treating Complex Diseases in Remote, Rural, and Underserved Communities

Sanjeev Arora, Summers Kalishman, Denise Dion, Karla Thornton, Glen Murata, Connie Fassler, Steven M. Jenkusky, Brooke Parish, Miriam Komaromy, Wesley Pak, and John Brown

3.1 Healthcare in New Mexico

With a population of 1.83 million residents scattered over 121,356 square miles, New Mexico is the sixth least populated and the fifth largest state in the country. The population is composed of 44.7% non-Hispanic white, 42.1% Hispanic, 9.5% Native Americans, and 3.7% other. Minorities make up over half the population in the state, making it one of two minority majority states in the United States. New Mexico has the largest concentration of Hispanics and the second largest concentration of American Indian/Native Americans in the country (U.S. Census Bureau, 2011). Rural poverty rates in New Mexico are as high as 22.2% (U.S. Department of Agriculture, 2008). There is a single academic medical center in the state. These factors contribute to the ongoing challenge of providing adequate health services to rural and frontier areas in New Mexico (Bureau of Business and Economic Research, UNM, 2009; U.S. Department of Health and Human Services, Human Resources and Services Administration, 2008).

The shortage of healthcare providers in rural areas, as well as the lack of access for patients to specialty care for chronic, complex health conditions, is a significant issue facing individual patients, families, and communities in New Mexico; similar challenges for patients with chronic, complex health conditions are faced by poor, rural, and medically underserved individuals, families, and communities around the globe. Only 20% of New Mexico's licensed physicians practice outside of urban areas, and few of them are specialists in complex diseases. Thus, patients and providers in primary care facilities in many rural communities lack access to medical specialists. In the absence of specialist support, patients in rural and medically underserved settings may remain undiagnosed and untreated, or may receive less-than-optimal care (Varkey et al., 2009).

S. Kalishman (✉)
University of New Mexico School of Medicine, Albuquerque, NM, USA
e-mail: skalishman@salud.unm.edu

A. Mc Kee, M. Eraut (eds.), *Learning Trajectories, Innovation and Identity for Professional Development*, Innovation and Change in Professional Education 7,
DOI 10.1007/978-94-007-1724-4_3,

The Project ECHO Model, which began in 2004, is an unprecedented collaboration between this center and the New Mexico Department of Health (NMDOH), the New Mexico Corrections Department (NMCD), the Indian Health Service (IHS), and community health hospitals and clinics in rural areas. The Project ECHO network currently has more than 21 partner clinics based in public health departments, prisons, Indian Health Service sites, Federally Qualified Health Centers, and rural primary care practices around the state (Arora, Geppert, Kalishman, et al., 2007a; Arora, Thornton, Jenkusky, et al., 2007b).

3.2 Project ECHO (Extension for Community Healthcare Outcomes)

The Project ECHO Model addresses complex and chronic conditions by linking providers in primary care practices with academic healthcare subspecialists. Its initial focus has been to develop effective and comprehensive treatment for the Hepatitis C Virus (HCV). In New Mexico, there are 32,000 reported cases of HCV, and less than 15% of patients infected with HCV have been treated (NM Department of Health Statistics, 2009). New Mexico has a higher mortality rate due to liver cancer than any other state, and the highest rate of chronic liver disease and cirrhosis deaths in the nation. Chronic liver disease, cirrhosis, and hepato-cellular cancer are three of the main outcomes of untreated HCV. National and state experts project that there will be 2,228 HCV-related deaths in New Mexico between the years 2010 and 2019 (CDC, 2009; NM DOH, 2009). Treatment permanently cures HCV in 45–70% of patients and prevents future complications such as cirrhosis, need for liver transplantation, and liver cancer. Eradication of infection also reduces the reservoir for transmission to other patients in correctional institutions and communities. Treatment entails injection therapy for a 6- to 18-month period and the intensive management of side effects.

The only current treatment of HCV (drug therapy with Interferon and Ribavirin) involves severe side effects, including moderate to severe depression, hemolysis, and neutropenia. Project ECHO works through outreach to community-based clinics, followed by weekly case-based, consultative education clinics focused on a complex disease and conducted via technology (web or telemedicine or cell phone access). This enables primary care providers to access the best practice standards of care and support for screening, managing, and treating patients whom they might diagnose but generally do not treat. Subspecialists share knowledge about best practice protocols using a case-based learning approach and co-manage patients with primary caregivers in rural communities and prisons.

Project ECHO uses teleconferencing and videoconferencing; Internet-based assessment tools; online presentations; and telephone, fax, and e-mail communications both to connect specialists with primary care providers in prisons and rural areas and to promote the use of identified best practices. Telemedicine and Internet connections enable specialists and primary care providers to co-manage patients with HCV infection, thus increasing the capacity of rural clinicians to provide treatment for HCV. Project ECHO participants must have access to the Internet and telephone service. Video conferencing is optional because it requires broadband access and a video camera, but its use enhances the interaction between the partners and the specialists. Project ECHO network partner organizations are recruited through statewide healthcare conferences, presentations, and partner contacts. Project ECHO network clinicians include pharmacists, nurse practitioners, primary care physicians, and physician assistants.

Once a provider organization joins the Project ECHO network, members of the UNM Project ECHO HCV team visit the site to conduct a one-day training workshop. Providers also train in Albuquerque at UNM-HSC HCV clinics and with ECHO staff. After completing orientation and training, network clinicians present and discuss their HCV patients during weekly 2-h telemedicine clinics. The clinics use a standardized, case-based format that includes discussion of treatment complications and psychiatric, medical, and substance use issues. During these clinics, network clinicians collaborate with specialists in gastroenterology, infectious disease, psychiatry, substance use, and pharmacology, as well as with other network clinicians.

Telemedicine and Internet connections enable specialists in the program to co-manage patients with complex diseases using best practice protocols, case-based knowledge networks, and learning loops. Learning loops are case-based educational experiences in which community providers learn through three main routes: (1) longitudinal co-management of patients with specialists, (2) other primary care providers on the network via shared case-based decision making, and (3) short didactic presentations on relevant topics, such as vaccination for hepatitis A and B and diagnosis of depression. These learning loops create deep domain knowledge about the content among rural providers, enabling them to provide the highest quality treatment for their patients. Systematic monitoring of treatment outcomes is an integral aspect of the project, which may also be generalizable to improving disease outcomes for other complex and chronic conditions in underserved areas.

ECHO uses regularly scheduled telemedicine clinics to provide a "knowledge network" for bringing together expert interdisciplinary specialists from UNM-HSC and community-based primary care providers. Community providers learn best practices in chronic disease management through "learning loops," in which they both co-manage diverse patients with expert specialists and simultaneously expand their knowledge through ongoing case-based learning. Over time, these learning loops create deep knowledge, skills, and self-efficacy in offering state-of-the-art care in health worker groups that lack specialty physicians. This is a crucial outcome, because specialists have limited time available, and a project based only on one-time consultations with specialists from the academic health center would have limited ability to expand care for patients with HCV, rheumatology, chronic pain, asthma, or diabetes. On the other hand, Project ECHO is designed to develop network clinicians' skills that enable them to deliver the highest quality specialty care with less need for specialist assistance, and without having to recruit, retain, and fund additional providers.

ECHO providers care for patients with Hepatitis C through their weekly telehealth clinics, where they identify patients they have screened for Hepatitis C treatment. Providers first have to apply the complex set of eligibility criteria that patients have to meet: they must have a support system, they should not smoke, they must not be using alcohol or other substances, they must have an acceptable score on the CES-D (Center for Epidemiological Studies Depression Scale), and they need to be screened on a wide array of laboratory tests prior to being moved into treatment. At the weekly telehealth clinics, providers present their patients; receive guided feedback from academic specialists in different fields (infectious disease, gastroenterology, and psychiatry); listen and observe other providers similar to themselves presenting HCV patients for screening, management, and treatment support; and listen and observe feedback given by academic specialists about patient cases managed by other primary care providers. Primary care providers receive direct feedback, receive answers to questions, observe role models, and interact with peers.

The ECHO Model uses disruptive innovation to support its knowledge network. In a one-to-many knowledge network, the expertise of a single specialist is shared with several primary healthcare providers, each of whom sees numerous patients. The flow of information in a knowledge network is NOT unidirectional; the specialists also gain invaluable feedback and case-based experience through the weekly consultations.

To support the provision of quality specialty care for HCV patients in a rural and underserved community, the ECHO Model engages community clinicians in weekly HCV clinical case presentations selected by the community providers from among their patients. This iterative learning with specialists increases the community providers' knowledge, self-efficacy, and skills. In addition, they have joined a community of clinical providers who also participate in these weekly case-based clinics. This approach supports the development of a community of practice among community providers based in community clinics, health and corrections departments supported by specialists from the academic health center.

3.3 Educational Theories Informing Project ECHO

Specific educational approaches and theories support the development of the Project ECHO partnership's focus on specialty training and skill development for health professionals in the workplace. To better understand how four of these educational theories contribute to Project ECHO, they are described in the context and framework of Project ECHO. They comprise the following:

(1) Deliberate practice (Ericsson, 2008)
(2) Social cognitive theory and self-efficacy (Bandura, 1986, 1991)
(3) Situated learning and community of practice (Lave & Wenger, 1991; Wenger, 1998)
(4) Adaptive expertise (Schwartz, Bransford & Sears, 2005; Bereiter, 1997)

3.3.1 Deliberate Practice

The primary care physicians, physician assistants, and nurse practitioners, who are the core learners in Project ECHO's HCV knowledge network, have opportunities for repeated and deliberate practice as they select, present, and manage HCV patients. This is integral to the facilitated learning and repeated practice approach used in Project ECHO. Project ECHO has adopted co-management in the care of 20 Hepatitis C patients by a primary care provider as the standard for certification and independent practice in HCV. Deliberate practice begins with learning through practice about the criteria that must be met for an HCV-diagnosed patient to be eligible to participate in treatment-screening criteria. When the provider screens a patient for potential treatment, the patient is presented. The patient may be rejected for treatment until certain prescreening criteria are met; the provider will represent that patient for treatment when those criteria change. If the patient is accepted for treatment, depending on the patient's genotype, the treatment will last from 6 to 18 months. There are a series of milestone points in the HCV protocol that require additional laboratory tests, depression inventory assessments, and assessment of function and well-being of the patient. Periodically these are presented by the provider to the ECHO clinics at biweekly or monthly intervals. In the intervening time between presentations, each primary care provider is expected to update laboratory data and records for best practice co-management with ECHO specialists. Each primary care provider has 24/7 access to subspecialists with whom they are co-managing patients.

The community primary care providers present the cases they have selected at the ECHO telehealth clinics, where they are expected to organize the case for presentation according to the best practice protocol for HCV patients. As they present the same patient at multiple clinics, and then present other patients, they develop more expertise in the protocol itself. They know the clinical history that is needed and the lab information required for presentation that adheres to the best practice protocol. It becomes increasingly familiar and second nature to them. They also become attuned to the questions to ask, and the problems that challenge them, for which they need or want additional guidance.

Patient safety and optimal care are the first priorities in Project ECHO. If a patient is deemed at risk, a provider may be advised to stop treatment immediately during the case-based ECHO clinic discussion. This discussion is followed with a direct call to the provider to further support the provider and discuss the reasons for the concern and decision. Giving providers rapid and direct feedback to become more expert in their HCV care is important for consistently achieving ECHO best practices. Usually, feedback within an ECHO clinic with community providers is also used to develop a teachable moment around an important protocol or best practice in HCV from which other providers can learn. The feedback centers around the issue and what can be learned, applied with a specific patient and generalized as well to similar patients. Specialists use feedback to a single provider to capitalize on teachable moments. Sometimes, feedback sessions precipitate requests to specialists from community providers for mini-didactic presentations. These sessions may include adjunct content related to the topic presented at the next clinic, sent to providers electronically, and placed on the ECHO HCV Web page. Deliberate practice relies on repeated case presentations, expert feedback, and self-regulation.

What amount of deliberate practice in HCV patient care is necessary and sufficient for primary care providers to achieve competence? Project ECHO's goal to develop primary care providers who can independently screen, manage, and treat HCV patients has raised questions about the number of HCV patients that a community provider might be expected to co-manage from screening through posttreatment prior to independent care. The current estimate for HCV patients is 20. The co-management and care of 20 patients by a primary care provider relieves neither the specialist's nor the primary care provider's time but provides the promise of future expansion of access to care by patients with HCV in underserved areas. This standard provides assurance that primary care providers will be well trained in the complex care of HCV patients.

3.3.2 Social Cognitive Theory and Provider Self-Efficacy

Social cognitive theory argues that three factors influence the likelihood of an individual changing his or her behavior. First, the individual must believe that the benefits of performing the new behavior will outweigh its costs. Second, the individual must have confidence in his or her ability to perform the specific behavior in a variety of circumstances, also known as self-efficacy. Third, there must be reinforcement of positive behavior changes from persons who are seen as role models or as experts (Bandura, 1986, 1991).

The ECHO Model of learning incorporates each of these three components in its HCV clinics, with a particular emphasis on enhancing provider self-efficacy. Community providers participate in Project ECHO knowing some of the dimensions of the cost of untreated care for their HCV patients: potential death from cancer or cirrhosis of the liver, shortened lives, poorer quality of life, the hopelessness that develops from lack of available treatment, and the impact of HCV on a patient's ability to work and on their families and communities. Providers who participate in ECHO and co-manage patient's treatment learn about the individual costs of treatment on patients as well as the benefits of delivering best practice care. Many of the patients who receive treatment for HCV meet the standard for cure; they are virus free six months after concluding treatment.

Providers recognize the implications of co-managing patients and seriously engage in learning the components of their care. They are also motivated to participate in weekly 2-h HCV teleconferences. During ECHO clinics, providers collaborate on patient management with several interdisciplinary specialists from psychiatry, infectious disease, and gastroenterology. These are seen as trusted experts who provide reinforcement for the provider's decisions and guidance for improved practices. Moreover, their elicited discussions about the nuances of care in authentic cases chosen from the community providers' panels build on providers' growing expertise in the co-management of the HCV patients.

Community providers often have knowledge about the patient essential to the patient's positive health outcome, such as deeper knowledge about the patient, the patient's family and support system, and the patient's relationship to the community. This can be used even more effectively as community providers develop self-efficacy and begin to take on an increasing role in delivering best practice care. This enables the expert team at UNM to gradually reduce their contribution to the smaller consultative role of ensuring patient safety and supporting provider confidence on an ongoing basis.

3.3.3 Situated Learning Theory

ECHO's iterative case-based learning, including the "learning loops" and co-management of patients during telemedicine clinics, drew upon situated learning theory. Learning requires both social interaction and collaboration, and teaching and instruction supports learners in knowledge construction and knowledge organization for learners' optimal assimilation and access (Vygotsky, 1978). Drawing on this model, ECHO specialists work with community providers to facilitate learning by providing learners with the opportunity to (1) extend their current skills and knowledge, (2) model the idealized version of the task, (3) engage learner's interest, (4) simplify tasks so they are manageable, and (5) motivate learners to pursue the task. All of these can be accomplished through the mentoring and consultation that interdisciplinary experts offer through ECHO.

Lave and Wenger (1991) elaborated on Vygotsky's work by describing in greater detail the learning process for individuals involved in communities of practice. The communities of practice within Project ECHO are multiple. Learning evolves from deeper and continuous participation in a community of practice that requires building technical knowledge and skill associated with the tasks (in this case, care of patients with HCV, a chronic, complex disease). Providers from different community clinics attend the telemedicine clinics and interact together. In addition, they note that this professional learning also requires the building of a set of relationships with others in that community of practice, since this community gives its members a sense of joint purpose and identity, identified as essential in chronic care practice in primary care (Soubhi, 2007). In the ECHO Model, situated learning is supported by collaborative learning, coaching, and mentoring with those more expert than oneself but also with one's peers (Parboosingh, 2002).

The level of interest among community providers in learning and in sharing expertise with each other is remarkable. There are providers who remain in their community clinics but regularly provide local presentations about HCV and about Project ECHO to their peer communities in the state. One community provider has become a faculty member in a separate ECHO clinic devoted to an additional chronic, complex disease. She has joined the ECHO-integrated addiction and psychiatry clinic, which includes opioid treatment with suboxone/buprenorphine in response to the large number of patients with opioid addiction in her community.

She remains active within the ECHO HCV clinic and has engaged other providers at her clinic in the care of HCV patients through ECHO. She is a co-faculty in buprenorphine certification training for providers from throughout the state as part of an additional ECHO clinic focused on training primary care providers in integrated addiction medicine and psychiatry. The community of providers in ECHO extends to providers other than physicians. Nurses who are participating in ECHO requested implementation of their own ECHO clinic to address knowledge, community of practice, and support for their practices and their learning. Training for community health workers, community health representatives, and promotoras for specialized disease care such as diabetes and addiction medicine is being developed using the Project ECHO Model to train and support specialized paraprofessionals who work in rural and underserved clinics.

3.3.4 Adaptive Expertise

Providers in Project ECHO HCV are learning about "best practices" for HCV based on routine and iterative exposure to the information and use of a standard protocol for screening, managing, and treating patients with HCV. These protocols and best practices are dynamic; they are updated within the Project ECHO HCV community with current HCV research.

Best practice expertise is similar to the "routine expertise" described by Schwartz et al. (2005) and represents the set of complex and sophisticated knowledge and skills that are integrated in patient care associated with unique, highly skilled expertise (Bransford et al., 2006). Routine expertise is honed from learning complex and sophisticated skills and competencies and in becoming more efficient with that knowledge and transforming it into integrated use. This is the expertise that each of the specialists is sharing with the community providers in their co-management of HCV patients with the providers, in the iterative case discussion, and in the supplemental didactic presentations they provide. It underlies corrective feedback as well as provides the framework they use when listening to the routine updates from the community providers about their patients.

Many HCV patients seen by community providers and presented in ECHO clinics also have comorbidities. The theory of adaptive expertise captures the duality of building on efficient and effective application of past knowledge in routine and familiar tasks with the challenge of adapting that expertise to innovative approaches to address practice-based problem solving that is not routine (Mylopoulos & Scardamalia, 2008). Adaptive expertise through an orientation to innovation infers new knowledge production in response to problem solving and creates the potential for ECHO providers to improve their future practice based on their shared new knowledge and practices that evolve as part of ECHO collaboration with peers, with ones' clinical team, and with specialists. Several providers involved in the ECHO clinics have demonstrated adaptive expertise and its application in their participation in ECHO. Two providers from one clinic developed an HCV screening tool that has been implemented as a best practice HCV screening tool for all patients in the participating community clinics. This protocol has been adopted by Project ECHO as a best practice screening tool and approach to screening for HCV in New Mexico and is being shared as a part of a replication effort of ECHO HCV clinics with another university.

Adaptive expertise is foundational to the problem-solving approaches used by the specialists at ECHO who interact with providers in the co-management of patients. In ECHO HCV clinics, there are three specialists who routinely provide support and co-manage patients with the community providers. While providing routine expertise, they are also listening to the pattern of comorbidities and patient problems that are being presented, the situational problems underlying cases with similar comorbidities, or concerns identified by the provider about systemic issues in the workplace. The specialists step back and often seek to figure out approaches to address them, in addition to co-managing patients with community providers. Educational researchers note that the path to adaptive expertise probably differs from the path to routine expertise (Bransford et al., 2006; Darling-Hammond & Bransford, 2005). Adaptive expertise requires that the expert relish challenges that require her to problem solve and may involve the expert in learning in new areas and applying this knowledge within a new area of expertise. ECHO specialists encounter a variety of problem-solving situations, and successfully consider and adapt solutions to them.

3.4 Collaboration

Since 2004, 21 different health organizations with clinic sites in New Mexico have joined the Project ECHO HCV telemedicine clinics. The outreach to providers has been on multiple levels—through presentations at clinics throughout the state, at professional and service organization meetings, as part of continuing professional education and updates, through word of mouth, and by referral to the Web.

ECHO providers themselves promote outreach within their communities about HCV prevention and treatment and Project ECHO. To generate interest among community members about HCV prevention, screening, and treatment, providers use several approaches. Providers in one community developed a well-attended health promotion/ disease prevention day associated with a health fair and a parade, and provided HCV screening and educational materials, and referral information to the clinic throughout the day. They created a festive event to promote HCV prevention and the resources available in the community for screening and treatment. They invited the ECHO specialists to participate in the events including the parade and the media coverage of the HCV-focused health promotion day. This model was also adopted by providers in other communities with similar success.

Providers have adapted their early experience with community outreach to use of media based on aspects of Project ECHO. Teams of providers and ECHO staff have developed several DVDs for outreach to patients and community members about HCV and to promote the ECHO HCV model, to recruit additional clinical sites and providers, and to tell the story of HCV and its impact on patients, families, communities, and the healthcare system. In one DVD, patients who are undergoing HCV treatment or who have completed HCV treatment are able to tell their story and the implication of treatment to them. The mayor and community officials as well as healthcare providers discuss the meaning of patients in their community having treatment when none existed previously. This video has been shown on the public television station throughout the state and coupled with a statewide call-in segment to provide information about the clinical sites for HCV screening and treatment that are connected with Project ECHO. Adaptive expertise in the use of the media is proliferating throughout the ECHO provider group, and a second DVD focused on integrated addiction and psychiatry was recently produced.

3.5 Methods and Approaches Used in Evaluation

What is the impact on primary care providers engaged in co-management of care with academic medical specialists? The screening, treatment, and follow-up care to assure effective treatment of an HCV patient require between 18 and 24 months of active care and two years of after-care to determine the patients' full response to HCV treatment. Given this considerable commitment from providers, we need to know what benefits they recognize, the challenges involved in their participation, and how it affects their professional and civic identities. How does their participation affect their practices, their interactions with their peers, and their role in their clinic and in the wider community? What are the implications for introducing a similar or modified model for application with other chronic, complex diseases?

Project ECHO has been evaluated by a range of complementary approaches, including patient outcomes, clinical site outcomes, and provider outcomes. The methods used to collect provider data include periodic surveys of primary care providers about their involvement with Project ECHO, their learning, and the benefits and barriers to their participation in the weekly Hepatitis C telehealth clinics. These surveys include both rated items and open-ended comment sections focused on the following:

- The provider's experience,
- The impact of their Project ECHO involvement on their practice, and
- The provider's assessment of the impact of Project ECHO on their organization.

The project's impact on provider knowledge and self-efficacy in treating Hepatitis C is assessed through mailed paper surveys administered when a provider joins Project ECHO at baseline and repeated every six months.

A retrospective self-efficacy questionnaire instrument about the components used in HCV patient care (screening, evaluation and treatment, patient education and clinic staff education, etc.) was developed and administered at the annual meeting of the Project ECHO partner providers, staff, and specialists.

Weekly observation of the Project ECHO Hepatitis C clinic is occurring, and a number of themes have been identified through the constant comparative method to structure the content analysis.

Annual meeting surveys with both rated items and open-ended comments are developed and administered at a Project ECHO annual meeting held in conjunction with continuing professional development and Project ECHO's continuing quality improvement efforts. In addition to surveys, informal discussion groups are held with Project ECHO participants to assess their preferences for future decisions within ECHO.

Each component of the evaluation has been collected and analyzed by two of the authors, SK and DD.

3.6 Results from Questionnaires

3.6.1 Who Are the Community Providers in Project ECHO?

Seventy-five providers (physicians, pharmacists, physician assistants, nurse practitioners) have presented patients in the ECHO HCV clinic. These providers represent 21 different healthcare organizations located throughout New Mexico.

Thirty-five providers have been involved with ECHO over a sustained period of time; the following data are based on their responses to a survey after participating in Project ECHO HCV clinics for six months. Twelve providers have been in practice for four years or less, another 12 have been in practice from 5 to 14 years, while six providers have been in practice for 15 or more years. Most of them practice in sites where they are the sole provider involved in Project ECHO HCV. The clinical organizations they represent include Federally Qualified Health Centers (FQHC), the New Mexico Department of Health (NMDOH) with a public health office near the Mexican border, Indian Health Service, and individual private practice physicians who serve low-income communities.

Several early primary care participants continue with Project ECHO; key to its growth has been interest by several community clinic medical directors who have supported and encouraged participation in the clinics. On average, 12 community providers participate in the weekly ECHO HCV clinics. Since the inception of HCV clinics in 2004, providers have participated in 318 HCV telehealth clinics during which 5,993 patient consultations occurred. Most of the HCV ECHO patient consultations serve patients from ethnic/racial minority groups (71% of patients from rural community health centers). As a result of these weekly clinics, 563 HCV patients have begun a 6- to 18-month treatment regimen. Two hundred thirty-one patients have successfully completed HCV treatment co-managed by community providers and ECHO specialists. Prior to the launch of Project ECHO, fewer than 1,600 rural residents in the state and no prisoners had received treatment for chronic liver disease in New Mexico.

3.6.2 Provider Self-Efficacy

Twenty-five direct care providers participating in the Project ECHO HCV Telemedicine Clinics rated their knowledge, skills, or competence before and after one year (or longer) of participation in Project ECHO. Providers rated themselves, both retrospectively and currently, on the following scale:

> 1 = none or no skill at all; 2 = vague knowledge, skills, or competence; 3 = slight knowledge, skills, or competence; 4 = average among my peers; 5 = competent; 6 = very competent; 7 = expert, teach others.

Table 3.1 shows that ECHO providers reported increased competence in each of the nine abilities, rating themselves as having vague or slight knowledge or skill at the time they joined ECHO HCV clinics to being competent or very competent in that knowledge and skill after participation in ECHO for six months or longer. The effect size for each item is large and so is the overall effect size for the mean comparison of the 9 items (Cohen, 1988). Providers are also responding positively to the expectations in the ECHO Model that they would be able to serve as local consultants about HCV questions and issues to other providers.

> Self-efficacy is important. Our team now knows that they are really capable to care for HCV patients in collaboration with our community physicians. Seeing that nurses, pharmacists and clinicians in a variety of settings can successfully treat HCV contributes to this.

3.6.3 Perspectives of Community Providers

Thirty-five primary care providers in underserved and rural community clinics who participate in the Project ECHO HCV telemedicine clinics rated the degree of learning associated with each of the following HCV clinical content topics after six months of participation in Project ECHO, Table 3.2. The topics were identified following observation of multiple clinics by the authors and in consultation with expert specialist providers in HCV screening, management, and treatment. Those who indicated NA were clinicians who were not providing direct care to HCV patients but who are located in the community clinics; they may be medical directors or other providers who are considering becoming involved in co-management of their patients in this chronic disease or in other telehealth clinics developed by Project ECHO. Qualitative data are coded by two researchers using the template approach (Crabtree & Miller, 1992).

Providers are reporting high levels of learning in each of the topics associated with the content in ECHO. While some practitioners start with greater knowledge in specific areas within HCV or behavioral health associated with HCV management and care, each provider who is engaged in treating patients reports increased learning in some area associated with ECHO HCV training. No providers report treating and managing HCV patients to be easier than they expected it to be.

Table 3.1 Project ECHO: direct care providers' assessment of their self-efficacy

$N = 25$ Direct care providers	Before		After			Effect size for the change[a]
	Mean	SD	Mean	SD	*p*-value	
1. Ability to identify patients who should be screened for HCV	4.2	(1.3)	6.4	(0.6)	<0.0001	1.8
2. Ability to identify suitable candidates for treatment for HCV	2.8	(1.2)	5.6	(0.8)	<0.0001	2.4
3. Ability to assess severity of liver disease in patients with HCV	3.2	(1.2)	5.5	(0.9)	<0.0001	2.1
4. Ability to treat HCV patients and manage side effects	2.0	(1.1)	5.2	(0.8)	<0.0001	2.6
5. Ability to educate clinic staff about HCV patients	2.8	(1.1)	5.8	(0.9)	<0.0001	2.5
6. Ability to educate and motivate HCV patients	3.0	(1.1)	5.7	(0.6)	<0.0001	2.4
7. Ability to assess and manage psychiatric comorbidities in patients with HCV	2.6	(1.2)	5.1	(1.0)	<0.0001	1.9
8. Ability to assess and manage substance abuse comorbidities in patients with HCV	2.6	(1.1)	4.7	(1.1)	<0.0001	1.9
9. Ability to serve as consultant within my clinic and in locality for HCV questions/ issues	2.4	(1.2)	5.6	(0.9)	<0.0001	2.8
Overall competence (average of 9 items above)	2.8*	(0.9)	5.5*	(0.6)	<0.0001	2.9

*Cronbach's alpha for the 9 *Before* ratings = 0.92, and Cronbach's alpha for the 9 *After* ratings = 0.86, indicating a high degree of consistency in the ratings on the 9 items.

[a]Effect size is the standard mean difference between paired post-participation and pre-participation ratings. It is calculated by using the average paired difference between post-participation and pre-participation ratings as the numerator and the standard deviation of the paired differences as the denominator. A classification of effect size offered by Cohen is: 0.2 = small, 0.5 = medium, and 0.8 = large. Cohen (1988)

Providers comment that effective approaches to learning used in Project ECHO are the case-based and iterative format with feedback from specialists to guide primary care providers learning.

> Access to more patients and cases for learning than just on my own. Having personal questions answered by a sub-specialist in real time with time for clarification.
>
> The structure in which to screen and treat patients and the reassurance that comes with having specialty expertise in decision making.

Table 3.2 Degree of learning in HCV clinical content areas

Degree of Learning	No learning	Limited degree of learning	Moderate degree of learning	High degree of learning	NA
1. General HCV information: etiology, transmission, genotype, etc.		3 (9%)	7 (20%)	19 (54%)	6 (17%)
2. Screening patients for HCV	1 (3%)	3 (9%)	8 (23%)	17 (49%)	6 (17%)
3. Identification of patients eligible for selection into HCV treatment		1 (3%)	7 (20%)	21 (60%)	6 (17%)
4. Interpretation of laboratory values associated with HCV		1 (3%)	11 (31%)	17 (49%)	6 (17%)
5. HCV treatment protocol by genotype	1 (3%)	3 (9%)	6 (17%)	19 (54%)	6 (17%)
6. Pharmacological management		3 (9%)	8 (23%)	18 (51%)	6 (17%)
7. Management of side effects associated with patients being treated for HCV		5 (14%)	5 (14%)	19 (54%)	6 (17%)
8. Management of HCV patients who are not eligible for treatment		4 (11%)	13 (37%)	12 (34%)	6 (17%)
9. Management of non-HCV patients with other GI problems/syndromes	3 (9%)	6 (17%)	13 (37%)	4 (11%)	9 (26%)
10. Screening HCV patients for behavioral health/substance abuse issues	1 (3%)	4 (11%)	8 (23%)	15 (43%)	7 (20%)
11. Treatment of behavioral health/substance abuse issues in HCV patients		5 (14%)	12 (34%)	11 (31%)	7 (20%)
12. Communication with patients and families about HCV	1 (3%)	3 (9%)	12 (34%)	13 (37%)	6 (17%)

The promise of access to specialists is something that providers in ECHO have experienced and is at the core of their participation.

> Access to specialists and expertise. Immediate access to assistance with problems/questions.
> Experts "advise when our patients are ready for treatment."

Learning from peers during the iterative presentation of complex patients also is essential to ECHO and the providers' learning.

> I identify the expertise of participants in helping manage complex patients, collegial interactions with peers and hearing other community members' patient presentations.

Providers identify ECHO as a tremendous resource with "fun, complex medical issues, a great learning opportunity, that provides great benefits to patients." Interest in treating HCV among community providers is generated because of the "recognition of how common it is in our patients," offers an opportunity for learning, and provides a break from "the drudgery of primary care."

Some providers recognize or come to recognize that HCV is a "major public health problem." Thus, HCV learning not only must include the disease components and content, for screening, management, and treatment, but also has to be situated within a wider model that links the disease and its impact with the wider public health functions of primary, secondary, and tertiary prevention, surveillance, and monitoring. As a result of Project ECHO's integration of agencies and organizations, including the Department of Health, the public health viewpoint is shared with providers who are interested in learning this wider model, which considers HCV as a disease, thus situating individual patient care within a model of community health.

Thirty-five primary care providers in underserved and rural community clinics who participated in the Project ECHO HCV telemedicine clinics rated their perceptions of the degree to which ECHO participation was a benefit to them, Table 3.3. The providers rated these items after six months of participation in Project ECHO.

3.6.4 Providers Identify the Beneficial Components

Providers indicate that ECHO helps them reconnect on multiple levels: with medicine, with their peers, and with a sense of being able to make a difference in their work.

> ECHO and participation in it "reduces burnout, increases enthusiasm, knowledge, and quality of care. [It has] increased camaraderie amongst providers, increases feelings of being able to work on something important that can facilitate positive change."

Some providers identify revitalization of interests and experience at their clinical sites, which for some is otherwise "stale and monotonous." Providers identify the multidisciplinary approaches emphasized in ECHO in which community providers and specialists listen and learn together from different disciplines centered on the patient's case.

> It has motivated me to learn more, understand more, and have more compassion toward patients with HCV or addictions.

Providers report that ECHO diminishes their professional isolation and engages them in additional learning. Some identify themselves as the local HCV expert in their community.

Table 3.3 Providers' perceptions of benefits associated with participation in Project ECHO HCV Network Telemedicine Clinic and co-managed care with specialists

Providers' perceptions of benefits	No benefit	Minor benefit	Moderate benefit	Major benefit	NA
1. Enhanced knowledge about management and treatment of HCV patients		1 (3%)	4 (11%)	30 (86%)	
2. Being well informed about symptoms of HCV patients in treatment		2 (6%)	5 (14%)	28 (80%)	
3. Achieving competence in caring for HCV patients		1 (3%)	3 (9%)	31 (89%)	
4. Self-efficacy: Belief in my ability to manage and treat HCV patients		2 (6%)	6 (17%)	27 (77%)	
5. Access to expertise in behavioral/mental health resources (in caring for HCV patients)		2 (6%)	3 (9%)	29 (83%)	1 (3%)
6. Access to expertise in pharmacology (in caring for HCV patients)		2 (6%)	9 (26%)	24 (69%)	
7. Enhanced skills in communication with HCV patients and their families	1 (3%)	4 (11%)	12 (34%)	17 (49%)	1 (3%)
8. Collegial discussions with peers about HCV patients		3 (9%)	5 (14%)	27 (77%)	
Perception of benefits, sum for 8 benefits	1 (<1%)	17 (6%)	47 (17%)	213 (77%)	2

[I am] able to teach staff about HCV screening, pretreatment work-up, and managing side-effects during treatment. I have been reading all the literature available on research and HCV treatment. I am able to be a resource person for the area in HCV.

20% of my time is now devoted to consultation with other doctors on Hepatitis C.

HCV and suboxone have become central to my clinical practice. I read anything I can on HCV and am engaged in a research project studying females with Hepatitis C and the roles of depression, alcohol use and drug use in their disease and treatment.

Thirty-five primary care providers in underserved and rural community clinics who participated in the Project ECHO HCV telemedicine clinics rated their perceptions of the barriers to providing care of patients with HCV in their clinical practices, Table 3.4. The providers rated these items after six months of participation in Project ECHO.

Table 3.5 shows that providers' attitudes are clearly not a major barrier, *but time, administrative support and clinical team (factors 1–3) and resources (factors 6–9)* are rated as major or moderate barriers to care by between *36% and 41%* of these ECHO HCV providers. More detail is added by the providers' comments about the barriers they identified as most significant to their participation. They fall into

Table 3.4 Barriers identified by providers to care of patients with HCV in their clinical practices

Barriers	Not a barrier	Minor barrier	Moderate barrier	Major barrier	NA
1. There isn't enough time in an office visit	2 (6%)	8 (23%)	16 (46%)	4 (11%)	5 (14%)
2. There isn't support from clinic administration	9 (26%)	7 (20%)	10 (29%)	3 (9%)	6 (17%)
3. My clinical team is not adequate to support a patient in treatment for HCV	7 (20%)	14 (40%)	7 (20%)	3 (9%)	4 (11%)
4. My attitude toward HCV treatment	30 (86%)	1 (3%)			4 (11%)
5. There are many patient problems that demand my attention. HCV is of less importance to manage and treat than other patient problems	20 (57%)	8 (23%)	2 (6%)		5 (14%)
6. Reimbursement for management and treatment of HCV is inadequate	15 (43%)	8 (23%)	2 (6%)	3 (9%)	7 (20%)
7. There aren't enough mental health resources available in my community to manage and treat patients with HCV	6 (17%)	11 (31%)	8 (23%)	6 (17%)	4 (11%)
8. Lack of access to substance abuse treatment	4 (11%)	12 (34%)	10 (29%)	6 (17%)	3 (9%)
9. HCV treatment is not affordable for most patients	8 (23%)	8 (23%)	8 (23%)	7 (20%)	4 (11%)

Table 3.5 Barriers summarized into three groups

Groups of barriers	Not a barrier	Minor barrier	Moderate barrier	Major barrier	NA or missing
1–3: Time, administrative support, clinical team	18 (17%)	29 (28%)	33 (31%)	10 (10%)	15(14%)
4–5: Attitudes	50 (71%)	9 (13%)	2 (3%)	0 (0%)	9 (13%)
6–9: Resources	33 (23%)	39 (28%)	28 (20%)	22 (16%)	18(13%)

time and clinic demands, productivity concerns, mental and behavioral health support, costs/medications and insurance, and administrations' support and productivity concerns.

> I'm fortunate to have time on my schedule blocked specifically for the HCV teleconference, but if I didn't have this time, I wouldn't usually be able to participate. Our clinic is too busy. The time constraint is why my colleague (MD) has not been able to participate in two months.
>
> Mental health and behavioral health availability (or lack thereof) is a major problem. The psychiatrists in [ECHO] are excellent, but I need more mental health professionals that can see and follow patients.
>
> Our patients are not working, have no income and no insurance. They have office visits on a sliding fee scale but we do not do labs.

Barriers are substantial for providers. They have significant patient care responsibilities, paper work, and referrals for other patients that need to be made. They may have multiple roles in their clinics; some providers are also administrators. They are faced with a substantial number of competing and urgent responsibilities that require attention. Many state that there are insufficient resources or staffing in their clinics to support them; others note that there is not enough physical space for them to participate in ECHO and see additional patients. In order to co-manage patients with the ECHO HCV specialists and to learn the different aspects of HCV care, providers must invest time in ECHO clinics and with patients that they select to co-manage with specialists to become confident about their decisions and knowledgeable about the HCV protocol. At the same time, the "other work" continues at their clinic and accumulates during the time they participate in ECHO HCV clinic. Providers describe how they are often challenged about their time spent in ECHO HCV clinics, and, for many, this is a major source of stress. At the end of an ECHO clinic, they have the work to complete for the ECHO HCV patients they are co-managing, as well as the other work associated with their normal clinic duties. For most community providers, participation in ECHO is treated as just additional clinical work and responsibility. None of their previous work was transferred elsewhere.

3.7 Findings from Annual Meeting Surveys

3.7.1 Care for Patients

The impact of HCV on patients is a substantial motivator for community providers to become engaged in Project ECHO HCV clinics. Community providers report that Project ECHO is a resource needed by their HCV patients. Some report that their participation in an ECHO HCV clinic offers the only hope for their patients (Project ECHO Annual Meeting Reports, 2006–2008). Providers recognize that by learning to care and co-manage patients with specialists, they provide a lifeline for their HCV patients. Similarly, providers are willing to accept responsibility for complicated HCV patient care, including the provision of 24-h access to patients for support while they are on treatment. They also learn that the side effects for patients on HCV treatment include the rapid onset of severe depression, severe anemia, and other blood disorders. Some patients may develop severe adverse reactions to treatment. However, providers are also convinced that the patient co-management advice they receive from subspecialists in ECHO is safe, effective, and best practice (Project ECHO Annual Meeting Reports, 2007–2008).

3.7.2 Broadened Networks and Expanded Interest in Learning

ECHO providers also note that they are engaged in interactions with other community clinics, and with organizations and agencies like the Department of Health and Department of Corrections, and the University of New Mexico Health Science Center with whom they had little or no previous connection prior to working with Project ECHO (Annual Meeting Reports, 2006–2008). Providers are building a relationship with their peers as well as with these organizations. Providers report an enhanced interest in learning and in reading about HCV as well as in other areas of medicine and indicate that they are assuming responsibility within their clinical sites as the local HCV expert (Project ECHO Six Month HCV Questionnaire Reports, 2006–2008; Project ECHO Annual Meeting Report, 2006–2008).

3.8 Community Providers Improving ECHO

Community providers also influence the direction of ECHO clinics with their inputs and their suggestions. The partnership includes routine site visits, regular meetings, and calls, in addition to the focused case-based discussions, questions and answers, and didactic presentations that are part of ECHO HCV clinics. To improve ECHO, providers suggest offering Web-based cases and identifying and generating "pearls" of learning from weekly clinics. They like DVDs to help them in sharing their knowledge and in training staff in the clinic, including transitions with an HCV patient from screening to initial treatment. DVDs and visual presentations that are supported with a paper protocol guarantee that each component of the initial screening and transition to treatment are followed (safety). Providers are interested in specific areas of additional training associated with side effects, comorbidities, and updates on recent practices with HCV treatment.

Prior to Project ECHO, rural providers lacked the knowledge resources to treat patients with HCV and were unprepared to deal with the treatment side effects, drug toxicities, treatment-induced depression, and other issues presented by this complex disease. Collaboration between specialists and rural providers in care of patients with HCV has resulted in patients in underserved and rural communities receiving best practice health care for HCV directly from their primary care providers in their own communities. Two hundred ninety-nine patients with HCV genotype 1 have been treated by community providers, with 179 successfully completing treatment (approximately 60%). This compares favorably with care provided during the same time period to patients at the academic health center. Approximately 65% of the HCV patients who have been treated by community providers are minority patients, a significantly larger proportion than those cared for at the academic health center. Outcomes of HCV patient treatment and care given by ECHO community providers are equivalent, or better, on all dimensions being studied, and a paper reporting these findings is now being prepared (Arora et al., 2011).

3.9 Links Between ECHO Model, Theories, and Collaboration

The four theories that informed the conceptualization of Project ECHO are relevant to the model today six years after its inception.

Deliberate Practice Theory: Currently, HCV community providers report that to master the HCV expertise and become proficient in the care of HCV patients, most indicate that they need to care for a minimum of 15 patients from screening through to treatment. They actively participate in weekly telehealth clinics that have been expanded in hours to accommodate the number of community clinicians who are presenting HCV patient cases. To reinforce deliberate practice and to more efficiently record and present patient data, an electronic HCV presentation form is now in use and an HIPPA-compliant version of the form is now available for others participating in the teleconference. The electronic form reinforces the routine required laboratory tests that need to be ordered and reviewed at each visit, the meaning of the laboratory values (normal, abnormal, and those that together indicate a more serious adverse prognosis for the patient). Similar deliberate practice with the medications and therapies reinforce the community clinicians' knowledge and skills in ordering medications for patients of different ages, weights, and heights—variables that have an impact on the dosage and expected response of patients to treatment. In addition to weekly clinics, specialists in ECHO use an intense two–three-day face-to-face course for introducing new providers to the chronic disease. These events can give 1–30 clinicians an intensive overview and initial training in knowledge and skills associated with that chronic disease. From these intense courses, the ECHO specialist can adaptively assess the clinical skills and background knowledge of the community clinicians, and revise and adapt the emphasis and effort in weekly case-based presentations, and didactic training should be best focused considering that group of individuals within the context of deliberate practice.

Social Cognitive Theory and Provider Self-Efficacy: This theory remains salient to the ECHO Model. Increasing numbers of clinical providers are involved in the co-management of HCV patients using the ECHO Model. Their commitment to caring for HCV patients in their communities, and to broader issues of co-managed chronic disease, is associated with many beliefs related to social cognitive and self-efficacy theory. They believe that their clinics provide the best option for HCV care and treatment because patients are both closer to home and get access to specialty care at a lesser cost. Moreover, their self-efficacy is rightly buoyed by the evaluation's report that Project ECHO's provision for HCV patients through co-management provided equivalent or better care than the care given by specialists at the academic health center (Arora et al., 2010). They identify appropriate patients to be screened, manage patients well, and have rates of effective treatment similar to those of specialists. Demonstration and feedback to clinicians during ECHO clinics provides the opportunity for clinical providers who recently joined the clinic as well as long-time participants to observe and to receive feedback and reinforcement as they gain expertise in HCV patient care.

Situated Learning Theory: In addition to training community clinicians to become experts in caring patients with HCV, this theory posits that the process of learning and participating in ECHO enabled participants to assume more active and expert roles within the domain of chronic diseases. The community clinician participants are becoming local experts in their communities, for each other, for their clinic peers and staff, and for the local community. Increasingly the community clinicians involved in HCV, or in another of Project ECHO's chronic, complex disease clinics, report that they are assuming the role of local expert within their clinic and in the larger healthcare community for the chronic disease in which they participate with ECHO. Not all clinicians assume this role, but a sufficient number are engaged and provide a clinical network of local expertise in specific diseases. Community clinicians are consultants to each other, enhancing their involvement with each other and their engagement in "best practice" chronic disease care.

Adaptive Expertise: In the ECHO Model, a specialist's expertise is first directed at teaching/facilitating community providers the mastery of the knowledge and skills associated for a specific chronic disease. In contrast, community providers are concerned not only with acquiring this knowledge but also with sharing their unique knowledge of the patient, the community, and the context when engaged in co-management decisions for the patient. What is routine knowledge for one may become complex, adaptive knowledge and expertise for another. Each is challenged to respond to the other's situation by developing alternate ways of thinking about problems that best support the melding of their dual levels of expertise.

Because community providers have now acquired unique levels of expertise, there are periods in the weekly clinics when the conversation centers on their special expertise in community knowledge and their adaptation of the chronic disease model within this unique context. One of the important components in educating community providers is that specialists build on these presentations to adapt their core knowledge in the weekly clinical case-based sessions. If a case presentation includes a patient with not one but two or three chronic complex conditions, there is an opportunity for both the specialist and the community clinician to develop adaptive expertise in the co-management of this patient. The knowledge and skill needed to address the patient's needs requires more than the interpretation of the problem, the laboratory values, and the management of therapy; it also requires understanding the complexities of life and culture unique to that patient and that community.

Patient's complex comorbidities and response to treatment, community-based cultural issues associated with specific disease, and adaptive response to new technologies such as electronic medical records and disease management tools are examples of problem-solving challenges presented within the ECHO Model. Each allows knowledge building, questioning, and improvement, hallmarks of adaptive expertise. Project ECHO's expansion to new chronic diseases and to training of different types of clinical support staff poses new opportunities as well as new theoretical challenges for adaptive expertise.

3.9.1 How Do These Knowledge Networks Contribute to Shared Knowledge Construction Among Academics and Practitioners?

The knowledge networks contribute to shared knowledge construction for academics and practitioners largely through the patient cases. The interaction between the academic and practitioner is organized around co-managed patient cases with specific diseases that are part of the community practitioner's panel of patients. Most of the community patients are poor, have lack of access to care, and often have multiple health problems including the chronic disease for which they are being co-managed with the specialist. Because of the complexity of the patients and the contexts in which practitioners provide care to their patients, they have unique knowledge that they share about the setting, context, and history of the patient. The academic has extensive background expertise about the specific disease that is shared. Knowledge networks are built from the shared co-management of patients between academics and practitioners. The practitioners provide a regular update report about co-managed patients during the weekly telehealth clinic. Over time, after listening to the iterative, case-based discussions, both academics and practitioners learn about the nonroutine dimensions associated with the patient case and the patient care. Community practitioners and academics have the opportunity to participate in collaborative problem solving in the development of adaptive approaches to address the complex, nonroutine patient cases—one dimension of care where shared knowledge construction among academics and practitioners commonly occurs.

Future plans for Project ECHO include a new focus on training community health workers, medical assistants, and others members of the clinical team with a focus on incorporating a team approach to visits and care for patients with chronic disease. In that process, Project ECHO has begun training community health workers who focus on a narrow range of knowledge, skills, and abilities in the care of patients with chronic disease. The community health worker training includes a two-day face-to-face training focused on incorporating the participants into a community of practice, developing and assessing their focused clinical knowledge and skills of chronic disease care. The multiday face-to-face training is then followed with six months of required weekly, case-based clinics in which the community health worker identifies patients from the clinic and presents them to her peers and to the specialists. The community health worker supports the clinician in assessment of vital signs, in reviewing and assessing the laboratory and pharmaceutical records, in assessing the patient depression index, and in conversing with the patient to assess his needs at that patient visit. This model diversifies the level of provider involved and is conceptualizing chronic disease care as a team education and training model.

3.9.2 What Lessons Can Be Learned from This Experience?

Project ECHO provides a model that works for authentic workplace education; it has been used effectively in educating community clinicians who deliver safe and effective chronic disease care to patients in rural areas and in prisons because of strength of collaboration between academics and community providers and their shared vision, to provide access to quality care for patients with chronic disease.

Theories of learning and behavior identified by ECHO continue to be salient as ECHO expands into new diseases and expands its training model to a more diverse team of community clinicians and health educators.

Use of iterative and deliberate practice, support for self-efficacy through role modeling, observation and feedback, and the development of community and adaptive problem solving to address unique challenges in ECHO are components of the ECHO Model that support this collaborative model of care for both academic specialists and community providers.

The ECHO Model for education and training in chronic complex disease management has the potential for replication and expansion to a variety of workplace settings, diseases, and issues.

Acknowledgments This work is supported by Agency for Health Research and Quality HIT grant 1 UC1 HS015135-04, and Agency for Health Research and Quality MRISP grant, R24HS16510-02, the New Mexico Legislature, the New Mexico Department of Health and the Robert Wood Johnson Foundation.

References

Arora, S., Geppert, C. M. A., Kalishman, S., Dion, D., Pullara, F., Bjeletich, B., et al. (2007, February). Academic Health Center Management of chronic diseases through knowledge networks: Project ECHO. *Academic Medicine, 82*(2).

Arora, S., Kalishman, S., Thornton, K., Dion, D., Murata, G., Deming, P., et al. (2010, September). Expanding access to hepatitis C virus treatment – Extension for Community Healthcare Outcomes (ECHO) project: Disruptive innovation in specialty care. *Hepatology, 52*(3), 1124–1133.

Arora, S., Thornton, K., Jenkusky, S. M., Parish, B., & Scaletti, J. V. (2007). Project ECHO: Linking University specialists with rural and prison-based clinicians to improve care for people with chronic hepatitis C in New Mexico. Public Health Reports. *122*(Supplement 2), 74–77.

Arora, S., Thornton, K., Murata, G., Deming, P., Kalishman, S., Dion, D., et al. (2011, June 9). Outcomes of treatment for hepatitis C virus infection by primary care providers. *New England Journal of Medicine*, *364*(23), 2199–2207. Epub 2011 Jun 1.

Bandura, A. (1986). *Social foundations of thought and action: A social cognitive theory*. Englewood Cliffs, NJ: Prentice-Hall.

Bandura, A. (1991). Social cognitive theory of self-regulation. *Organizational Behavior and Human Decision Process, 50*(2), 248–287.

Bereiter, C. (1997). *Situated cognition and how to overcome it. Situated cognition: Social, semiotic, and psychological perspectives* (pp. 281–300). Hillsdale, NJ: Lawrence Erlbaum.

Bransford, J. D., Vye, N. J, Stevens, R., Kuhl, P., Schwartz, D., Bell, P., et al. (2006). Learning theories and education: Toward a decade of synergy. In P. Alexander & P. Winne (Eds.), *Handbook of educational psychology* (2, 209–244). Mahwah, NJ: Erlbaum.

Centers for Disease Control and Prevention (2009). Retrieved January 6, 2009, from http://www.cdc.gov/

Cohen, J. (1988). *Statistical power analysis for the behavioral sciences* (2nd edn). Hillsdale, NJ: Lawrence Erlbaum Associates.

Crabtree, B. F., & Miller, W. L. (1992). A template approach to text analysis: Developing and using codebooks. In B. F. Crabtree & W. F. Miller (Eds.), *Doing qualitative research* (pp. 93–109). Newbury Park: Sage.

Darling-Hammond, L., & Bransford, J. D. (2005). *Preparing teachers for a changing world: What teachers should learn and be able to do*. San Francisco, CA: Jossey-Bass.

Ericsson, K. A. (2008). Deliberate practice and acquisition of expert performance: A general overview. *Academic Emergency Medicine, 15*, 988–994.

Health Professional Shortages Area at U.S. (2008). Department of Health and Human Resources, Health Resources and Services Administration. http://www.hrsa.gov/

Institute of Medicine of the National Academies. State of U.S.A. (2008). *Health indicators*. Washington, DC: The National Academies Press.

Lave, J., & Wenger, E. (1991). *Situated learning: Legitimate peripheral participation*. Cambridge, MA: Cambridge University Press.

Mylopoulos, M., & Scardamilia, M. (2008). Doctors' perspectives on their innovations in daily practice: Implications for knowledge building in health care. *Medical Education, 42*, 975–981.

New Mexico Department of Health. (2009). Retrieved January 6, 2009, from http://www.health.state.nm.us/

Parboosingh, J. T. (2002). Physician communities of practice: Where learning and practice are inseparable. *The Journal of Continuing Education in the Health Professions, 22*, 230–236.

Project ECHO Annual Meeting Report. (2006). *Internal report based on survey and discussion groups*.

Project ECHO Annual Meeting Report. (2007). *Internal report based on survey and discussion groups*.

Project ECHO Annual Meeting Report. (2008). *Internal report based on survey and discussion groups*.

Project ECHO Hepatitis C Six Month HCV. (2006–2008). *Report based on survey of ECHO HCV providers*.

Schwartz, D. L, Bransford, J. D, & Sears, D. (2005). Efficiency and innovation in transfer. In J. Mestre (Ed.), *Transfer of learning: Research and perspectives*. Greenwich, CT: Information Age Publishing.

Soubhi, H. (2007). Toward an ecosystemic approach to chronic care design and practice in primary care. *Annals of Family Medicine, 5*, 264–269.

United States Department of Agriculture, Economic Research Service (2008). Retrieved January 11, 2008, from http://www.ers.usda.gov/StateFacts/NM.HTM

University of New Mexico, Bureau of Business and Economic Research (2009). Retrieved January 6, 2009, from http://www.unm.edu/~bber/

U.S. Census Bureau: State and County QuickFacts. Last Revised: Friday, 03-Jun-2011 15:23:14 EDT.

U.S. Department Health and Human Services, Human Resources and Services Administration. (2008). Retrieved December 27, 2008, from http://www.hhs.gov/

Varkey, A. B, Manwell, L. B, Williams, E. S, Ibrahim, S. A, Brown, R. L, Bobula, J. A, et al. (2009). Separate and unequal: Clinics where minority and nonminority patients receive primary care. *Archives of Internal Medicine, 169*(3), 243–250.

Vygotsky, L. S. (1978). *Mind and society: The development of higher mental processes*. Cambridge, MA: Harvard University Press.

Wenger, E. (1998). *Communities of practice: Learning, meaning and identity*. New York: Cambridge University Press.

Chapter 4
Using Simulation and Coaching as a Catalyst for Introducing Team-Based Medical Error Disclosure

Lynne Robins, Peggy Odegard, Sarah Shannon, Carolyn Prouty, Sara Kim, Douglas Brock, and Thomas Gallagher

4.1 Background

Practitioners face many barriers to disclosing errors to patients, including embarrassment, fear of litigation, and minimal training in how to discuss them. Clinicians frequently lack opportunities to observe or practice error disclosure in the workplace. Efforts at teaching error disclosure skills often focus on a one-on-one physician–patient interaction and neglect the inter-professional context. Lack of consensus about which healthcare team members should be involved in error disclosure to patients and families hampers both instruction and change in practice. In this chapter, we describe a funded research project intended to align clinical practice with what we know to be true about medical errors: they are made in teams, and patients want to be told when errors occur.

The importance of open and honest communication with patients following adverse events and errors in their care is gaining increasing recognition (Gallagher, Denham, Leape, Amori, & Levinson, 2007; Gallagher, Studdert, & Levinson, 2007; The Full Disclosure Working Group, 2006). As awareness of error disclosure has increased, so too have calls for change in the way that errors are routinely handled (Gibson & Singh, 2003; Shapiro, 2008; Sharpe, 2004). In the United States, as in other countries, regulators, hospitals, accreditation organizations, and legislators have developed standards, programs, and laws to encourage transparent communication with patients and families following adverse events (American Society for Healthcare Risk Management of the American Hospital Association, 2003; Amori, 2006; The Joint Commission, 2007). Several research studies suggest that health professionals themselves strongly endorse the general principles of disclosure but struggle with how to put these principles into practice (Blendon et al., 2002; T. H. Gallagher, Garbutt et al., 2006; Gallagher Waterman, Ebers, Fraser, & Levinson, 2003; Garbutt et al., 2007; Loren et al., 2008). Recent national surveys suggest that patients may learn about less than 30% of errors (Blendon et al., 2002;

L. Robins (✉)
University of Washington, Washington, DC, USA
e-mail: lynner@u.washington.edu

A. Mc Kee, M. Eraut (eds.), *Learning Trajectories, Innovation and Identity for Professional Development*, Innovation and Change in Professional Education 7,
DOI 10.1007/978-94-007-1724-4_4, © Springer Science+Business Media B.V. 2012

Schoen et al., 2005; The Kaiser Family Foundation/Agency for Healthcare Research & Quality/Harvard School of Public Health, November 2004). Even when healthcare workers do disclose errors, they frequently omit critical information, such as why the event happened and how recurrences might be prevented (Gallagher et al., 2003, 2006).

Clinicians often lack confidence in their ability to conduct these difficult conversations and fear that disclosure will prompt litigation (Gallagher et al., 2003; Gallagher, Waterman, et al., 2006). These fears are not unfounded as the consequences of failed disclosures can be substantial, including patient dissatisfaction and loss of trust, an increased risk of litigation, and lost opportunities to learn from such events how to prevent recurrences (Berlinger, 2005; T. H. Gallagher et al., 2003; Kachalia et al., 2003; Mazor et al., 2006). For any individual clinician, disclosure is a relatively infrequent occurrence which makes it difficult to develop strong disclosure skills *through practice* (Kaldjian et al., 2007; Waterman et al., 2007). Additionally, the emotional distress that often accompanies an error can make it difficult for an individual provider to objectively analyze the event, decide whether disclosure is appropriate, and formulate an appropriate disclosure plan (Waterman et al., 2007; White et al., 2008). Thus, institutional culture at the practitioner level is usually too strong for disclosure policies to be implemented, and the hope of avoiding both cost and loss of reputation may also be dominant at the management level.

The notion of error disclosure as a team undertaking is gaining currency, replacing previous views of error disclosure as the responsibility of an individual healthcare provider (usually the attending physician) (Gallagher, Denham, et al., 2007; Shannon et al., 2009). A recent study reported that nurses view the disclosure process as a team event rather than as a physician–patient conversation though, in reality, they are often excluded from error disclosure discussions. Nurses reported that because they are excluded from these conversations, they often find themselves communicating with patients in ethically compromising ways after an error has occurred (Shannon et al., 2009). This finding highlights the need for organizations to improve the quality of error disclosure by integrating the entire healthcare team into the disclosure process, though nurses *expressed doubt* that policies alone can change disclosure practice. Decisions about when and how to disclose are too complex and context specific to benefit from a procedural recipe, and organizations often have so many policies in place that they are difficult to remember and implement with regularity (Shannon et al., 2009). Although there is acceptance that errors are made by teams rather than by individuals and that a team approach to error disclosure fits more easily within a blame-free framework for discussing errors, team-based error disclosure is not yet the norm.

Some institutions are training “disclosure coaches” to help clinicians improve and become more comfortable with disclosure. Discussions among team members following an error are often *highly emotionally charged,* and a skilled “disclosure coach” (i.e., individuals skilled in disclosure who can provide “just-in-time” training to the involved healthcare workers) can mediate difficult planning conversations and help team members to avoid blaming one another. A coach can also

(1) guide the team toward appropriate disclosure strategies
(2) help *team members* to anticipate likely patient questions and formulate thoughtful responses
(3) articulate an *explicit apology* that effectively conveys *sincere regret*

Following the *disclosure conversation* with the patient, the coach can then help the team debrief, consider what went well and what they might have done differently during the disclosure, and provide *emotional support* to distraught team members.

The National Quality Forum's *Safe Practices for Better Healthcare* explicitly calls on organizations to provide healthcare workers with around-the-clock access to disclosure coaches (Gallagher, Denham, et al., 2007). At organizations where this model is being implemented, medical directors, clinical managers, department chairs, or other hospital administrators generally fill the role of disclosure coach. However, little has been written to guide efforts to teach effective disclosure coaching techniques or how to conceptualize the role of the disclosure coach in the overall process of communicating with patients about errors. We received funding to mount a research project intended to align clinical practice with what we already know about medical errors: they are made in team contexts, discussion about the error needs to occur among the team, and patients want to be told about errors that have occurred in their care.

4.2 Research Project Description

At the University of Washington, we used a pre-/post-research study to assess whether participating in team-based disclosure simulation training improved clinicians' knowledge, attitudes, and skills needed for disclosing harmful errors to patients and team discussions about improving their collective practices to reduce errors. This two-year project was funded by the Agency for Healthcare Research and Quality to explore the use of coaching and simulation in error disclosure skill development for an inter-professional team. We trained professionals from the fields of risk management and officers in patient or medication safety to become disclosure coaches who help teams to discuss harmful errors and to plan whether and how to disclose errors to patients. Participants included 38 teams of physicians and nurses and 12 disclosure coaches from five different healthcare organizations in the Seattle area.

Prior to participating in the simulations, clinicians' baseline knowledge, attitudes, and skills regarding team communication, safety culture, and disclosing errors to patients were assessed using an interactive Web assessment (Kim et al., 2011). (Figure 4.1 illustrates the flow of the study and its component parts.) All the simulations were videotaped for later analysis to determine how effectively team members communicated with each other and with the patient about the event. At the completion of the simulations, participants repeated the Web assessment to determine the impact of the simulation on their knowledge, attitudes, and skills.

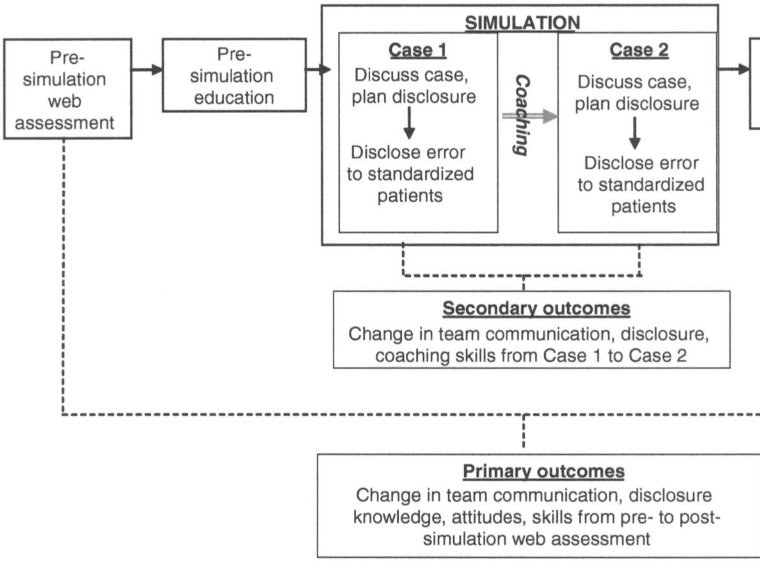

Fig. 4.1 Project components

4.3 Description of Simulation in Action

We chose simulation for our educational intervention due to its potential to raise clinician awareness of the team approach to error disclosure and provide objectives-based experiential instruction, practice, and feedback in a risk-free environment. Our intent was to promote the development of competence and confidence in performing effective team error disclosure and increase the likelihood that an inter-professional team approach to disclosure would be adopted at our institution. Delivery of traditional didactic continuing education has been largely discredited as a method for changing behavior (Davis et al., 1999), and passive dissemination of information about research findings is similarly ineffective (Bero et al., 1998). Evidence indicates that interactive teaching/learning formats are more effective than noninteractive ones, and multiple exposures to professional education activities are more effective than a single exposure. Joint active learning experiences are also considered necessary preparation for inter-professional collaboration (Mann et al., 2009).

Simulation is particularly well suited for presenting an education challenge like disclosure because it both requires and stimulates learners to respond to the challenge as if they were interacting in the workplace context. As an educational modality, simulation is widely used to address gaps in learners' clinical experience and has been shown to be effective in fostering skills acquisition when deliberate practice and feedback are incorporated (Issenberg et al., 2005). Educators seeking to improve inter-professional collaboration, communication, and trust have demonstrated that bringing professionals together for team training in simulated workplace environments is an educationally powerful experience and provides opportunities for purposeful dialogue about roles, shared and separate competencies, values, and professional biases (Ker, Mole, & Bradley, 2003). There is evidence that simulation training is especially effective in enhancing communication skills generally (Driskell, 1998; Marinopoulos et al., 2007). Practicing in realistic settings and receiving targeted feedback specifically enhance the communication skills needed for effective team communication and disclosure (Morey et al., 2002). We hoped to promote behavior change through simulation by giving nurse-physician teams opportunities to experience firsthand the benefits of collaborating to conduct error disclosure (Adelson, Vanloy, & Hepburn, 1997).

We developed two surgical and two medical error case scenarios based on actual incidents. Our stated learning objectives were that participants would

(1) demonstrate effective team communication skills when discussing medical error, responsibility and blame, source of error, and prevention of future errors;
(2) apply knowledge of error disclosure principles in planning the content of the disclosure (including whether and how to disclose the event to the patient and defining team members' roles); and
(3) conduct an effective disclosure of the error to a standardized patient based on the plan the team had discussed.

To guide the development of our simulation scenarios, scripts, coding templates, coaching points, and Web assessment tool, we compiled a list of communication behaviors and topics considered essential for the effective conduct of each phase of error disclosure being simulated: first discussing the medical error and planning for disclosure to the patient, and then conducting the error disclosure itself (see especially Gallagher, Studdert, et al., 2007). During the discussion and planning phase of the simulation, we expected team members to achieve mutual agreement that an error had occurred, avoid blaming one another, solicit each other's perspective, negotiate differences of opinions, agree to fully disclose, plan team roles for the disclosure, and anticipate patients' reactions. During disclosure to the patient, we expected teams to explicitly *(a) state that an error had occurred, (b) provide an upfront apology, (c) respond forthrightly to questions, (d) exhibit patient-centered communication skills, (e) demonstrate blame-free disclosure with each team member acknowledging their role, (f) communicate a plan to prevent future errors, and (g) discuss follow-up with the patient.*

The premise of the simulations was that the members of a surgical or medical team had recently been involved in a harmful error and therefore needed to meet to discuss the event and how it happened, plan whether and how to disclose the event to the patient, and then perform the disclosure to the patient according to their plan. The main features of the four cases are summarized below:

1. The Case of the Retained Sponge (Surgery)

- *Surgical residents were unaware* that surgeon always performed complete abdominal cavity examination before closing.
- A *scrub nurse new to general surgery* and unaware of protocol did not cue residents to perform a final wound examination.
- There was a *false correct sponge count*, possibly due to a miscount of bagged sponges, a sponge falling back into the bucket after being counted, a sponge being counted twice, etc.
- In the case hospital, there was no policy to routinely take *post-op radiographs* after abdominal surgery.

2. The Case of the Missing Specimen (Surgery)

- Patient admitted for vaginal bleeding.
- Surgeon excised mass from cervix, patient bleeds profusely.
- Surgeon, attending to bleeding, places *specimen on back table*, neglecting to tell nurses.
- Bleeding eventually controlled amidst *hectic operating room activity* including blood transfusion.
- Circulating nurse took break, *without telling relieving nurse* that no specimen had been received from scrub tech.
- Lab called later in day to say that *no specimen was found* in submitted container.
- Patient doing well post-op, but surgeon is worried about implications of lost mass.

3. The Case of the Blood Thinner Overdose (Medicine)

- Patient suffered hip fracture and had successful surgical repair.
- A fluid balance problem was diagnosed post-op, and transferred to Medicine Service.
- At the time of transfer, MD diagnosed a deep vein clot in lower leg and placed patient on enoxaparin (a blood thinner dosed by weight); asked for *weights and ins/outs*.
- Patient had massive lower intestinal bleed.
- *Incorrect weight recorded* in medical record (75 kg, not 150 kg).
- *RN had not recorded new order for weights*, and *MD never checked weights*.
- Patient was transfused and stabilized.
- Patient believes that bleeding was due to recurrence of ulcer.

4. The Case of the Insulin Overdose

- A patient with diabetes and COPD admitted.
- MD wrote "7U," *using an unapproved abbreviation,* rather than the approved "7units" on admission orders.
- RN *mistook "7U" for "70," checked with second nurse*, gave *70 units of insulin.*

- RN discovered patient unresponsive in room at bedtime.
- Patient successfully treated for hypoglycemia, spent the night in ICU, now fine.

At the beginning of every simulation session, a research team member briefed the participating nurse, physician, and risk manager about the expectations and logistics for the simulations, explaining that teams would complete *two different simulated cases*, one after the other, each consisting of two distinct phases: (1) *team planning* and (2) *error disclosure to the patient*. In between the two cases, a risk manager observer coached them using a prescribed rubric that incorporated reflection and the collaborative identification of behaviors to change to improve performance in the second simulation.

The nurses and physicians who participated in the simulations were experienced professionals. We trained actors from a professional troupe known as Effective Arts to perform in the roles of a standardized team member and a standardized patient who had experienced a harmful error. The actor who played the role of a hospital administrator/standardized team member was trained to facilitate teams' interactions *using prompts* when necessary to promote discussion about *how the error occurred, whether and how the error should be disclosed, who should disclose the error,* and *how the disclosure should be performed.* The actor was also trained to prompt team members to practice key skills often overlooked during error disclosure planning. For example, teams often neglected to anticipate and rehearse responses to potentially challenging patient questions or expressions of emotion. In these instances, the actor was trained to pose questions that would prompt these behaviors. Sample prompts might include, "Well, what are you going to say to the patient when she asks you who is to blame for making this mistake?" or "How will you respond to the patient who angrily shouts 'you could have killed me' and wants to know who is going to be fired for this?'" If a team neglected to discuss how they would actually begin the disclosure conversation and what role each team member would play during the disclosure, the facilitator would prompt, "Who is going to begin the conversation about what happened?" or "How are you going to manage the conversation with the patient – what role will each of you take?" This standardized prompting both enabled participant learning and provided insight into clinicians' current knowledge, skills, and attitudes about error disclosure in general and team error disclosure in particular. The facilitator's role emulated the role that an error disclosure coach might play during actual error disclosure planning sessions – identifying gaps in team approaches to planning for disclosure, prompting targeted instruction and rehearsal, and setting the stage for a more effective planning and disclosure.

We had initially developed a standardized pharmacist role for the medical scenario; however, training an actor to play the role proved difficult in the beta testing phase of the simulations. Clinicians reported that the actors were not able to convincingly "carry out" the role of the pharmacist due to their lack of content knowledge. They could not, for example, respond to clinicians' requests for medication information during the disclosure. Actors reported equal difficulty training for this very content-oriented role. We then selected a hospital administrator role for the standardized team member to eliminate medical-oriented content from the role without sacrificing authenticity.

In addition to the facilitated interaction, a modified improvisational acting approach was employed to promote a realistic discussion that was consistent with a particular team's communication style and dynamic. Effective Arts actors were trained to play the roles of the four different patients that had been harmed and to adjust their responses to teams in accordance with the team's demonstration of (or failure to demonstrate) targeted skills effectively. That is, *the actors judged how truthful, forthright, apologetic, or empathetic they perceived the team's communication to be and adjusted their reactions accordingly to simulate more realistic interactions.* For example, if during a disclosure a team failed to explicitly state that they had made an error, the actor/standardized patient would repeatedly ask "how could this have happened" until the team explicitly stated that they had made an error and provided a truthful accounting of how it occurred (based on the facts of the simulation scenario). Or, if the team did not offer an early explicit apology, the standardized patient was instructed to "turn up the emotional heat" until the team offered an apology. Conversely, when a team was forthright about having made an error and then effectively offered an upfront, explicit apology, the actor was instructed to demonstrate more understanding toward the team.

Practising risk managers from participating organizations participated in the simulation experience as disclosure coaches, providing feedback to the teams about their performance.

The way in which we set the tone for the simulations was influenced by feedback received from clinicians during pilot testing of the scenarios and *research findings about patients' preferences and expectations for error disclosure.* Having learned that clinicians were inexperienced in team error disclosure and in some cases resistant to the notion, we acknowledged at the outset of our simulations that we were asking them to do something new. We gave teams permission to conduct their disclosures in the ways they thought would be best for their patients, noting that some teams preferred for the entire team to go in, while others preferred for the physician to go in by themselves. But we also encouraged participants to "try on" team error disclosure to see how it felt and to be mindful of its benefits and drawbacks during the simulation. We specifically challenged teams choosing to have the physician do the disclosure alone in the first case to try disclosing as a team in the second case (unless they thought it was really ill-advised for the patient). By framing team error disclosure as something new or "novel," we sought to allay clinicians' anxieties about making "mistakes" or not performing well.

4.4 Description of Disclosure Coaching in Action

While educational activities like simulation training can influence cultural norms and create institutional environments supportive of behavior change, coaching is regarded as the essential ingredient for the transfer of learning into practice

(Showers, 1982). Our trained on-site coaches will be available after this project's funding cycle ends to provide institutional support for and reinforcement of the model of team error disclosure we introduced in our simulations by offering *just-in-time coaching* and *formal continuing education.* They can additionally provide *emotional support* before and after teams engage in error disclosure conversations with patients and families.

We trained risk managers to provide targeted feedback to team members using an "*Ask-Tell-Ask*" coaching format that we hoped they would adopt for use in actual error disclosure situations, primarily during planning discussions. The coaching model is a variation of the "one minute preceptor," which combines principles of adult learning with techniques of time-limited teaching and is widely used in clinic settings where feedback and teaching have to be conducted "on the fly." These features of the model fit with what risk managers told us about error disclosure discussions with clinicians: that they occur most often "on the fly" when a distressed clinician phones for advice about how to discuss an error with a patient or family in a soon-to-occur meeting. *Ask-Tell-Ask* incorporates Knowles et al.'s (1984) principles that teaching and learning are enhanced when teachers take the time to elicit their adult learners' prior knowledge and beliefs, diagnose their learning needs, and provide targeted instruction to address gaps and misunderstandings. Prior knowledge is the starting point for new instruction and a baseline for monitoring learners' changing attitudes and perceptions during the instructional process. *Ask-Tell-Ask* can be used iteratively to assess learners' evolving understanding of a topic or concept after exposure to planned experiential activities, thus mirroring Kolb's (1984) experiential learning cycle. In sum, the model assists learners in developing their knowledge structures and provides teachers a means of assessing whether learners are advancing toward appropriate learning goals (Bell, 1982a, 1982b; Bell & Purdy, 1985).

In the simulations, we encouraged risk manager/coaches to *postpone "telling" participants how to improve their performance and instead to ask teams to reflect on what went well, identify areas for improvement, and plan and rehearse selected skills to accomplish their goals for improvement.* We instructed coaches to listen to team members, customize their feedback, and *provide targeted instruction incorporating two relevant learning "pearls" rather than a generic laundry list of do's and don'ts.* This coaching model represented *a significant shift from risk managers' current practice* of offering didactic, generalized preparation for disclosure. As a coaching tool, the model is attractive because it fosters collaborative partnership between coaches and learners, requiring both parties to listen to and learn from each other.

We also explicitly acknowledged the wealth of experience that our coaches brought to the simulations. Many were already practising "disclosure coaches" at their institutions, providing just-in-time guidance to clinicians about what to disclose to patients and how to disclose it. But we asked them to expand their role to become educators as well, so as to provide instruction and enduring institutional support for changes in clinical practice. To these ends, we specifically requested that they (1) use the *Ask-Tell-Ask* coaching rubric, (2) coach teams rather than individuals to perform team rather than individual error disclosures, and (3) address practitioners' discomfort when performing team disclosure since it is not the current norm in clinical practice. To lessen their concerns about performing these new skills in the context of simulations, we provided a one-page handout outlining the *Ask-Tell-Ask* rubric and identifying a prioritized set of feedback targets comprising the essential content components of effective error disclosure and the communication behaviors necessary for effective team error disclosure planning and performance. They were advised that they should provide feedback on one content component priority (a familiar task) and one team component priority (a less familiar task associated with coaching teams). These coaching priorities represent a subset of the behaviors we targeted for learning. They are the ones we considered most important for effective error disclosure and are summarized below:

Content components of disclosure (essential in individual and team disclosures)

1st *Make an Explicit Apology*: During the actual disclosure, patients and families want clinicians to offer an explicit apology for errors that have occurred. Clinicians find this very difficult to do both emotionally and in terms of "finding the right words." An explicit apology conveys regret and acknowledges team responsibility for the error that was made.

2nd *Respond to Patient Emotion*: During the actual disclosure, clinicians often are unsure or overwhelmed about how to respond to the patient's emotional reaction (such as sadness, anxiety, anger, etc.). Patients want to have the professional acknowledge the impact of the event upon the patient.

3rd *Empathetic Disclosure of Core Content*: During the actual disclosure, patients want to be told about the error honestly but compassionately. This includes an explicit statement that an error occurred, what happened in simple but truthful language, the implications for the patient's health, and then to solicit the patient's questions and answer truthfully.

Team Components of Disclosure (Behaviors specific to team disclosures)

1st Anticipate patient reactions: During team planning for disclosure, all team members need to discuss aloud how each of them will work together to convey their desired TEAM message. Team members often fail to anticipate how patients will respond to error disclosure and plan an effective response. For example, if a patient responds to the disclosure of an error by asking which individual is to blame, team members need to be able to respond to the patient's blaming behavior and help each other to cope with a difficult situation.

2nd Solicit Multiple Views: During team discussion of the error, teams often neglect to solicit every person's view of how the error occurred instead allowing one person to dominate the discussion.

3rd Respond to Team Member's Emotions: During team discussion of the error and planning for disclosure, teams tend to ignore each other's emotional reactions to the error rather than responding empathetically to each other's emotions. If team members' emotions are not addressed, they may leak into the actual disclosure to the patient.

The application of the *Ask-Tell-Ask* model to disclosure coaching during the simulations was straightforward. At the outset of any disclosure coaching session, a coach would ask the team members to reflect on their experiences during the first simulation and then elicit and discuss their plans for the subsequent disclosure simulation. Team members' responses gave coaches insight into team members' readiness to perform the second disclosure by revealing (a) their knowledge about the content and communicative process of an error disclosure event, (b) their beliefs about how the error occurred, (c) their roles in it, and (d) their emotional states. Answers given to the "*Ask*" portion of the rubric informed the coaches' instruction or "Tell." During the "*Tell*" portion of a coaching interaction, coaches delivered a limited number of learning "pearls" targeted to team members' specific needs. The final "*Ask*" was comprised of coach/caregiver discussion and planning for the next concrete experience.

For example, teams frequently failed to explicitly apologize for their error during simulated disclosures, offering instead vague expressions of sympathy. In these instances, coaches were encouraged to explore the team's knowledge about apology in error disclosure and to prompt reflection on improving their approach to apologizing in the next simulation. The coach might make an observation such as: "*It seemed the patient wanted an apology from the team. How could your apology have been more explicit?*" Based on the team's replies, the coach would then offer a learning pearl, "telling" them, for example, "Research has shown that patients want their providers to offer an early unprompted apology that explicitly acknowledges the team's role in an error. When you express sympathy to your patients by saying *'I'm sorry that this has happened to you'*, you convey regret that something bad has happened to the patient, but the words fall short of conveying that you accept responsibility for the error. Statements such as *'I'm sorry for my role in the error that occurred in your care yesterday'* or *'I feel responsible for what happened to you; I am so sorry'* are more explicit."

Coaches were encouraged to follow-up their learning pearls by "asking" "*Is this something you would be willing to try in the next simulation – to make your apology more explicit?*" This suggestion often prompted pushback and discussion about risk management's attitudes toward apology and litigation and provided opportunities for teaching and learning about institutional and governmental policies surrounding apology. After reassurance that explicit apology was recommended, teams most often agreed to try a more explicit apology in the next simulation; some even rehearsed wording.

4.5 Assessment of the Intervention

A variety of data types were collected to assess the effectiveness of our simulation/coaching intervention, including data collected via an interactive Web-based tool (primary outcome measure), videotapes of teams performing error disclosure in two simulated scenarios with coaching provided between the first and second scenario, and debriefs with all participants.

We developed an interactive Web-based tool to assess the simulation/coaching intervention's impact on clinicians' skills related to inter-professional team communication about medical error and error disclosure as well as their knowledge and attitudes. Our "*Web-based Team-Oriented Medical Error Communication Assessment Tool*" incorporates innovative methods developed by Mazor and her colleagues (Mazor et al., 2007), who used short video vignettes followed by an open-ended question designed to trigger "actual" responses to patients on video. Mazor was able to distinguish meaningful differences in physicians' real-world communication skills. We hoped that our tool would be similarly able to distinguish the skills, knowledge, and attitudes of clinicians who participated in our simulation/coaching intervention from controls who did not.

We wrote open- and closed-ended questions to test participants' capability to correctly identify and evaluate exemplary and undesirable behaviors portrayed in video segments and to provide written feedback to team members about how to improve their team communication and error disclosure to the patient. Our goal was to capture both knowledge and recognition-level demonstrations of skill as well as higher order skills (e.g., providing feedback) requiring the synthesis and evaluation of information (Kim et al., in press). Question types included multiple choice, Likert-type scale, and open-ended questions requiring short written answers. For example, one multiple-choice stem was *"How would you approach disclosing this event to a patient?"* Answer options included *"no reference to adverse event or error," "mention adverse event but not error,"* and *"explicit statement that error occurred."* Likert-type scale questions assessed an examinee's global impression of an interaction. For example, *"How effectively has this team planned their disclosure to the patient/family?"* or *"How effective was the team in presenting a plan to a patient to prevent future error?"* (Scale: Not at all effective to extremely effective.) An example of a short-answer question was *"What aspects of this team's disclosure planning seemed most effective from your perspective?"* An example of an open-ended question associated with a shorter, focused video segment was *"What is the most important thing you would say to this team?"*

Development of the assessment tool's questions and scenarios progressed in tandem with the development of our team simulations and our coaching protocols. With the project nearly over, we began creating a scoring system, which proved to be more time consuming than anticipated. Our inter-professional research team, comprised of individuals from general internal medicine, nursing, pharmacy, and medical education, met to review participants' quantitative and qualitative responses to each Web assessment question and to try to reach agreement about standards for correctness and completeness of their responses. Reaching consensus about how to evaluate team member's (physician, nurse, pharmacist) overall effectiveness in facilitating team communication was difficult, in part because *team error disclosure*, in contrast with error disclosure by a single physician, is an *evolving concept* and clinicians' roles and responsibilities in its performance are not yet standardized. We have wrestled with how much we can expect nurses and pharmacists to assert themselves during team error disclosure planning, given the current hierarchical nature of clinician relationships. (Members of our research team have differing opinions about whether scoring standards should be in alignment with expectations for physician, nurse, and pharmacist roles as currently conceived or with those we imagine possible in the future.) This has also complicated the assessment of nuanced individual behaviors in a team because it is unclear, for example, whether silence signals agreement with what another team member has proposed (taking the position that restatement is unnecessary) or, whether it is an artifact of the clinical hierarchy and signals a reticence to voice disagreement.

Where participants were asked to view videos as an observer and provide feedback outlining "the most important thing you would say to the team," we have been challenged to come up with a scoring rubric that awards the greatest number of points to the most skilled clinicians, who identified the most critical behavior(s) and also provided cogent justification for their selections. We wanted to be able to distinguish the most skilled clinicians from those who responded by identifying key behaviors, but gave insufficient or no justification, or those who identified behaviors considered less central to the performance of an effective error disclosure.

It may turn out that the Web-assessment offers greatest value as a teaching/learning tool. User responses to the instrument have been positive with a sample of 99 early users rating the overall quality of the tool as good on a scale from 1 poor to 5 excellent: (mean = 4.1, SD = 0.97), the user interface design as innovative (mean = 4.1, SD = 0.83), intuitive to use (mean = 3.9, SD = 1.0), engaging (mean = 4.2, SD = 0.95), and instructionally valuable (mean = 4.2, SD = 0.88). Preliminary reliability analyses with 78 intervention participants demonstrate acceptable internal consistency within related subgroups of items (alpha = 0.89–0.70).

We videotaped the simulations and coaching sessions as a means of assessing teams' baseline knowledge, attitudes, and skills in planning for and conducting (a) error disclosure with patients (evident in the first simulation and brought out during the coaching sessions), (b) coaches' ability to implement the ask-tell-ask coaching rubric (coaching session), and (c) the effects of participating in a simulation and receiving coaching (second simulation). We also developed coding schemes for the simulation and coaching sessions with an eye towards describing changes in team behavior from the first simulation to the second (with our learning objectives informing our coding categories) and exploring the relation between coaching and behavior change.

For example, a key learning objective was that teams become skilled at anticipating the range of possible emotions a patient might express after the disclosure of an error and to plan (and even rehearse in some cases) appropriate empathic responses. We coded videos of the team simulations so we could examine when teams accomplished this objective. Codes indicated whether teams (a) anticipated or planned responses to their patients' emotions, (b) anticipated or planned responses to their patients' emotions with prompting from the standardized team member, or (c) did not anticipate or plan responses to their patients' emotions. Table 4.1 illustrates the codes we created to capture team communication about how they would respond to the full range of patients' reactions following disclosure of an error during the planning phase of the simulation. With reference to this example,

Table 4.1 Team planning for patient reaction to disclosure of an error

Team behavior	CODE and definition of team plan for response	Illustrative verbatim examples (from planning sessions)
Team plans for patient reaction to error disclosure	SILENCE: Silence or no response/nonverbal comfort	Plan no response to patient
	CALM: Calm, unflustered response	"I think it is best to just be calm."
	NV_POS: Nonverbal – pos: touch, moving in, etc.	"If they cry, I might give them a pat."
	NV_NEG: Nonverbal – neg: moving back, crossing arms, etc.	"If they get angry, I just move back."
	FACTS: Provide facts	"If she has lots of questions, let's just give her lots of information."
	ACKNOWL: Acknowledge/affirm the patient's emotional response	"If she is upset, I think we need to acknowledge this could have been serious."
	ARGUE: Argue with emotion	"I just think when patients get too upset or make too big a deal out of errors, you can try to put it into perspective."
	APOLOGIZE: Respond with apology	"If the patient seems upset, I just find it is best to apologize."
	RESCUE: Step in to help colleague if they get into trouble	"If she starts to focus on the insulin being given then I will step in to emphasize that this wasn't just your error but an error for all of us."
	PREVENT: Discuss how a similar future error will be prevented.	"If he is worried, we'll tell him that we're working on changes that will prevent this from ever happening again."
	REASSURE: Reassure the patient	"If she is worried, we can reassure her that there is no lasting harm from the error."
	OTHER: Other plan to respond to patient's emotion or reaction.	Other planned response.

if a team failed to plan for their patient's emotional responses to error disclosure, we expected coaches to make a point of noting this omission and providing information about its importance (especially if the team became flustered and unable to respond to the patient during the disclosure portion of the simulation). The coaching codes will enable us to capture and categorize the behavioral targets of our coaches' instruction (which should match coded team performance deficits and difficulties). It will also provide a means of assessing coaches' implementation of the *Ask-Tell-Ask* rubric.

We developed global rating scores for the simulation and coaching portions of our intervention to facilitate analysis of the relation of coaching to the incorporation of coached behaviors as well as error disclosure quality. Coaches received a top score of 10 points if they incorporated selected behaviors likely to promote changes into their coaching. These included using the Ask-Tell-Ask rubric (5 points), making an explicit request for change (2 points), receiving an explicit agreement from the team that they would change (1 point), providing two explicit teaching pearls (1 point), and summarizing their coaching points (1 point). No points were awarded if they moved right into the "tell" portion of their coaching, opened with a rambling set of sequences, or opened the session with closed or leading questions. If coaches started a coaching session with an open "ask" question, they received one point; if they started with an open "ask" question and followed up with teaching points in the "tell" portion of their coaching, they received three points.

Global scores for *team planning* were based on their effectiveness in

1. planning disclosure to the patient
2. facilitating open communication
3. planning for the patient's needs
4. the overall quality of the interaction between team members

Global scores for *team disclosure* were based on

- overall effectiveness of their disclosure
- quality of explicit apology
- quality of explanation for how the error occurred
- support for patient emotion
- sincerity of communication and
- quality of team communication with the patient.

During development of these coding schemes, we were challenged in our ability to capture both the content and the process elements of what occurred in the simulations. For example, we wanted to code when clinicians expressed an emotional response to having participated in an error situation ("I feel terrible that I gave that much insulin to this patient") and their colleague's response to that statement ("Well, it wasn't just your error. I used an abbreviation I shouldn't have"). In addition, we wanted to code how the team responded to scripted triggers and prompts the actors used in the simulations. Our coding scheme allows for coding the trigger and the team's response to that trigger. We also wanted to code general team interactions such as one team member's efforts to help another team member participate more actively by asking them a question, sometimes rhetorical, and waiting for a response or rescuing their colleague when he or she was at a loss for words or being uncomfortably targeted by the patient. Finally, we wanted the coaching coding scheme to be linked to the other coding schemes in a way that would allow us to track whether gaps or strengths during the planning and disclosure segments were identified and discussed in the coaching segments. We believe that the coding described is granular enough to allow us to track changes in behavior from simulation to simulation and global enough to be able to make statements about the value of simulation and coaching in effecting change.

4.6 Preliminary Findings

We learned that although the case scenarios were vetted, some participants questioned their authenticity; others expressed difficulty imagining they would have made the errors described. We encouraged the former participants to "throw themselves into" the situations and roles described and see what happened. At the other end of the continuum were the clinicians who reported that the simulations were "real enough" to be stressful. To address the concerns of this latter group, we scheduled post-simulation debriefings that afforded participants the opportunity to express their emotions and decompress while we learned more about their perceptions of the experience (e.g., case fidelity, the pluses and minuses of planning as a team to disclose and team error disclosure, etc.) Although the analyses of our Web-based assessment and videotapes are not completed, we have been able to review nurses', physicians', and risk managers' transcribed debriefing sessions to gain some insight into the impact of our intervention on participants' knowledge, skills, and attitudes.

Initial reviews of the debriefs suggests that clinicians found participating in team simulation and role play to be challenging, but worthwhile for the experience of having to find the words to respond in the moment to their inter-professional team members and the standardized patients. As one physician observed,

> It's one thing to see it on the video and say, 'Oh, that's what I'll do.' But then, when the patient gets angry or sad, or whatever, or interrupts you or you can't control the conversations so you just have to kinda let it be dynamic.

Participating in the simulations also raised clinicians' awareness of the benefits of disclosing errors to a patient as a team. Physicians commented that they felt more at ease when they disclosed errors with their nurse colleagues:

> I've been familiar with error disclosure in the past in terms of apologizing and explaining and making a plan for prevention, but it's been more thought of as solo. So, I think that the new aspect with this was with a team approach, which I think seemed to make it more comfortable and more effective.

Additionally, physicians praised their nurse team members for their ability to communicate empathically and effectively with patients:

> The big learning point for me was to work with the nurse who was so exceptionally skilled and be able to use her skills in the team... they're usually more skilled than the physicians in communicating with patients and families... to have the ability to use that nurse and then to see how effectively she could communicate in that environment, I think was a good learning point for me.

Nurses, who often felt as if they were most responsible for the errors that were made because they were on the "front lines" reported feeling more comfortable disclosing errors in teams because they felt more supported. As one nurse observed,

> In both of the scenarios, I felt personally like I'm the one who made the mistake. And so it was really good to be part of a team and to have that not be really the team's impression... that X. is a bad nurse and should get fired. So that was really good to be able to just share that it's really a systems problem, not a personal problem.

From their vantage point, the coaches were able to discern and describe how nurses and physicians reacted to working in teams to plan for and disclose errors together, often for the first time. In some cases, they felt that team members were able to work synergistically, performing team error disclosures that were most likely better and more effective than either one of them would have performed alone. As one coach noted,

> Within seconds, they became a team and I believe it was much easier for them to be more personal and say "I am so sorry" and "I did this" because they had another person that was going to be saying the same thing... And so, for the patient, it made a huge difference. Because each . . . the physician or the nurse, each of them added something that the other one didn't add. So it kinda covered all bases for the patient.

In general, coaches observed that nurses tended to be more attuned to the patients' emotional needs and were better able to communicate the facts of a case using language that was understandable to them than the physicians. In contrast, coaches described physicians as more authoritative than nurses and possessing superior clinical knowledge and hence the ability to provide more detailed explanation of how errors had occurred. Coaches described physicians' presence in disclosures as essential, lending weight to the interaction and promoting the belief that action would be taken to redress the causes and consequences of the error.

The coaches commented on the resistance to team disclosure they encountered:

> You know, I saw some reluctance, because the doctor is in that power position and used to being in control and taking complete accountability for whatever happens in the care of the patient. And so I saw a little bit of reluctance, in the nurse, not feeling necessarily like an equal partner in this, because I do feel that the docs feel that the bottom line is they're responsible.

Overall, however, nurses expressed the opinion that team error disclosure was optimal because it gave them a voice and a presence in patient care:

> I think it's really important, if nursing wants to be seen as an equal member of the health care team, then they need to be equally accountable for errors that happen.

The risk managers reported that they liked using the coaching rubric because it gave them a standardized way to "coach on the fly." One risk manager had already begun to reframe her everyday approach to working with clinicians using the rubric:

> I just talked to somebody the other night who had to disclose and so I kind of think to myself, "Ok, I've got x number of minutes and I need to get the story from them." So that's kind of the *ask*, right? And then I need to *tell* them the two or three most important things, based on what they've told me. And then I need to *ask* them again, "Ok, what are you going to do?"

> And that's been helpful. I've allowed them to talk more, for me to try to figure out where they're going with their thinking and then customize my advice back, according to that.

The *Ask-Tell-Ask* approach to identifying clinicians' learning needs and then providing targeted coaching was appealing to the coaches:

> The thing that I found useful was the focus on keeping it simple and just keeping to a few points. We've always emphasized more going over the records and that type of thing, but I ... you know, I appreciated the advice on responding to patients' emotions and getting that apology up front there.

Risk managers also appreciated the value of helping to facilitate clinician self-learning through reflection:

> I will become more of a facilitator, having gone through the simulations, because I can see some areas where I can push them differently. Risk management tends to be the answer man and the fix-it people. And I think this is a good opportunity to allow them [the clinical team] to fix it.

Overall, debriefs with the risk managers who acted as disclosure coaches in our study suggest that they enjoyed taking on the role of educator, focusing on helping teams to identify their own deficits and learning needs, and providing guidance in rehearsing and preparing for difficult conversations rather than dictating institutional regulations or offering generalized instruction that might not be relevant or helpful.

4.7 Discussion and Next Steps

Our intervention sought to improve inter-professional team communication and promote the concept of team error disclosure to individual clinicians and institutional representatives through the use of simulated authentic scenarios. We recognize that simulation is only one strategy in a multidimensional set of strategies needed to change the way error disclosure is currently practiced. Organizational culture change also needs to occur to foster, enable, and support changes in the disclosure practices of individual providers that result from educational initiatives such as ours. Studies of practice change suggest that institutional resources will need to be invested in information dissemination, instruction, team building, feedback and consultation, practitioner engagement, systems change, formulation of policies and procedures, assessment of performance and outcomes related to practice changes, and campaigns explaining how changes in disclosure practice are aligned with the organizational mission (Adelson et al., 1997).

Although research suggests that nurses are more dissatisfied with how error disclosures are routinely handled than physicians and more likely to perceive the value of moving to team disclosure (Adelson et al., 1997), both physicians and nurses expressed increased interest in team error disclosure after participating in the simulations. Risk managers' participation in the educational intervention afforded them a first-hand look at the "current competence" and "current practice" of nurses and physicians within their organizations. It also provided opportunities to reflect on and begin to formulate coaching strategies to aid practitioners in performing effective and empathic team error disclosure.

In the near term, we anticipate that our videotape-based analyses will reveal that the clinicians who participated in our simulations were able to improve the quality of their error disclosures with targeted instruction. In the long term, our hope is that nurses and physicians at our institution will feel more supported when they face the challenging task of disclosing an error to a patient – both because they will be able to receive just-in-time coaching from coaches more skilled at providing instruction and because team-based error disclosure will become the institutional norm. Culture change can be slow. But the risk managers we trained as disclosure coaches will remain in place well after our project's completion and can potentially enable and reinforce changes at the individual practitioner level as well as the organizational level to foster the learning begun with these simulations.

References

Adelson, R., Vanloy, W. J., & Hepburn, K. (1997). Performance change in an organizational setting: A conceptual model. *The Journal of Continuing Education in the Health Professions, 17*, 69–80.

American Society for Healthcare Risk Management of the American Hospital Association. (2003). *Disclosure of unanticipated events: The next step in better communication with patients*. Chicago: American Society for Healthcare Risk Management.

Amori, G. (2006). *Pearls on disclosure of adverse events*. Chicago: American Society for Healthcare Risk Management.

Bell, A. (1982a). Treating students' misconceptions. *The Australian Mathematics Teacher,* 2, 11–13.

Bell, A., & Purdy, D. (1985). *Diagnostic teaching—Some problems of directionality*. Shell Centre for Mathematical Education, University of Nottingham, England.

Bell, A. W. (1982b). Diagnosing students′ misconceptions. *The Australian Mathematics Teacher, 1*, 6–10.

Berlinger, N. (2005). *After harm: Medical error and the ethics of forgiveness*. Baltimore: The Johns Hopkins University Press.

Bero, L., Grilli, R, Grimshaw, J. M., Harvey, E., Oxman, A. D., & Thomson, M. A. (1998). Closing the gap between research and practice: an overview of systematic reviews of interventions to promote the implementation of research findings. *British Medical Journal, 317*, 465–468.

Blendon, R., DesRoches, C. M, Brodie, M., Benson, J. M., Rosen, A. B., Schneider, E., et al. (2002). Views of Practicing Physicians and the public on medical errors. *New England Journal of Medicine, 347*, 1933–1940.

Davis, D., O'Brien, M. A., Freemantle, N., Wolf, F. M., Mazmanian, P., & Taylor-Vaisey, A. (1999). Impact of formal continuing medical education: do conferences, workshops, rounds, and other traditional continuing education activities change physician behavior or health care outcomes? *JAMA, 282*(9), 867–874.

Driskell, J. E. (1998). Stress exposure training. In J. Cannon-Bowers & E. Salas (Eds.), *Making decisions under stress – Implications for individual and team training*. Washington, DC: American Psychological Association.

Gallagher, T. H., Denham, C., Leape, L., Amori, G., & Levinson, W. (2007). Disclosing unanticipated outcomes to patients: The art and the practice. *Journal of Patient Safety, 3*(3), 158–165.

Gallagher, T. H., Garbutt, J. M., Waterman, A. D., Flum, D. R., Larson, E. B., Waterman, B. M., et al. (2006). Choosing your words carefully: how physicians would disclose harmful medical errors to patients. *Archives of Internal Medicine, 166*(15), 1585–1593.

Gallagher, T. H., Studdert, D., & Levinson, W. (2007). Disclosing harmful medical errors to patients. *New England Journal of Medicine, 356*(26), 2713–2719.

Gallagher, T. H., Waterman, A. D., Ebers, A. G., Fraser, V. J., & Levinson, W. (2003). Patients' and physicians' attitudes regarding the disclosure of medical errors. *JAMA, 289*(8), 1001–1007.

Gallagher, T. H., Waterman, A. D., Garbutt, J. M., Kapp, J. M., Chan, D. K., Dunagan, W. C., et al. (2006). US and Canadian physicians′ attitudes and experiences regarding disclosing errors to patients. *Archives of Internal Medicine, 166*(15), 1605–1611.

Garbutt, J., Brownstein, D. R., Klein, E. J., Waterman, A., Krauss, M. J., Marcuse, E. K., et al. (2007). Reporting and disclosing medical errors: pediatricians' attitudes and behaviors. *Archives Pediatrics and Adolescent Medicine, 161*(2), 179–185.

Gibson, R., & Singh, J. P. (2003). *Wall of silence: The untold story of the medical mistakes that kill and injure millions of Americans*. Washington, DC: Lifeline Press.

Issenberg, S. B., McGaghie, W. C., Petrusa, E. R., Lee Gordon, D., & Scalese, R. J. (2005). Features and uses of high-fidelity medical simulations that lead to effective learning: A BEME systematic review. *Medical Teacher, 27*(1), 10–28.

Kachalia, A., Shojania, K. G., Hofer, T. P., Piotrowski, M., & Saint, S. (2003). Does full disclosure of medical errors affect malpractice liability? The jury is still out. *Joint Commission Journal on Quality and Patient Safety, 29*(10), 503–511.

Kaldjian, L. C., Jones, E. W., Wu, B. J., Forman-Hoffman, V. L., Levi, B. H., & Rosenthal, G. E. (2007). Disclosing medical errors to patients: attitudes and practices of physicians and trainees. *Journal of General Internal Medicine, 22*(7), 988–996.

Ker, J., Mole, L., & Bradley, P. (2003). Early introduction to interprofessional learning: a simulated ward environment. *Medical Education, 37*(3), 248–255.

Kim, S., Brock, D., Prouty, C., Odegard, P., Shannon, S., Robins, L., et al. (2011). A web-based team-oriented medical error communication assessment tool: Development, preliminary reliability, validity, and user ratings. *Teaching and Learning in Medicine*, *23*(1), 68–77.

Knowles, M., et al. (1984). *Andragogy in action: applying modern principles of adult learning*. San Francisco: Jossey-Bass.

Kolb, D. (1984). *Experiential learning*. Englewood Cliffs, NJ: Prentice Hall.

Loren, D., Klein, E. J., Garbutt, J., Krauss, M. J., Fraser, V., Dunagain, W. C., et al. (2008). Medical Error disclosure among pediatricians: choosing carefully what we might say to parents. *Archives Pediatrics and Adolescent Medicine, 162*, 922–927.

Mann, K. V., McFetridge-Durdle, J., Martin-Misener, R., Clovis, J., Rowe, R., Beanlands, H., et al. (2009). Interprofessional education for students of the health professions: the "Seamless Care" model. *Journal of Interprofessional Care, 23*(3), 224–233.

Marinopoulos, S. S., Dorman, T., Ratanawongsa N, Wilson LM, Ashar BH, Magaziner JL, et al. (2007). *Effectiveness of continuing medical education. Evidence Report/Technology Assessment No. 149 (Prepared by the Johns Hopkins Evidence-based Practice Center, under Contract No. 290-02-0018.) AHRQ Publication No. 07-E006*. Rockville, MD: Agency for Healthcare Research and Quality.

Mazor, K. M., Haley, H. L., Sullivan, K., & Quirk, M. E. (2007). The video-based test of communication skills: description, development, and preliminary findings. *Teaching and Learning in Medicine, 19*(2), 162–167.

Mazor, K. M., Reed, G. W., Yood, R. A., Fischer, M. A., Baril, J., & Gurwitz, J. H. (2006). Disclosure of medical errors: what factors influence how patients respond? *Journal of General Internal Medicine, 21*(7), 704–710.

Morey, J., Simon, R., Jay, G. D., Wears, R. L., Salisbury, M., Dukes, K. A., et al. (2002). Error reduction and performance improvement in the emergency department through formal teamwork training: evaluation results of the MedTeams project. *Health Services Research, 37*(6), 1553–1581.

Schoen, C., Osborn, R., Huynh, P. T., Doty, M., Zapert, K., Peugh, J., et al. (2005). Taking the pulse of health care systems: experiences of patients with health problems in six countries. *Health Aff (Millwood), Suppl Web Exclusives,* W5-509–525.

Shannon, S., Foglia, M., Hardy, M., & Gallagher, T. (2009). Disclosing errors to patients: Perspectives of registered nurses. *Joint Commission Journal of Quality and Patient Safety, 35*(1), 5–12.

Shapiro, E. (2008). *Disclosing medical errors: Best practices from the "leading edge"*. Retrieved January 22, 2009, from http://www.ihi.org/IHI/Topics/PatientSafety/SafetyGeneral/Literature/DisclosingMedicalErrorsBestPracticesLeadingEdge.htm

Sharpe, V. (2004). *Accountability: Patient safety and policy reform*. Washington, DC: Georgetown University Press.

Showers, B. (1982). *Transfer of training: The contribution of coaching*. Eugene, Oregon: Center for Educational Policy and Management.

The Full Disclosure Working Group. (2006). *When things go wrong: responding to adverse events*. A consensus statement of the Harvard Hospitals. Boston: Massachusetts Coalition for the Prevention of Medical Errors.

The Joint Commission. (2007). *Hospital Accreditation Standards, 2007*. Oakbrook Terrace, IL: Joint Commission Resources.

The Kaiser Family Foundation/Agency for Healthcare Research & Quality/Harvard School of Public Health. (November 2004). *National survey on consumers' experiences with patient safety and quality information*. Retrieved October 6, 2005, from http://www.kff.org/kaiserpolls/upload/National-Survey-on-Consumers-Experiences-With-Patient-Safety-and-Quality-Information-Survey-Summary-and-Chartpack.pdf.

Waterman, A. D., Garbutt, J., Hazel, E., Dunagan, W. C., Levinson, W., Fraser, V. J., et al. (2007). The emotional impact of medical errors on practicing physicians in the United States and Canada. *Joint Commission Journal of Quality and Patient Safety, 33*(8), 467–476.

White, A., Waterman, A., McCotter, P., Boyle, D., & Gallagher, T. (2008). Supporting health-care workers after medical errors: Considerations for health care leaders. *Journal of Clinical Outcomes Management, 15*(5), 240–247.

Chapter 5
Leader Development in Dynamic and Hazardous Environments: Company Commander Learning Through Combat

Nate Allen and D. Christopher Kayes

5.1 Introduction

> The biggest thing is, you know, whenever you are surrounded by chaos always to remember to assess. Now I always tell myself to remind myself to continue to assess. (Company Commander #18)

To understand leadership in a highly dynamic and hazardous context, it makes sense to view the experience through the eyes of leaders. Here is how one leader, a US Army company commander in Iraq in 2005, described a developmental experience he had in combat:

> I've never seen enemy fire like that. We had 20 to 30 insurgents together shooting straight up at us while our ground forces were in contact. . . . It was a situation where you've been taught the way to do it your entire career, and that just wasn't working. (Company Commander #1)

In this context, information needs are constantly changing and the leader faces chaotic interdependent systems, ambiguities, complexities, and novel situations. In such an environment, the individual experiences, in the words of Karl Weick, a sense of "vu jade – the opposite of déjà vu: I have never been here before, have no idea where I am, and have no idea who can help me" (Weick, 1993, pp. 633, 634). The context itself is constantly changing, but what is the leader experiencing? Again, the words of a company commander prove the most instructive:

> You . . . are going to these classes. You sit in an educational environment. And they say: "Your soldiers' lives are in your hands," and you kind of laugh, "Okay; got it. They are in my hands." . . . They say you are responsible and everything, but you don't fully realize how important it is until you are there and you experience it first hand. . . . You talk about lives of your soldiers in your hands. And this time people are actually dying. (Company Commander #13)

In a few short sentences, this company commander described his sense of profound responsibility, and his heightened awareness of the consequences his decisions have on others. But this is just one dimension of the experiences that form the

---

N. Allen (✉)
National Defense University, Washington, DC 20319-5066, USA
e-mail: nate.allen@us.army.mil

A. Mc Kee, M. Eraut (eds.), *Learning Trajectories, Innovation and Identity for Professional Development*, Innovation and Change in Professional Education 7,
DOI 10.1007/978-94-007-1724-4_5, © Springer Science+Business Media B.V. 2012

foundation for learning in combat. In this chapter, we explore the nature of several such experiences and how they lead to deep learning in highly dynamic and hazardous situations.

In an attempt to generate greater understanding of the increasingly critical area of leader learning and development, one of the researchers traveled to Iraq during the fall of 2005 to interview 53 company commanders about their learning experiences. One guiding question formed the basis for this study: What characteristics are associated with the learning developed through company commanders' experiences in combat?

This study follows in a tradition of research that has explored leadership in action teams working in a complex, dynamic, and hazardous context. Naturalistic decision-making literature, for example, has focused on how experts make decisions and has contrasted these expert decisions with the decisions of novices (see, for example, Klein, 1998). The underlying assumption of this approach is that experts make better decisions than novices. Much of the work on naturalistic decision making has emerged from observing experts, conducting detailed case studies, and using critical incident interviews. The result of much of this literature is a map of the decision-making process of experts to better understand how the best leaders make decisions in highly dynamic and hazardous contexts.

A closely related stream is the research on organizational sensemaking. This literature is broad and diverse; however, one of its major contributions is the attempt to understand the nature of decision making as a retrospective process (see, for example, Weick, 1995). In contrast to the naturalistic decision-making approach, the sensemaking approach is more concerned with how leaders make sense of their immediate actions and how these actions influence new actions. Both the naturalistic decision-making as well as the sensemaking traditions assume that experience plays an important part in how leaders respond in these contexts.

These two traditions represent unique but connected approaches to understanding the nature of leadership experience. While existing literature contributes significantly to our understanding of leadership in a highly dynamic and hazardous context, there is less understanding about the process whereby leaders learn from their experience in this milieu. In other words, much of the research focuses on the end state of decision making but says less about the nature and personal outcomes of developmental experiences. In this regard, this chapter furthers awareness of the process of leader development and extends our understanding of the acquisition of expertise in hazardous environments. The following section presents a conceptual framework for this exploration based on experiential learning theory.

5.2 Our Conceptual Framework

This study draws on two theoretical traditions, experiential learning (Kolb, 1984; Mezirow, 1991) and leader development, to better understand how leaders learn in highly dynamic and hazardous contexts. Such contexts create situations in which there is no way to predict the future or prepare leaders for every contingency they will face—situations that demand adaptive capacity in which effective leaders learn from their experiences in an ongoing manner. Thus, experience-centered learning theories are optimally equipped to address leader learning in combat.

5.2.1 Experiential Learning Theory

We drew on Kolb's (1984) process model of experiential learning to guide our thinking because it integrates several learning theories and has proven a useful model to study learning in practice-based settings such as combat. Experiential approaches view learning as an ongoing process where new knowledge is created as past and current experiences are reflected upon and integrated (Kolb, 1984; Knowles, 1980; Mezirow, 1991). Kolb described learning as the "process whereby knowledge is created through the transformation of experience" (Kolb, 1984, p. 38). Mezirow (1991) built upon the notion of experience as the basis for learning by suggesting that meaning is constructed from experience—or, in his words, "to make meaning is to construe or interpret experience" (Mezirow, 1994, p. 4). In this regard, knowledge emerges when the learner effectively constructs meaning from his or her own personal experience. Kolb (1984) popularized the term *experiential learning* as a model that builds upon Lewin's (1951) thinking and described learning as four steps in a continuous process.

- *Concrete experience* initiates the learning process by engaging with the world. For example, experiential learning involves engaging directly in combat in contrast to reading stories or studying past combat scenarios in a classroom.
- *Reflective observation* involves being mindful of and reflecting upon what is happening during and after the experience. This might include identifying outcomes (both expected and unexpected), becoming aware of opportunities for improvement, and comparing what actually occurred with what was planned.
- *Abstract conceptualization* is the direct result of reflective observation. In this step the learner turns observations into advice for the future—generalizing from the specific. This advice incorporates past learning and experience and guides future action.
- *Active experimentation* requires that the learner process options for new action based on the learning constructed from reflected-upon concrete experience and then apply these options to future experiences—thus moving the learner back to the first step in the cycle (concrete experience).

Figure 5.1 provides a version of Kolb's learning cycle.

These four steps provide two important considerations for leader development in combat. First, for Kolb, emotions play an important part in learning. In fact, the terms *experience* and *emotions* are often used interchangeably. As we discuss next, the emotional nature of combat leadership is a key element in learning to be a leader. Leaders must learn to work in a context of volatile and intense emotions. Second, the cycle time of learning accelerates in combat. Thus, a leader must learn to cycle through the four-stage cycle at a more rapid pace than traditional leadership.

Fig. 5.1 Experiential learning cycle

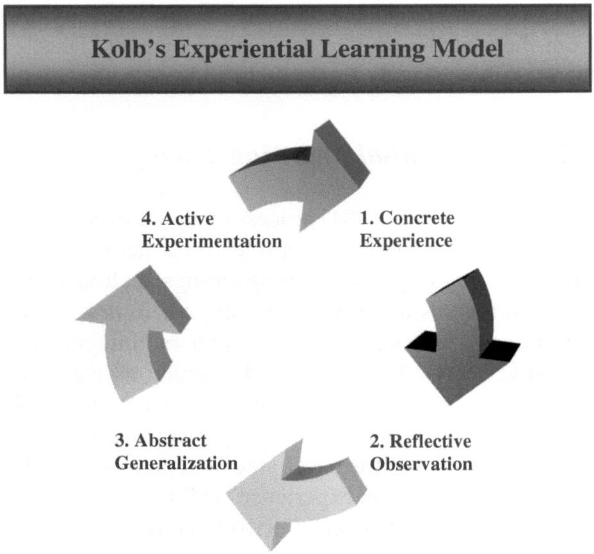

5.2.2 Leadership Development and Learning

Like the learning literature, knowledge on leader development is diverse in underlying assumptions. While this chapter focuses on the more individual (e.g., cognitive and affective) aspects of leader development rather than on the more socially oriented dimensions, this emphasis on individual learning should not be construed as an endorsement of a purely individualist perspective (for a contrast to the individualist perspective, see Reynolds & Vince, 2005). We fully believe that this type of deep learning occurs through both individual reflection and feedback from others. The importance of feedback in leader development cannot be overstated. The developmental impact of feedback combined with support provided in a trusted mentoring relationship leads to the most developmental of learning experiences and facilitates the leader's ability to make sense of his or her experiences, identifying strengths to be leveraged and weaknesses to be overcome (McCauley, Moxley, & Van Velsor, 2004).

Rather, due to the nature of our research question and our research protocol, we focus our attention on the leader development literature that parallels learning theory's focus on cognitive and affective experience. For example, Kouzes and Posner (1995) claimed that it is through experience that leaders learn both to become leaders and to improve their leadership abilities. Among experiences that leaders described as developmental, Kouzes and Posner (1995) discovered a common theme: key learning experiences were *challenging* (Kouzes & Posner, 1995). McCall (1998) supported the notion that challenging experiences prove the most developmental: "The intellectual repartee of the classroom has a certain appeal, but when asked to recount events that changed them significantly, successful executives ... described powerful, challenging experiences" (McCall, 1998, p. 62). In order for challenging experiences to be the basis for learning, McCall added that these experiences required self-awareness (a sense of personal strengths and weaknesses) and a willingness to confront one's deeply held assumptions in the learning process. Here the link between experiential learning and leader development should be clear: challenging experiences enhanced by self-awareness (e.g., reflective observation) and the willingness to confront assumptions (abstract conceptualization) lead to development.

Further, researchers at the Center for Creative Leadership found that novel and challenging experiences proved the most significant in a leader's growth. They added three additional elements to the existing learning framework: the need for (1) pre-experience preparation, (2) post-experience assessment, and (3) an ongoing supportive context (McCaulley et al., 2004).

These traditions provide an understanding of how leaders learn from experience. Neither experience alone nor the nature of the experience itself can lead to developing leaders. Both the experiential learning and leader development literature support the conclusion that leaders learn from experience and that the context in which each experience is situated plays a significant role. There is, however, less understanding about the leader's learning experiences in a context that is highly dynamic and hazardous.

5.3 Methodology

To develop a better understanding of how leaders develop in a highly dynamic and hazardous context, one researcher traveled to Iraq to study US Army company commanders in combat. Case study with a multiple-case design (in which each participant was a case) was then used to explore the interviews, applying a process of analytic induction (Yin, 2003). The research process was iterative in nature. The data, the research questions, and the interview questions were assessed in an ongoing manner to ensure alignment with the purposes of this study. When we study experience, we are tapping into the emotional content of the leader in the form of their narratives, or descriptions of their direct experience (see Dey, 2007). Throughout this chapter you will see firsthand, how these experiences are described by the leaders themselves.

5.3.1 Participant Selection

Rubin and Rubin discussed the principle of completeness in discerning at what point enough participants have been interviewed: "You choose people who are knowledgeable about the subject and talk with them until what you hear provides an overall sense of the meaning of a concept, theme, or process" (Rubin & Rubin, 1995, p. 73). Potential participants for this study were identified through ongoing purposive sampling from company commanders in Iraq. A diverse perspective was developed based on branch or type of command (16 armor, 14 infantry, 7 aviation, 5 field artillery, 2 engineer, 1 air defense artillery, 1 special forces, 2 medical, 1 chemical, 1 ordnance, 2 military intelligence, 1 quartermaster, and 1 signal commander), prior combat experience (36 with prior combat experience and 17 with no prior combat experience), time in command (ranging from 2 weeks to 35 months, with an average of 14 months), time commanding a company in combat (ranging from 2 weeks to 20 months, with an average of 7 months), region in Iraq (four distinctly different regions in Iraq), and unit (four different divisional level units). Additionally, two of the 53 commanders were national guard and four were headquarters company commanders now leading their second company.

5.3.2 Data Collection

The primary data collection method comprised in-depth qualitative interviews. Seidman's (1998) approach to qualitative data collection inspired the research because it values the role of experience and meaning-making (pp. 7, 8; see also Weiss, 1994). Conducting research in a combat setting created several logistical challenges. For example, traveling between interviews required moving with combat logistics patrols, and schedules did not often allow for multiple meetings with the same subject. Thus, the research resulted in the use of only two interviews for eight participants and only one interview for 45 participants to create understanding around life and work context. However, the interview approach led to long interviews that opened up issues that might otherwise have required second or even third interviews. Thus, the time spent with each participant averaged 2 h and 23 min.

5.3.3 Data Analysis

Data generated from both field notes and transcribed interviews were analyzed in an ongoing manner throughout the study. The data were coded using the open coding process, such that codes emerged from analytic induction of the data and from participant characterization (Berg, 1989; Miles & Huberman, 1994). A start list (Miles & Huberman, 1994) of sensitizing concepts from the experiential learning literature was used, modified, and built upon. Both within-case and cross-case analyses (Miles & Huberman, 1994) were conducted, comparing and contrasting the relationships, themes, and patterns that emerged. As new patterns and themes were identified, transcripts were reviewed and coded, accounting for developing constructs. Subsequently, representative quotes from the interviews were collated for descriptions of each theme. This enabled the portrayal of the themes and patterns in this report to be based upon the authentic voice of the participants (Miles & Huberman, 1984). To facilitate the management of this process with the large amount of data generated in over 126 h of interviews, the software package *Atlas.ti* was used.

5.3.4 Possible Sources of Bias

In this study, there was a risk of bias related to participants' level of authenticity and openness. This concern was addressed through personal engagement in the participants' context, discussion with each participant about how confidentiality would be ensured, and the positioning of the researcher *as a learner* in the process of negotiating the researcher–participant relationship. Additionally, openness with the participants in the research process was engendered because the researcher had himself commanded a company and was a fellow Army officer. Thus, the ability to leverage the common shared experiences was important.

Another potential source of bias was related to preconceived assumptions. As an insider, the researcher was what Lincoln and Guba (1985) referred to as *emic*: As a result of underlying assumptions, the researcher may not go deep enough in conversation to pull out the multiple meanings attached to an experience (Lincoln & Guba, 1985). At the same time, we believe that past experience in the profession provided intuition on questions to ask in order to facilitate a more meaningful generation of knowledge. Thus, while there were risks of preconceived mental models interfering with the inductive process, we believe that the benefits of trust and an intuitive understanding of organizational culture provided great benefit to the process of meaning-making.

5.3.5 Limitations and Member Check

Due to the limited scope of this study with regard to the environment (combat) and participants (company commanders in the Army), claims of transferability to diverse leaders in different environments are limited. Furthermore, the interpretive nature of this research and the purposive process of sampling used preclude claims for absolute transferability to other company commanders in combat. However, having said this, due to the thick description of both context and personal experience that in-depth interviewing and participant observation afford, readers are able to discern for themselves what might seem reasonably transferable from the knowledge generated in this study.

Lincoln and Guba (1985) described the use of a member check as significant in establishing the credibility of a qualitative study. To accomplish this, face-to-face, one-on-one sessions were conducted with three company commanders on May 18 and 19, 2006, upon their return to the United States. During this session, each commander reviewed his or her interview excerpts along with summaries of the results and implications of this study. We are very encouraged by their response. All three felt that the analysis accurately reflected their and their peers' experiences. In fact, two of the commanders (unsolicited) expressed the sense that as they were reading, they were gaining a language to describe their experiences—a language that they did not have before. Concepts that were previously implicit were made explicit for them in the text. Furthermore, all three communicated that this study should be made available to the profession as a means to prepare the next generation of leaders for the rigors of combat.

5.4 Learning Experiences in Combat

Review of the interviews revealed four characteristics of the types of experiences related to learning in combat. Like Kouzes and Posner, who indicated that challenging experiences are essential to leader development in executives, this study revealed several characteristics of the nature of experiences that lead to learning in combat. We called these experiences "molten" in nature, as they share, metaphorically, characteristics of molten lava. Furthermore, they were characterized by a profound sense of responsibility, intense affect, and embodied feedback. We describe each in turn.

5.4.1 The Molten Experience

Molten experiences are chaotic, complex, volatile, and ambiguous. They are unpredictable, with threads from multiple, simultaneous, and overlapping experiences woven together. Moreover, they may demand that the leader wear multiple hats, requiring him or her to agilely shift from one role to another—roles that, in some situations, may require the leader to hold opposing viewpoints simultaneously. And finally, within each of these experiences and multiple potential roles, there is ongoing information oscillation—which consists of either too much, not enough, or conflicting information. There is something about leading through experiences like these that is highly developmental.

The commanders in this study illustrated powerfully the molten nature of combat-related developmental experiences. Company Commander #6 described the level of volatility and information oscillation succinctly: "About 2 weeks into the operation it all blew up in our faces . . . I've felt out of control, where I am fighting for information and feeling like I'm losing the bubble. . . . You talk about fog of war." Commanders #1 and #19 shared a sense of ambiguity and dilemma: "It was a situation where you've been taught the way to do it your entire career, and that just wasn't working" and "You have no idea who is bad or good and some of the people are bad who you think are good." Commanders #12 and #13 illustrated how fluid these experiences were: "That's the way it happens. You conduct a mission expecting one thing and then another happens" and "You go out on one mission and it would end up turning into 20 different missions." Commander #13 depicted the chaos: "Hearing the screaming, hearing the gunfire. Yeah, you feel the chaos." And Commander #47 shared the reality of multiple, simultaneous experiences: "I've had instances where an IED [improvised explosive device] goes off, at the same time I'm talking to a member of the Iraqi police, and I have a platoon out with an Iraqi Army patrol." These experiences were extreme, and yet these commanders were not just trying to survive them as individuals; they were leading people through them. And, in so doing, they felt an incredible amount of responsibility for the consequences of their decisions and actions.

5.4.2 Profound Responsibility

Company commanders found that the experiences they identified as developmental had given them a sense of profound responsibility, and linked to the leader's cognitive and affective recognition that he or she had an overwhelming amount of authority and power and that there was a significant risk in the decisions they had to make. In combat, this sense of profound responsibility includes the conviction that leaders are responsible for the lives of those in their care—as well as the lives of noncombatants and wounded insurgents. Furthermore, there is a sense of moral responsibility for the actions their soldiers take. In this regard, the knowledge generated in this study supports the notion that an experience has the potential to be developmental when the leader in that experience carries a significant amount of authority, while at the same time recognizing that there are substantial implications regarding his or her competence and character. We catch a glimpse of this sense of profound responsibility when the following company commanders shared their experiences with the interviewer:

> I could hardly pull myself away from the radios to rest. ... Every time we went out we were shot at, and the greatest fear I had was for my guys, especially when I wasn't out there with them. (Company Commander #1)

> We all have fear when we roll out the gate. My fear is not so much for myself anymore. Yeah, I'm afraid of being blown up and the effect it would have on my family. Now I fear more and more for my guys. I feel so responsible for them. ... I feel like I have a contract with my soldiers and their families—you know, mom and dad and people who love them—to ensure they are taken care of, and if they aren't being provided quality leadership I need to address it. (Company Commander #4)

> I couldn't get sleep whenever guys were out at night and I wasn't with them. I either had to be with them or I was on the radio. (Company Commander #12)

> And people did look to me for answers. What really felt good about it all was when I had all these things under control. I started to feel: Okay. I'm in charge of some stuff now. I felt responsible. ... And everything going on was because of me and my guys. And then you start feeling: I can't sleep, I can't go down because I'm responsible. ... It put everything more in perspective. And every decision you make will impact people and has weight. Every night I don't go to sleep until my last convoy is in; doesn't matter if it's 3:00 or 4:00 in the morning. I feel obligated: my duty is to make sure I'm available for them. ... The most stressful events for me were when I wasn't out with my men. Even when something was going on, I'd try to talk them through it on the radio. Absolutely one of the most stressful situations is not being able to affect the situation. Without being there I couldn't see what they were seeing. (Company Commander #13)

> I think one thing combat does—and it's not that you are cavalier before—but it increases your respect for the awesome responsibility that you have. (Company Commander #21)

As depicted, the commanders in this study reflected a deep sense of responsibility—a sense of responsibility both profound and enduring. For example, Commander #22 reflected: “For months and days on end, you really are responsible and in charge in your area, and you are the authority on every level.” And Commander #25 related: “It’s a very sobering experience for me because I realize the decisions I make affect my [own] and my soldiers’ lives and the people of Iraq. My actions can be a credit or discredit to my nation. I’m kind of like: ‘Wow’; it’s very sobering that you have the ability to affect all those things.” In reflecting upon and absorbing what these commanders shared about the degree of responsibility they felt, one cannot help but sense the level of emotion aroused in these types of experiences.

5.4.3 Intense Affect

The molten nature of the experience and the profound sense of responsibility it developed also created intense emotional affect. Experience often triggers an emotional response, but in the case of combat, the emotional response is more complex, more deeply felt, and of stronger intensity. Intense affect describes how the experiences identified as developmental by participants in this study were charged with emotion—emotion ranging from sheer rage, anger, and fear to relief, joy, and love—emotion experienced both by the leaders and by those around them. One cannot help but experience this dynamic as the participants in this study described their experiences.

> I heard them tell my pilots over the radio, “You are clear to engage.” And the net went silent. I felt like my heart was ripped out of my chest as I waited for my guys to come up on the net. (Company Commander #1)

> Before some missions I’d get a knot in my stomach, knowing they were vulnerable. In spite of this fear, you make the decision you have to make, knowing you could lose a soldier. (Company Commander #2)

> Trying to figure out my role in the whole grieving process was tough. We were all very emotional and crying and I found myself in the role of a grieving friend and a commander providing strength for the men. I think I was a little more stand-offish than I should have been. (Company Commander #7)

The commanders in this study communicated an incredible range of emotions both in themselves and in others. Commanders #6 and #18 described: “That was the first time I’ve ever felt this intense hatred for all Iraqis. You have to work through that. The thing that really held me together was I knew my soldiers were feeling all of the same things” and “I know I wanted to punch the insurgents we captured. I wanted to hurt them, and I know if I wanted this because of my love for that soldier we lost, I surely know his battle buddy felt that.” Through these comments and others like them, the participants in this study expressed the intensity of emotion that comprised their developmental experiences. A great proportion of this emotion was related to the unfathomable outcomes of their decisions and actions—what is described in this study as embodied feedback.

5.4.4 Embodied Feedback

Embodied feedback describes feedback that manifests itself in such a way that it is experienced by all the senses and leaves a lasting impression. Such feedback holds a mirror up for the leader, enabling sight of issues the leader might otherwise miss. While embodied feedback might include verbal and written forms, it goes beyond this conceptually to provide deeper meaning and sustained impact. This might include tangible failure, success, loss of a soldier, loss of a critical piece of equipment, or a personal crisis of limitations. There is no way for the leader to avoid the impression that embodied feedback delivers. It is in the moment, it is raw, it is in your face, it is not couched in politically correct terms, it is uncompromising. The experience of embodied feedback leads us to consider the learning process of reflective observation in the broadest possible terms. During reflective observation, the leader in combat must continue to gather information from the environment, even after the initial experience evaporates. Reflection in combat is not just an "intentional process" moving inside oneself, but includes a continued scanning for external stimuli.

The embodied feedback is not unlike Mezirow's (1994) conceptualization of disorienting dilemmas: experiences that demand self-examination and often result in what he described as perspective transformation. The following leader comments about losing a soldier demonstrates this:

> I lost three soldiers in one day—it devastated the company. No matter how many times you think of it, you are never prepared for picking up pieces and parts of your men. ... I felt a lot of anger. ... (Company Commander #6)

> When we lost our first two soldiers in the company, there were distinct things we could go back and say we could have done differently and we potentially could have avoided that. (Company Commander #21)

Commanders #2 and #31 expressed: "The lessons you learn in combat are ones you learn for the rest of your life. ... [Why?] Because of the cost of the decisions you make" and "The biggest thing about this environment is that your mistakes have potentially life/death, success or failure, victory or defeat implications. ... In combat the results are immediate and tangible. ... Over here when someone does die, it gets your attention pretty damn quick." In summary, this type of feedback demands attention and leaves an impression on the soul of the leader that cannot be discounted or forgotten.

5.5 Implications for Learning and Development

This study suggests that company commanders in combat are developing important competencies related to effective leadership. While the context of combat requires specific skills related to time-critical and highly consequential decisions, many of the competencies leaders learn in combat are generalizable. Four of the most critical outcomes include judgment, innovation, resilience, and compassion.

5.5.1 Leader Development in Combat

Reviewing data from this study suggests that existing models of experiential learning provide a stable foundation for exploring how leaders turn raw experiences into developmental opportunities in the combat context. Two additional considerations, however, may add to our understanding of how this learning is different in combat.

First, certain aspects of the learning cycle take on new dimensions in combat. The data revealed that the combat environment accelerates the learning cycle. The four processes of concrete experience, reflective observation, abstract conceptualization, and active experimentation occur so quickly as to become indistinguishable from each other. Rather than the deliberate and step-by-step process described by Kolb, learning in combat is better conceived as a series of interlocking actions and thoughts, whereby knowledge is constantly being created and recreated (see Klein et al., 1993).

Second, the notion of learning from past experience reveals only part of the puzzle of learning in combat. For example, the abstract conceptualization phase of learning may present a problem for the combat leader. Learning in combat often provides no prior knowledge or working theory on which to base action or judge past events. Therefore, new knowledge must be generated and current situational understanding must be constantly challenged and reviewed. Leadership in combat may be particularly challenging because one persistently enters novel situations.

Also, learning through active experimentation confronts two challenges in a combat situation. First, actions are more time critical. Second, actions are of higher consequence. In combat, there is little time to test out hypotheses, revaluate, and test again. Action requires almost immediate movement to another action.

5.5.2 Compassion and Resilience

Resilience describes the individual who bounces back after significant trauma or stress and adapts while maintaining his or her sense of self. The leaders in this study were developing resilience and gaining confidence. Things that might have created stress in the past began to seem routine, and the leaders were developing a hardiness that allowed them to remain calm for a prolonged period of time. They were learning to sustain both themselves and their soldiers. As one leader described it, "I think I've learned more of a sense of trying to find an inner peace or calm I guess. And knowing ways to not get stressed out or let the anxiety get to me because it's constant. I've learned a lot better how to relate with soldiers and lieutenants and the whole visualization of everything. . . . I guess I've learned that I can stand up in a firefight." (Company Commander #5)

Themes of resilience emerged throughout the study in phrases such as "we went out again and got back into the fight" (Company Commander #1) and "we ended up holding our positions there for 2 days against indirect fire, RPG [rocket-propelled grenade], and small arms fire—we never gave ground" (Company Commander #3). Like emotional aspects of judgment, resilience required constant nurturing as this leader describes:

> For a few hours [after witnessing the death of a fellow soldier] I felt like, "I can't make it through this." I knew I had to. But I felt like ... "How am I going to make it?" And then I looked at my soldiers and knew I had to for them. (Company Commander #6)

The commanders in this study communicated that not only were they developing resilience but they were also personally experiencing how critical resilience is for effectiveness in the combat environment. In many cases, leaders were developing a sense of efficacy and a capacity to sustain both themselves and their organizations under the stress of combat.

Compassion was another aspect of leader development as Commander #4 can attest:

> I'm much more empathetic as a leader of my soldiers because I know what they are going through. ... You know, sharing the hardship. I would say because of everything these soldiers have gone through and that I've gone through with them, there probably isn't anything I wouldn't do for them. I'm better at caring for my soldiers. (Company Commander #4)

Company Commander #4 demonstrates an important aspect of leadership in a molten environment: compassion. Compassion defines the heart of the leader. It enables him or her to extend beyond self and sacrifice for others; compassion is love in action. Through shared hardship with soldiers and experiencing potentially unfathomable loss, the company commanders in this study were deepening in compassion and were becoming more fully aware of the critical role compassion played in their practice of leadership. This reality was communicated as company commanders shared what they were experiencing:

> I let them just talk it all out, letting them say exactly what's on their mind. Let them call it "bullshit," "stupid," and everything else. At that point you are the commander but you can't go army strict, and you have to be compassionate and understanding and explain things through and not confront. And you can't say, "Private, that's disrespectful." That's not what they need to hear at that time. In many ways they are looking to be heard. They need an opportunity to express themselves. And at no other time do they need to hear from you [more] and express themselves to you than at the loss of a comrade. (Company Commander #5)

> It's made me think so much more on the personal dynamics of combat. ... To the point where that soldier is not a machine, he's a human being. And it really made me start to understand. Before this, I thought the whole PTSD [post-traumatic stress disorder] thing like, "Come on, it's a bunch of crap." But I'm more sympathetic now to the fact that human beings are a fragile organism. Just the whole personal thing of seeing these men going from back at home and having wives and families and doing things the rest of America does, and then coming here and getting knocked off the horse. And then getting back on the horse and going at it. The respect I have for these guys is tenfold of what I originally had. (Company Commander #25)

The company commanders in this study compellingly expressed a deepening and expanded capacity in the area of compassion. The crucible experiences of combat were serving to shift compassion from an abstract concept to a concrete reality. What once was head knowledge was now a matter of heart. As one company commander observed, "I learned the importance of compassion. ... There are times to be compassionate and to be human."

In reflecting upon these learning outcomes, it is significant to note that the attributes of innovation and resilience are in healthy tension and harmony. Just as the rider of a horse requires tension and harmony to stay upright in the saddle, so these two attributes keep each other in check. Innovation enables the leader to adapt, create, and both respond to and impact the environment. At the same time, resilience enables the leader to innovate while not losing a sense of self or drifting away from core values. Furthermore, resilience without innovation would result in stagnation, rigidity, and loss of relevance. In like manner, the attributes of judgment and compassion are in balance. Compassion without judgment results in naïveté and a misappropriation of attention and resources, while judgment without compassion results in a sterile and nonhuman dispensation of authority. Accordingly, judgment and compassion enable the developing leader to do the right thing in the right manner.

5.5.3 Judgment and Decision Making

The word *judgment* elicits images of sage-like discernment and wisdom born of experience and age. To trust in a leader's judgment is to trust in his or her character and competence. In this section we describe and provide examples of how judgment emerges as a key developmental outcome in combat. We describe two dimensions to judgment—emotional intelligence (related to affect) and decision making (related to cognition and character).

One of the most important areas of judgment that emerged in this study was participants' ability to reconcile the emotional dimension of their work with their decision making. One comprehensive model that includes both emotional and cognitive demands is Goleman's (1995) concept of emotional intelligence, which integrates four capabilities—self-awareness, self-regulation, other-awareness, and the ability to influence others' emotions. The model of emotional intelligence is enacted in the company commander who knows his or her own strengths as well as points of vulnerability. The leader stands acutely aware of the complexity and volatility of emotions in this context, especially the emotions of fear and anger. One leader reported, "I was extremely angry and acted out of emotion. The fact that I exposed myself and my men in anger is a learning point" (Company Commander #22). Yet awareness alone is not enough; the ability to manage oneself in such a way that these emotions have no impact on effective actions and do not impede sound and ethical decision making and behavior is also crucial. Company Commander #2 described it this way. "If [a particularly molten situation] were to happen again, I would not have reacted so quickly, especially in the firing of my platoon sergeant. I think I made some hasty decisions in my anger that put my battalion commander in a tight spot."

Furthermore, emotional intelligence is seen in the leader who is also aware of his or her subordinates' fear, anger, and diverse affective responses, and with these in mind is able to ensure that effective and moral action is taken in spite of the emotions raging within. The following commander illustrates his own developing self-awareness and its impact on others: "The most important thing is you have to talk to your men and motivate them through professionalism rather than anger. The easiest thing to do at that point is [to motivate through common anger], but if anger is in control then bad decisions will be made" (Company Commander #18). Commander #25 provides guidance on how to redirect these emotions:

> There was also a point in time when I could see my guys looking at the detainees we'd taken as if they would like to beat the shit out of them. I could tell if I gave the word, they would beat those guys up in a second. I told them, "We aren't doing anything to the prisoners." I then told my leaders to get the soldiers focused on working on their vehicles, and I put my first sergeant in charge of the detainees. I was trying to refocus their energies. (Company Commander #25)

Importantly, managing these emotions must constantly be managed. Commander #41 describes the continuing struggles of managing emotions in a molten context.

> It's stressful every day out here. ... And that can be exhausting in itself, ... So working under that kind of pressure and staying calm. If I freak out, then shit's really going to hit the fan. Part of it is constant practice of all these—like when a car bomb blew up out here and casualties going to hospital—it's almost because I'm desensitized to stuff like that, I'm able to stay calm and lead through it: "Okay, we've got to do this now." That's what it is—practice, I guess. Practice and constantly telling yourself to stay calm and think through the situation.

These leaders portray the degree to which learning experiences informed judgment in the awareness and management of emotions (both in self and in others). As one leader commented, "We had a day down and then we were back at it. I talked to my guys, 'We are angry but we are professional soldiers. We won't do anything immoral or unethical.' You want to deal with that anger, but it would not honor the lives of those men to commit murder in their names." (Company Commander #6)

These experiences also served to inform cognitive aspects of judgment, as depicted by participant comments related to sensemaking and decision making. The cognitive aspects of judgment or decision making is observed when leaders take actions that are based on their awareness of their own intuition and values, when they discern the intent of others, and when they reflect on the need to create the space necessary for cognition. These leaders were developing their ability to synthesize, gain clarity, and take action.

> My intuition told me the enemy was gathering to the south of me from the direction we had entered the district. So instead of going back, I directed my unit to depart out the east side of the city into the desert and circled back around to the south. (Company Commander #2)
> This leader points to the emergence of cognitive judgment in the form of pattern recognition from experience. Cognitive decision-making capacity is enhanced when leaders draw on their experience to make informed judgments about their environments. As Company Commander # 3 said, "You learn to see the presence of the abnormal and the absence of the normal."

Perhaps the most important aspect of judgment came in greater awareness of the limitations and consequences of actions. As one leader reflected,

> I can't tell you how many times you'll get an order that says to go do this or go execute that, and in a lot of cases those decisions aren't good decisions because we don't fully understand the situation. We don't know what we don't know. You have to start off by understanding your area—you have to fully assess your area. (Company Commander #36)

5.5.4 Innovation

Leaders who innovate are generative, creative, able to think outside the box, and willing to challenge the norm; they are adaptive as learners and creative in problem solving. Furthermore, innovative leaders facilitate an ongoing innovation management process within their organizations. A significant aspect of innovation is the capacity to adapt. However, in environments like combat, being adaptive is necessary but not sufficient. One insight that emerged from this study is that immersion in a highly complex and dynamic environment creates awareness of the need for innovation and enhances the capacity to innovate. The following quotations illustrate junior officers becoming aware of the importance of innovation. "What I learned?" he asked, "I guess, to be creative wherever you can. If higher [headquarters] is telling you that you have to do this, you have to break away from the mentality that you don't have guys in that specialty area. We can't just do our specialty areas" (Company Commander #5). Importantly, Company Commanders learned to go beyond their training and to interpret established doctrine in the context of the molten environment. "You have to [learn new things]—you are grasping on core competencies you haven't developed or haven't used in a long time. Ninety percent of the stuff we are doing now is not stuff I've trained the company for" (Company Commander #49). Company Commander #17 explained it this way:

> There have been times with my platoons [in an engineering company] where they have been tasked out, and they've been out on a mission to reduce an IED [improvised explosive device] or do a cache search; and then information comes down and the next thing you know they are transitioning to a cordon and search of an area in town. And there have been times where the information they gathered from stopping a vehicle, for whatever reason, leads them to cordon and search and a hit on a house where they end up finding weapons or bomb-making material. And that's something we've never trained on—it's not anywhere in the engineer manual. But that's what we are called upon to execute out here. Because if we don't act upon the information coming in, what are the chances of getting the enemy? (Company Commander #17)

Another Company Commander, a pilot, described how he developed a new attack strategy that involved approaching a target by descending horizontally, from above the target. He explains:

> In our strategy, I wanted to use standoff from the enemy, [from a vertical sense not a horizontal sense. ... We were talking about [attacking the enemy] from altitudes we had never fought at because we had always stayed low before. It was just a concept in the beginning and we still had a lot of questions: Can we even shoot a hell fire missile while diving from high altitude? ... I think that the number one thing I've learned based on the success we've had is that leaders have to be willing to challenge the norm, they need to take risks, and they need to [be] creative. You have to be flexible and you have to adjust. You've got to understand the limitations and capabilities of your men and equipment and shape and shift

> based on the situation. If you aren't willing to challenge the norm, it may mean you pass an opportunity for absolute and unprecedented success. What it really comes down to for junior leaders is they have to be in an environment where being creative and thinking out of the box is encouraged. And as we shift from one battlefield to another, we adjust and maybe we even develop new techniques and tactics. We aren't tied into just what the manual says. (Company Commander #31)

In the company commanders' experiences related above, one can sense an entrepreneurial flare in the mindset of these leaders and their practice of innovation and innovation management. Company commanders in Iraq are in many ways entrepreneurs who, with their teams, innovatively create new knowledge in the face of molten situations. They are deepening their understanding that entrepreneurial freedom and constant innovation are necessary for effectiveness in environments that are dynamic and hazardous.

5.6 Conclusions and Final Insights

In conclusion, we want to emphasize that this chapter only summarizes our preliminary findings. Thus, more work is needed to further our understanding of the nature of leader development in a dynamic and hazardous context. Preliminary findings from this study revealed that developmental experiences in this environment are molten in nature and are characterized by profound responsibility, intense affect, and embodied feedback. Such experiences result in four primary learning outcomes: compassion, resilience, innovation, and judgment. Of course, not all leaders embedded in a highly dynamic and hazardous environment will develop these leadership abilities, nor are these outcomes preordained. In other words, these outcomes do not arise automatically; however, our belief is that these outcomes are more likely to occur when leaders engage in the learning cycle and subject their experiences to reflection, abstraction, and testing.

A key recommendation from this study centers around the assumptions on which traditional training and education is based in most organizations. The institutional Army has taken a primarily cognitive approach to the development of leaders, with minimal training and development initiatives intentionally focused on the awareness and management of affect both in self and in others. This study serves to recognize and reinforce the significance that emotion plays in leaders' lives. In some cases, the affective component of a leader's developmental experience is more significant than the cognitive. Other noncombat organizations may not be too dissimilar in this emphasis on cognitive rather than on emotional skills.

In closing, we would like to comment on an overarching theme that resonated throughout the interviews and, in some ways, was a part of every facet of this research. This theme is the expression and continued development of professional identity.

> Commanding a company in combat is the defining moment in my life. ... I've put the past 8 years into this—a lot of soldiers have sweat and bled to get us where we are today, and

> the battery as a whole has grown so much. Some of that I've enabled them to do. I've been a part of enabling them to become something they couldn't be. (Company Commander #4)
>
> We got word a couple of hours later that he had died during surgery. That night I went into the company area and was in awe of my noncommissioned officers at work. The company had been waiting for several hours—waiting on the word. We were all basically staying in the basement of a small house. I parked the vehicle, dropped my gear, and walked over to where we were living. As I got downstairs there was a sense of purpose, not stress, in the air. There were some guys being emotional. I remember seeing at each door a noncommissioned officer talking to each soldier. And inside each room for the guys not getting one on one, noncommissioned officers were sitting with the guys in the room counseling. And as I walked through the company each person I came across—every soldier was meeting with a noncommissioned officer. In the heat of the moment, in the time of need of counseling, seeing that self-healing going on—that's been my proudest moment of command, to see the noncommissioned officer corps at its best. I guess I would say we talk about our jobs and we talk about it as a profession—constant study, we live in a microcosm of society, and we train ourselves to do a job. And we basically do blue-collar work, but counseling and other professional facets you wouldn't find in a blue-collar environment. And seeing these guys truly caring for their boys and doing what leaders do. (Company Commander #22)

In this chapter, we have focused on the learning outcomes of leaders in combat. Our research suggests that these outcomes provide the foundation for the development of leaders working in a highly complex and dynamic environment, and these Army officers offer lessons for others working in highly dynamic and complex environments.

In terms of professional development, the lessons expressed by these company commanders and their experiences are serving to create a sense of solidarity and commitment to the greater profession in ways that are powerful and likely not replicable in any other environment. These leaders are learning what it means to be a member of the profession and what it means to behave as a professional. One leader (Company Commander #22) sums up the importance of professional growth and the molten experience. "Our Army went collectively untested for a period of time but yet this came up—we were agile and prepared for Iraq. Along with that agility—one moment we can be doing humanitarian assistance and giving kids a piece of candy, the next moment we can be in intense combat, then mourning the loss of a soldier, and then back the next day handing a piece of candy to a kid. And to see all that going on inherently. It ultimately goes back to the strength of our profession."

If the experiences shared herein are viewed as idiosyncratic events, one might miss this. However, if viewed as if they are the shared experience set of the whole, or the collective profession—as if they are an experience set of one—we deepen our understanding of what it means to lead and learn in a profession that experiences dynamic and hazardous environments.

References

Berg, B. L. (1989). *Qualitative research methods for the social sciences* (3rd ed.). Boston: Allyn Bacon.

Dey, I. (2007). Grounding categories. In A. Bryant & K. Charmaz (Eds.), *The Sage handbook of grounded theory* (pp. 167–190). Los Angeles, CA: Sage.

Goleman, D. (1995). *Emotional intelligence*. New York: Bantam.
Klein, G. A. (1998). *Sources of power*. Cambridge, MA: MIT Press.
Knowles, M. S. (1980). *The modern practice of adult education: From pedagogy to andragogy*. Englewood Cliffs, NJ: Prentice Hall.
Kolb, D. (1984). *Experiential learning: Experience as the source of learning and development*. Englewood Cliffs, NJ: Prentice-Hall.
Kouzes J. M., & Posner, B. Z. (1995). *The leadership challenge*. San Francisco: Jossey Bass.
Lewin, K. (1951). *Field theory in social science*. New York: Harper & Brother.
Lincoln, Y. S., & Guba, E. G. (1985). *Naturalistic inquiry*. Beverly Hills, CA: Sage.
McCall, M. W., Jr. (1998). *High flyers: Developing the next generation of leaders*. Boston: Harvard Business School Press.
McCauley, C. D., Moxley R. S., & Van Velsor, E. (Eds.) (2004). *The center for creative leadership handbook of leadership development*. San Francisco: Jossey-Bass.
Mezirow, J. (1991). *Transformative dimensions of adult learning*. San Francisco: Jossey-Bass.
Miles, M. B., & Huberman, A. M. (1994). *Qualitative data analysis* (2nd ed.). Thousand Oaks, CA: Sage Publications.
Reynolds, M., & Vince, R. (Eds.). (2005). *Organising reflection*. London: Ashgate.
Rubin, H., & Rubin, I. (1995). *Qualitative interviewing the art of hearing data*. Thousand Oaks, CA: Sage.
Seidman, I. (1998). *Interviewing as qualitative research* (2nd ed.) New York: Teacher College Press.
Weick, K. E. (1993). The collapse of sensemaking in organizations: The Mann Gulch disaster. *Administrative Science Quarterly, 38*, 628–65.
Weick, K. E. (1995). *Sensemaking in organizations*. Thousand Oaks, CA: Sage.
Weiss, R. S. (1994). *Learning from strangers: The art and method of qualitative interview studies*. New York: The Free Press.
Yin, R. K. (2003). *Case study research design and methods* (3rd ed.). Thousand Oaks, CA: Sage.

Chapter 6
Managers' Teaching and Leading in the Workplace: An Exploratory Field Study

Robert E. Saggers and Alenoush Saroyan

6.1 Introduction

Leadership and education have been identified as two leverage points to meet the challenges of the twenty-first century (Kennedy, 1993). The manager's role in employee productivity, satisfaction, and retention is increasingly recognized (Buckingham and Coffman, 1999; Cohn, Khurana & Reeves, 2005; Fitz-Enz, 1997). Despite this, prominent leadership researchers have talked for some time about a leadership crisis (Bennis, 1999; Kotter, 1990). Corporate executives consistently identify a leadership gap as the top business issue facing their organizations (Weiss & Molinaro, 2005). This is backed by a recent survey of corporate training and development professionals conducted by Blanchard (2006), who found that developing potential leaders was rated as the top challenge.

Meanwhile, leadership itself continues to be enigmatic for scholars and practitioners alike (Heymann & Heifetz; 2004; Wren, 2002). Barker (1997) questions the viability of training leaders, when there is no agreement on what constitutes effective leadership or even the traits and behaviors that contribute to it. Leadership understanding appears not to have progressed much in the past 36 years since Stogdill (1974) observed, "There are almost as many definitions of leadership as there are persons who have attempted to define the concept" (p. 2). Northouse more recently remarked that "as soon as we try to define leadership, we immediately discover leadership has many different meanings" (2000, p. 2).

Addressing these issues involves thinking differently about what leadership is and how it is developed.

Parts of this chapter were presented at the 2009 annual meeting of the American Educational Research Association, San Diego, CA.

R.E. Saggers (✉)
School of Continuing Studies and Faculty of Education, McGill University, Montreal, QC, Canada
e-mail: Bob@robertsaggers.com

A. Mc Kee, M. Eraut (eds.), *Learning Trajectories, Innovation and Identity for Professional Development*, Innovation and Change in Professional Education 7,
DOI 10.1007/978-94-007-1724-4_6, © Springer Science+Business Media B.V. 2012

6.2 Leadership and Education

The relationship between education and leadership has been recognized since the days of the early Greek philosophers. Plato's philosopher king was not only a thinker but also a teacher of others (Ozmon & Craver, 1999, pp. 16, 17). The transition to a knowledge-based economy (Drucker, 1993; Stewart, 1997) necessitates strengthening this bond and is forcing corporations to transform themselves into *learning* (Senge, 1990) and *teaching* (Tichy & Cohen, 1998; Tichy, 2004) organizations. The demarcation between formal education and workplace training is blurring, a convergence noted by Lowyck (1996) and de Moura and de Oliveira (1996). Today's corporations are increasingly concerned about education and training, with some taking a much wider perspective than others and involving executives as corporate university faculty (Betof, 2009). Interest in viewing managers as facilitators of on-the-job learning is also growing (see Eraut, Chapter 2). Meanwhile, academics are questioning how they prepare tomorrow's managers and leaders (Bennis & O'Toole, 2005; Mintzberg, 2004).

6.2.1 What Is Leadership?

Despite a plethora of definitions, several themes have emerged in recent years. Leadership is perhaps best viewed as a purposeful shared social process, not restricted to a person in particular, and those led are recognized as part of the leadership process (Hughes, Ginnett, & Curphy, 2006). This is reflected in Northouse's (2006) definition of leadership "as a process whereby an individual influences a group of individuals to achieve a common goal" (p. 3). It suggests that if we want to better understand leadership, we should approach our inquiry from a systems perspective (Senge, 1990) and look at those being led when assessing leadership effectiveness (Daniels & Daniels, 2007; Kelley, 1992; Tichy & Cohen, 1998).

There is a tendency to think about leaders and managers differently. The prevailing view, however, is that while management and leadership are different processes, leaders and managers are not different people (Kotter, 1990; Mintzberg, 1973). Leadership and management may be best viewed as an activity system (Engeström, 1987) of two overlapping, interdependent, and complementary processes that includes both the leader and those being led (Hughes et al., 2006; Rost, 1994). Organizations today need managers who can lead and leaders who can manage, and a core competency of future *manager-leaders* will be their ability to be continual learners (Meister, 1998) and teachers (Covey, 2004) that facilitate the learning of others.

6.2.2 Leadership Theory and Research

Research into leadership and the factors that influence leader effectiveness has increased over the years from an initial focus on leader traits and behaviors

(Bennis & Nanus, 1985; Blake & Mouton, 1964; Gardner, 1993; Mintzberg, 1973) to the more recent cognitive (Gardner, 1995; Sternberg, 2003), affective (Goleman, Boyatzis, & Mc Kee, 2002), and situational (Blanchard, 2007; Blanchard, Zigarmi, & Zigrami, 1985; Hersey & Blanchard, 1969) dimensions of leadership.

Hollander (1978) conceived of leadership as an integrative framework of three elements: *leader, followers,* and *situation*; Bass (1990) also treated leadership as an interactive process. It is also consistent with two popular leadership models that emphasize the managers' role in employee development and provide a useful lens for better understanding the relationship between managerial leading and teaching. The first is Hersey and Blanchard's situational leadership model (1969, 1982) and its subsequent elaboration, differentiated as *situational leadership II* (SLII), by Blanchard et al. (1985) and Zigarmi, Edeburn, and Blanchard (1997). This posits four leadership styles based on the extent to which the manager exhibits directive or supportive behavior and argues that effectiveness reflects the appropriateness of a style to an employee's current development level, relative to a specific task or goal (see *development level* and *leader style* in Fig. 6.1).

The second model, *transformational leadership,* was first identified by Burns (1978) and was further developed by Bass (1985), and Bass and Avolio (1994). This differentiates between two differing manager orientations, transactional and transformational, and argues that long-term managerial effectiveness depends on transformational leadership (Bass, 1997).

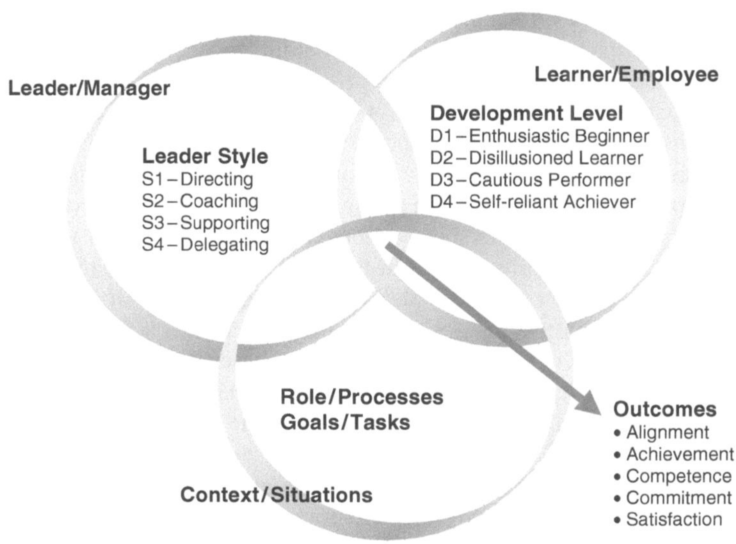

Fig. 6.1 A proposed model adapted from Hughes et al. (2006) that links learning outcomes to the interactive leader framework and situational leadership II theory (Blanchard et al., 1985)

6.2.3 Leadership Education/Development

Despite the continuing myth that *leaders are born, not made*, several leadership scholars (Bennis & Nanus, 1985; Daloz-Parks, 2005; Gardner, 1993; Hughes et al., 2006; Kouzes & Posner, 2001) believe that leadership is more widely distributed than people might think. Leadership can be learned and taught even though, according to Doh (2003), some elements (knowledge, skill) are more readily taught than others (attitudes).

There is no shortage of leader/manager competency models. Most major organizations have developed their own (Conger & Benjamin, 1999; Tichy & Sherman, 2005; Vicere & Fulmer, 1998); some are organizational level specific and recognize that managers need different competencies as they ascend the organizational hierarchy (Charan, Drotter, & Noel, 2001); others are generic (Gebelein, Stevens, Skube, Lee, Davis, & Hellervik, 2001; Whetten & Cameron, 2005; Zenger & Folkman, 2002), while yet others are based on a theoretical perspective (e.g., Bass & Avolio, 1994; Goleman et al., 2002; Kouzes & Posner, 1995). Most, if not all, recognize the development of others as a key competence for managers, but neglect to specify the behaviors linked to managerial teaching. Kouzes and Posner (2006) contend that the "best leaders are teachers" and "the best way to learn something [including leadership] is to teach it to somebody else" (pp. 20–26), but they offer no empirical evidence to support their claim.

Educational research has the potential to offer much to management knowledge and practice. Teaching, like leadership, is described as a "complex, dynamic, ill-structured process" (Leinhardt, 1993, p. 1). Much of what has been learned over the past 50 years about learning theory and instructional practice (see Gredler, 2001) has direct relevance to understanding and promoting leadership competencies. One aspect that is most relevant to the topic of this chapter is the way teaching has been conceptualized. Ramsden (1992), for instance, has identified three "theories" or conceptions of teaching. His first theory depicts teaching as the "transmission of authoritative content or the demonstration of procedures," casting students as "passive recipients of the wisdom of a single speaker" (p. 111). This view is somewhat akin to transactional leadership or more conventional views of management, where the power and authority remain in the hands of one person, in this case the instructor. Ramsden's second theory defines teaching in terms of organizing student activity. This activity is seen as the end and not a means to intended learning. A similar distinction between activity- and results-based leadership was made by Schaffer (1990) and Ulrich, Zenger and Smallwood (1999). Ramsden's third theory casts teaching as making learning possible and the instructor as the facilitator of that learning. The similarities between this latter theory and a transformational leadership that empowers the "learner" and facilitator in the educational process are evident. Others have proposed similar notions about teaching conceptions, and, while there may be some disparity at the micro level, there is consistency and robust empirical support about two broad clusters of conceptions: teacher centered and student centered (Åkerlind, 2003, 2004; Gow & Kember, 1993; Saroyan, Dagenais, & Zhou, 2008; Samuelowicz & Bain, 2001). Taking these two categories into account, it is not hard to see similarities between ways of conceptualizing teaching and ways of conceptualizing leadership. *Based on the teaching literature, one can hypothesize that transformative leaders and managers are likely to devote more time to employee development, and among them the most effective are likely to be those who take an "employee-centered" approach when they engage in teaching their charges.*

6.3 Methodology

The catalyst for this study came, on the one hand, from the observed emerging interest of managers being conceptualized as teachers and, on the other hand, from the lack of a conceptual framework to describe managerial teaching and the paucity of empirical evidence to support the claim that managerial leadership effectiveness is linked to employee development.

For the purpose of this study, leadership is patterned on the SLII model (Blanchard et al., 1985; Zigarmi, Blanchard, O'Connor, & Edeburn, 2005), described in the "Introduction" section of this chapter, and defined as the process by which a manager supports the development of employees to accomplish job tasks and mutually agreed upon goals through the appropriate use of directive (e.g., telling, demonstrating, instructing, etc.) and supportive (e.g., explaining, encouraging, asking/listening, etc.) behaviors.

6.3.1 The Three Hypotheses and Design Framework

The proposed blended leadership model provided the basis for the following research-directed hypotheses:

1. Managers who are perceived by employees to spend more time teaching will be viewed by their employees to be more flexible, effective, and productive.
2. Employees will exhibit higher satisfaction with managers they perceive to generally spend more time teaching.
3. Employees who indicate that their manager taught them[1] the SLII model after attending a one-day workshop will view their managers as more flexible, effective, and relatively more productive than the employees of managers who did not teach.

A single-group pre-test/post-test design was used as it is particularly suited to investigating changes within variables that are generally stable or resistant to change, e.g., leadership behavior and employee perceptions (Gall, Borg, & Gall, 1996).

[1] Defined as any directive or supportive behavior used by the manager to facilitate employee learning. Employees were asked to respond to the following question on the post-instructional intervention survey: "My manager taught me the leadership model that he/she learned in the workshop" (yes/no).

The study took place both in the *classroom* in which practising managers were *taught* SLII in a one-day workshop and in the *workplace* in which the managers were to subsequently *teach* their employees this conceptual leadership model and practice using it with them. Manager teaching, patterned after the *Merriam-Webster Online Dictionary* (2007) definition, was broadly defined as any action undertaken by the manager to impart information so that employees could *know both* what situational leadership is and *how* to use it in the workplace.

6.3.2 The Instructional Intervention

The intervention was a one-day workshop for managers, designed according to activity systems theory (Engeström, 1987) and informed by theories of social learning (Bandura, 1977), social constructivism (Vygotsky, 1978), and situated learning (Collins, Brown, & Newman, 1989). The learning goals were based on the taxonomies developed by Bloom (1956); Krathwohl, Bloom, and Masia (1964); and Simpson (1972). The subsequent instructional design was also influenced by Anderson's (1982) three-stage learning theory for which participants were expected to learn what to do (*declarative knowledge*) and how to do it (*procedural knowledge)* and practice doing it (*tuned procedural stage)*.

The flow of the workshop followed the instructional sequence proposed by Gagné and Biggs (1979). This entailed the following steps: (a) attention was gained by getting participants to focus on their own best leader/manager examples and providing them with research evidence to support the leader/manager role in employee satisfaction, performance, and retention; (b) learners were informed of the learning objectives and given the opportunity to voice their expectations; (c) each concept was introduced in a way that built on participant experience and prior learning; (d) each content was then presented; (e) learners were guided on how to apply each concept through instructor modeling; (f) participants were given the opportunity to practice; (g) feedback was then given to participants on their performance; (h) participants were able to assess their own performance as situational leaders; and (i) a post-workshop teaching activity was presented to enhance learning retention/transfer. The sequence of steps "c" thru "g" was repeated for each of the main concepts covered in the workshop (i.e., diagnosing employee development, matching leadership style, and partnering for performance).

Presentations were kept to a minimum in favor of *instructor-guided plenary discussions*. *Experiential* (activities, followed by debriefing), *authentic* [linking the material to participant experience, providing feedback on their own leadership styles from the Leader Behaviour Analysis Questionnaire they did prior to the workshop[2] (Blanchard, Hambleton, Zirgami, & Forsyth, 2005) self-assessing their own development level as situational leaders after the workshop], and *cooperative* (participants learning together) *learning* were emphasized. These are all

[2] A sample of the report provided to the managers during the workshop is provided in Appendix 1.

approaches consistent with adult education principles (Brookfield, 1987; Cranton, 2000; Mezirow, 1977). A deliberate attempt was made to embed the following instructional activities within the workshop design to reinforce the manager role as teacher:

Peer teaching (Annis, 1981; Brown, 1992) – working in triads, each participant had two case studies (one to diagnose developmental level and the other to match the appropriate leadership style). They first had to analyze each case and then teach the other participant(s) how they came to their solution using the concepts presented.

Peer coaching (Swafford, 2000) – working in pairs, each participant was asked to think about a performance issue they were facing. They then took turns describing their issue and coaching each other using the SLII model and the "partnering for performance" worksheet provided.

Micro teaching (Amundsen, Winer, & Gandell, 2004) – working in triads, participants took turns playing the manager (teacher), employee, and observer. Each had to teach the purpose of SLII, plus one of the main phases of the model (e.g., diagnosing, matching, or partnering) to the designated employee, after which the observer provided feedback to the manager and coached on suggested improvements.

The key to this study was post-workshop action by the participating managers to apply their learning by teaching the SLII model to their employees. Since the researcher had little control over this, three additional strategies were added to facilitate learning transfer. The first focused on "preparation for future learning" (Bransford & Schwartz, 2001) by emphasizing "meta-teaching" (i.e., teaching about teaching), conceptual instructional methods, critical reflection, and dynamic assessment. The second added some post-workshop contact with the managers to prompt manager action. A day or two after the workshop, managers were e-mailed the PowerPoint slides and asked to contact the instructor if they needed any additional direction or support. Then managers were e-mailed again, a couple of weeks later, to see if they had taught their employees SLII. The third was to e-mail the employees about four weeks after their manager had attended the workshop and ask them if their manager had yet talked to them about the workshop and taught them the SLII model.

The workshop was facilitated by the lead author, who has extensive experience teaching situational leadership and workshop facilitation. A description including the learning goals, instructional methods, content summary, and resources used is provided in Appendix 2.

6.3.3 The Participants

About 140 contacts were made through e-mails, telephone calls, face-to-face meetings and a "university blog" to identify organizations and individuals willing to participate. This generated consent forms from 24 managers and 72 of their employees (three employees per manager). In order to be included in the study, managers needed to have attended the workshop, completed both pre- and post-surveys, and have at least one employee that had participated; employees needed to have

Table 6.1 Description of participating organizations

	Size		Sample	
Sector	(number of employees)	Ownership	Managers $N = 20$	Employees $N = 43$
Consulting —Information services	300	Public	4	9
Distribution	5,000	Private	5	11
Food services	10	Private	1	2
Manufacturing				
Consumer goods	400	Public	2	3
Pharmaceutical	1,500	Public	1	2
Transportation equipment	4,000	Public	2	4
Mining	2,000	Public	1	3
Software development	150	Private	4	9

completed both pre- and post-surveys. Four managers and 29 employees did not meet the criteria for inclusion. The resultant sample comprised 20 managers and 43 employees that report to them from eight different organizations (details in Table 6.1).

6.3.4 Data Collection

Approval was obtained from the Institutional Ethics Review Board; then informed consent was subsequently received from all managers and their employees prior to data collection. Data were collected on two occasions: pre (one month before the managers' workshop) and post (about four months after that workshop). Although information was collected from each group, using a secure online survey, this chapter is confined to the employee data (see Saggers, 2009, for a review of the managers' data).

Employees were asked to complete the "other" versions of the following:

(a) *LBAII – Leader Behavior Analysis II* (Zigarmi et al., 1997) – an instrument that asks employees to select from four actions, each based on a specific leadership style, what they believe their manager would do in different situations; and
(b) The transformational leadership scale items from the *MLQ – Multi-Factor Leadership Questionnaire* (Bass & Avolio, 2000) – one of which asks employees to indicate the extent to which their manager spends time teaching.

Items from the *LAP – Leader Action Profile* (Zigarmi, Zigrami, Edeburn, & Blanchard, 2000) – indicating employee satisfaction with their manager were also

Table 6.2 Description of variables and instruments

Variables	Measurement characteristics	Instrument	Range of scores
Independent			
• Employee perception of manager time spent teaching	Repeated measure, ordinal	MLQ	0–4
• Employee indication of manager teaching SLII after attending workshop	Fixed measure, nominal (yes/no)	Post-survey	n/a
Dependent			
Employee perception of			
• Manager leadership style – flexibility	Repeated measure, ordinal	LBAII – other	0–30
• Manager leadership style – effectiveness	Repeated measure, ordinal	LBAII – other	20–80
• Manager's productivity compared to other managers in company	Repeated measure, ordinal	Pre-/post-survey	0–10
• Employee satisfaction with manager	Repeated measure, ordinal	LAP	6–36

included, and *employees were asked in the post-survey to indicate if their manager met with them to teach employees about what he or she learned during the leadership development workshop.*

A list of the variables studied is presented in Table 6.2. Data were analyzed using both correlations and analysis of variance.

6.4 Results and Discussion

Table 6.3 presents a summary of the correlation analyses. Except for manager style flexibility, all the variables are significantly correlated to employee perception of manager time spent teaching: employee satisfaction ($p < .005$) and their perception of their manager's relative productivity ($p < .01$). Manager effectiveness after SLII training was also seen to be positively correlated with employee perception of managerial teaching ($p < .05$). This suggests that, *even though employees saw their manager's use of the various leadership styles (flexibility) staying the same, they saw their managers being more effective in their use of the different leadership styles.*

Separate repeated measures analysis of variance (ANOVA) followed by post-hoc analyses were done for each of the hypotheses.

Hypothesis 1 – Managers who are perceived by employees to spend more time teaching will be viewed by their employees to be more flexible, effective, and productive.

Table 6.3 Pearson product correlations between employee perception of manager time spent teaching and selected variables from pre- and post-workshop surveys

	R	
	Pre-survey	Post-survey
Manager relative productivity	0.38*	0.48*
Employee satisfaction with manager	0.52**	0.63**
Manager leadership style flexibility	0.01	0.23
Manager leadership style effectiveness	−0.07	0.32***

Note: *$p < 0.01$; **$p < 0.005$; ***$p < 0.05$.

The first two of the five possible answers to the MLQ item on frequency of manager teaching were combined to give four fairly equal groups for analysis: Group 1 – "not at all" or "once in a while" ($n = 10$); Group 2 – "sometimes" ($n = 12$); Group 3 – "fairly often" ($n = 13$); Group 4 – "frequently, if not always" ($n = 8$).

This hypothesis was only partly supported. The time managers devoted to teaching did not significantly affect employee perceptions about their manager's leadership style flexibility or effectiveness, but did positively affect employees' perceptions of their manager's relative productivity. Figure 6.2 presents a comparison of how each employee rated their manager's productivity relative to other managers at their company before and after SLII training. *It suggests that managers on the pre-survey whose employees indicated that they "frequently, if not always" taught (group 4) were viewed as being more productive than those managers who were seen to teach "not at all" or "once in a while" (group 1).*

An ANOVA for pre-productivity confirmed statistical significance, F (3, 39) = 2.79, p = .05. The results of the ANOVA for post-productivity are presented in

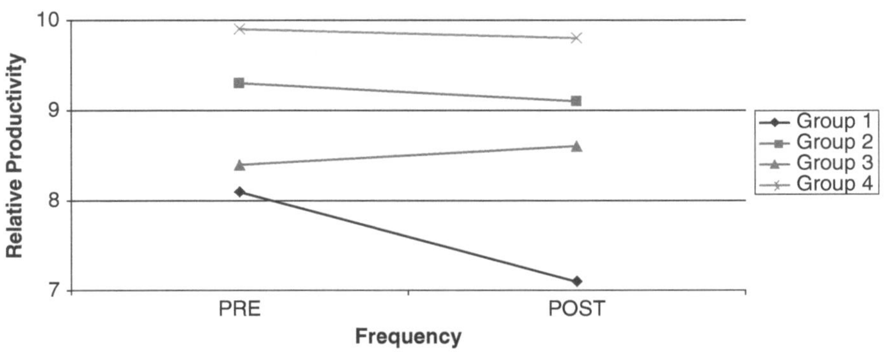

Fig. 6.2 Employee perception of their manager's relative productivity based on the frequency employees reported their manager spent teaching

Table 6.4 Analysis of variance for relative productivity

Source	*df*	*F*
Between subjects		
Post-teach frequency	3	3.55^*
Error	39	
Within subjects		
Time	1	3.96^*
Time × post-teach frequency	3	3.40^*
Error (time)	39	

Note: $^*p < 0.05$.

Table 6.4 and show a main effect as well as a time and interaction effect. Post-hoc analyses using Tukey's *HSD* (Honestly Significant Differences) test were done to control for Type 1 error, i.e., saying an effect is statistically significant when it is not. The following results were statistically significant: group 1 < 4, $HSD = 1.18$; group 1 < 2, $HSD = 1.06$; group 3 < 4 $HSD = 1.17$. The post-hoc result for interaction resulted in one statistically significant change: Group 1, $HSD = 0.94$. The statistically significant time effect was also due to this one group (decreased from $M = 8.1$, $SD = 2.4$ to $M = 7.1$, $SD = 2.7$), since the other groups did not change.

This finding suggests that *it is not so much the frequency of time spent teaching, but how teaching is used and in which context.* This confirms the predictions of situational leadership theory (Hersey & Blanchard, 1982), SLII theory (Blanchard et al., 1985), and Hughes et al.'s (2006) interactional framework. Managers who were seen to spend the least amount of time teaching were perceived by their employees to be less productive, a finding consistent with the leadership competency research (e.g., Bass, 1985; Blanchard, 2007; Kouzes & Posner, 1995; Ulrich et al. 1999).

Hypothesis 2 – Employees will exhibit higher satisfaction with managers they perceive to generally spend more time teaching.

This hypothesis was supported: employee perception of the frequency of time that managers spend teaching and coaching significantly affected employee satisfaction. Employees were more satisfied with managers who were observed to teach. Figure 6.3 compares the level of employees' satisfaction, both before and after SLII training, with their estimates of the time their managers spent on their teaching: 1 (10 managers) = "not at all" or "once in a while"; 2 (12 managers) = "sometimes"; 3 (13 managers) = "fairly often"; 4 (8 managers) = "frequently, if not always".

These graphs suggest that *an employee's satisfaction increases with the frequency of their manager's teaching.* An ANOVA for pre-manager SLII training confirmed statistical significance, $F\ (3, 39) = 4.26$, $p < .01$, while the ANOVA results for post-employee satisfaction presented in Table 6.5 show a main effect as well an interaction effect. Once again, post-hoc analyses using the Tukey's *HSD* test were done. The main effect was simply due to the overall lower mean for Group 1

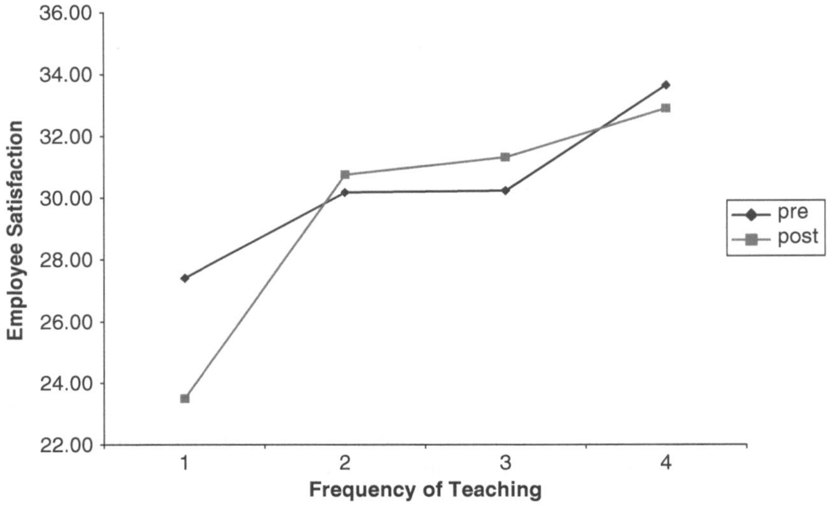

Fig. 6.3 Employee satisfaction with manager based on the extent to which employees perceived their manager to spend time teaching

Table 6.5 Analysis of variance for employee satisfaction

Source	*df*	*F*
Between subjects		
Post-teach time	3	7.77*
Error	39	
Within subjects		
Time	1	1.64
Time × post-teach time	3	3.82**
Error (time)	39	

Note: *$p < 0.001$; **$p < 0.05$.

($M = 25.4$) versus Group 4 ($M = 33.3$), $HSD = 6.46$. The interaction effect resulted from Group 1 being only lower than group 4 at pre-test, but lower than all other groups at post-test: Group 1 < 2, $HSD = 3.64$; Group 1 < 3, $HSD = 3.58$; and Group 1 < 4, $HSD = 4.03$.

This result is similar to that found for employee perception of relative productivity; managers who were seen by their employees to spend more time teaching generated higher employee satisfaction. Main and interaction effects resulted primarily from those managers who were not seen to teach at all or teach only once in a while. This would seem to indicate that *there may be a threshold level of manager teaching needed for employee satisfaction and positive attributions, beyond which there is no noticeable impact.* More teaching is not necessarily viewed positively, especially when it is not appropriate. This finding is consistent with the blended interactional and SLII model used in this study.

Hypothesis 3 – Employees who indicate that their manager taught them the *situational leadership* II model after attending the workshop will view their managers as more flexible, effective, and relatively more productive than the employees of managers who did not teach.

The hypothesis was only partially supported. Leadership style flexibility and relative productivity were not seen to be affected by manager post-workshop teaching of the SLII model to their employees, while leadership style effectiveness was significantly affected.

Both the "teach" and "non-teach" managers were perceived by their employees to be almost identical in their leadership style effectiveness on the pre-survey; on the post-survey, the "teach" managers increased, while their "non-teach" colleagues decreased in the view of their employees. This relationship is demonstrated in Fig. 6.4.

Table 6.6 presents the results of the ANOVA. There was also a "time by teach interaction." On the pre-survey, both groups of managers were perceived as the same by their employees. On the post-survey, however, employees who said that their manager taught them after the workshop ($n = 19$) perceived their managers to be more effective in their selection of leadership styles (pre $M = 47.3$, $SD = 7.6$; post $M = 52.7$, $SD = 7.9$), while employees who said that their manager did not

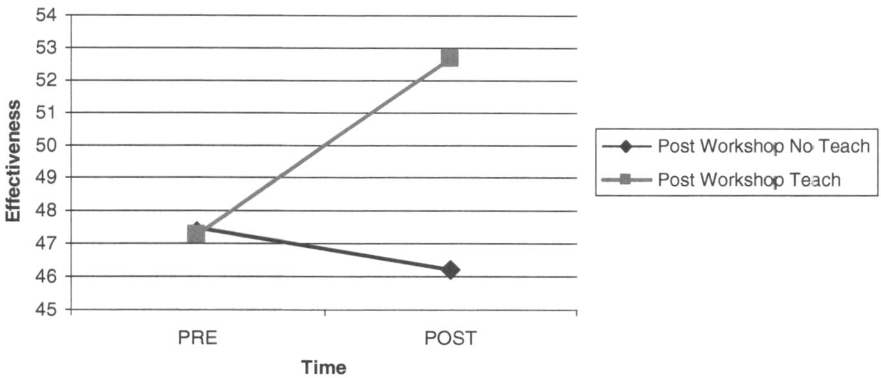

Fig. 6.4 Employee perception of manager leadership style choices as a function of post-workshop teaching of employees by managers

Table 6.6 Analysis of variance for employee perceived manager leadership style effectiveness based on manager teaching employees after SLII workshop

Source	*df*	*F*
Between subjects		
Post-workshop manager teaching	1	3.33
Error	41	3.33
Within subjects		
Time	1	3.80
Time × post-workshop teaching	1	9.63*
Error (time)	41	

Note: $^{*}p < 0.01$.

teach them ($n = 24$) saw their managers less effective in their leadership choices (pre $M = 47.5$, $SD = 4.3$; post $M = 46.2$, $SD = 6.7$). Post-hoc analyses using Tukey's *HSD* test were done once again. There were two statistically significant results. The "teach" group increased effectiveness from pre ($M = 47.3$) to post ($M = 52.7$), $HSD = 4.34$. At the post-test, the teach group (employees who said "yes" that their managers taught them the SLII model) had higher effectiveness scores than the "no teach" group ($M = 52.7$ and $M = 46.2$, respectively), $HSD = 4.11$. These results basically say the same thing in different ways: *employees in the "post workshop – no teach" group did not see their managers change to select more effective leadership actions, unlike the employees in the "post-workshop teach group" who did see it.*

These results and the earlier ones for employee satisfaction and perception of manager productivity surfaced an interesting finding; both the "no post-teach" and "not teaching at all/once in a while" groups dropped from pre- to post-test. This would seem to indicate that a possible *reverse* Hawthorne effect may have occurred. Another possible explanation might be what Cha and Edmondson (2006) have theorized as the *hypocrisy attribution dynamic*, a process that leads to employee disenchantment with the leader. In either scenario, employees may have had heightened expectations of their managers due to their participation in a leadership study and having taken leadership training; when they see no noticeable change in their manager's behavior resulting from it, they are likely to be disappointed and thus have a lower opinion of their manager. Organizations would therefore be prudent to follow through and support leadership development initiatives, lest it become a "double-edged sword ... and have unintended negative consequences" (Cha & Edmondson, 2006, p. 57).

As employee satisfaction has been linked to positive outcomes, e.g., productivity (Leimbach, 1994), employee engagement (DuBois, 2005), and talent retention (Buckingham & Coffman, 1999; Cohn et al., 2005; Fitz-Enz, 1997), organizations would probably benefit from ensuring that their managers meet the threshold level for teaching, instituting post-manager teaching as part of their leadership development programs, and encouraging/supporting managerial teaching.

6.5 Conclusion

Even though exploratory in nature, this study provides empirical evidence to support the view that a conceptual leadership model can be learned during a one-day classroom-based workshop and subsequently applied in the workplace. Moreover, the best leaders may indeed be those who incorporate teaching in their leadership practice. Managers who teach compared to those who do not were seen to be relatively more productive and to generate higher levels of satisfaction in those they manage. Post-workshop teaching by managers of what they learned (i.e., the SLII model) helped them to become more effective situational leaders in the eyes of their employees. Given this finding, it would be worthwhile to explore why more managers did not follow through and teach their employees after the workshop.

More clarity, also, is needed about the role of managers as teachers and the nature of managerial teaching activities, as well as the role of organizations in promoting and nurturing it. Continuing this line of inquiry could lead to an opportunity for an interdisciplinary approach to bridge educational/leadership management science research and leadership/management practice, not to mention, increasing our knowledge about leadership and how it is developed in the workplace.

Appendix 1: Sample Participant Report on Leadership Style

Introduction

As part of the pre-work for this workshop, you were asked to put yourself in 20 different situations and then to select what you would do from the various options provided. These items are from the *Leader Behavior Analysis II* questionnaire (Blanchard et al., 2005) and are designed to assess your leadership style flexibility and effectiveness.

Flexibility

According to the Situational Leadership II model, leadership style is based on the extent to which leaders tend to use directive and supportive behaviors. Four leadership styles are identified: S1 (Directing), S2 (Coaching), S3 (Supporting), and S4 (Delegating). Your results were as follows:

3 S3	13 S2
S4 1	S1 3

Your primary leadership style (your highest score, the one you tend to use most frequently) is ***Coaching***; you do not have a secondary leadership style (styles that you chose four or more times tend to be used frequently) as all the other styles need developing (styles that you chose three or less times tend to be used less frequently or rarely; i.e., ***Delegating***, ***Supporting,*** and ***Directing***).

Style flexibility refers to the extent that you tend to use the different styles. Style flexibility scores range from 0 to 30, the mean score is 17, and the normative data ranges from 16 to 20. Your style flexibility score is ***14***.

Effectiveness

In order to be effective as a leader, not only do you need to be flexible, but you must also use the most appropriate style for the situation. Style effectiveness scores range from 20 to 80, the mean score is 54, and the normative data ranges from 50 to 58. Your effectiveness score is ***53***.

Conclusion

Compared to other managers taking this instrument, you fall below the average range for style flexibility and within the average range for style effectiveness. You can improve by learning to use the directing, supporting, and delegating styles when appropriate and more accurately diagnosing the development level before choosing a leadership style.

Appendix 2: Description of Instructional Intervention

Learning objectives	Learning domain	Learning level
1. Describe the difference between management and leadership	Cognitive	Analysis
2. Apply the interactive leadership model	Cognitive	Synthesis
3. Diagnose employee development level	Cognitive	Analysis
	Affective	Responding
	Psychomotor	Guided Response
4. Match appropriate leadership style to employee development level	Cognitive	Analysis
	Affective	Responding
	Psychomotor	Guided Response
5. Demonstrate how to partner for performance	Cognitive	Analysis
	Affective	Responding
	Psychomotor	Guided Response
6. Self-assess development level on being a situational leader	Cognitive	Evaluation
7. Continue leadership development	Cognitive	Synthesis/Evaluation
	Affective	Valuing
	Psychomotor	Guided Response/Mechanism

Instructional sequence

Time	Instructional activity/content	Tools/materials[a]
8:30	Welcome ■ Introductions, participant expectations (capture on flip chart) ■ Workshop ground rules/agenda/learning objectives	PWB[b]; FC; PP
9:00	Exercise 1: Best leader vs. "best-manager" ■ Two groups – one brainstorms what their best leader did and how it made them feel, while the other does it for their best manager ■ Each group presents their results	FC

9:15	Presentation ■ Management versus leadership ■ Interactive Leadership Model ■ Manager-leader's role ■ Research on importance of manager to employee performance and satisfaction ■ Leadership/management development – transitioning from an individual contributor to leading others, requires people to think, feel, and act differently	PP
9:30	Plenary Discussion ■ Introduction to SLII ■ Diagnosing development levels (D1 through D4) ■ Participants asked to share examples of when they were at each level	PP
9:45	Exercise 2: Peer teaching on diagnosis in triads ■ Each participant given a case study in which they diagnose an employee's development level ■ Teach the other participants how they identified the development level ■ Plenary debriefing to ensure correct diagnosis and get feedback on participant teaching	PWB
10:00	Health Break	
10:15	Plenary Discussion/Exercise 3: Directive vs. supportive behavior ■ Examples of directive–supportive behavior ■ Same groups as Exercise 1 – review list previously generated and indicate if behavior was directive or supportive ■ Each group presents their results	PP; FC
10:30	Plenary Discussion ■ Review of the four leadership styles (S1 through S4) ■ Participants asked to share personal examples	PP
10:45	Exercise 4: Peer teaching on matching leadership styles to employee development level ■ Each participant given a case study in which they have to match the appropriate leadership style ■ Teach the other participants how they identified the appropriate leadership style ■ Plenary debriefing to ensure correct leadership style match and get feedback on participant teaching	PWB
11:00	Exercise 5: Match/mismatch role-play ■ Each participant given a specific role (either D1 through D4 or S1 through S4) ■ Four separate role-plays, each lasting about 3 min (each development level with each leadership style) ■ After each role-play, participants note their observations about the appropriateness of the style used (i.e., match or mismatch) ■ Plenary debriefing on participant observations and exploring impact of matching/mismatching leadership style to development level (e.g., employee satisfaction, productivity, commitment)	Role-play instructions; PWB; FC
12:00	Lunch	

13:00	Exercise 6: Debriefing on LBAII-self results on manager leadership style flexibility/effectiveness ■ Research findings on leadership styles before SLII training ■ Each participant gets a report on their leadership style flexibility and effectiveness ■ Individual reflection on report through guided questions ■ Plenary debriefing of participant reflections and questions	PP; PWB; Personal Report
13:30	Presentation – Partnering for performance/conversation starters ■ Integrating the Interactive Leadership and SLII models ■ Review the partnering for performance process (reaching agreement on goals, employee development level, manager leadership style/behaviors, follow-up actions) ■ Tips on what managers say to employees when using each leadership style	PP; PWB
13:45	Demonstration – Using the Partnering for Performance Worksheet ■ Use personal example to walk participants through the partnering for performance process ■ Solicit/answer participant questions	PWB
13:50	Exercise 7: Peer coaching in pairs on individual-specific issues ■ Participants individually reflect on a performance issue they currently have with an employee ■ Take turns describing their issue and coaching each other using the SLII model and partnering for performance worksheet ■ Plenary debriefing of participant reflections and questions	PWB
14:30	Health Break	
14:45	Presentation – Ongoing development – teaching to learn and to lead ■ Summary of personal/organizational benefits ■ Suggestions for post-workshop developmental actions ■ Linkage between personal involvement and learning retention ■ Importance of developing others to leader role (link back to Exercise 1 results) ■ Review post-workshop teaching activity and adult learning principles	PP; PWB
15:00	Exercise 8: Planning to teach direct reports SLII/peer micro-teaching in triads ■ Each participant take turns as manager (teacher), employee, and observer ■ Individual preparation to teach the others the purpose of SLII, plus one of its key steps (diagnosing, matching, or partnering) ■ Teaching sessions followed by observer feedback and coaching ■ Plenary debriefing on participant performance and questions	PWB
16:00	Plenary Discussion ■ Testimonial from previous workshop participant ■ Review of participant expectations/workshop objectives ■ Closing quotes about the importance of learning by doing	PP; Posted FC
16:15	Workshop evaluation, including self-assessment on participant development level	Evaluation Form
16:30	End	

[a]PWB = Participant workbook; FC = Flip chart/markers; PP = PowerPoint slides.
[b]Included all PowerPoint slides, exercises, and resource material used in the workshop.

References

Åkerlind, G. (2003). Growing and developing as a university teacher – variations in meaning. *Studies in Higher Education, 28*(4), 375–390.

Åkerlind, G.S. (2004). A new dimension to understanding university teaching. *Teaching in Higher Education, 9*, 363–376.

Amundsen, C., Winer, L., & Gandell, T. (2004). Designing teaching for student learning. In A. Saroyan & C. Amundsen (Eds.), *Rethinking teaching in higher education: From a course design workshop to a faculty development framework* (pp. 71–94). Stirling, VA: Stylus.

Anderson, J. R. (1982). Acquisition of cognitive skill. *Psychological Review, 89*, 396–406.

Annis, L. F. (1981). The processes and effects of peer tutoring. *Human Learning, 2*, 39–47.

Bandura, A. (1977). *Social learning theory*. Englewood Cliffs, NJ: Prentice-Hall.

Barker, R. A. (1997). How can we train leaders if we do not know what leadership is? *Human Relations, 50*(4), 343–362.

Bass, B. M. (1985). *Leadership and performance beyond expectations*. New York: The Free Press.

Bass, B. M. (1990). *Bass and Stogdill's handbook of leadership* (3rd ed.). New York: Free Press.

Bass, B. M. (1997). Does the transactional-transformational leadership paradigm transcend organizational and national boundaries? *American Psychologist, 52*(3), 130–139.

Bass, B. M., & Avolio, B. J. (Eds.). (1994). *Increasing organizational effectiveness through transformational leadership*. Thousand Oaks, CA: Sage.

Bass, B. M., & Avolio, B. J. (2000). *MLQ – Multifactor Leadership Questionnaire: Technical report, leader form, rater form and scoring key for MLQ Form 5x-Short*. Redwood City, CA: Mind Garden.

Bennis, W. (1999). *Managing people is like herding cats*. Provo, UT: Executive Excellence Publishing.

Bennis, W., & Nanus, B. (1985). *Leaders: The strategies for taking charge*. New York: Harper & Row.

Bennis, W. G., & O'Toole, J. (2005). How business schools lost their way. *Harvard Business Review* (May), 96–104.

Betof, E. (2009). Leaders as teachers: Unlock the teaching potential of your company's best and brightest. San Francisco: Berrett-Koehler.

Blake, R. R., & Mouton, J. S. (1964). *The managerial grid*. Houston: Gulf Publishing.

Blanchard, K. (Ed.). (2006). *2006 Corporate issues survey*. San Diego: Ken Blanchard Companies.

Blanchard, K. (Ed.). (2007). *Leading at a higher level: Blanchard on leadership and creating high performing organizations*. Upper Saddle River, NJ: Pearson, Prentice-Hall.

Blanchard, K., Hambleton, R., Zigarmi, D., & Forsyth, D. (2005). *LBAII: Leader behavior analysis II questionnaire*. Escondido, CA: The Ken Blanchard Companies.

Blanchard, K., Zigarmi, P., & Zigarmi, D. (1985). *Leadership and the one-minute manager*. New York: William Morrow.

Bloom, B. S. (Ed.). (1956). *Taxonomy of educational objectives: The classification of educational goals. Handbook 1, cognitive domain*. New York: McKay.

Bransford, J. D., & Schwartz, D. L. (2001). Rethinking transfer: A simple proposal with multiple implications. In A. Iran-Nejad & P. D. Pearson (Eds.), *Review of research in education* (pp. 61–100). Washington, DC: American Educational Research Association.

Brown, A. L. (1992). Design experiments: Theoretical and methodological challenges in creating complex interventions in classroom settings. *The Journal of the Learning Sciences, 2*(2), 141–178.

Brookfield, S. B. (1987). *Developing critical thinkers*. San Francisco: Jossey-Bass.

Buckingham, M., & Coffman, C. (1999). *First break all the rules: What the world's greatest managers do differently*. New York: Simon and Schuster.

Burns, J. M. (1978). *Leadership*. New York: Harper & Row.

Cha, S., & Edmondson, A. C. (2006). When values backfire: Leadership, attribution, and disenchantment in a values-driven organization. *The Leadership Quarterly, 17*, 57–78.

Charan, R., Drotter, S., & Noel, J. (2001). *The leadership pipeline*. San Francisco: Jossey-Bass.
Cohn, J. M., Khurana, R., & Reeves, L. (2005). Growing talent as if your business depended on it. *Harvard Business Review, 83*(10), 63–70.
Collins, A., Brown, J. S., & Newman, S. E. (1989). Cognitive apprenticeship: Teaching the craft of reading, writing and mathematics. In L. B. Resnick (Ed.), Knowing, *learning, and instruction: Essays in honor of Robert Glaser* (pp. 453–494). Hillsdale, NJ: Lawrence Erlbaum.
Conger, J., & Benjamin, B. (1999). *Building leaders: How successful companies develop the next generation*. San Francisco: Jossey-Bass.
Covey, S. R. (2004). *The 8th habit: From effectiveness to greatness*. New York: Free Press.
Cranton, P. (2000). *Planning instruction for adult learners* (2nd ed.). Toronto: Walls & Emerson.
Daloz-Parks, S. (2005). *Leadership can be taught*. Boston: Harvard Business School Press.
Daniels, A. C., & Daniels, J. E. (2007). *Measures of a leader*. New York: McGraw-Hill.
de Moura, C., & de Oliveira, J. B. A. (1996). Convergence between education and training. In C. Tuijnman (Ed.), *International encylopedia of adult education and training* (2nd ed., pp. 18–22). Paris: Pergamon.
Doh, J. P. (2003). Can leadership be taught? Perspectives from management educators. *Academy of Management Learning and Education, 2*(1), 54–67.
Drucker, P. F. (1993). *Post capitalist society*. New York: HarperCollins.
DuBois, P. (2005). *Le sentiment d'appartenance du personnel*. Montreal: Les Editions Quebecor.
Engeström, Y. (1987). *Learning by expanding: An activity-theoretical approach to developmental research*. Helsinki: Orienta-Konsultit. [Electronic version]. Retrieved October 20, 2005 from http://lchc.ucsd.edu/MCA/Paper/Engestrom/expanding/toc.htm
Fitz-Enz, J. (1997). *The 8 practices of exceptional companies: How great organizations make the most of their human assets*. New York: AMACOM.
Gagné, R. M., & Biggs, L. J. (1979). *Principles of instructional design*. New York: Holt, Rinehart & Winston.
Gall, M. D., Borg, W. R., & Gall, J. P. (1996). *Educational research: An introduction* (6th ed.). White Plains, NY: Longman.
Gardner, H. (1995). *Leading minds: An anatomy of leadership*. New York: Basic Books.
Gardner, J. G. (1993). *On leadership*. New York: Free Press.
Gebelein, S., Stevens, L. A., Skube, C. J., Lee, D. G., Davis, B. L., & Hellervik, L. W. (2001). *Successful manager's handbook* (6th ed.). Minneapolis, MN: Personnel Decisions International.
Goleman, D., Boyatzis, R., & Mc Kee, A. (2002). *Primal leadership: Realizing the power of emotional intelligence*. Boston, MA: Harvard Business School Press.
Gow, L., & Kember, D. (1993). Conceptions of teaching and their relationship to student learning. *British Journal of Educational Psychology, 63*, 20–33.
Gredler, M. E. (2001). *Learning and instruction: Theory into practice*. Upper Saddle River, NJ: Merrill Prentice Hall.
Hersey, P., & Blanchard, K. (1969). Life cycle theory of leadership. *Training and Development Journal, 23*, 26–34.
Hersey, P., & Blanchard, K. (1982). *Management of organizational behaviour: Utilizing human resources*. Englewood Cliffs, NJ: Prentice-Hall.
Heymann, P., & Heifetz, R. (2004). The intellectual architecture of "leadership". Retrieved July 1, 2005 from http://www.ksg.harvard.edu/leadership
Hollander, E. P. (1978). *Leadership dynamics: A practical guide to effective relationships*. New York: Free Press.
Hughes, R., Ginnett, R., & Curphy, G. (2006). *Leadership: Enhancing the lessons of experience* (5 ed.). New York: McGraw-Hill Irwin.
Kelley, R. (1992). *The power of followership: How to create leaders people want to follow and followers who lead themselves*. New York: Doubleday Currency.
Kennedy, P. K. (1993). *Preparing for the twenty-first century*. New York: Random House.

Kotter, J. (1990). *A force for change: How leadership differs from management*. New York: Free Press.
Kouzes, J., & Posner, B. (1995). *The leadership challenge* (2nd ed.). San Francisco: Jossey-Bass.
Kouzes, J., & Posner, B. (2001). Bringing the leadership lessons from the past into the future. In W. Bennis, G. Spreitzer, & T. Cummings (Eds.), *The future of leadership: Today's top leadership thinkers speak to tomorrow's leaders* (pp. 81–90). San Francisco: Jossey-Bass.
Kouzes, J., & Posner, B. (2006). *A leader's legacy*. San Francisco: Jossey-Bass.
Krathwohl, D. R., Bloom, B. S., & Masis, B. B. (1964). *Taxonomy of educational objectives: The classification of educational goals. Handbook 2: Affective domain*. New York: McKay.
Leinhardt, G. (1993). On teaching. In R. Glaser (Ed.), *Advances in instructional psychology* (pp. 1–54). Hillsdale, NJ: Lawrence Erlbaum & Associates.
Leimbach, M. P. (1994). *Business performance, employee satisfaction and leadership practices*. Eden Prairie, MN: Wilson Learning.
Lowyck, J. (1996). Learning in the workplace. In C. Tuijnman (Ed.), *International encylopedia of adult education and training* (2nd ed., pp. 414–418). Paris: Pergamon.
Meister, J. C. (1998). *Corporate universities: Lessons in building a world-class work force*. New York: McGraw-Hill.
Mezirow, J. (1977). Perspective transformation. *Studies in Adult Education, 9*, 100–110.
Merriam-Webster Online Dictionary. (2007). Retrieved February 18, 2007, from http://www.merriam-webster.com/dictionary/teach
Mintzberg, H. (1973). *The nature of managerial work*. New York: Harper and Row.
Mintzberg, H. (2004). *Managers, not MBAs*. San Francisco: Berrett-Koehler.
Northouse, P. (2006). *Leadership theory and practice* (4th ed.). Thousand Oaks, CA: Sage.
Ozmon, H. A., & Craver, S. M. (1999). *Philosophical foundations of education* (6th ed.). Upper Saddle River, NJ: Prentice-Hall.
Pratt, D., & Associates. (1997). *Five perspectives on teaching in adult & higher education*. Malabar, FL: Krieger.
Ramsden, P. (1992). *Learning to teach in higher education*. London: Routledge.
Rost, J. C. (1994). *Leadership for the twenty-first century*. Westport, CN: Praeger.
Saggers, R. E. (2009). *The efficacy of manager teaching to enhance leadership learning and effectiveness*. Unpublished doctoral dissertation, McGill University, Montreal, QC.
Samuelowicz, K., & Bain, J. D. (2001). Revisiting academics' beliefs about teaching and learning. *Higher Education, 41*(3), 299–111.
Saroyan, A., Dagenais, J., & Zhou, Y. (2008). Doctoral students' conceptions of learning and teaching: Formation for change. *Instructional Science*. [Electronic Version]. Retrieved November 27, 2008 from http://dx.doi.org/10.1007/s11251-008-9071-8
Schaffer, R. H. (1990). *The breakthrough strategy*. New York: Collins Business.
Senge, P. (1990). *The fifth discipline: The art and practice of the learning organization*. New York: Currency Doubleday.
Simpson, E. (1972). *The classification of educational objectives in the psychomotor domain*. Washington: Gryphon House.
Sternberg, R. J. (2003). WICS: A model of leadership in organizations. *Academy of Management Learning and Education, 2*(4), 386-401.
Stewart, T. A. (1997). *Intellectual capital*. New York: Currency Doubleday.
Stogdill, R. M. (1974). *Handbook of leadership: A survey of the leadership*. New York: Free Press.
Swafford, J. (2000) Teachers supporting teachers through peer coaching. In B. Moon, J. Butcher, & E. Bird (Eds.), *Leading professional development in education* (pp. 107–115). New York: Routledge Falmer.
Tichy, N. M. (Ed.). (2004). *The cycle of leadership: How great leaders teach their companies to lead* (pp. 285–394). New York: HarperCollins.
Tichy, N. M., & Cohen, E. (1998). The teaching organization. *Training & Development Journal, 52*(7), 27–33.

Tichy, N. M., & Sherman, S. (2005). *Control your own destiny or someone else will*. New York: Harpers Collins.
Ulrich, D., Zenger, J., & Smallwood, N. (1999). *Results-based leadership*. Boston: Harvard Business School.
Vicere, A. A., & Fulmer, R. M. (1998). *Leadership by design*. Boston: Harvard University Press.
Vygotsky, L. S. (1978). *Mind in society*. Boston: Harvard University.
Weiss, D. S., & Molinaro, V. (2005). *The leadership gap: Building leadership capacity for competitive advantage*. Mississauga, ON: Wiley.
Whetten, D. A., & Cameron, K. S. (2005). *Developing management skills* (6th ed.). Upper Saddle River, NJ: PrenticeHall.
Wren, J. T. (2002). A quest for a grand theory of leadership. [Electronic Version]. Retrieved July 1, 2005, from www.leadershiplearning.org/community/files/download?version_id=1230
Zenger, J. H., & Folkman, J. (2002). *The extraordinary leader: Turning good managers into great leaders*. New York: McGraw Hill.
Zigarmi, D., Blanchard, K., O'Connor, & Edeburn, C. (2005). *The leader within: Learning enough about yourself to lead others*. Upper Saddle River, NJ: Pearson Prentice Hall.
Zigarmi, D., Edeburn, C., & Blanchard, K. (1997). *Getting to know the LBAII: Research, validity and reliability of the self and other forms* (4th ed.). Escondido, CA: Blanchard Training and Development Inc.
Zigarmi, D., Zigarmi, P., Edeburn, C., & Blanchard, K. (2000). *Situational leadership II: LAP – leader action profile*. Escondido, CA: The Ken Blanchard Companies.

Chapter 7
Professional Identity Formation and Transformation across the Life Span

Muriel J. Bebeau and Verna E. Monson

7.1 Professional Identity and the Status of Professions in Contemporary Society

Examining the foundational elements of professional identity and their link to unmet health needs in society is at a critical juncture. Some (e.g., May, 1999) argue that the growing disparities result from market forces that are usurping the practice of professions and reducing them to trade organizations. Indeed, Colby and Sullivan (2008) point out that the professional status of an occupation can change as the field professionalizes or de-professionalizes over time. Even though the defining characteristics of professions are generally agreed upon, the commitment to assume full responsibility to place the interests of patients or clients before the self, or full commitment to putting the welfare of society before the welfare of the profession, may become weakened as individual professionals and the profession as a whole lose sight of the profession's public purposes. Indeed, the public purposes of professions may never have been fully understood.

In their book *Good Work,* Gardner, Csikszentmihalyi, & Damon (2001) used extensive evidence to contrast professions that are more or less well aligned with their public purposes. For example, they described journalism as a misaligned field. They cited medical genetics as an example of a profession that, at the time of data collection, appeared to be authentically well aligned. Many factors, they argued, including an increased push for market share and profits, a technology-driven increase in the pace of work, degradation of newsroom culture through budget cuts, and corporate rather than family ownership, have "intruded on their domain's integrity, obstructing [the journalists'] capacity to pursue the mission of good reporting" (p. 128). This contributed to a de-professionalization over time.

Commenting on the alignment of the dental profession with its public purpose, Welie (2004c) observes, "By definition, dentistry does not qualify as a profession

M.J. Bebeau (✉)
Department of Primary Dental Care, School of Dentistry, University of Minnesota, Minneapolis, MN 55455, USA
e-mail: bebea001@umn.edu

A. Mc Kee, M. Eraut (eds.), *Learning Trajectories, Innovation and Identity for Professional Development*, Innovation and Change in Professional Education 7,
DOI 10.1007/978-94-007-1724-4_7, © Springer Science+Business Media B.V. 2012

when and to the extent that the interventions performed are purely elective instead of medically indicated. It therefore behooves dentists who focus their practices on aesthetic interventions to clearly state that they are not professionals. Doing so does not mean they are incompetent, dishonest or otherwise immoral. It simply means that the ethical structure of their practices differs from that of professional dentists." He remarks that the ethical structure of such a dental practice "is akin to that of an interior designer rather than an oncologist" (p. 676).

Similarly, the intrusion of market language and market models of health-care delivery has put medicine in serious danger of abandoning, or at least marginalizing, the profession's central values and public duties. In the foreword to Stern's (2006) book, *Measuring Medical Professionalism*, Jordon Cohen highlights the central tensions faced by medicine.

> Whether by intent or otherwise, our country has chosen to rely on the commercial marketplace in an effort to control the escalating costs of health care. As a consequence, medicine is increasingly being viewed by policy makers and others as no different from any other commercial entity. In their view, medicine is just another business. Witness the terminology that has crept into common usage: doctors are commonly referred to as providers; patients, as consumers; health care services, as commodities. As a salient reminder of the fundamental differences between commercialism and professionalism, consider their starkly contrasting mottos. Commercialism's is *caveat emptor*, buyer beware. Medicine is *primum non nocere*, first do no harm. (p. viii)

The danger posed by commercialism, Cohen argues, comes not from adopting sound business practices, but in adopting its core ideology. "Self interest, the dominant paradigm of the market place, is the very antithesis of the self-sacrifice called for by medicine's commitment to the primacy of our patient's interest" (p. viii). Clearly, the outward manifestations of professionalism may help to maintain public trust, just as a customer service orientation may serve as an antidote to crass commercialism. However, such outward manifestations may not sustain the profession or the professional unless they are linked to a moral identity that not only keeps self-interest in check but also guides and promotes a doctor–patient relationship based upon trust. Cohen's remarks speak more loudly to the professional's individual responsibility than to the profession's collective responsibility. Both elements, we will argue, are dimensions of a fully formed professional identity.

Reflecting on the need for professional socialization of medical residents, Leach (2008) raises these questions: "How do we preserve and nurture authentic human and moral reflexes in our young learners? How do we foster authentic professionalism and moral development in young people when the context in which young people are being formed is itself morally challenged?" (p. 512). When referring to authentic professionalism, Leach is distinguishing outward professionalism (as manifested by particular behaviors) from the quality of the professional's inner life. "Transcendence of self-interest is not a technique—it is a way of being. The resident, in addition to learning the science and art of medicine, must also learn a new way of being in the world in order to become a fully-developed professional. The resident's journey is an inner journey. We have a heavy obligation to help them" (p. 515).

Assuming that it is possible to more effectively educate for professional identity formation—after all, professional schools have not exactly ignored their responsibility to socialize students to the profession's values—we need to ask whether Leach's assumption, that students need to learn "a new way of being," is true. Is it true for everyone, or just for some? Are students entering professional school primarily self-interested? Is the current generation more self-interested than previous generations, as seasoned professionals often assert? Do a professional's value commitments change over time? How do entering students understand professional role expectations? Are their conceptions aligned with the professions' values and expectations? If not, is it possible to influence development within the limits of our resources? If not, shouldn't we screen for these qualities?

7.2 Challenges to the Formation of a Professional Identity

This section examines six key challenges to the formation of an ethically based professional identity[1]:

1. Are young people today more self-centered than those in earlier generations?
2. How do professional school students understand professional and societal exceptions? Are their conceptions aligned with the professions' values and expectations?
3. How do moral exemplars understand professional and societal expectations?
4. How do professionals disciplined by a licensing board understand professional and societal expectations?
5. Is it possible to influence development within the limits of our resources?
6. Should professional schools try to matriculate students who exhibit a willingness to be connected and committed to professional and societal exceptions?

7.2.1 Are Young People Today More Self-Centered Than Those in Earlier Generations?

New evidence supports the presence of generational shifts in perceptions of self-importance and individual priorities that present challenges for educators concerned with instilling in students a sense of responsibility toward others. For example, college freshmen have increasingly replaced the goal of developing a meaningful philosophy of life during college with a new interest in finding employment that provides a secure future (Pryor, Hurtado, Saenz, Santos, & Korn, 2007). Similarly, college students increasingly score higher than earlier generations on measures of self-esteem (Twenge & Campbell, 2001) and on measures of individualistic traits (Twenge, 1997), which, in turn, are highly correlated with psychological measures of narcissism. Recent cross-temporal meta-analyses have shown increases over time

[1] Portions of the literature review in this section also appear in Bebeau (2008).

on narcissism scales (Foster, Campbell, & Twenge, 2003; Twenge, Konrath, Foster, Campbell, & Bushman, 2008), suggesting generational shifts in feelings of entitlement and self-importance. For example, Newsom, Archer, and Trubetta (2003) reported that in the 1950s, only 12% of respondents agreed with a statement in the MMPI (Minnesota Multiphasic Personality Inventory – Butcher, Graham, Williams, & Ben-Porath, 2000), "I am an important person," whereas by the late 1980s, 77% of female and 80% of the male respondents agreed with the statement.

Consistent with other findings indicating an increased emphasis on the self, Thoma and Bebeau (2008) observed a narrowing of social reasoning as measured by the Defining Issues Test (DIT).[2] It appears that moral judgment development for entering professional school students and college students is currently less mature and driven by more personal considerations than it has been in previous cohorts. Two analyses support this conclusion. First, our access to large data sets maintained by the Center for the Study of Ethical Development[3] and used to establish norms for the measure enabled us to investigate trends in data sets collected at various intervals over the past 30 years. Statistically significant declines were observed in the most recent samples from both college students and graduate students. Because samples depicted in Fig. 7.1 were drawn from many regions of the country and from a range of educational institutions, and we know that some contextual variables such

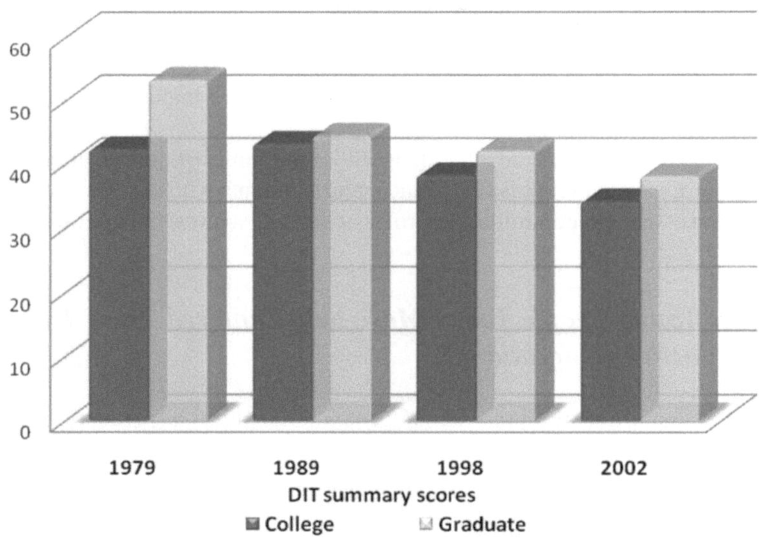

Fig. 7.1 Declines in DIT summary scores for four composite samples used to construct norms. *Note*: The smaller mean difference between college students and graduate students evident in the 1989, 1998, and 2003 composite samples is attributable to a broadening of criteria for defining what constitutes graduate education

---

[2] A measure of life span moral judgment development (Rest, 1979).

[3] Information about the Center is available at: http://www.ethicaldevelopment.ua.edu/

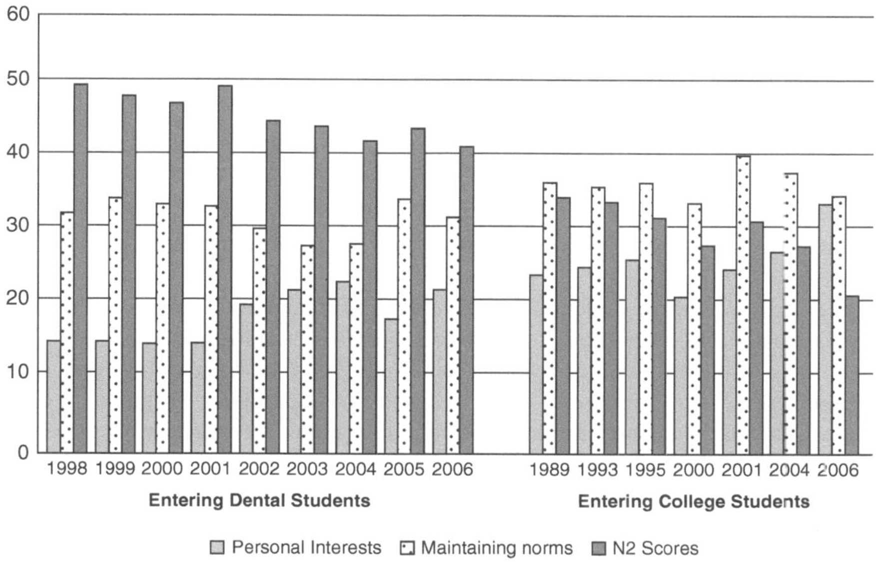

Fig. 7.2 DIT scores by class for two long-term cross-sectional samples collected within clearly defined settings

as education (liberal arts vs. technical, region of the country, public vs. religious affiliation) are related to the level of moral judgment (Maeda, Thoma, & Bebeau, 2009), we reasoned that observed differences in DIT scores could be attributed to an unintended selection bias. Thus, we next checked for declines in two long-term cross-sectional samples collected within clearly defined settings. Figure 7.2 depicts declines in mean DIT summary scores (N2) over time for college students at a Southern university and declines over time for entering professional school students at a Midwestern university.

These findings suggest that students may not be as well prepared as they once were to reason about social issues or to make moral judgments more appropriate for professional practice. Particularly troubling is the increase in personal interest reasoning (Fig. 7.2) within the past 10 years. For persons working in professions, preference for personal interest reasoning has been shown to be a liability when making context-specific moral decisions (Thoma, Bebeau, & Bolland, 2008). The recent observations join a body of literature demonstrating connections between moral judgment development (thought) and a wide range of pro-social behaviors (actions). Examples include interactions between moral judgment and ethical actions for professionals—recently summarized by Bebeau and Monson (2008), between moral judgment and political reasoning and choices (Crowson, DeBacker, & Thoma, 2007), and between moral judgment and decisions about real-life moral situations (Thoma, Hestevold, & Crowson, 2005).

Young people do learn from their environment and their culture. The question of concern for educators, of course, is not that self-esteem is unimportant, but whether self-esteem and self-importance are being developed at the expense of other essential personal qualities such as self-control and self-discipline, or important competencies such as the ability to self assess.[4]

7.2.2 How Do Professional School Students Understand Professional and Societal Exceptions? Is Their Conception Aligned with the Professions' Values and Expectations?

Several studies confirm students' undeveloped understanding of professional roles and responsibilities, even though they may express a desire to "help others through the practice of the profession." A longitudinal study of doctoral students aspiring to become researchers (Anderson, 2001) revealed that, upon entry to graduate education, students could not articulate basic expectations for integrity in research. Interestingly, they were not able to do so later in their program either. Anderson concluded that students do not intuit the values of the discipline and do not seem to learn them from either mentors or the hidden curriculum.

Similarly, entering dental students (Bebeau, 1994) could not articulate professional expectations, sometimes even after explicit instruction. Some students seemed to lack a conceptual framework for key professional concepts—like responsibility for self-regulation and professional monitoring. They conflate professional reporting of dishonesty or incompetence with "tattling,"[5] and the usual socialization process seems to develop a sense of camaraderie among peers that contributes to a reluctance to engage in self-regulation—one of the hallmarks of a profession.

When Rennie and Crosby (2002) explored Scottish medical students' perceptions of the duty to report misconduct and their actual commitment to do so, less than 40% said they should report and only 13% said they would. Further, the proportion who thought they should report declined over the years of medical school. When interviewed about the reluctance to report, students indicated that it wasn't that misconduct should not be addressed—it was just, they thought, *that someone else should do it* [emphasis added]. Similarly, 65% of students from a prominent U.S. medical school (Feudtner, Christakis, & Christakis, 1994) expressed discomfort at challenging members of the medical team over perceived wrongdoing.

A recent analysis of Minnesota senior dental students' reflective essays on the easiest and hardest professional expectations to fulfill[6] found that 44% of the 91 students perceived professional self-regulation and professional monitoring to

---

[4] The Alverno College Faculty (Loacker, 2000) describe self assessment as an individual's ability to observe, analyze, and judge his or her performance on the basis of standards of professional practice, and then determine how to improve it.

[5] In the United States, "tattling" is the term used to describe the childish act of telling an authority (usually a teacher or an adult) about another's misdemeanor, usually for the purpose of getting the other in difficulty. In the United Kingdom this is called "snitching."

[6] Students were asked to reflect (based on clinical experience to date, and portfolio entries) on what they now viewed as the easiest, the hardest, and the second hardest expectations of the professional

be the hardest responsibilities to fulfill, whereas achieving the knowledge of the profession and meeting responsibilities for lifelong learning were considered the easiest. Putting patients' interests before the self and serving the underserved were considered difficult, but not as difficult as questioning a superior about a judgment that seemed questionable or admitting an error in one's own judgment. Our curriculum studies (Bebeau & Monson, 2008; You, 2007) reveal that even when professional expectations about self-regulation are well understood, reluctance to report instances of misconduct comes both from uncertainty about how to do so and from the negative reactions of colleagues that often follow such actions.

Professional students learn from their environment. Unless professional socialization includes appropriate practice in confronting real or perceived misconduct, it is unlikely that factors that seem to work against professional self-regulation can be overcome. The next two sections contrast the understanding of professional expectations shown by those highly regarded by their peers and those disciplined by a licensing board.

7.2.3 How Do Moral Exemplars Understand Professional and Societal Expectations?

In an attempt to understand what psychologists had referred to as the "thought/action problem," Colby and Damon (1992) interviewed 23 individuals who had led lives of committed moral action. What characterized these moral exemplars was the high degree of unity between the self and morality. The men and women interviewed had pursued their individual and moral goals simultaneously, viewing them as one and the same. They do not deny the self, but define it with a moral center. Similarly, none of the 10 dental exemplars interviewed by Rule and Bebeau (2005), following Colby and Damon's criteria for nomination, saw their moral choices as an exercise in self-sacrifice. Rule and Bebeau's findings echo Colby and Damon's (1992) observations of the extraordinary integration of the self and morality. "Time and again we found our moral exemplars acting spontaneously, out of great certainty, with little fear, doubt, or agonized reflection. They performed their moral actions spontaneously, as if they had no choice in the matter. In fact, the sense that they lacked a choice is precisely what many of the exemplars reported" (p. 303). Janet Johnson, a dental resident who, after unproductive discussions with her supervisor and then hospital administration, reported her supervisor for flagrant disregard for basic requirements for safe administration of sedation for anxious and uncooperative patients, illustrates this conviction. Unlike the residents who preceded her in the position and took no

to fulfill. Portfolio entries written during the first semester of the first year relevant to this activity included (a) the *Professional Identity Essay* written as a baseline assessment and (b) an essay "What does it mean to you to become a professional?" written as part of a course exam following a series of learning activities designed to enhance understanding of professional and societal expectations.

action, she said, "There was no way I could leave the situation the way it was" (Rule & Bebeau, 2005, p. 66).

Rule and Bebeau's (2005) in-depth study of dental moral exemplars illustrates many of the tenants of developmental theory. For example: (1) Exemplars are aware of transformations in their identity as it has unfolded across the life span. They can articulate professional expectations and are aware that their concepts of professionalism (e.g., service to society, professional regulation, etc.) have undergone transformations since initial professional education. They are aware that they now think of these responsibilities differently than they did as young professionals. (2) Exemplars appear to have constructed "self-systems" (i.e., a stage 4 identity) that provide an internal compass for negotiating and resolving tensions among these multiple, shared expectations. (3) Exemplars are self-aware, reflective, and highly effective practitioners. They are aware of their competence, their values, and the forces that shaped their identity. They are able to critically assess aspects of their profession while remaining strongly committed to it. Viewed as authentic persons, they become leaders and change agents within their profession.

We also know from studies of competence development that self reflection and self assessment are important dimensions of professional growth and that the ability to self assess is a capacity that does not develop in the absence of instruction and practice (Mentkowski & Associates, 2000).

7.2.4 How Do Professionals Disciplined by a Licensing Board Understand Professional and Societal Expectations?

We now compare Rule and Bebeau's (2005) exemplary dentists with an analysis of 41 mid- and late-career professionals referred for ethics instruction by a licensing board (Bebeau, 2009a, 2009b). When asked to articulate professional and societal expectations—concepts that are fully and rather spontaneously expressed with little prompting by exemplary dentists—all but three of the 41 professionals referred for an ethics assessment had difficulty (Bebeau, 2009a, 2009b). Whereas change in the ability to articulate responsibilities that resulted from instruction was highly valued by these 38 referred practitioners, the frequency with which these concepts were omitted at pretest helped to illuminate reasons for their moral failings. For example,

- 76% of the respondents made no reference to the responsibility to *abide by the profession's code of ethics.*[7]
- 68% made no reference to the *responsibility for lifelong learning.*

---

[7] The six italicized statements in this section represent a synthesis of ideas drawn from the sociological and professional ethics literature. For a more extensive discussion of these six expectations of a professional, see Bebeau and Kahn (2003).

- 55% made no reference either *to placing the interest of patients before the self* or to the profession's collective responsibility *to place the oral health interests of society before the interests of the profession.* Of the 42% who did articulate the obligations to put patient interests before self, only one individual also articulated the broader sense of commitment described by Rule and Welie (2009).
- 45% made no reference to *acquiring the knowledge of the profession to an external set of standards.*
- 39% omitted any reference to the responsibility for *self-regulation and monitoring of one's profession or to membership in professional associations.*[8]
- While almost everyone mentioned a responsibility *to serve society*, 34% seemed to limit this service to those who could afford care. Interestingly, some expressed an unbounded sense of responsibility toward others—a willingness to compromise the self that bordered on martyrdom. Thus, the 15 individuals cited for some version of Medicaid or insurance fraud seemed to support the referrals' assertions that their actions were motivated by a desire to help a patient who seriously needed care for which they were unable to pay.

In sum, when the issues for which they were disciplined were examined for this group, it became evident that conceptions of professional responsibility were not part of self-understanding and did not guide decision making. Further, 38 of the 41 referrals who completed a specially designed ethics course said that the instruction on professional values was the most inspiring dimension of instruction and contributed a renewed sense of professionalism (Bebeau, 2009b).

Interestingly, when the same instruction is provided to entering professional school students, at least 20% complain (anonymously, of course) that the instructor is "imposing values" and they "should be able to develop their own values." One student, on the first draft of a self assessment that accompanied a learning plan, likened his highly individualistic approach to identity formation to what he perceived to be admirable about his approach to creative expression. He opined:

> When taking ceramics courses in undergrad I would make a conscious effort to not look at the numerous examples of other artists' work that were strung all over the studio walls. The reason I made this effort was to avoid squashing my own creativeness so that I would know, deep down, that the art I was doing was completely original, unique and uninfluenced by concepts that other people had already entertained. In certain ways, I feel that my development as a professional should also be of my own doing, utilizing my *own* morals and freewill in developing strategies that will maximize my ability to deliver quality oral care. There are certain concepts that I have plucked from this University's accepted doctrine of ethical parameters that I do feel are applicable to my unique professional development.

---

[8] However, 47% partially attended to one or more of the three dimensions of this responsibility: (1) to monitor one's own practice to assure that processes and procedures meet ever-evolving professional standards; (2) to report dishonest, incompetent, or impaired professionals; and (3) to join one's professional associations, in order to participate in the setting of standards for the continuation of the profession. The latter is not a legal, but rather an ethical, responsibility (Bebeau & Kahn, 2003).

Like his highly individualistic approach to creative development, this student sees the development of his professional identity as highly individualistic, honoring only his *own* morals and free will. Further, he deliberately separates his approach from that of the profession he has chosen to join, which clearly requires its practitioners to use the profession's own value frameworks. While we might hail his autonomy, and recognize the need for professional autonomy, it is unclear that he understands fully what it means to learn, and indeed, blocks himself from engaging content that he thinks might undermine his individualism. This student was not helped during his undergraduate education to see that:

> Creative ideas, even those that are radically new, are firmly planted on ideas that came before. There are always antecedents to any creative idea. The reason that it sometimes looks like an idea comes out of nothing is because we observers are ignorant of the knowledge base of the individual producing the new idea. (Weisberg, 2006. p. 53)

Indeed, students like the one quoted above might even be frustrated with faculty practitioners who reflect on their professional values and experiences in the classroom, and see these values and experiences as irrelevant to their own future plans. We see from the studies cited above that it is possible to identify shortcomings in understanding of professional and societal expectations and the viewpoints that accompany them. What seems more challenging is to work out effective strategies for challenging perspectives that seem, at least to the experienced professional, as less developed.

7.2.5 Is It Possible to Influence Development Within the Limits of Our Resources?

Young people are naturally more self-centered rather than other-centered. Becoming other-centered is a marker of moral maturity and a distinguishing feature of individuals who have led lives of committed action (Colby & Damon, 1992; Rule & Bebeau, 2005). Unlike professional students entering dental education (Bebeau, 1994) and dentists referred for ethics instruction by a licensing board (Bebeau, 2009a), the dental exemplars interviewed by Rule and Bebeau (2005) not only clearly articulated their professional expectations, but also reflected on how their perceptions of those responsibilities developed over a lifetime of professional practice. They noted that when they were young professionals, they did not see their professional responsibilities in the same way that they see them today. They expressed considerable insights into their own professional identity formation, and they saw their sense of obligation to society and their profession as growing and changing over time. Toward the end of their career, they saw professional and community service as what they must do, rather than what would simply be good to do if one were so inclined.

Dr. Jack Echternacht, a general dentist from Brainerd Minnesota, best known for his decades-long struggle to fluoridate his town's water supply, conceptualizes as obligation what others might express as "beyond the call of duty." He says, "I believe that if one lives in the community and makes his livelihood from it, he should return that benefit by participating in the activities of the community to better it in any way that he can" (Rule & Bebeau, 2005, p. 16).

Similarly, Dr. Jerry Lowney, an orthodontist from Norwich, Connecticut, uses every bit of his power, privilege, position, and knowledge to serve the poorest of poor in Haiti. What began as a survey trip to Haiti in 1981 with his friend, a Roman Catholic bishop, where he performed some extractions for the poor, turned into a life-changing event for him. Through grant writing, connections with Mother Teresa's religious order, fundraising, and huge investments of his own time and money, he now manages a multimillion-dollar general health-care facility in one of the poorest regions of Haiti. In reflecting on what he does, he says simply, "To whom much is given, much is expected" (Rule & Bebeau, 2005, pp. 75–92).

Dr. Donna Rumberger, a practitioner in New York City, nominated for her dedication and effectiveness in launching programs to help others, works through organized dentistry to create programs that enable dentists to volunteer their services—not to promote self-interest, but to benefit the lives of others. Examples include a program to restore the oral health of poor women in need of jobs, and a Skate Safe program for inner-city children in Harlem. For Dr. Rumberger, helping others is central to her identity. She says, "Doing good for others is doing good for me" (Rule & Bebeau, 2005, p. 101).

Such examples are consistent with the perspectives of developmental psychologists such as Blasi (1984) and Kegan (1982), who have long argued that people differ in how deeply moral notions penetrate self-understanding. Understanding the self as responsible is the bridge between knowing the right thing and doing it. If, as psychologists have argued, identity formation is a lifelong developmental process, we educators should not expect young people to come fully prepared to take on professional roles and responsibilities, or to demonstrate the kind of integration of personal and professional values that are exhibited by exemplars in the profession. The main question then is not whether young people are self-centered rather than other-centered, but the degree to which societal influences may be inhibiting, rather than enhancing, the development of the moral self.

Three recent studies raise concerns. The first, by Forsythe, Snook, Lewis, and Bartone (2002), suggests that students entering college are more self-centered than other-centered. The second, initiated by Snook (2007), suggests that post-baccalaureate programs are not currently selecting the more mature and developed student for graduate education. Both studies used the Kegan interview schedule (Lahey, Souvaine, Kegan, Goodman, & Felix, 1988), an extensive, in-depth tool to code stages of identity development, with well-trained raters using a well-validated assessment method. The third study (Monson, Roehrich, & Bebeau, 2008) supports the findings of the second, although it used a less rigorous measure than the other two.

In the first study, begun in the late 1990s, Forsythe et al. (2002) extended their research into the identity development of military leaders by adding longitudinal follow-ups on selected military cadets, based on the rigorous coding of Kegan interviews. These researchers found that

(1) Entering cadets (college freshmen) were less developed than theorists had assumed;
(2) Cadets did develop, particularly between the second and fourth years, although it was unclear whether the development could be attributed to the educational experience;
(3) Identity formation was associated with leadership—cadets perceived as effective leaders by their peers, their superiors, and their subordinates had made the key transitions in identity formation that enabled them to attend to the interests of others; and
(4) Advanced levels of identity formation (the integration of professional and personal values and an other-centered focus) characterized military leaders who were selected for career advancement and additional professional development.

Forsythe and his military educator colleagues were also concerned about the 30% of West Point cadets who had not achieved key transformations in identity by graduation—transformations that would enable the broad internalized understanding of the codes of ethics and other professional standards required for effective leadership. These graduates remained at stage 2 to stage 2/3, characterized by a predominant focus on personal needs and wants. Forsythe and colleagues concluded,

> Cadet development programs will not be successful in instilling desired values in these less mature cadets unless the broad educational environment in which they operate promotes identity development toward a shared perspective on professionalism. (p. 374)

While the Forsythe study was in progress, the Army had commissioned a position paper (see Swain, 2007) to more clearly define role expectations. Four professional roles of the military professional (leader of character, servant of the nation, warrior, and member of the profession) were defined. As these role expectations were being vetted throughout the military, educators at the United States Military Academy (USMA) began to strengthen leader development by including coursework that required cadets to articulate the requirements of each role and to write reflective essays (see Bebeau & Lewis, 2003) on how their experiences presented challenges to meeting role expectations for their level of development and some examples of how they had either managed or failed to live up to these role expectations.

By comparing levels of identity formation across the career trajectory for a military leader, Forsythe and colleagues concluded that being self-centered rather than other-centered, and focused on individual needs and wants (a stage 2 to stage 2/3), might be typical of entering college students, but would not be what military educators would envision for college graduates about to enter the military profession nor, for that matter, what educators would expect for college graduates about to enter a post-baccalaureate professional school. Expectations should be guided by the following:

- In random sample studies of adults, approximately 5% remain at stage 2 (Kegan, 1994, pp. 194, 195), and 58% of adults have not achieved stage 4 (Kegan & Lahey, 2009, p. 27);
- More than a third of military cadets had not completed the transition to stage 3 by the end of their senior year (Forsythe et al., 2002; Lewis, Forsythe, Sweeney, & Bartone, 2005); and
- Based upon a comparison between cadets and a matched sample of college students, Lewis et al. (2005) estimated that college students progress at approximately the same rate as military cadets, observing that only 19% of college graduates had begun the transition to stage 4.[9]

So educators should not expect entering dental and medical professionals to exhibit the more advanced (stage 4) phase of identity formation typical of the fully formed professional. Nor should they expect students entering professional school to exhibit the integration of personal and professional values, and consistency between espoused ideals and actions. Indeed, such integration may not even be completed by the end of professional education. Put simply, advanced levels are rarely achieved until after considerable professional experience.

Given these observations of identity development across the college years and also that the more advanced seniors were also the better military leaders (Bartone, Snook, Forsythe, Lewis, & Bullis, 2007), these researchers were concerned to find that a substantial proportion of entering professional school students appear to be "less developed" psychosocially than previous research would suggest. Extending their work beyond the military context, Snook (2007) interviewed a sample of 26 MBA students at the beginning and end of a highly selective, two-year program, and found extraordinary variability among the 26 study participants, echoing the findings of Kegan and Lahey's (2009) meta-analytic studies.[10] Ten of the 26 exhibited the stage 2 to 2/3 identity, typical of entering college students (Bartone et al., 2007); seven exhibited the stage 3 to stage 3/4 identity of college seniors (that is, cadets considered to be effective leaders for their level of professional achievement as entry-level military leaders). Nine of the 26 MBA students exhibited the stage 4 to stage 4/5 identity characteristics of the senior military officers this team had previously studied (Forsythe et al., 2002). Moreover, only 7 of the 25 MBA students who were interviewed 18–20 months later exhibited developmental change. Of these seven, six exhibited *slight* change (i.e., moved up the ladder 1/4 step), and

[9] To establish the equivalency of the cadet population with the general population of college students, Lewis et al. (2005) administered the Kegan interview to a sample of college students from a state university that were matched to cadet samples based on standardized scores. Although the cadets scored slightly higher on the Kegan assessment, the differences were not statistically significant.

[10] Although lower stages of identity formation are characteristic of early adulthood and advanced identity levels achieved with midlife (if achieved at all), Kegan and Lahey (2009, p. 14) identified ample variability in identity level across all ages of the lifespan, suggesting higher levels of identity formation are more prevalent than previously estimated (Kegan, 1994, pp. 194–195). According to Kegan and Lahey "...six people in their thirties ... could all be at different places in their level of mental complexity, and some could be more complex than a person in her forties" (p. 14).

one student moved from a solid stage 3 perspective to stage 3/4 transition. Given the age of the students (a mean age of 27, with a range of 23–35, and no relationship between age and identity), one might have expected that change would have been more pronounced in those who were least developed; but only three of the 10 stage 2/3 students exhibited any change. Based on experience with interventions for the moral judgment development of adult learners, change is usually more pronounced for those who are least developed, and with mature accomplished learners, self-interest moral arguments are often readily apparent, once their inadequacy is challenged.

In the third study, Monson, Roehrich, and Bebeau (2008) coded essays written by entering dental students in response to probe questions aimed at eliciting a student's sense of professional identity. Preliminary evidence (Monson & Hamilton, in press) suggests that inferences made from written responses to open-ended questions are comparable to inferences made from an interactive interview method. Further, these researchers have been able to classify student statements that seem to reflect different stages of identity formation and to validate their judgments against other developmental measures, like Rest's (1979) Defining Issues Test (DIT). When essay responses written by dental students in a classroom setting were compared to those used in their admissions essays, they seemed less developed than the lofty ideals expressed in their admissions essays would suggest. Most attended to image or personal rewards of the professional life. What distinguished 37 of the 97 entering students who appeared to have a more developed sense of the moral self (what Baxter Magolda & King (2004), borrowing Kegan's language, refer to as "self-authoring") was a greater tendency to integrate other-directed concerns such as access to care, serving medical assistance patients, and volunteering to help those in need—as key aspects of the self.

The studies cited here support the influence of culture on the establishment of a value system that may or may not be aligned with a moral identity. The studies also confirm that not all entering college students or students entering a post-baccalaureate program possess an identity consistent with professional and societal expectations of professionals. On the other hand, the studies also confirm that identity formation is a lifelong process, subject to influence by both culture and context. Educators' professional responsibility is to attend to both selection and identity formation.

7.2.6 Should Professional Schools Try to Matriculate Students Who Exhibit a Willingness to Be Connected and Committed to Professional and Societal Expectations?

Studies that illustrate immature personal attributes in the applicant pool for professional education, or an undeveloped professional identity during or after professional education, quite naturally raise questions about the possibility of selecting for moral maturity and/or for desirable personal attributes. Past efforts to select for desirable traits using admissions interviews or other screening devices have had only limited success. However, for educators concerned with both selection and development of an other-centered professional identity, recent work by Eva, Reiter, Rosenfeld, and Norman (2004) is gaining professional educators' attention. Eva and colleagues developed and validated a Multiple Mini-Interview (MMI; a kind of "medical school admissions OSCE[11]") that is cost-effective and provides better predictions of the clerkship performance of physicians than the standard admissions interview—which, for all the effort and cost involved, has not been able to reliably discriminate those who are likely to have problems as students or practitioners. The MMI has recently been adapted for dentistry and is being tested in a predictive validity study by Lantz (personal communication, August 2007) at the University of Michigan. These MMIs comprise 6–12 short encounters designed to reveal the capabilities that faculty value most in their students: critical thinking, ethical decision making, knowledge of the health-care system, and effective communication skills.

7.3 Overcoming the Challenges: Deliberate Socialization for Professional Identity Formation

Having established the potential for selection and formation of a professional identity, we turn to strategies to overcome the effects of culture and context on identity formation. At a minimum, each profession should assert its commitment to place the interests of others before the self and its awareness of the profession's collective social responsibility for health.

7.3.1 Assessing for Identity Formation

Three strategies have been used to assess identity formation: standardized inventories, open-ended interviews, or open essays. A good example of a standardized inventory is the *Professional Role Orientation Inventory* (PROI) developed by Bebeau, Born, and Ozar (1993), to assess action tendencies and underlying values.[12] Individuals can assess themselves against group norms, and educators can use group scores to estimate educational effectiveness. The PROI, for example, is derived from philosophers' observations of different models of professionalism that appear to guide professional practice. An interpretive guide enables educators

[11] Objective Structured Clinical Exams (OSCEs) are used in assessing medical student competencies in one-on-one patient clinical interviews, clinical examination, communication, and interpersonal skills (Harden, Stevenson, Downie, & Wilson, 1975).

[12] Another example, designed for law and medicine, is the *Professional Decisions and Values Test* (PDV) created by Rezler et al. (1992).

(1) to engage students or professionals in a self assessment of the model of professionalism (commercial, guild, service, agent) that is most closely aligned with the individual's role conception,
(2) to compare one's self to others in the profession, and
(3) to set personal learning goals.

Two of the four PROI rating scales (Authority and Responsibility) have proven useful as an outcome measure of a curriculum's effectiveness in promoting a sense of professional authority and responsibility that is consistent with particular models of professionalism.[13] Recently, You (2007) explored gender differences in the ethical abilities (sensitivity, reasoning, identity [PROI scales], implementation[14]) of five cohorts of dental students who completed an ethics curriculum as part of their four years of professional education. Male and female students did not differ on PROI scales as freshmen, but women seniors gave significantly higher ratings than their male colleagues to items eliciting their views about the commitment to serve others (e.g., to patients who cannot pay for their services, to colleagues whose competence may be questionable, to third-party payers, etc.). Change on the PROI, and on two other developmental measures—the DIT and ethical implementation (PPS scores) included in You's (2007) study—supports the notion that students' conception of their responsibility changes over the four years of the curriculum, that the change is measurable, and that enhanced identity, as measured by the PROI, may have accounted for the fact that the dental women were significantly[15] more effective than their male colleagues in applying moral ideals to the resolution of ethical problems (PPS scores).

The second strategy is to elicit conceptions of identity through the individually administered subject–object interviews developed by Kegan and his colleagues (Lahey et al., 1988), but this is time consuming for routine use rather than research. This brings us to the third strategy: the use of essay responses to open-ended questions administered in a supervised setting. Whereas the professional school admissions essay is a potential source of information about identity formation, the essay may reflect coaching and, therefore, may not authentically represent the student's level of identity formation. Monson et al. (2008) found that *Professional Identity Essay* responses elicited in a monitored setting do provide evidence of

---

[13] The Autonomy and Agency scales assess the probability that an individual will act upon his or her role concept. The scales are useful for remediation courses as part of disciplinary action (Bebeau, 2009b).

[14] The Minnesota dental ethics curriculum uses well-validated measures of the four components of morality described by James Rest (See Bebeau, 1994; Bebeau & Monson, 2008, for a discussion of Rest's theory and for descriptions and a review of construct validation studies of the measures used in You's study.)

[15] You (2007) reported an effect size of .57, favoring females, for the difference between male and female dental students' mean scores on eight assignments that required third- and fourth-year students to demonstrate effective problem solving and interpersonal interaction skills.

conceptual differences in students' understanding of professional roles and responsibilities that align with Kegan's criteria for stages and transition phases of identity formation. These same essay responses, together with the student's admissions essay and the adapted descriptions of Kegan's stages (See Table 7.1), have been used as part of a reflective exercise that helps students examine their professional identity, compare it to ways others see professional roles and responsibilities at various stages across the life span, and set some learning goals for themselves. The validity of this approach is further supported by Monson and Bebeau's (2009) analysis of learning plans and their relationship to *Professional Identity Essays* and admissions essays.

To explore the potential usefulness of qualitative analysis of admissions essays for stages of identity formation, Monson and Bebeau (2009) selected 10 admissions essays and *Professional Identity Essays*, and used two artifacts present in first-year dental student course portfolios. We wondered whether we could estimate the level of identity formation by reading admissions essays and whether our estimates would be similar to the levels we assigned based on our reading of the *Professional Identity*

Table 7.1 The evolving professional identity

Robert Kegan (1982) suggests that all human beings are continuously involved in a process of constructing meaning. As individuals gain an increasing amount of experience in an extremely complex world, they construct progressively more complex systems for making sense of it. Similarly, each person constructs an understanding of what it means to be a professional, and a professional's understanding may be qualitatively different from that of the general public.

Kegan's five levels of identity transformation were adapted for the professions by Bebeau and Lewis (2003) to enable educators to coach professional students, as they reflect on their evolving professional identity. Three levels of identity formation, typically evident among aspiring professionals, are described here. For a fuller description, see Bebeau and Lewis (2003) or Bebeau and Rule (2005).

The Independent Operator

These individuals look at themselves and the world in terms of individual interests and concrete, black-and-white role expectations (their own, others', their employer's, etc.). Personal success is paramount. It is measured by concretely accomplishing individually valued goals and enacting specific role behaviors.

How the typical *Independent Operator* understands professionalism. These individuals understand professionalism as meeting fixed, concrete, black-and-white role expectations, rather than a broader understanding of what it means to be a professional. Motivation for meeting standards is wholly individual and based on a desire to be correct and effective. Said one aspiring professional, "*There are professional guidelines and codes that shape your life.*"

The Team-Oriented Idealist

Unlike *Independent Operators* who view themselves and others as individuals, each with his or her own agendas and interests, *Team-Oriented Idealists* view themselves and others as having shared interconnections. Their capacity to make sense of the world, by taking multiple perspectives simultaneously, profoundly changes their sense of self and how they understand social reality—as shared experiences, psychological membership, and the internalization of social expectations and societal ideals. While *Team-Oriented Idealists* still possess and can articulate *individual* interests and specific behavioral goals, individual interests are no longer central.

Table 7.1 (continued)

How the *Team-Oriented Idealist* understands professionalism. Unlike *Independent Operators*, these professionals are both idealistic and internally self-reflective. They understand and identify with (or worry that they are not yet fully identified with) their chosen profession. They no longer see professionalism as enacting specific behaviors or fixed roles (the *Independent Operator's* view). Rather, the *Team-Oriented Idealist* sees professionalism as meeting the expectations of those who are more knowledgeable and legitimate, and even more professional. As one professional remarked, "*We must always hold ourselves to the highest expectations of society.*" Because their identity is grounded in others, and particularly external authorities, the *Team-Oriented Idealist* is vulnerable to "going along with others" for the sake of "getting along," and can have difficulty seeing boundaries between self and other.

The Self-Defining Professional

If a *Team-Oriented Idealist* is characterized by embeddedness in and identification with a set of shared or collective identities, *the Self-Defining Professional* forges a personal system of values and internal processes for evaluating those shared identities. *Team-Oriented Idealists* often find themselves torn among multiple shared identities (e.g., dentist, parent, spouse, etc.) with no easy way of coordinating them. As one's responsibilities multiply, life as a *Team-Oriented Idealist* often becomes one of constantly trying to balance the felt obligations of multiple identities. The self system of the *Self-Defining Professional* provides an internal compass for negotiating and resolving tensions among these multiple, shared expectations. Conflicts among the inevitable competing pulls of various roles and their attendant obligations are negotiated by adherence to one's own internal standards and values.

How the *Self-Defining Professional* understands professionalism. These individuals, unlike *Team-Oriented Idealists,* are no longer identified solely with external expectations of their professional role. Instead, having freely committed themselves to being a member of the profession, they have constructed a self-system comprised of personal values integrated with those of the profession. These provide principles for living. While their identity is not wholly embedded in their profession, they have created a vision of the "good" profession that is grounded in reflective professional practice. As *Self-Defining Professional* continue to transition to the next level (Kegan's (1982) *Humanist* or Rule & Bebeau's (2005) *Moral Exemplar*), they are able to stand aside from their own profession and even look across professions. They critically assess aspects of the professions, yet remain strongly committed. They are authentic persons who may emerge as leaders within the profession. Thus, *Self-Defining Professional* can become change agents within their profession.

Transitions

In the lifelong process of identity development, individuals spend a considerable amount of time (typically many months) in the transition between stages. Transitions are characterized by the process of encompassing one's current way of making meaning within the broader and more complex framework of the next developmental stage. Both stages may be demonstrated, with the higher stage expressed in a tentative and less-well-articulated manner. Research (Forsythe et al., 2002) suggests that many college-age students are in the transition between the *Independent Operator* and the *Team-Oriented Idealist*, whereas the transition between the *Team-Oriented Idealist* and the *Self-Defining Professional* is more typical of early- to mid-career professionals. Rarely is full transformation to the *Self-Defining Professional* evident before mid-career.

Essays (Monson et al., 2008). In 2 of the 10 cases, the applicant's admissions essays suggested more advanced development than the *Professional Identity Essay* (written under supervision) or other artifacts in the portfolio, likely the result of coaching or the availability of model essays and references. Developmental differences were apparent in the way meaning was constructed relative to four themes commonly addressed in the admissions essay: (1) dentistry as lifestyle vs. privilege, (2) dentist as aesthetician vs. healer, (3) independent services provider vs. change agent, and (4) expectations of the nature of the dentist's work.

Two admissions essays from the sample, which appeared to be authentic reflections of identity based on consistency with judgments we made on the *Professional Identity Essay* and other artifacts in the portfolio, were chosen to illustrate the potential for distinguishing matriculating students who have made key transitions in identity formation from those who have not.

Both Sam and Danielle[16] were admitted to professional school based upon current admissions criteria. Sam's conception of being a dentist centered on helping people enhance their physical appearance through cosmetic procedures, which Sam viewed as central to achieving well-being, which he described as helping the patient "get their smile back." He saw dentistry as providing a satisfying lifestyle that fits with his goals for personal achievement. For Danielle, becoming a dentist centered on the prospect of fulfilling a personal mission that had evolved through her work with special-needs patients that began in high school, continued through college, and beyond. Danielle described "learning from" a particular patient—about the patient's perspectives, and how well-being had little to do with external beauty. For Danielle, becoming a dentist was about overall health and serving the patient from the patient's perspective —and not about imposing her ideals or achieving an aesthetic ideal. Becoming a dentist was viewed as a privilege granted to those who were committed to serve.

In our judgment, Danielle illustrates a more mature conception of personal and social responsibility illustrative of the more mature identity of some college graduates. Her understandings of her identity were apparent in both her admissions essay and her *Professional Identity Essay*. The question of interest is whether the educational experiences described below will promote Sam's development and whether the educational experience will solidify and advance Danielle's.

7.4 Developing a Professional Identity Consistent with Societal Expectations

In an earlier section, we established that students entering professional school or graduate school do not intuit professional and societal expectations from the culture or usual socialization process. Hence, the profession has a clear responsibility to

[16] Danielle and Sam are pseudonyms, and salient facts from their essays were altered slightly to preserve student confidentiality.

clarify these expectations and to stress the profession's public duties. In this section, we describe strategies for raising student consciousness about what people fundamentally believe they should be able to expect from persons in society that are accorded the power and privileges granted to the most essential professions.[17] Students themselves expect that persons in positions of authority over their health and well-being should be held to higher standards than the ethic of the marketplace. The following active learning strategies are based on the literature reviewed herein and reflect the authors' ongoing evaluation of the strategies:

1. Eliciting understanding of professional expectations
2. Using moral exemplars to help students set aspirational standards for the formation of a professional moral identity
3. Engaging students in self assessment, reflection, and development of a learning plan to achieve their professional moral identity
4. Providing feedback on self assessment and the learning plan
5. Engaging students and professionals in periodic reflection on professional and societal expectations

7.4.1 Eliciting Understanding of Professional Expectations

An important first step for introducing a curriculum in professional ethics is to engage students in thinking about the ethical expectations they have of doctors, dentists, lawyers, teachers, and other persons who might use the term *professional* to describe their occupation. Approaches might include the following:

- A news clipping of a doctor or lawyer who has breached rather ordinary ethical standards of conduct (e.g., driving while intoxicated) challenges students to ask themselves why the story is so prominently featured as "news".
- Developing a continuum from less to more professionalized groups based upon one or more references (e.g., Hall, 1975).
- Discussing Welie's (2004a) questions: "Is the label 'professional' simply synonymous with other, less eloquent adjectives such as 'competent', 'reliable', or 'decent'? Is any person who does what he or she has agreed to do, and does it well, a professional? Is any occupation that issues a list of dos and don'ts a profession?" (p. 529). Developing some consensus on features that distinguish occupations helps students to consider how society and the professions have arrived at a set of expectations (see also Welie, 2004b).

[17] We find it helpful to draw students' attention to sociologists' (Hall, 1975) observations about the emergence of professions over time—that the amount of power and privilege granted by society is in direct proportion to the extent to which the practice of that profession is deemed essential to the health and welfare of society.

Another goal is to help students articulate what ethicist May (1999) refers to as the three marks of a profession, and what Bebeau and Kahn (2003) have defined as six expectations (p. x, see items in italics; see also footnotes 6 and 7) of a professional. The six (though there could be more or less) are a synthesis of several sources (e.g., Hall, 1975; May, 1999). After students have agreed on the importance of these six, they reflect on their admissions essays and their *Professional Identity Essays* to see how many of the six professional expectations were part of their initial understanding. Students then share their insights with one another and discuss their personal commitments to the expectations. At this point we have found it helpful for students to examine their profession's code of ethics to see where and how each of these expectations is expressed.

7.4.2 Using Moral Exemplars to Help Students Set Aspirational Standards for the Formation of a Professional Moral Identity

Following discussion, students have been assigned (in groups of three) to read 1 of 10 stories of dental exemplars (Rule & Bebeau, 2005) and to present (to the class) (1) how the exemplar they read about lived up to each of the six expectations and (2) how the individual came to see professional expectations as he or she developed across the life span of professional practice. Presentations from small groups have given the class an opportunity to learn about each of the exemplars in the text. Students have been encouraged to set aspirational goals for themselves, while faculty help them to view professional identity formation as a lifelong developmental process. This experience has been followed by a panel discussion with professionals who have been disciplined by the licensing board for violations of the state dental practice act.[18] These dentists are asked to discuss their personal experience in living up to the six expectations, where they fell short, and how they have modified their activities to address personal shortcomings.[19] At the conclusion of instruction, students write one-page essays on a midterm exam to express their new understanding of each of the six expectations of the dental professional. These are judged for clarity, coherence, and completeness of expression. Interestingly, despite ongoing efforts to improve the instruction (Bebeau, 1994), students continue to reveal

[18] Arranging for students to interact with disciplined professionals may not be as difficult as it may appear. In the United States, every state board of medical or dental practice publishes the disciplinary cases and many states require that disciplined individuals engage in some kind of community service. It merely takes a creative ethics educator to initiate it. Our colleagues in legal education regularly invite lawyers who have been convicted of "white collar crime" to hold discussions with law students. Such learning opportunities are very powerful, especially when accompanied with a program that also uses positive mentors.

[19] In Minnesota, sanctioned dentists may be required to complete an ethics course as part of the board's disciplinary action. See Bebeau (2009a, 2009b) for a discussion of the procedures and outcomes of such a curriculum.

misunderstandings of professional expectations on this test. Such findings support the need for ongoing reflection on professional expectations.

7.4.3 Engaging Students in Self Assessment, Reflection, and Development of a Learning Plan

As a key concluding professional identity formation activity for the first semester, students have been asked to "Prepare a one- to two-page typed, single-spaced summary that reflects your assessment of your professional ethical development and your plans to enhance your development with respect to (1) professional identity formation and (2) ethical reasoning and judgment." Students have been asked to review documents in their course portfolio—their admissions essay, their responses to the *Professional Identity Essay,* the earlier self assessment following the lectures, their notes on the exemplars, and the panel discussion—and to write a paragraph summarizing new insights developed and challenges they see themselves facing, as they begin to understand and meet professional and societal expectations. Then, students have been invited to study Kegan's descriptions of the stages and transition phases of the *Evolving Professional Identity* (Table 7.1) and view sample essay responses[20] that illustrate the stages and transition phases. Students are then invited to "Rate your level of identity formation. Support your judgment with statements from documents *you have written* (i.e., entries in your portfolio). Be sure to cite yourself. Using the descriptions of the stages and transition phases of the *Evolving Professional Identity Essay*, describe an area you believe you need to further develop. Indicate what you will do to enhance your development in this area."[21]

7.4.4 Providing Feedback on the Self Assessment and Learning Plan

Using a rubric to guide assessment of the essay, faculty write supportive comments to either confirm the student's self assessment of identity or to engage a student in further reflection on the definitions and evidence from the student's portfolio. Students are encouraged to review and resubmit whenever directions have been misunderstood, inconsistencies between the definitions and cited evidence were evident,

[20] In addition to the descriptions included in Table 7.1, the authors prepared an extensive set of examples of student responses to the various essay questions that are organized under the levels of identity formation they have been judged to represent. These are available upon request.

[21] Similar directions have been given with respect to self assessment of ethical reasoning and judgment, based upon feedback from measures of moral judgment development students completed at the beginning of the semester. This activity, though a useful part of self assessment of professional identity formation, is not addressed here.

or further clarity has been requested. In some instances, personal tutorials have been held. The assessment and learning plan remains in the portfolio for later review and subsequent reflection.

7.4.5 Engaging in Periodic Reflection on Professional and Societal Expectations

An ethics course portfolio has been maintained across the educational experience and requires periodic reflection on all dimensions of professional ethical development—not just identity formation. The portfolio provides students with a record of their accomplishments. Reflection on clinical experiences and 6–8 weeks of outreach experience (now required of dental graduates) is important, but is unlikely to accomplish their purposes unless accompanied by reflective activities (Henshaw, 2006). In addition to reflection, students have needed opportunities to affirm their commitments to personal and social responsibility with mentors who also serve as expert assessors. For example, members of the American College of Dentists—an organization committed to promoting ethics and professionalism—meet individually with dental seniors to assess their performance on a measure of ethical sensitivity (Bebeau, 1983), a program that has been in place for more than 20 years. The American College of Dentists is currently involved in a national initiative to provide more extensive ethics training to enable their members to serve as effective advocates for the professional identity formation of students and graduates entering the profession (Ozar, 2008).

7.5 Influence the Collective Profession to Focus on Its Public Purposes

Engaging communities of practitioners in self assessment and in reflection that is tied to professional and societal expectations is challenging, particularly for professions that tend to practice in isolation from other health professions, and also from each other. As Welie and Rule (2006) observe, dentistry is a profession with a long history of disconnectedness. Dentistry is typically practiced not only in isolation from other branches of medicine but also in solo practices that often compete for patients. Such isolation does not foster peer review or communities of practitioners who work to address health disparities in their communities. The consequence of such disconnectedness to the professions' public purposes is no more apparent than in Minnesota, where there is currently a legislative initiative to train and license mid-level providers. Whether development of mid-level providers will actually address the access to care problem is speculative, but the movement itself is reflective of the profession's need to attend to their public duties. Two strategies are proposed to address what Rule and Welie (2009) describe as a symptom of a systemic condition.

7.5.1 Engaging Students in Collective Endeavors to Address Health Disparities and Build Skills in Self Assessment and Peer Review

Students form strong bonds during professional education. A four-year program can provide frequent opportunities to engage in self assessment and peer review of their developing technical abilities and their moral competencies. To foster personal growth, students have been invited to reflect on these issues at least once at the end of the first two years, and then at the end of each year of clinical experience. Additional suggestions are offered here to promote personal and social responsibility:

(1) Invite students to *identify both positive and negative moral models* to help them set aspirational goals for themselves.
(2) Provide *definitions of the virtues of medical practice* (e.g., Pellegrino & Thomasma, 1983) as a tool for reflection on students' own competences and their positive and negative models.
(3) Promote *respect for self and others.* When students are engaged in the identification of negative examples, hold open discussions in which students practice civil, honest, and constructive comments. The professional school must be vigilant in promoting open dialog and constructive opportunities for feedback. We suggest that schools avoid using anonymous evaluations where students can make disparaging remarks about their fellow students and faculty and are not held accountable for what they write, because students in a professional school should be expected to speak directly about problems.
(4) Maintain a *climate of openness* to reflection on action, but be vigilant about a climate that fosters gossip and hearsay.
(5) Structure *collaborative public health projects*, where students work in groups to design and implement a health promotion or disease prevention project within an identified community (e.g., a program to *Get Sour on Sour Candy*). Many schools already participate in the American Dental Association's Give Kids A Smile® program, a nationally sponsored one-day effort to provide care to children with restorative needs. Such programs, while helpful, do not address the more important need for oral health promotion and disease prevention.

7.5.2 Engaging the Profession in Renewal of Its Collective Duties

Rule and Welie (2009) have devised strategies to promote connectedness within the dental profession. Engaging the practicing community to take up their public duties and address the access to care problems in their community is no small task. One place to start is by educating for social responsibility. This chapter has attempted to establish that fostering personal and professional responsibility not only is possible, but is also the duty of the profession and the professional education community.

7.6 Summary and Conclusion

It is easy to agree that educators in the professions should do more to foster an ethical professional identity among tomorrow's professionals, especially in the face of the substantial body of evidence suggesting that many students entering professional education have not achieved key transitions in identity formation that prepare them for the other-centered roles that society and the profession expect of them. It is more difficult to agree on how to craft both the culture and the curriculum of professions education to accomplish these ends. Educators can often identify persons ill-suited for professional practice after the fact. They have been less successful in differentiating students who are most likely to grow and become the other-centered professionals society requires.

We have argued that to foster a moral identity consistent with professional and society's expectations, schools need to (1) engage students in formative assessments of their identity (Monson & Hamilton, in press), (2) create effective strategies to challenge immaturity, (3) provide role models and frequent opportunities for students to reflect on who they are and who they are becoming, and (4) honor those whose behavioral expressions reflect an other-centered moral maturity. In concert with efforts to facilitate the development of an inner life of reflection and authenticity, schools must counter the unintended effects of narrowly focused undergraduate education that reinforces individualism and may be displayed as egocentrism or arrogance. Professions education is most effective when it (1) fosters a culture that is founded on respect for all students, faculty, and staff—what O'Toole and Bennis (2009) term "a culture of candor" in which there is an organizational default to communicate directly and honestly—and (2) reinforces the responsibility of the professions to society by integrating content dealing with disparities in health care within the entirety of the curriculum and co-curriculum from day one.

We are at a critical juncture in history demanding change to remedy increasing disparities in health-care delivery. Professions education plays a critical role in fostering authentic professionalism, in which the profession's responsibility to society is woven into the fabric of both curriculum and culture. Rather than responsibility that is imposed, a constructivist approach to professional identity formation motivates change from within that integrates personal and professional values.

References

Anderson, M. (2001). What would get you in trouble: Doctoral students' conceptions of science and its norms. *Proceedings of the ORI conference on research on research integrity*. Washington, D.C.: Office of Research Integrity.

Bartone, P. T., Snook, S. A., Forsythe, G. B., Lewis, P., & Bullis, R. C. (2007). Psychosocial development and leader performance of military officer cadets. *The Leadership Quarterly, 18*, 490–504.

Baxter Magolda, M., & King, P. M. (2004). *Learning partnerships: Theory and models of practice to educate for self-authorship*. Sterling, VA: Stylus Publishing, LLC.

Bebeau, M. J. (1983). Professional responsibility curriculum report: American College fellows serve as expert assessors. *Journal of the American College of Dentists, 50*(2), 20–23.

Bebeau, M. J. (1994). Influencing the moral dimensions of dental practice. In J. Rest & D. Narvaez (Eds.), *Moral development in the professions: Psychology and applied ethics* (pp. 121–146). New York: Erlbaum Associates.

Bebeau, M. J. (2008). Promoting ethical development and professionalism: Insights from educational research in the professions. *University of St. Thomas Law Journal, 5*(2), 366–403.

Bebeau, M. J. (2009a). Enhancing professionalism using ethics education as part of a dental licensing board's disciplinary action: Part 1 An evidence-based process. *Journal of the American College of Dentists, 76*(2), 38–50.

Bebeau, M. J. (2009b). Enhancing professionalism using ethics education as part of a dental licensing board's disciplinary action: Part 2 Evidence the process works. *Journal of the American College of Dentists*, *76*(3), 32–45.

Bebeau, M. J., Born, D. O., & Ozar, D. T. (1993). The development of a Professional Role Orientation Inventory. *Journal of the American College of Dentists, 60*(2), 27–33.

Bebeau, M. J., & Kahn, J. (2003). Ethical issues in community dental health. In G. M. Gluck & W. M. Morganstein (Eds.), *Jong's community dental health* (5th ed., pp. 425–446). St. Louis, MO: Mosby.

Bebeau, M. J., & Lewis, P. (2003). *Manual for assessing and promoting identity formation.* Minneapolis, MN: Center for the Study of Ethical Development, University of Minnesota.

Bebeau, M. J., & Monson, V. E. (2008). Guided by theory, grounded in evidence: A way forward for professional ethics education. In L. Nucci & D. Narvaez (Eds.), *Handbook on moral and character education* (pp. 557–582). Hillsdale, NJ: Routledge.

Blasi, A. (1984). Moral identity: Its role in moral functioning. In W. M. Kurtines, & J. L. Gewirtz (Eds.), *Morality, moral behavior, and moral development* (pp. 129–139). New York: Wiley.

Butcher, J. N., Graham, J. R., Williams, C. L., & Ben-Porath, Y. S. (2000). *Development and use of the MMPI-2 content scales*. Minneapolis, MN: University of Minnesota Press.

Colby, A., & Damon, W. (1992). *Some do care: Contemporary lives of moral commitment.* New York: Free Press.

Colby, A., & Sullivan, W. M. (2008). Formation of professionalism and purpose: Perspectives from the preparation for the professions program. *University of St. Thomas Law Journal, 5*(2), 404–427.

Crowson, H. M., DeBacker, T., & Thoma, S. J. (2007). Are DIT scores empirically distinct from measures of political identification and intellectual ability? A test using post-9/11 data. *British Journal of Developmental Psychology, 25*(2), 197–211.

Eva, K. W., Reiter, H. I., Rosenfeld, J., & Norman, G. R. (2004). The ability of the multiple mini-interview to predict clerkship performance in medical school. *Academic Medicine, 79(10 Suppl),* S40–42.

Feudtner, C., Christakis, D. A., & Christakis, N. A. (1994). Do clinical students suffer ethical erosion? Students' perceptions of their ethical and personal development. *Academic Medicine, 69*, 670–679.

Forsythe, G. B., Snook, S., Lewis, P., & Bartone, P. T. (2002). Making sense of officership: Developing a professional identity for 21st century army officers. In D.M. Snider, & G. L. Watkins (Eds.), *The future of the army profession* (pp. 357–378). Boston: McGraw-Hill.

Foster, J. D., Campbell, W. K., & Twenge, J. M. (2003). Individual differences in narcissism: Inflated self-views across the lifespan and around the world. *Journal of Research in Personality, 37,* 469–486.

Gardner, H., Csikszentmihalyi, M., & Damon, W. (2001). *Good work: When excellence and ethics meet.* New York: Basic Books.

Hall, R. H. (1975). *Occupations and the social structure* (2nd ed.). Englewood Cliffs, NJ: Prentice-Hall.

Harden, R. M., Stevenson, M. Downie, W. W., Wilson, G. M., (1975). Assessment of clinical competence using objective structured examination. *British Medical Journal, 1*:447–451.

Henshaw, M. (2006). Service-learning. Oral health disparities and the shift in dental education. In J. V. M. Welie (Ed.), *Justice in oral health care. Ethical and Educational Perspectives* (pp. 261–283). Milwaukee: Marquette University Press.

Kegan, R. (1982). *The evolving self*. Cambridge, MA: Harvard University Press.

Kegan, R. (1994). *In over our heads: The mental demands of modern life*. Cambridge, MA: Harvard University Press.

Kegan, R., & Lahey, L. (2009). *Immunity to change: How to overcome it and unlock the potential in yourself and your organization*. Cambridge, MA: Harvard Business Press.

Lahey, L., Souvaine, E., Kegan, R., Goodman R., & Felix, S. (1988). *A guide to the subject object interview: Its administration and interpretation*. Cambridge, MA: Harvard University Graduate School of Education, Subject-Object Research Group.

Leach, D. C. (2008). Medical professionalism and the formation of residents: A journey toward authenticity. *University of St. Thomas Law Journal*, *5*(2), 512–521.

Lewis, P, Forsythe, G.B., Sweeney, P., Bartone, P., Bullis, G., & Snook, S. (2005). Identity development during the college years: Findings from the West Point Longitudinal Study. *Journal of College Student Development*, *46*(4): 357–373.

Loacker, G. (Ed.). (2000). *Student self assessment at AlvernoCollege*. Milwaukee, WI: Alverno College Institute.

May, W. F. (1999). Money and the professions: Medicine and law. In The future of callings—An interdisciplinary summit on the public obligations of professionals into the next millennium. *William Mitchell Law Review*, *25*(1), 75–102.

Maeda, Y., Thoma, S. J., & Bebeau, M. J. (2009). Understanding the relationship between moral judgment development and individual characteristics: The role of educational contexts. *Journal of Educational Psychology, 101*(1), 233–247.

Mentkowski, M., & Associates. (2000). *Learning that lasts: Integrating learning, development, and performance in college and beyond*. San Francisco: Jossey-Bass.

Monson, V. E., & Bebeau, M. J. (2009, May). *Dental student professional identity development: Themes illustrative of developmental stage differences*. Paper presented at the American Educational Research Association Annual Meeting, Denver, CO.

Monson, V. E., & Hamilton, N. W. (in press). Ethical professional (trans)formation: Early career lawyers make sense of professionalism, *University of St Thomas School of Law*. Retrieved from http://ssrn.com/abstract=1733282

Monson, V. E., Roehrich, S. A., & Bebeau, M. J. (2008, March). *Developing civic capacity of professionals: A methodology for assessing identity*. A paper presented at the American Educational Research Association Annual Meeting, New York.

Newsom, C. R., Archer, R. P., & Trubetta, S. (2003). Changes in adolescent response patterns on the MMPI/MMPI–A across four decades. *Journal of Personality Assessment*, *81*(1), 74–84.

O'Toole, J., & Bennis, W. (2009, June). What's needed next: A culture of candor. *Harvard Business Review,* 54–61.

Ozar, D. (2008). The future of dental ethics: What to hope for and the challenges of getting there. *Journal of the American College of Dentists, 75*(1), 25–29.

Pellegrino, E. D. & Thomasma, D. C. (1983). *The virtues of medical practice*. New York: Oxford University Press.

Pryor, J. H., Hurtado, S., Saenz, V. B., Santos, J. L., & Korn, W. S. (2007). *The American freshman: Forty year trends*. Los Angeles: Higher Education Research Institute, UCLA.

Rennie, S. C., & Crosby, J. R. (2002). Students' perceptions of whistle blowing: Implications for self-regulation. A questionnaire and focus group study. *Medical Education*, *36*(2), 173–179.

Rest, J. (1979). *Development in judging moral issues*. Minneapolis: University of Minnesota Press.

Rezler, A. G., Schwartz, R. L., Obenshain, S. S., Lambert, P., McGibson, J., & Bennahum, D. A. (1992). Assessment of ethical decisions and values. *Medical Education, 26,* 7–16.

Rule, J. T., & Bebeau, M. J. (2005). *Dentists who care: Inspiring stories of professional commitment*. Chicago, IL: Quintessence Publishing Co, Inc.

Rule, J. T., & Welie, J. V. M. (2009). The access to care dilemma: Symptom of a systemic condition. *Dental Clinics of North America*, *53*(3) 421–433.

Snook, S. (2007, August). *Teaching leadership in business schools*. Address at the Annual Academy of Management Meeting, Philadelphia, PA.

Stern, D. T. (2006). *Measuring medical professionalism*. New York, NY: Oxford University Press, Inc.

Swain, R. (Spring 2007). Reflection on an ethic of officership. *Parameters*, pp. 4–22.

Thoma, S. J., & Bebeau, M. J. (2008, March). *Moral judgment competency is declining over time: Evidence from twenty years of Defining Issues Test data*. Paper presented at the annual meeting of the American Educational Research Association, New York.

Thoma, S. J., Bebeau, M., & Bolland, A. (2008). The role of moral judgment in context-specific professional decision making. In F. Oser & W. Veugelers (Eds.), *Getting involved: Global citizenship development and sources of moral values* (pp. 147–160). Rotterdam, The Netherlands: Sense Publishers.

Thoma, S. J., Hestevold, N., & Crowson, M. (2005, March). *Describing and testing a contextualized measure of adolescent moral thinking*. Paper presented at the American Educational Research Association, Montreal, Canada).

Twenge, J. M. (1997). Changes in masculine and feminine traits over time: A meta-analysis. *Sex Roles*, *36*(5/6), 305–325.

Twenge, J. M., & Campbell, W. K. (2001). Age and birth cohort differences in self-esteem: A cross-temporal meta-analysis. *Personality and Social Psychology Review*, *5*, 321–344.

Twenge, J. M., Konrath, S., Foster, J. D., Campbell, W. K., & Bushman, B. J. (2008). Egos inflating over time: A cross-temporal meta-analysis of the narcissistic personality inventory. *Journal of Personality*, 76(4), 875–902.

Weisberg, R. W. (2006). *Creativity: Understanding innovation in problem solving, science, invention, and the arts*. Hoboken, NJ: Wiley.

Welie, J. V. M. (2004a). Is dentistry a profession? Part 1. Professionalism defined. *Journal of Canadian Dental Association*, *70*(8), 529–532.

Welie, J. V. M. (2004b). Is dentistry a profession? Part 2. The hallmarks of professionalism. *Journal of Canadian Dental Association*, *70*(9), 599–602.

Welie, J. V. M. (2004c). Is dentistry a profession? Part 3. Future challenges. *Journal of Canadian Dental Association*, *70*(10), 675–678.

Welie, J. V. M., & Rule, J. T. (2006). Overcoming isolationism. Moral competencies, virtues and the importance of connectedness. In J. V. M. Welie (Ed.), *Justice in oral health care. Ethical and educational perspectives* (pp. 97–125). Milwaukee: Marquette University Press.

You, D. (2007). *Interrelationships and gender differences among components of morality for dental students*. Unpublished dissertation, University of Minnesota

Chapter 8
The Role of Reflection in Medical Practice: Continuing Professional Development in Medicine

Sílvia Mamede, Remy Rikers, and Henk G. Schmidt

8.1 Introduction

In modern times, the works of John Dewey established the grounds for the notion of *reflection on experience* as the basic mechanism for learning and improvement of practice (Dewey, 1933; Boud, Keogh, & Walker, 2000). According to Dewey (1933), "reflection on experience," or "reflective thought" as he named it, is triggered by an episode that provokes a state of uncertainty, perplexity, or doubt and leads the individual to search for possible explanations or solutions. This happens through what he conceptualizes as a five-stage process of reflective thought, which comprises the following: (1) a state of doubt, perplexity, or uncertainty due to an emerging difficulty in understanding an event or solving a problem; (2) definition of the difficulty by thoroughly understanding the nature of the problem; (3) occurrence of a suggested explanation or possible solution for the problem, constructed through inductive reasoning; (4) rational elaboration of ideas produced through abstract, deductive thought focusing on implications of explanations or possible solutions previously considered for the problem; (5) testing resultant hypotheses by overt or imaginative action, thereby verifying whether conditions required by suggested explanations are actually present or expected results from proposed solutions do, in fact, occur.

Dewey (1933) conceived reflection on experience as a learning loop that involves first perception of relations between elements in a problematic, challenging situation, and then understanding of connections between one's own actions and its consequences. Only when reflection provides meaning to an experience can it become a source of further learning. Nurturing and sustaining habits of reflective thought require general attributes such as open-mindedness, commitment to detect and solve problems, and intellectual responsibility for the careful consideration of

S. Mamede (✉)
Scientific Researcher, Department of Psychology T13-33, Erasmus University Rotterdam, 3062 PA, Rotterdam, The Netherlands
e-mail: mamede@fsw.eur.nl

A. Mc Kee, M. Eraut (eds.), *Learning Trajectories, Innovation and Identity for Professional Development*, Innovation and Change in Professional Education 7,
DOI 10.1007/978-94-007-1724-4_8, © Springer Science+Business Media B.V. 2012

any proposed solution. Moreover, reflective thought depends on a skilled mind, able to maintain control over its five stages. Problem setting, for example, often demands careful observations. Appropriately characterizing difficulties at hand requires preventing acceptance of the first ideas that come to mind and suspending judgments until the nature of the problem has been extensively explored. Constructing coherent hypotheses relies on the selection and organization of facts that are sometimes fragmentary and discrepant. Openness and cultivation of various alternative solutions are required, thereby avoiding final conclusions until further evidence about the problem is available. The final stage in the reflective thought process, verifying the appropriateness of any explanations or solutions, demands critical skepticism, questioning of underlying assumptions, and careful searching for relevant evidence (Dewey, 1933).

More recently, other authors have built upon Dewey's ideas to conceptualize "critical thinking." Their contributions highlight affective dimensions involved in reflection on experience. According to Brookfield (1987), challenging one's own assumptions and exploring alternatives are the core elements of critical thinking. Engaging in critical thinking depends on awareness of the context and influences on one's own understandings, the recognition that hidden assumptions shape one's own perceptions, and acceptance of possible alternative ways of thinking. Another essential requirement for critically thinking on one's own practice is commitment to ask oneself difficult questions, to review past experiences and current beliefs and values, and to face the challenge of changing oneself to enable new perspectives and future actions to be seriously considered (Boyd and Fales 1983; Brookfield, 1987).

Schön's influential works on professional expertise generated the construct of "reflective practice." According to Schön (1983), professionals, in their daily activities, make judgments and decisions largely based upon tacit knowledge. In routine situations, actions are carried out largely spontaneously, without requiring prior intellectual operations, guided by what Schön named "knowing-in-action," the characteristic mode of ordinary practical knowledge. Practice, Schön highlights, involves an element of repetition; a professional tends to encounter similar situations again and again. As long as practice is stable, knowing-in-action becomes increasingly automatic and tacit, and it works well, leading to the expected outcomes so long as the situation remains within the boundaries of what professionals have learned to see as normal (Schön, 1983). As a counter-side effect of this "over-learning," however, professionals may become less and less subject to surprise, thereby failing to recognize unusual situations that require special attention. Professionals, indeed, tend to be selectively inattentive to phenomena that elude categories of their practical knowledge. A "reflective practitioner," however, would realize when a phenomenon at hand, such as an unexpected outcome or unexplained problem, does not fit his or her ordinary categories of knowing-in-action. A process of "reflection-in-action" would then lead professionals to surface and criticize their own initial understandings of the phenomenon and reframe the problem within the dynamics of the situation. The decisions to be taken, the ends to be achieved, and the means to be used would be identified. Through critically reviewing his or her initial understanding of the problem and developing more complex representations of the situation, the professional could generate solutions. Their validity would be verified in a next step, through analyzing scenarios and consequences, or pros and cons of each alternative, whose adoption would enrich the professional's knowledge structure and practice. Besides reflection that occurs in the midst of performance, professionals engage in "reflection-on-action," a reconstructive mental review that occurs later on, after the event. Reflection-on-action, Schön suggests, would allow reflective practitioners to return to a problematic situation, reordering facts, and thinking on alternative solutions and their consequences. Attention would be directed not only to reframing the problem, but also to one's own performance in searching for generalizable conclusions. Thus, learning from experience could lead to practice improvement (Schön, 1983).

Reflective practice has been increasingly discussed in studies on professional work in several fields. The literature on teacher expertise has explored the nature of reflection on practice and examined approaches for developing reflective teachers (Francis, 1997; Hatton & Smith, 1995). The notion of reflection as a core component of expertise has also been widely used in nursing, where the literature has discussed the meaning of reflection on practice, skills required for reflective practice, and strategies for its development in student and professional nurses (Atkins & Murphy, 1993; Maynard, 1996; Pierson, 1998).

Critically reflecting upon one's own practice has been emphasized as a requirement for professional competence in medicine. The need to develop reflective doctors has led to discussions about how educational strategies based on reflection on experience can best be used in both undergraduate and postgraduate training (Arseneau, 1995; Heidenreich, Lye, Simpson, & Lourich, 2000; Scott Smith & Irby, 1997; Snadden, Thomas, Griffin, & Hudson, 1996).

The characteristics and attributes of a reflective doctor have also been explored. For example Epstein (1999) suggests that "mindful practice" leads doctors to become conscious of their own reasoning processes, and therefore embedding "mindfulness" into their practice helps physicians to develop the capability to both observe their patients and monitor themselves during their clinical encounters. Physicians' decision-making may also be informed by a large body of personal knowledge, beliefs, values, and experiences that are not entirely known to them. Hence, their perceptions and interpretations of features encountered in a patient's problem are influenced by this tacit knowledge. Mindfulness would help physicians to become more aware of their own reasoning processes by questioning their judgments. Although Epstein recognizes the subjective basis of his construct of "mindful practice," he suggests that its characteristics include general attributes such as an open mind, the willingness to search for their prejudices, the tolerance to examine their own areas of incompetence, all through the "active observation of oneself, the patient and the problem," critical curiosity, and peripheral vision.

The concept of metacognition, suggested by some authors, also emphasizes reflection on one's own thinking processes as a crucial condition for appropriate decision-making in clinical cases. Metacognition requires the ability to explore a broader range of possibilities than those initially apparent, and the capacity to examine and critique one's own decisions and to select strategies to deal with the demands of decision-making in particular cases and contexts (e.g., Croskerry, 2003a; Graber, Gordon, & Franklin, 2002).

Recent research has provided empirical evidence of the nature of reflective practice in medicine. Starting from a theoretical model constructed on the basis of the literature, Mamede and Schmidt (2004) explored the behaviors and reasoning processes of 202 primary health-care physicians when dealing with complex, unusual cases. The findings of this study led them to propose that reflective practice in medicine has a multidimensional structure that draws on at least five sets of behaviors, attitudes, and reasoning processes. Thus, responding to the complex problems encountered in professional practice requires the following skills and dispositions:

(1) *Deliberate Induction*: a tendency to search for alternative explanations, e.g., other diagnostic hypotheses beyond the initial ones that come to mind, when responding to difficult or unexpected problems.
(2) *Deliberate Deduction*: a tendency to explore the consequences of these alternative explanations. Through logical deduction, reflective physicians would, for instance, explore signs and symptoms that might be present if any one of these "alternative hypotheses" were to be true. This could lead to predictions that might be tested against new data.
(3) A willingness to *Test* these predictions extensively against the data encountered in the case at hand and *Synthesize* new understandings about the problem.
(4) An attitude of *Openness toward Reflection* as a means of solving patient problems. Physicians who show this attitude tend to engage in reflective, thoughtful reasoning in response to a challenging problem, instead of just discarding the problem. In doing so, they learn to handle better the uncertainty and ambiguity that characterize periods of reflection.
(5) *Meta-reasoning*: the capability to reflect about one's own thinking processes and to critically review one's own conclusions, assumptions, and beliefs about a problem.

The authors emphasize that these five components of reflective practice do not constitute a strategy to be followed step by step. They represent several dimensions that may overlap and occur in the moment of the action, as well as during reflection after the event as part of a reflexive physician's reasoning. Studies have shown that physicians differ in the extent to which they engage in reflective practice. Reflective approaches are adopted quite often by some physicians when dealing with complex or unexpected problems. But others rarely or never appear to use them (e.g., Mamede & Schmidt, 2004; Mamede & Schmidt, 2005). The factors that compel (or prevent) doctors to engage in reflection are still under investigation (Mamede, Schmidt, Rikers, Penaforte, & Coelho-Filho, 2007). What would be the consequences of these differences in engagement in reflective practice for the quality of clinical judgments?

8.2 Diagnostic Performance and Medical Errors

Reflection on one's own practice has been recognized as a key requirement for appropriate performance in medicine. Value attributed to reflection has grown in recent years as complexity, uncertainty, and fallibility have been acknowledged as inherent to clinical judgments (GMC, 1993; Maudsley & Strivens, 2000). Traditional views of medical decisions usually present them as being conscious applications to particular patients' problems of well-defined rules derived from objective, well-established scientific knowledge bases (Maudsley & Strivens, 2000). In fact, however, clinical judgment is susceptible to multiple influences and usually marked by ambiguity and restricted certainties. Several reasons, intrinsic to medical knowledge and practice, determine this. First, new advances in research continuously modify the medical knowledge base (Maudsley & Strivens, 2000). Second, medical knowledge, despite its continuous growth, will always be insufficient to tell doctors what should be done in a particular case. Doctors always need to interpret the scientific literature in the light of every patient's unique configuration of disease, personal characteristics, and needs for care (Hall, 2002; Kempainen, Migeon, & Wolf, 2003; Tonelli, 1998). Third, doctors cannot be seen as neutral observers that objectively examine and interpret a patient's problem to make decisions. Every physician brings to a clinical encounter a body of knowledge constituted by both theoretical knowledge from medical education and knowledge acquired through experience. This body of knowledge is always idiosyncratic: doctors' experiences, values, and perspectives, often not entirely known to them, influence their perception and interpretation of findings presented by a patient (Kalf & Spruijt-Metz, 1996; Malterud, 2002). Instead of an entirely objective, rational application of scientific knowledge and rules, medical judgments depend largely on interpretation, and decisions are often taken under a certain degree of uncertainty. Clinical decisions, therefore, are subject to failures, which, in reality, are not as rare as the profession likes to think.

Medical mistakes and their adverse effects have raised increasing concerns over the past decade (Graber et al., 2002; Hall, 2002; Kempainen et al., 2003). Reports have highlighted them as important causes of morbidity and mortality, (Bion & Heffner, 2004) and the well-known Institute of Medicine's 1999 report "To Err is Human" indicated that in the USA, between 44 000 and 98 000 deaths per year were attributable to clinical mistakes (Institute of Medicine, 1999). If the lower estimate is considered, deaths due to adverse events exceed the deaths attributable to motor vehicle accidents, breast cancer, or AIDS. Similar problems have been reported in several countries (Bion & Heffner, 2004). Diagnostic errors, which correspond to a high proportion of all medical mistakes, have received particular attention. Efforts have been directed toward understanding the types and origins of diagnostic errors, thereby opening avenues for exploring means for their prevention. According to Kassirer and Kopelman (1991), errors could occur in several stages of the diagnostic process: generation of hypotheses, hypotheses refinement through data gathering and interpretation, and diagnosis verification. More recently, Graber et al. (2002) classified diagnostic errors in three major categories. "No-fault errors" occur when the correct diagnosis would hardly be expected. Atypical presentations of diseases exemplify this first category. Failures imputed to flaws in the health system that negatively affect doctors' performance are described as "system-related errors." "Cognitive errors," the third category, arise from "inadequate knowledge or faulty data gathering, inaccurate clinical reasoning or faulty verification." Misperceptions and misinterpretation of evidence from a patient's clinical history, for example, can lead to failures in the generation or refinement of hypotheses (Elstein & Schwartz, 2002). Difficulties in reframing the initial explanation for a problem have also been pointed out as stemming from underlying experienced doctors' errors (Eva, 2002).

Attention has also been directed to potential distortion of diagnostic reasoning caused by the use of heuristics. Medical heuristics have been defined as "mental shortcuts or maxims that are invoked, largely unconsciously, by clinicians to expedite clinical decision making" (Kempainen et al., 2003). Heuristics emerge from professional experience, personal theories, and medical tradition and do not necessarily have a scientific basis. They may, however, be a powerful guide in the hands of experienced doctors, allowing them to overcome uncertainty and to take timely and efficient decisions (Kempainen et al., 2003; McDonald, 1996). On the other hand, biases that originated from the use of heuristics have also been extensively explored as causes of cognitive errors, and this literature has repeatedly cited examples of failed heuristics that lead to distortions throughout the various stages of the diagnostic process (Bornstein & Emler, 2001; Croskerry, 2003b; Kempainen et al., 2003; McDonald, 1996).

Minimizing diagnostic errors requires understanding the nature of clinical reasoning. Throughout the past decades, research on clinical reasoning has generated substantial empirical evidence on how physicians make diagnoses. Two main modes of processing clinical cases – analytic and nonanalytic – have been shown to underlie diagnostic decisions. Experienced doctors diagnose common problems largely by recognizing similarities between the case at hand and examples of previously seen patients. As experience grows, this so-called pattern-recognition, nonanalytic mode of clinical reasoning tends to become largely automatic and unconscious. Complex or uncommon problems, however, may trigger an analytic mode of reasoning, in which clinicians arrive at a diagnosis by analyzing signs and symptoms, relying on biomedical knowledge when necessary.

Cognitive psychology research indicates that these two different types of reasoning result from diverse kinds of knowledge used for diagnosing cases. According to Schmidt and Boshuizen (1993), medical expertise development entails a process of knowledge restructuring, and, therefore, knowledge structures available to medical students and physicians change throughout training and practice. In the first years of their training, medical students develop rich networks of biomedical knowledge explaining causal mechanisms of diseases. This biomedical knowledge is gradually "encapsulated" or integrated with clinical knowledge. With clinical experience, illness scripts (i.e., cognitive structures containing few biomedical knowledge but a wealth of clinically relevant information about a disease) are formed, and examples of patients encountered are stored in memory. Experienced physicians' diagnostic reasoning is characterized largely by nonanalytic processing that relies extensively on illness scripts, examples of patients, and encapsulated knowledge. Later research (Charlin, Tardif, & Boshuizen, 2000) showed that illness scripts play a crucial role not only in hypotheses generation, but also in organizing the search for additional data and interpretation of evidence, in order to refine hypotheses and verify diagnoses. However, the diverse knowledge structures developed throughout training do not appear to decay but remain as layers in memory, and earlier acquired structures may be used to deal with problems when necessary. For example, physicians have been shown to make use of knowledge of pathophysiological processes to understand signs and symptoms in a patient when cases are unusual or complex and immediate explanations do not come to mind. Indeed, expert clinicians' reasoning seems to be characterized by complexity and flexibility, and apparently different mental strategies are adopted to meet the demands of different problems.

Thus, appropriate decision-making relies largely on clinicians' capacity to think critically about their own diagnostic reasoning, and this attribute is judged to be as important as a well-structured knowledge base (Maudsley & Strivens, 2000). By becoming aware of their own reasoning processes and checking its grounds, doctors can recognize biases and avoid distorted judgments (Epstein, 1999; Graber et al., 2002; Croskerry, 2003b). Reflective practice, therefore, emerges from the recent research on clinical decisions as a crucial process for doctors to use for preventing diagnostic errors and improving their performance.

A physician that is open to reflection tends to recognize more possible difficulties when solving a problem and to accept uncertainty while further exploring the problem instead of searching for a quick solution. By engaging in reflective practice, physicians would bring to consciousness and critically examine their own reasoning processes. Patients' problems would, therefore, be explored more thoroughly; alternative hypotheses would be more easily considered and more extensively verified. Clinical judgments would improve, and errors could be reduced. Although theoretically justified, these statements have only recently been supported by empirical studies. Experimental studies with internal medicine residents have explored the effects of the two main modes of reasoning – nonanalytic and reflective – on the quality of diagnoses. Residents were asked to diagnose simple and complex cases by following, in each experimental condition, instructions that led to either a nonanalytic or a reflective approach. Reflective reasoning was shown to improve accuracy of diagnoses in complex clinical cases, whereas it made no difference in diagnoses of simple, routine cases. When physicians engaged in reflection to solve complex cases, the diagnostic scores were 64% higher than when they solved the cases through automatic reasoning (Mamede, Schmidt, & Penaforte, 2008). In a subsequent study with internal medical residents, this positive effect of reflective reasoning on the diagnosis of difficult, ambiguous clinical cases was reaffirmed (Mamede, Schmidt, Rikers, Penaforte, & Coelho-Filho, 2008).

These recent studies indicate that diagnostic decisions could be improved by adjusting reasoning approaches to situational demands. While nonanalytic reasoning seems to be highly effective for solving routine cases, complex, unusual, or unique clinical problems require physicians to shift to more analytic, reflective reasoning. This statement, however, is not so simple and obvious as it seems at first sight. As nonanalytic reasoning is inherently associated with expertise development, how would experienced physicians, who tend to reason highly automatically, recognize when a problem requires further reflection? It has been demonstrated that physicians do shift to analytic reasoning approaches, but the conditions that break down automaticity are still under investigation. An experimental study with medical residents indicated that, as might be expected, the complexity of the case seems to be one of these conditions (Mamede et al., 2007). However, not only characteristics of the case itself may trigger reflection, but contextual information may also play a role. In another study with residents, the information that other physicians had previously incorrectly diagnosed the case was sufficient on its own to lead participants to adopt a reflective approach (Mamede, Schmidt, Rikers, et al., 2008). It is likely that other factors related either to the context in which the case is solved or to physicians' characteristics may restrict or favor reflection. For example, a study exploring correlates of reflective practice suggested that physicians with more years of practice, and those working in primary care settings in which high standards of performance are not so much valued, tend to engage less frequently in reflection for diagnosing patients' problems (Mamede & Schmidt, 2005).

Reflection upon experience has also been considered to be a key factor for promoting lifelong learning (Boud et al., 2000; Boyd & Fales, 1983). The attributes linked to meta-reasoning in studies on reflective practice in medicine are of particular interest, because meta-reasoning was shown to involve a disposition to continue to reflect about complex cases even after their completion, e.g., a willingness to review one's own approach in cases referred to specialists in order to visualize what could be improved (Mamede & Schmidt, 2004). This disposition to reflect upon one's own decisions after the event has passed exemplifies Schön's concept of "reflection-on-action" (Schön, 1983). Hence, it is reasonable to expect that reflective practice could have a positive influence in minimizing repetition of errors, thereby improving clinical performance throughout life.

Reflective practice in medicine also comprises dimensions encountered in the construct of "deliberate practice" (Ericsson & Charness, 1994; Ericsson, 2004). Research on expert performance has appointed deliberate practice as the key mechanism for the acquisition of expertise. High levels of expert performance are directly related to the amount of professional practice. Experience by itself, however, is not enough to lead to expert performance. It has to be associated with deliberate practice, defined as effortful activities aimed at improving one's own current performance level. Deliberate practice differs from other domain-related activities, such as routine work, in the sense that it is oriented toward the recognition and overcoming of weaknesses in one's performance (Ericsson & Charness, 1994). Thus, deliberate practice is expected to occur when practitioners are faced with difficult or unexpected problems, provided that they have the capability to critically reflect upon their performance in order to identify gaps and deficiencies in their own practices. By engaging in deliberate practice, therefore, practitioners can progressively improve their own performance. Although the two concepts differ in some aspects, several dimensions of reflective practice in medicine can be seen as similar to constituents of deliberate practice. From a theoretical point of view, reflective practice could then be expected to promote expertise acquisition and development throughout professional life.

Reflection is not always an individual process. The literature on continuing medical education has increasingly emphasized educational approaches based on reflection upon practice that takes place in groups. Some well-known formats are the peer review groups that have been largely adopted, for example, in family medicine (Grol & Lawrence, 1995; Beyer, Gerlach, Flies, & Grol, 2003) or the teams of professionals from different backgrounds that work together to continuously review their experience and improve their practice (Rushmer, Kelly, Lough, Wilkinson, & Davies, 2004).

8.3 Implications for Medical Education and Further Research

Research on reflective practice in medicine has generated empirical evidence on the role of reflection in clinical diagnoses. Some implications may be drawn from research findings to medical education, but many questions remain to be investigated.

The relative effectiveness of the different reasoning modes in relation to diverse situations demands further investigation. It is well known that the nonanalytic reasoning characteristic of expert works well in many cases, and indeed the limits of reflective approaches in real life of medical practice also need to be addressed. In the "real world" of medical care, careful exploration of alternatives and critical examination of own thinking may be a hard, sometimes even an unrealistic, task. Clinical judgments may have to be done under stress and severe time constraints. It is also known, however, that there is space for improving clinical reasoning, and hence medical diagnosis, through the enhancement of reflective approaches. Reflection has been shown to lead to better clinical performance in troublesome situations, and there may be a potential for improving reflective approaches that still remains unexplored.

Research on medical expertise has shown that nonanalytic reasoning emerges "naturally" from training and experience (Norman, 2000; Norman & Brooks, 1997). The studies on the effect of reflective reasoning on diagnostic performance suggest that medical education should be concerned with the refinement of analytic reasoning and the development of ability to flexibly combine nonanalytic and reflective approaches. This might include enhancing awareness of factors possibly influencing one's own judgments and ability to critically reflect on their grounds. Studies are still required for exploring whether and how reflective practice could be taught, thereby verifying how effective strategies aimed at promoting reflection in clinical teaching actually are (Smith & Irby, 1997). Training for enhancing metacognition has been emphasized by the literature as a strategy to reduce cognitive errors. Croskerry (2003a) has suggested the adoption of cognitive forcing strategies as a debiasing approach to deal with potential pitfalls in clinical reasoning. Universal, generic, and specific cognitive strategies are proposed, and several of the examples provide replicate behaviors and processes inherent to reflective practice. Metacognitive training for making medical students and practicing physicians aware of potential biases in clinical reasoning and able to incorporate cognitive forcing strategies is suggested as potentially effective to minimize risks of cognitive errors in diagnoses. Other possibilities for improving cognition and consequently diagnostic reasoning have been explored. Reports of successful initiatives in the medical domain already exist (Graber, Gordon, & Franklim, 2002). Further exploration of educational strategies to enhance reflective approaches in clinical reasoning is certainly a requirement and may offer promising perspectives in facing cognitive diagnostic errors.

A key question that requires further investigation refers to factors that trigger reflection and physicians' ability to realize that they face a problem that demands special attention, which would lead them to adopt a reflective approach. Studies have explored some of these factors, such as complexity of clinical cases and contextual information, but there are certainly others still to be identified (Mamede et al., 2007; Mamede, Schmidt, Rikers, et al., 2008). Research has also shown that reflective physicians are more likely to recognize when they are faced with a complex, unusual problem and engage in reflection, but it is not clear how and why they shift from nonanalytic to more reflective reasoning approaches, whereas others seem not to do so.

References

Arseneau, R. (1995). Exit rounds: A reflective exercise. *Academic Medicine, 70*(8), 684–687.

Atkins, S., & Murphy, K. (1993). Reflection: A review of the literature. *Journal of Advanced Nursing, 18*, 1188–1192.

Beyer, M., Gerlach, F. M., Flies, U., & Grol, R. (2003). The development of quality circles/peer review groups as a method of quality improvement in Europe. Results of a survey in 26 European countries. *Family Practice, 20*, 443–451.

Bion, J. F., & Heffner, J. E. (2004). Challenges in the care of the acutely ill. *Lancet, 363*, 970–977.

Bornstein, B. H., & Emler, C. A. (2001). Rationality in medical decision making: a review of the literature on doctors' decision-making biases. *Journal of Evaluation in Clinical Practice, 7*(2), 97–107.

Boud, D., Keogh, R., & Walker, D. (2000). *Reflection: Turning experience into learning*. London: Kogan Page.

Boyd, E. M., & Fales, A. W. (1983). Reflective learning: Key to learning from experience. *Journal of Humanistic Psychology, 23*, 99–117.

Brookfield, S. D. (1987). *Developing critical thinkers*. San Francisco: Jossey-Bass.

Charlin, B., Tardif, J., & Boshuizen, H. P. (2000). Scripts and medical diagnostic knowledge: theory and applications for clinical reasoning instruction and research. *Academic Medicine, 75*(2), 182–190.

Croskerry, P. (2003a). Cognitive forcing strategies in clinical decision making. *Annals of Emergency Medicine, 41*(1), 110–120.

Croskerry, P. (2003b). The importance of cognitive errors in diagnosis and strategies to minimize them. *Academic Medicine, 78*(8), 775–780.

Dewey, J. (1933). *How we think*. Boston: Heath.

Elstein, A. S., & Schwartz, A. (2002) Clinical problem solving and diagnostic decision-making: Selective review of the cognitive literature. *British Medical Journal, 324*, 729–732.

Epstein, R. M. (1999). Mindful practice. *Journal of the American Medical Association, 282*, 833–839.

Ericsson, K. A. (2004). Deliberate practice and the acquisition and maintenance of expert performance in medicine and related domains. *Academic Medicine, 79*(1), 70–81.

Ericsson, K. A., & Charness, N. (1994). Expert performance: Its structure and acquisition. *American Psychologist, 49*, 725–746.

Eva, K. W. (2002). The aging physician: Changes in cognitive processing and their impact on medical practice. *Academic Medicine, 77*(S1), 1–6.

Francis, D. (1997). Critical incident analysis: A strategy for developing reflective practice. *Teachers and Teaching: Theory and Practice, 3*, 169–188.

General Medical Council. (1993). *Tomorrow's doctors: Recommendations on undergraduate medical education*. London: General Medical Council.

Graber, M., Gordon, R., & Franklin, N. (2002). Reducing diagnostic errors in medicine: What's the goal? *Academic Medicine, 77*, 981–992.

Grol, R., & Lawrence, M. (1995). *Quality improvement by Peer review*. Oxford: Oxford University Press.

Hall, K. H. (2002). Reviewing intuitive decision-making and uncertainty: The implications for medical education. *Medical Education, 36*, 216–224.

Hatton, N., & Smith, D. (1995). Reflection in teacher education: Towards definition and implementation. *Teaching & Teacher Education, 11*, 33–49.

Heidenreich, C., Lye, P., Simpson, D., & Lourich, B. A. (2000). The search for effective and efficient ambulatory teaching methods through the literature. *Pediatrics, 105*, 231–237.

Institute of Medicine. (1999). *To err is human: Building a safer health system*. Washington, DC: National Academy Press.

Kalf, A. J. H., & Spruijt-Metz, D. (1996). Variation in diagnoses: Influence of specialists' training on selecting and ranking relevant information in geriatric case vignettes. *Social Science and Medicine, 42*, 705–712.

Kassirer, J. P., & Kopelman, R. I. (1991). *Learning clinical reasoning*. Baltimore, MD: Williams and Wilkins.

Kempainen, R. R., Migeon, M. B., & Wolf, F. M. (2003). Understanding our mistakes: A primer on errors in clinical reasoning. *Medical Teacher, 25*(2), 177–181.

Malterud, K. (2002). Reflexivity and metapositions: Strategies for appraisal of clinical evidence. *Journal of Evaluation in Clinical Practice, 8*(2), 121–126.

Mamede, S., & Schmidt, H. G. (2004). The structure of reflective practice in medicine. *Medical Education, 38*, 1302–1308.

Mamede, S., & Schmidt, H. G. (2005). Correlates of reflective practice in medicine. *Advances in Health Sciences Education, 10*, 327–337.

Mamede, S., Schmidt, H. G., & Penaforte, J. C. (2008). Effects of reflective practice on the accuracy of medical diagnoses. *Medical Education, 42*, 468–475.

Mamede, S., Schmidt, H. G., Rikers, R. M. J. P., Penaforte, J. C., & Coelho-Filho, J. M. (2007). Breaking down automaticity: Case ambiguity and shift to reflective approaches in clinical reasoning. *Medical Education, 41*, 1185–1192.

Mamede, S., Schmidt, H. G., Rikers, R. M. J. P., Penaforte, J. P., & Coelho-Filho, J. M. (2008). Influence of perceived difficulty of cases on physicians' diagnostic reasoning. *Academic Medicine, 83*(12), 1210–1216.

Maudsley, G., & Strivens, J. (2000). "Science", "critical thinking" and "competence" for Tomorrow's doctors. A review of terms and concepts. *Medical Education, 34*, 53–60.

Maynard, C. A. (1996). Relationship of critical thinking ability to professional nursing competence. *Journal of Nurse Education, 35*, 12–18.

McDonald, C. J. (1996). Medical heuristics: The silent adjudicators of clinical practice. *Annals of Internal Medicine, 124*(1), 56–62.

Norman, G. R. (2000). The epistemology of clinical reasoning: Perspectives from philosophy, psychology, and neuroscience. *Academic Medicine, 75*(S9), 127–135.

Norman, G. R., & Brooks, L. R. (1997). The non-analytical basis of clinical reasoning. *Advances in Health Sciences Education Theory and Practice, 2*, 173–184.

Pierson, W. (1998). Reflection and nursing education. *Journal of Advanced Nursing, 27*, 165–70.
Rushmer, R., Kelly, D., Lough M., Wilkinson, J. E., & Davies, H. T. O. (2004). Introducing the learning practice – II. Becoming a learning practice. *Journal of Evaluation in Clinical Practice, 10*(3), 387–398.
Schmidt, H. G., & Boshuizen, H. P. A. (1993). On acquiring expertise in medicine. *Educational Psychology Review, 5*, 1–17.
Schön, D. (1983). *The reflective practitioner: How professionals think in action*. New York: Basic Books.
Scott Smith, C., & Irby, D. M. (1997). The roles of experience and reflection in ambulatory care education. *Academic Medicine, 72*, 32–35.
Snadden, D., Thomas, M. L., Griffin, E. M., & Hudson, H. (1996). Portfolio-based learning and general practice vocational training. *Medical Education, 30*, 148–52.
Tonelli, M. R. (1998). The philosophical limits of evidence-based medicine. *Academic Medicine, 73*, 1234–1240.

Chapter 9
From Nurse to Advanced Nurse Practitioner: Mid-Career Transitions

Debra Sharu

This chapter describes the learning experiences, professional progression and identity formation of UK ANPs by drawing on evidence gathered by the author's longitudinal study of the first year of practice, during which their new roles and identities were developed and consolidated. Learning in Nurse Practitioners (LiNP) was linked to two nationally funded projects (ESRC) awarded to the Universities of Sussex and Brighton. The first project on mid-career professional learning (part of the Learning Society Programme) included nurses' learning at work. The second project, Early Career Learning at Work *(ECLW),* studied learning in the first three years of employment of chartered accountants, engineers and hospital nurses. All three projects had the same three research questions, which enabled a great deal of cross comparison:

(1) What is being learned?
(2) How is it being learned?
(3) What are the main factors affecting this learning in the workplace?

LiNP's answers to these questions revealed a number of characteristics unique to ANPs. Not only were they far from being novices, but they also became innovative, pioneering members of the nursing profession. Hence this aspect of the ANP role resulted in adapted versions of the theoretical models developed by the ECLW team.

The first research question produced a model of learning trajectories specific to ANPs. The second question showed that rapid, or slow, changes in role took many different forms, shaped both by each individual's previous trajectory profiles and by the learning environments in which their changes were occurring. The third research question provided considerable insight into what particular support was required at the various developmental stages and how contextual and organisational factors affected the range and quality of the acquired skills. Of particular note was the pivotal part played by workplace managers and medical facilitators in fostering

---

D. Sharu (✉)
Practitioner Development UK Ltd., Gosport, Hants, UK; University of Cumbria, Cumbria, UK
e-mail: DMSW@pduk.net

A. Mc Kee, M. Eraut (eds.), *Learning Trajectories, Innovation and Identity for Professional Development*, Innovation and Change in Professional Education 7,
DOI 10.1007/978-94-007-1724-4_9,

ANPs' knowledge and skills development. Their enhanced professional persona, the degree of success and the speed at which it was attained were all directly linked to the level of support available to them at work.

9.1 Introduction

The nurse practitioner concept originated in the United States in the 1960s and was imported into the UK in the 1980s. Since its inception, resistance in the UK to the introduction and recognition of an autonomous nurse that practices within a more advanced, independent remit has been considerable. While the new title of Advanced Nurse Practitioner (ANP) has now been adopted, the long anticipated creation of an Advanced Nurse Register has been slow to materialise (Nursing & Midwifery Council, 2009; Royal College of Nursing, 2010). In the meantime, numerous factors have led to practice developments in which nurses have increasingly trained for, and taken up posts as, advanced practitioners. This demand from both employers and nurses has become increasingly prevalent for a number of reasons: increasingly more complex patient requirements, patients' need for more choice and more accessible health care, reduced junior doctors' hours, recruitment and retention of staff, new primary care personal initiatives for medical services, government initiatives and the nurses themselves (Por, 2008). In order to understand the change process encountered by this group of professionals, it is essential to look at the forces that have contributed to ANP professional formation and progression.

First, a shortage of doctors in particular settings has created the need for specialised nurses to provide services previously within the exclusive domain of medicine. This has been particularly relevant in primary care where there continues to be an acute shortage of general practitioners (GPs),[1] especially in inner city areas. This problem has been compounded by the continuing shift away from healthcare delivery in hospital settings to primary care. Longer GP opening times, guaranteed patient registration at a local open practice and more access to nurses at first contact with patients have all been highlighted, along with improved care for patients with long-term conditions (Department of Health, 2006). In some areas, polyclinics are now providing a comprehensive network of community-based facilities in which primary, community and some secondary care services are co-located (Department of Health, 2007; Barr, 2010).

ANPs now work with patients who have urgent/acute conditions and long-term chronic conditions. Hence ANPs require a wide range of skills, a broad knowledge base and the ability to deliver specific aspects of care. When necessary, ANPs confer, work with or refer to specialist healthcare professionals to provide optimal patient care (Royal College of Nursing, 2010). An official definition of their role is the following statement from the UK Nursing & Midwifery Council:

[1] GPs are community doctors who focus on primary care.

> Advanced nurse practitioners (ANPs) are highly skilled nurses who can take a comprehensive patient history and carry out physical examinations. They use their expert knowledge and clinical judgment to identify the potential diagnosis, referring patients for investigations where appropriate. ANPs make final diagnoses and decide on and carry out treatment, including the prescribing of medicines, or referring patients to an appropriate specialist. They use their extensive practice experience to plan and provide skilled and competent care to meet patient's health and social care needs, involving other members of the health care team as appropriate. Advanced Nurse Practitioners also ensure the provision of continuity of care including follow-up visits, assessing and evaluating, with patients, the effectiveness of the treatment and care provided making changes as needed. ANPs work independently, although often as part of a health care team. They provide leadership, making sure that each patient's treatment and care is based on best practice. (Nursing & Midwifery Council, 2005)

Nurse-led services such as Walk in Centres, Urgent Care Centres and Minor Injury Units have also developed in response to the government's agenda and public needs. With the advent of GP contracts, Out of Hours clinics have sprung up along with an increasing number of specialty clinics designed to meet specified patient care targets such as heart and kidney disease management. Meeting the needs of specific patient populations has become a prime motivator in skills development for ANPs. Many are now managing more complex patients due to the increase in numbers of elderly patients. Others have gone on to specialise in areas such as dermatology or cardiology where there are particular gaps in service provision. All of these events have served to increase the opportunities and demands for more advanced qualified practitioners, with ANPs taking the lead in many instances (Lillyman, Saxon, & Treml, 2009).

Changes in the nature of health care have seen both a reduction in the average length of hospital stays and the growth of day surgeries. This combination of changing need and patterns and new technological developments has enabled some clinicians to expand their practice into different areas of work. Traditional skills that were once reserved for the acute care setting and performed by medical doctors have now moved to outpatient clinics and primary health care where nurses, as well as their medical colleagues, are delivering services.

Expansion of nursing roles has also been encouraged by the nursing profession, whose unions and professional bodies have urged nurses both to fill the gap and to practice according to their competence. The Royal College of Nursing (RCN) has been the strongest advocate of title protection and regulation in the UK in order to promote a clear perception of the role by both the health profession and the public. For more than 15 years, the RCN has devised accreditation guidelines for nurse practitioner degree courses and constantly lobbied for official recognition (Royal College of Nursing, 2010). During this time, ANPs have been accountable for their practice in the same way as other registered nurses, and their employers, often local GPs, have been accountable for managing their work within their demonstrated competence. After a considerable amount of time and research into the various options pertaining to expansion of nursing roles, the British nursing board, the Nursing & Midwifery Council (NMC), agreed to recommend the recognition of the broader category in which the ANP role fits, Advanced Nurse Practitioner.

Government support has, however, been limited and regulation of advanced practice is still pending.

When considering the development and expansion of the ANP role, one must also give credence to the motivation and drive that individual nurses have shown in their decisions to follow this professional path. While government and professional drivers have been very significant in the progression of the role, its ultimate success depends on interplay between this new context and the individuals who carry it through. Many of the nurses who chose to become ANPs had very little support from their employers and colleagues. Until recently, those that took up the role often had to fund their own training programme and put in clinical practice time outside the designated working day. This is not a usual pattern for a society in which training and support from one's employer are increasingly expected to be a part of the job, and this highlights the dedication that these individuals have shown in pushing professional boundaries forward (Main, Dunn, & Kendall, 2007).

For many, the motivation has been to advance their career while staying clinically focused. Prior to the introduction of the ANP role, nurses who wanted to climb the professional ladder either had to seek a managerial position that took them away from patient care or became academics, which often allowed them only minimal time to remain clinically active. The ANP's remit emphasises advanced clinical skills that are conducted within an autonomous fashion, allowing the practitioner not only to remain in the front lines, but also to make a considerable contribution to the improvement of the health service. Clinical focus, therefore, has been the primary motivator for ANP role development (Carryer, Gardner, Dunn, & Gardner, 2007). Hence, workplace learning is where the bulk of this development takes place.

9.2 Advanced Nurse Practitioners: Role Transition—an American Perspective

The majority of the research on ANP role transition comes from the United States. Studies can be found as early as the 1970s (Malkemes, 1974; Knafl, 1978), but it was not until the 1990s that work was done on the challenges encountered by ANP graduates. Brown and Olshansky's landmark study (1998) focused on the turbulence characterised during the practitioner's first year of practice after obtaining their master's degree. The advanced beginner stage (Benner, Tanner, & Chesla, 1996), in particular, was found to be especially challenging, as they had to enhance their formal knowledge, establish themselves in the practice environment and recreate their self-understanding of their role as a nurse. Many found that the changes they had to undergo were more complex than those previously encountered in former nursing roles. This was despite having completed the minimum standard of 500 clinical hours required by all US ANP master's programmes.

Brown and Olshansky identified four stages that new graduates experienced. Stage 1, *laying the foundation*, involved recuperating from formal education, negotiating the bureaucracy, looking for a job and worrying. Negotiating bureaucracy included obtaining an advanced practice licence and then sitting a national certification examination. American ANPs work within a well-regulated and well-structured system. They must complete two hurdles, a master's degree course followed by a certification examination specific to their practice focus (women's health, paediatrics, etc.). This examination is generally undertaken once the ANP has gained additional clinical experience. Although British nurses are not required to complete a certification examination or a minimum number of clinical hours during ANP training, the unclear nature of what is expected from an ANP can be a major form of stress at this stage (Sharu, 2011).

Another striking difference between the two systems is that ANPs in the UK frequently stay in the same, relatively small, organisation as before, so they have to transform themselves both in their own eyes and in the eyes of the people that they worked with in their previous roles. On the contrary, ANPs in the United States usually have to seek out new employment when they finish their degree. There are advantages in coming in as a new face, but they still have to prove themselves.

Stage 2 of the Brown and Olshansky model, *launching*, was defined as the first three months of practice in which the practitioner went from being a competent nurse to an uncertain advanced beginner. They began to feel like a legitimate ANP, but safely getting through the day was both an effort and an achievement. This created a great deal of anxiety for the novices, who then started building internal support systems to help meet new professional challenges. Stage 3, *meeting the challenge,* and Stage 4, *broadening the perspective,* were less stressed, because they began to feel more competent and confident, understood the system better and got involved with more complex skill development.

This study, along with other American investigations, has highlighted a number of commonalities in ANP transitions. These include feelings of being disconnected, changes in identities and role relationships, losses, distress and anxiety, as well as feelings of gain, satisfaction and happiness (Schumacher & Meleis, 1994; Brown & Draye, 2003).

A more recent qualitative American study by Heitz, Steiner, and Burman (2004) used a more theoretical model for describing both pre-graduation and post-graduation phases. Instead of mapping successive phases, they formulated six central categories: *extrinsic obstacles* or stressors, *intrinsic obstacles, turbulence, positive extrinsic forces, positive intrinsic forces* and *role development.* Although the central categories were found to be the same in both phases, the defining characteristics differed.

Extrinsic obstacles encountered during both phases involved issues in the clinical site related to events, situations or people. Some student ANPs had negative experiences such as an unhelpful preceptor style, lack of mentoring or staff resistance, and this was often continued after the ANP had graduated. Defensive encounters with others in the workplace frequently resulted in the ANPs having to defend their role. *Intrinsic obstacles* for student ANPs were described in terms of sacrifices (either personal or emotional), self-perception and role confusion (RN or ANP?), and these gave way to self-doubt and disillusion once the graduate entered Phase II (Heitz et al., 2004).

The external and internal barriers encountered in both phases gave rise to alternating emotions and perceptions, which Heitz (2004) described as *turbulence*. Stability was achieved through the influences of *positive extrinsic and intrinsic forces*. *Positive Phase I outside factors* included influences of people such as academic tutors or preceptors, events and situations. *Positive inside factors* were identified as life experiences, acceptance of self-responsibility and 'optimistic self-talk'. For the new ANP graduate, central outside forces focused on professional support by colleagues, networking and approval from lay people. *Intrinsic positive factors* during this latter phase were role immersion, acceptance and 'optimistic self-talk'. *Role development* transpired once the practitioner was able to overcome the negative obstacles and emerge as an independent ANP with a deeper understanding of the dimensions of the role (ibid.).

A crucial factor for successful health provider transition and professional development is the provision of positive support by colleagues, managers, doctors, ANP facilitators and patients. This has been borne out by research evidence from the UK and the United States pertaining to both nurses and ANPs (Heitz et al., 2004; Caballero, Blackman, & Miller, 2005; Steiner, McLaughlin, Hyde, Brown, & Burman, 2008).

9.3 LiNP: A Study of New Advanced Nurse Practitioners Over Time

The first year of practice after qualification is particularly important, because this is when new professionals have to strengthen their practical expertise and develop their new professional identity. While some research has been conducted on this crucial period of ANP professional development in North America, very little has been done in the UK. Learning in Nurse Practitioners (LiNP) was designed as a longitudinal investigation of the work-based learning of a group of novice ANPs, who had just graduated from British university programmes focused on the ANP role. Evidence of both formal and informal learning at work was collected by a series of interviews and observations over approximately one year. This involved two initial pilot studies, preliminary interviews of the 14 ANPs and further interviews and observational visits to the participant's respective places of employment. This data set was amplified by face–to-face and telephone interviews with managers and facilitators.

Although the literature in Section 8.2 discussed the role of significant others in the workplace, the nature of this support was limited to inter-personal relations and paid little attention to the key factors affecting the progression of new ANPs. However, Chapter 2 in this book draws attention to Eraut's work on the importance of the manager and experienced colleagues in developing learning for both mid-career and newly qualified professionals, and LiNP, was strongly influenced by his two major studies. The more recent, Early Career Learning at Work: Project LiNEA (Eraut, Maillardet, Miller, & Steadman, 2006) provided an analytic framework based on early career development of new graduate engineers, accountants and nurses. This research was preceded by the Learning Society project, Development of Knowledge and Skills in Employment (Eraut, Alderton, Cole, & Senker, 2000), which explored work-based learning in mid-career professionals, including experienced nurses. Their conclusions were that the majority of learning was unplanned and unspecified and could not easily be separated from daily work activities. Apart from the individual learner's personal characteristics, the most important factors for learning were the nature of the work, the way it was organised and managed, the immediate workplace climate and the wider organisational culture. Eraut and Hirsh (2007) also argued that the traditional concept of the manager as staff developer needs to be reassessed. Support of learning and professional development through the allocation and structuring of work and the creation of a climate that promotes informal learning should be an integral part of the managerial role.

The LiNP focus incorporated elements of both investigations through its use of a cohort of experienced nurses who were in the middle of their professional careers but were embarking on a new dimension of expanded practice. By choosing this professional pathway, these individuals had been placed in a position that combined aspects of both mid-career and early career development. All observations and discussions were transcribed and analysed using a NUD*IST (N6) computer research package. Categories and themes derived from findings from the two University of Sussex studies were adapted to form a final theoretical framework that addressed three central questions:

(1) What is being learned?
(2) How is it being learned?
(3) What are the main factors affecting this learning in the workplace?

9.4 Contexts for Learning Before, During and After the ANP Qualification

The first pre-requisite for becoming an ANP in the UK is to be an experienced Registered General Nurse (RGN). Many nurses that wish to become ANPs will then enter a B.Sc. or master's-level advanced practice programme. There are no set standards for ANP degree preparation, but the RCN does recommend that certain core courses are included. Basic standards of clinical practice in the workplace are outlined with 500 h suggested as being the minimum requirement. Advanced practice domains and competencies adapted from the American National Organisation of Nurse Practitioner Faculty (NONPF) offer a framework on which to base an agreed standard of practice (Royal College of Nursing, 2010).

A number of universities have been accredited by the RCN, thereby guaranteeing a certain level and focus of provision. However, the completion of an RCN accredited course, or any other ANP degree-level programme, is not obligatory for using the title of either a nurse practitioner or an Advanced Nurse Practitioner (Scottish

Executive, 2008). This has resulted in considerable confusion, because practitioners carrying the same title and claiming to perform the same role will have very different levels of preparation.

This phenomenon has created an interesting mix of nurses who enter ANP courses. Some have been practicing in a more autonomous role for months, even years before proceeding with formal training. Others have had little exposure or opportunity to extend their practice before entering university. This varied background has a considerable effect on nurses' experiences of their transition. While all course entrants are health professionals with many years of experience in the clinical environment, those that have had greater levels of clinical autonomy often feel more able to cope at first. They have essentially taken the first steps before embarking on the official journey (Sharu, 2011).

The concept of autonomy is an integral part of the concept of advanced practice, and the main focus for ANPs is working *autonomously* with patients in the clinical environment (Scottish Executive, 2008). This key motivator for becoming an ANP is intrinsically linked with the concept of an ANP's identity, and their ability to work more independently is seen as the paramount indicator of higher level competence and proficiency. It provides more continuous patient care and offers a better service to their patients and their employers.

All the respondents in LiNP either mentioned this as a prime reason for undertaking ANP training or referred to it over the course of the study.

> Linda: It appealed to me. I felt I could do things independently. It felt very nice to be able to make your own decisions. In the past you just did things because you had to do them. This one was very much a thinking job.

> Beth: I decided to do it. It seemed to be more of a variety of things to do, you were much more independent and you could see the patient through rather than relying on anybody else.

The core concepts of the ANP role are frequently cited as autonomy, pioneering professional, clinical leadership, expert practitioner and researcher (Royal College of Nursing, 2010). All neophyte ANPs in the LiNP investigation supported these perceptions and saw themselves as initially striving to attain four out of these five central remits. Autonomy in practice and expert practitioner were paramount, with promoter of the role and clinical leader as something that came with the territory, something that was part of breaking new ground. Only the researcher role was perceived as less important. Research would be only a very small part of what these new ANPs were doing, but might develop further in the future.

> Tom: To start a new service is part of the role. To boost the image and acceptance of ANPs ...Working clinically as an ANP, seeing patients with undiagnosed conditions, managing them, perhaps referring them on. Educating other nurses. To a large extent clinical on the job teaching of investigations, diagnosing and treatment. No management or research. Not research at the moment, maybe in the future ... To promote the ANP role ... To start new things. Lots of learning, not an easy ride. Certain resistance to it. To show people that Advanced Nurse Practitioners are consistent. To show people about ANPs. When I start other ANPs will start. This will give it a new boost.

To achieve a degree of clinical autonomy, ANP students need to hone their clinical skills and become proficient in assessing, diagnosing and managing patients with a variety of presentations. This can be as simple as seeing a patient with a straightforward skin infection to a patient who has multiple problems such as diabetes and heart failure. To develop these skills, both formal and informal components are required. This is reflected in student evaluations of their academic training and clinical facilitation as ANP students. Technical/medical role behaviours are highly valued by novice ANPs as these are the areas where they feel most inadequate. Thus courses that offer this sort of training are seen as the most valuable, and the theory that relates to everyday practice and the application of practical skills is the most appreciated. This has also been found to be true in other countries (Humbert, 2005; Carryer et al., 2007; Sharu, 2011).

Facilitator support is the linchpin for developing the everyday skills that are seen as central to becoming an expert practitioner (Tanner, Pohl, Ward, & Dontje, 2003; Sharu, 2011). LiNP participants unanimously referred to learning from doctors, specialists and other ANPs that were based either within their practice or within easy access as the best way of learning in the clinical setting.

> I had 5 doctors and I had an ANP mentor as well that I met with once a week. Clinically I learnt the most from one of the newer doctors. He was very good at making things comprehensible. He was good at explaining things. I needed to look at the patient and discuss things. We would have a clinical session almost on the spot.

Although most UK ANP programmes provide formal training in the classroom or online for these core skills, there is no formal requirement for on-the-job training. This is in sharp contrast to the American requirement for all students to complete a minimum of 500 h before qualifying as an ANP (NONPF, 2008). Although some higher education institutions in the United States have clinics attached to the university which provide a ready-made venue for clinical training, the majority mirror the situation found in the UK, where students' support and access to appropriate patients have to be negotiated with their medical colleagues. This could range from exposure to a broad spectrum of patients and problems to a very narrow choice of learning opportunities.

Most higher education institutions expect students to assess their own learning needs, together with their work-based medical colleagues. Indeed this appears to be part of the development of the role. The student has to learn how to access and then negotiate ways of getting what they need (Griffith, 2004). At the time of the LiNP investigation, the novice ANPs had been doing this for at least 2–3 years with varying degrees of success. This appeared to be partly due to 'lucky or unlucky circumstances', but may also have been influenced by the personal agency of the prospective ANPs and their ability to promote themselves and seek out what they required.

The variability of facilitator input was reflected in participant responses. While some were full of praise, others were not. Those that had poor support relied more heavily on peers and had to seek further for the help they needed. This was seen as less than optimal, with several of them leaving their original practices to work in environments that were perceived to be more ANP friendly.

> I did not have a facilitator while I was going through the course. It was more important for me to get through the day. I did visit other clinics and other NPs but unfortunately my surgery did not give me the help they promised. I was supposed to see so many patients and work as an ANP student for so many hours a week but that didn't happen. It was not the best way.

> When I failed my physical OSCE, they allocated me a doctor. They did this for 4 weeks and then it stopped. It was all very hit and miss. We'll give you support in a crisis.

However, the practice manager explained:

> We have had a problem with our student ANP, yes. She needed to be able to inform the others in the practice of her role parameters and areas of competency. The GPs aren't aware of the role. Unless we know what the ANP wants to see, I can't just guess. When she failed the OSCE we were surprised because we thought that she had been taught all that on her course.

The extent to which formal and informal support was available in the workplace was often indicated by the organisation's understanding of the added value that the student ANP could bring to the practice. This was also linked with what the facilitators and managers anticipated would be provided by the academic institutions.

> Barbara's GP: There is no standard role for an ANP. We don't know what an ANP does. We needed a better understanding of what an ANP does. We know what others do, for example Health Visitors and counsellors.

> Beth's GP: Having an Advanced Nurse Practitioner that can work with me and support the practice and patient load is very important. It will benefit all of us. I try my best to find as much time as I can to work with her. I have done this from the start of her studies and of course will continue to do so. Of course I will have to do this less and less as time goes on. It is what we all want.

These issues of workplace support and learning often remain after the students have finished their degrees. Indeed, they become even more prominent as support from academia and the student peer structure dissipates. Novice ANPs in primary care often find themselves isolated when trying to develop their practice further.

There were various reasons why some of the ANPs had a smoother, quicker transition than others. Some of it had to do with who they were as individuals, their level of confidence and their ability to assert themselves. Some of it depended on the micro-politics of the workplace, its perceptions of the nurse concerned and its ability to provide support (Sharu, 2011). Rapid progress often indicated high levels of facilitator and practice support, while slower progress often indicated a lack of workplace support. LiNP found that student ANPs who experienced difficulty in transition had usually received little or no support during their ANP training from employers with only a limited understanding of what to expect from an ANP.

Critical features of the nurse practitioner to ANP transition highlighted by the participants over the year were as follows:

- Learning to become more efficient in the use of their time, and handling patients at a more rapid pace
- Recognising potential urgent patient presentations and how to manage them
- Being able to make independent diagnoses and sound management judgements based on their assessments
- Learning about proper referral systems, when and how to access them within the context of an autonomous practitioner
- Learning a variety of new procedures with different levels of guidance
- Varying levels of support and acceptance from colleagues and ancillary staff
- Limited contact with other ANPs
- Variable access to further continuing professional development (CPD) was often constrained by finances, staffing shortages and the value placed on the ANP by their employers
- Variable access to facilitator support
- Limited opportunities for peripheral learning due to time constraints and isolation
- Negotiating their new roles

Novices' concerns were often centred on these issues. While all participants voiced concerns to some degree, the ANPs who were thwarted in their development and progressed more slowly were understandably more anxious.

Griffith (2004) found that ANP students' experience of their role transition in the workplace involved both transforming the workplace and addressing those factors that affected their learning. A third category, 'pioneering spirit', encompassed the contribution of individual's personal attributes to their ability to transform their workplace and embrace the learning required to fulfil their new remits. Aspects of all three categories were areas of concern for the novice ANPs in the LiNP study, and these did not begin to dissipate until the novices had been in practice for at least six months. Some of these concerns were resolved by the end of the year, while others remained to a lesser degree.

At the start of the study, four main areas were highlighted: striving to make safe and accurate patient assessment and management decisions, being accountable for these decisions, getting appropriate and sufficient facilitator support and recognition and acceptance by others of the professional status of the ANP roles. These areas are reflected in a learning trajectory model adapted from the Project LiNEA study (Eraut et al., 2005).

9.5 Learning Trajectories: A Model for Representing What Has Been Learned

LiNP's response to the first key question 'What is being learned?' was based on complexity, lifelong learning and holistic performances (Eraut et al., 2006; Eraut & Hirsh, 2007). Their data was presented as a typology of learning trajectories that develop and progress or regress in different ways and at different periods over

Task Performance

Speed and fluency
Complexity of tasks and problems
Range of skills required
Communication with a wide range of people
Collaborative work

Awareness and Understanding

Other people: colleagues, customers, managers, etc.
Contexts and situations
One's own organization
Problems and risks
Priorities and strategic issues
Value issues

Personal Development

Self evaluation
Self management
Handling emotions
Building and sustaining relationships
Disposition to attend to other perspectives
Disposition to consult and work with others ***(within the context of the new ANP role).***
Disposition to learn and improve one's practice
Accessing relevant knowledge and expertise
Ability to learn from experience
How to fight one's corner
Self promotion
Becoming a change agent
Developing a new professional persona

Teamwork

Collaborative work
Facilitating social relations
Joint planning and problem solving
Ability to engage in and promote mutual learning

Role Performance

Prioritisation
Range of responsibility
Supporting other people's learning
Leadership/***Pioneership***
Accountability
Supervisory role
Negotiating one's own role
Delegation
Handling ethical issues
Coping with unexpected problems
Crisis management
Keeping up-to-date
Self auditor
Autonomy

Academic Knowledge and Skills

Use of evidence and argument
Accessing formal knowledge
Research-based practice
Theoretical thinking
Knowing what you might need to know
Using knowledge resources (human, paper-based, electronic)
Learning how to use relevant theory (in a range of practical situations)

Decision Making & Problem Solving

When to seek expert help
Dealing with complexity
Group decision making
Problem analysis
Generating, formulating and evaluating options
Managing the process within an appropriate timescale
Decision making under pressurised conditions

Judgement

Quality of performance, output and outcomes
Priorities
Value issues
Levels of risk

Fig. 9.1 The LiNP progression typology for learning in the workplace

a person's whole career (Fig. 9.1). The contexts for using these trajectories are professional performances, which usually need an appropriate combination of trajectories. Hence progression in a trajectory depends on the range and complexity of its contribution to those performances in which they were used. Thus development is more reflective of what happens in the workplace, the type of work carried out and the opportunities and challenges that one encounters during one's career (Miller & Blackman, 2005). While all the practitioners in the LiNP study did not progress at the same rate and there were variations in the focus of their development, a definite pattern unique to ANPs emerged when the participants were interviewed and observed. The items in bold italics were added to Eraut et al.'s (2005) typology to accommodate the LiNP study.

9.6 Patterns of Progress for New ANPs

9.6.1 Just Qualified

The foremost issues of concern for all the novices at the beginning of the LiNP study were *performing correct assessments* and *making appropriate management decisions* for patients that presented with a variety of conditions. Thus their key trajectory areas were task performance, decision making and problem solving, personal development, and role performance. Feelings of preparedness and confidence depended on previous work and ANP training experiences, feelings about their learning and workplace facilitation during their course and their views of the adequacy and relevance of what they had been taught. All the ANPs were unsure whether their skills and their knowledge base were sufficient for the extended remit they had chosen.

> Diane: Examine the patients. That is where I haven't got the confidence. I am so comfortable in my Practice Nurse role ... Drugs. More about primary health care problems. Investigations, blood tests and things like that. Differential diagnoses Patient management for different conditions. That is the sort of things you need to know when the patient is in front of you.

Although the degree of uncertainty varied with each individual, all ANPs voiced major concerns about being accountable and responsible for patients that previously fell within a doctor's remit. They were afraid that they would miss something or make an incorrect decision. Professional accountability and the perceptions that they were taking on greater responsibility made it even more urgent for them to attain proficiency in the demands of everyday clinical practice.

> Ron: I know how to recognise erectile dysfunction. In those areas I have always been the assistant. I have not been the leader in showing people how to use vacuum devices, how to use constriction rings. Things like that. I have never been in position to be that person who is deciding what is best for that person I am now that person and must be responsible for these decisions.

These concerns regarding accountability led to frequent referrals being made to the GPs or consultants during the initial phase of the novices' independent practice. This pattern is not unusual and has been noted in observations of ANP referral patterns and experiences of working in similar roles (Rosen & Mountford, 2002). The implications of making an incorrect decision and being held accountable for that decision were not new for these experienced practitioners, but it was understood that one part of becoming more independent and gaining the acceptance and respect of colleagues was that ANPs would eventually *knock on the GP's door less often.* Fewer responsibilities could be laid at the doctor's door. To be accountable, the ANPs needed to be safe practitioners, become competent and eventually expert, and they needed to make sure that they had the confidence to do this. The most direct way of achieving this goal was *to refer and confer if at all in doubt until they felt they had it right.*

This in turn caused concern for some over sufficient access to adequate facilitator support and knowing when to seek expert help. The challenge was to develop their assessment skills so they could perform these skills more fluently, gradually building them up to a point where they felt confident in applying them to a growing range of patient presentations. These skills needed to be performed in conjunction with accurate decision making and problem analysis, thus highlighting once more the importance of task performance and decision making/problem analysis.

> Learning at the moment, in response to what you see, makes having the GP around very important. Some of the GPs in this practice are very approachable, but others don't want to know. When a resistant one is the only person I can refer to, I find this quite stressful.

All the ANPs also had some degree of uncertainty about the direction that their expanded role would take them, due to the evolving and often ill-defined nature of the role. This placed a considerable amount of importance on being able to define what they were expected to do, frequently having to negotiate boundaries and promote themselves and their new professional persona. Those practices with a clear idea of the ANP role were better able to provide more targeted support.

> Polly: I get prioritised patients. The receptionists are beginning to triage again. I think that they are only triaging minor things to me. They are triaging things like sore throats, earaches or rashes. I would like to see more of a cross section. I would like them not to have to go down the line of what they currently say: Is this something an Advanced Nurse Practitioner can deal with? It is changing their current perceptions of what an ANP can and can't do.

The emphasis on these subcategories and the LiNP typology amendments reflect the groundbreaking aspects of this role. Challenges included learning how to recreate themselves into an ANP, recognising and communicating their limitations and goals, educating others about ANPs and coping with an increased range of responsibility. The categories of *personal development* and *role performance* are therefore of considerable importance at this stage.

While these four areas were of most concern for the newly qualified ANPs, learning in other areas was also progressing. Examples included the following:

Awareness and understanding: The novices were very focussed on their own practice but not on the wider picture.

Teamwork: They were starting to work collaboratively, and many were at the beginnings of establishing a new team and changing work relations.

Academic knowledge and skills: Formal training was put on hold for many who felt that they needed a rest. The use of knowledge sources and artefacts was certainly evident, but reliance on working with facilitators and asking questions was far more frequent. Reading up on patients' conditions and exchange of artefacts were evident.

Judgement: Assessment of risk and priorities was ingrained in many of the decisions that these ANPs had to make, but fluency and confidence in dealing with such decisions in this broader role were yet to be developed.

9.6.2 Six Months Later: Consolidation

Six month into the study, it was noted that the novice ANPs were starting to consolidate what they had learned. The same areas maintained their prominence, but a shift in subcategory focus was noted. ANP levels of confidence and competence were very variable at this point. Those that had experienced relatively smooth transitions with supportive practices were moving at a quicker pace than their less-fortunate colleagues. All, however, were at some level of skills consolidation and were in the process of building a deeper and more extensive skills and knowledge base.

The challenges of *decision making and problem solving, role and task performance* continued to mainly centre on problem analysis, but more complex patients were beginning to be dealt with. When to seek help was not as strong an issue, although access to support was still problematic for some. The range of skills needed was growing in relation to the type of patients the practitioners dealt with. Clinical skills in assessing, diagnosing and managing patients remained the area of most concern. However, as confidence increased, concern regarding accountability decreased.

Challenges regarding role promotion and definition still remained prominent for the majority of the ANPs. Levels of autonomy were increasing, and those that were encountering barriers in these areas tended to leave their practice at this point. Self-evaluation and management along with beginning to build sustainable relationships was coming into play towards the end of the six-month period. Consulting with other healthcare providers within the context of the new ANP role was also starting to take shape.

Learning in the other areas was also noted. Examples included the following:

(1) *Awareness and understanding*: A broader comprehension of the strategic perspective was being developed through the workings of their own personal agenda and the wider perspective of the ANP role and that of their whole organization.
(2) *Teamwork*: The ANPs were gradually developing and promoting mutual learning with colleagues and in some cases with their facilitators.
(3) *Academic knowledge and skills*: More theoretical thinking was being applied, and many of them were increasing relevant aspects of their formal knowledge.
(4) *Judgement*: The practitioners were beginning to look at their own outputs and outcomes as measures of performance quality.

9.6.3 Twelve Months After Graduation: More Solid

At this point on the continuum, the participants were either more settled in their original place of employment or working in their new jobs. They were comfortable when dealing with routine patients at the beginning of this time frame, and, by the end of the first year, they were handling more complex difficult presentations. There was still concern about knowledge and skills deficits in specific areas, but these had become more targeted and appeared less daunting. Credibility with their colleagues and other professionals was established, and autonomy in role performance pervaded practice. The ANPs were working more comprehensively across all eight areas.

The ANPs' dependence on medical colleagues to support them diminished considerably. Many of the participants were seeking out more specialist practitioners. Some had firmly established themselves in their role and were independently referring to a wide range of link health providers, while others were still finding resistance from colleagues in accepting their new role. There was, however, some degree of increased acceptance by colleagues and patients for all the ANPs.

The practitioners had a greater understanding of what their learning needs were, and more of them were seeking *academic knowledge and skills*. Some of the participants were involved with the non-medical prescribing courses, and the continued challenge of dealing with more complex patients remained. Roles were widening for many of them. Some were teaching others, and several were working on par with their medical colleagues. *Role performance* was still a prominent area with the shift more towards increasing the range of responsibility, supporting other people's learning, leadership and keeping up to date. *Awareness and understanding* of the bigger picture was easier now. Many elements of the role had become automatic, so task performance was less of a challenge. Collaboratively working with others had become easier as the ANP became more of a known entity.

9.7 After the First Year: What Next?

The LiNP investigation explored the first year of ANP post-graduate practice, learning and development, but professional learning did not stop at this point. Green, Gorzka, and Kodish (2005) described further learning as a shift in focus prompted by practitioners continuing gains in experience and expertise. Although little formal research has been done on the more seasoned ANPs, the author's role as a provider of short formal continuing professional development (CPD) courses enabled her to gather evidence from six years of evaluations and discussions with ANPs, and this has revealed a number of interesting conclusions.[2]

[2] Practitioner Development UK is a private organisation that offers CPD courses for ANPs and other healthcare practitioners. The author is the founding director.

The continuing trend of constant change in patient requirements and the frequent reallocation of job workload has continued ANPs' ongoing need to update and expand existing skills or develop new ones. The more experienced practitioners still find the opportunity to liaise with other colleagues invaluable. Many work in isolation and find discussion with others on CPD courses helpful either for confirming their own practice or for learning new techniques and approaches from other participants, the lecturers and course material.

Although the experienced ANPs appear to be more self-directed and clearer on their learning needs, managers along with clinical medical and nursing leads continue to be pivotal in providing ANPs access to formal and informal training. This may involve funding, allocation of workload and/or time for attending events and specialty clinics. Many managers and clinical leads commission formal courses with only minimal assessment of what the ANPs actually require. Follow-through with opportunities to reinforce formal learning through informal learning in the workplace is still hit or miss, and this can greatly impact on practitioner expertise development, confidence and job satisfaction (Eraut et al., 2006).

Both formal and informal learning remain key elements in strengthening the success and long-term viability of the role for the novice and more practiced ANP. The provision of optimal opportunities to facilitate this process remains essential for the fostering of professional role development. Employers as well as practitioners need to maintain a broader approach to ANP practice growth, focusing on learning rather than training. We hope that this discussion will contribute to this process and be viewed by other professions in their own promotion of professional development and higher levels of service.

References

Barr, F. (2010). 100 polyclinics to shake-up London. Retrieved September 18, 2010, from http://www.e-health-insider.com/news/5605/100_polyclinics_to_shake-up_london

Benner, P., Tanner, C. A., & Chesla, C. A. (1996). Expertise in nursing practice. New York: Springer Publishing.

Brown, M. A., & Draye, M. A. (2003). Experiences of pioneer nurse practitioners in establishing advanced practice roles. *Journal of Nursing Scholarship*, *35*, 391–397.

Brown, M. A., & Olshansky, E. F. (1998). Becoming a primary care nurse practitioner: Challenges of the initial year of practice. *The Nurse Practitioner*, *23*, 46–66.

Caballero, C., Blackman, C., & Miller, C. (2005, April). Nursing taking action: Symposium on early career professional learning presented at the AERA Conference, Montreal.

Carryer, J., Gardner, G., Dunn, S., & Gardner, A. (2007). The core role of the nurse practitioner: Practice, professionalism and clinical leadership. *Journal of Clinical Nursing*, *16*(10), 1818–1825.

Department of Health. (2006). *Our health, our care, our say: A new direction for community services White Paper*. London: HMSO.

Department of Health. (2007). *Our NHS, our future*. London: HMSO.

Eraut, M., Maillardet, F., Miller, C., & Steadman, S. (2006). Early career learning at work: Project LiNEA Final Research Report for ESRC/TLRP, University of Sussex.

Eraut, M., Alderton, J., Cole, G., & Senker, P. (2000). Development of knowledge and skills at work. In F. Coffield (Ed.), *Differing visions of a learning society* (pp. 231–262). Bristol: Policy Press.

Eraut, M., & Hirsh, W. (2007) *The significance of workplace learning for individuals, groups and organisations*. SKOPE: Department of Economics, University of Oxford.
Eraut, M., Maillardet, F., Miller, C., Steadman, S., Ali, A., Blackman, C. et al. (2005). What is learned in the workplace and how? Typologies and results from a cross-professional longitudinal study. *EARLI biannual conference*, Nicosia.
Green, R., Gorzka, P., & Kodish, S. (2005). Education achieving excellence in practice: A model for continuing education for nurse practitioners. *Journal of the American Academy of Nurse Practitioners, 17*(11), 452–459.
Griffith, H. (2004). Nurse practitioner education: Learning from students. *Nursing Standard, 18*, 33–41.
Heitz, L. J., Steiner, S. H., & Burman, M. E. (2004). RN to FNP: A qualitative study of role transition. *Journal of Nursing Education, 43*, 416–420.
Humbert, J. (2005). Ten years of nurse practitioner education in Ontario. *Canadian Nurse, 101*(3), 8–9.
Knafl, K. A. (1978). How nurse practitioner students construct their role. *Nursing Outlook, 26*, 650–653.
Lillyman, S., Saxon, A., & Treml, H. (2009). Community matrons and case managers: Who are they? *British Journal of Community Nursing, 14*(2), 70–73.
Main, R., Dunn, N., & Kendall, K. (2007). Crossing professional boundaries: Barriers to the integration of nurse practitioners in primary care. *Education for primary care, 18*(4), 480–487.
Malkemes, L. C. (1974). Resocializatoin: A model for nurse practitioner preparation. *Nursing Outlook, 22*, 90–94.
Miller, C., &. Blackman, C. (2005, December). The *shape of the learning curve: Trajectories of workplace learning*. Paper presented at the Researching Work and Learning Conference, Sydney.
NONPF. (2008). Criteria for evaluation of nurse practitioner programs : A report on the task force for quality nurse practitioner education. Retrieved April 17, 2009, from http://www.nonpf.com/NONPF2005/NTFCriteriaWebVersion0208.pdf
Nursing and Midwifery Council. (2005). *Implementation of a framework for the standard for post registration nursing – decision*. Agendum 27.1 December 2005/c/05/160. London: NMC
Nursing and Midwifery Council. (2009). *NMC projects on the go*. Retrieved February 19, 2009, from http://www.nmc-uk.org/aArticle.aspx?ArticleID=3196
Por, J. (2008). A critical engagement with the concept of advancing nursing practice. *Journal of Nursing Management, 16*(1), 84–90.
Rosen, R., & Mountford, L. (2002), Developing and supporting extended nursing roles: The challenges of NHS walk-in centres. *Journal of Advanced Nursing, 39*, 241–248.
Royal College of Nursing (RCN). (2010). *RCN competencies: Advanced nurse practitioners*. London: RCN.
Schumacher, K. L., & Meleis, A. I. (1994). Transitions: A central concept in nursing. *Image Journal of Nursing Scholarship, 26*, 119–127.
Scottish Executive. (2008). *The advanced practice tool kit*. Retrieved March 2, 2009, from http://www.advancedpractice.scot.nhs.uk/home.aspx
Sharu, D. (2011). *Learning in the workplace: A study of primary health care advanced nurse practitioners (ANPs) in their first year of postgraduate employment*. Saarbrucken, Germany: LAP Lambert Academic Publishing.
Steiner, S., McLaughlin, D., Hyde, R., Brown, R., & Burman, M. (2008). Role transition during RN-to-FNP education. *Journal of Nursing Education, 47*(10), 441–447.
Tanner, C. L., Pohl, J., Ward, S., & Dontje, K. (2003). Education of nurse practitioners in academic nurse-managed centers: Student perspectives. *Journal of Professional Nursing, 19*, 354–363.

Chapter 10
Learning from Conceptions of Professional Responsibility and Graduates Experiences in Becoming Novice Practitioners

Tone Dyrdal Solbrekke and Ciaran Sugrue

10.1 Introduction

We invite you to join with us in considering the complexity of professional responsibility. Our point of departure is the moral philosopher Larry May's statement: '*The idea of professional integrity or professional responsibility is intimately connected with the way a group of people comes to regard itself, and the way that society comes to regard that group*' (May, 1996, p. 109). We draw on classical as well as more recent theories on professional responsibility in dialogue with data from an empirical study on the experiences of student professionals in transition from higher education to work life.[1] The primary purpose is to foreground some evidence and speculations that may help us to develop a more elaborate understanding of what is at stake regarding the challenges to 'professional responsibility' by the mechanisms of 'accountability' as we define them.

In most Western societies, professionals with specialised knowledge are assigned particular *responsibilities* and granted a specific status and levels of autonomy to live out the normative mandate of committing to the ideals of putting service before profit, of being willing to handle conflicts between societal and individual interests, speaking out in the interest of the broader society and deploying expertise in

This chapter is an elaboration on an earlier publication: Solbrekke (2008a).

[1] The theoretical perspectives and empirical data we draw on is restricted to the western part of the world in a cultural and political sense. Including perspectives from systems with other cultural and political traditions would of course have enriched, and complicated, the discussion on professional responsibility – an elaboration impossible within the limitations of this chapter. However, even within the frames of European countries, our cultural biases and interests influence the way we approach the problem.

T.D. Solbrekke (✉)
Faculty of Education, Institute for Educational Research, University of Oslo, 0318 Oslo, Norway
e-mail: t.d.solbrekke@uv.uio.no

A. Mc Kee, M. Eraut (eds.), *Learning Trajectories, Innovation and Identity for Professional Development*, Innovation and Change in Professional Education 7,
DOI 10.1007/978-94-007-1724-4_10, © Springer Science+Business Media B.V. 2012

the interest of democracy (Barnett, 1997; Durkheim, 1957/2001; Freidson, 2001; Sullivan, 2005).[2]

Although studies show that most professionals take their responsibilities seriously and strive to do good work, examples of unethical work and ignorance of the social aspect embedded in professional responsibility are also evident (Gardner, 2008). It is generally accepted internationally that trust in professions and professionals has declined. In the absence of trust, reaction to unacceptable professional behaviour is often to impose more restrictive demands for greater (externally prescribed) accountability (Bovens, 2005). This externally driven accountability agenda is motivated by the belief that the quality of professional work will be enhanced in the interest of the public through the adoption of various accounting mechanisms (Dubnick, 2006). The function of strategies deployed by the 'accountability movement' (Hoyle & Wallace, 2009) is to reduce the ambiguity of professional practice by obliging professionals to adhere to, and be accountable for, prescriptive policy standards of quality and making their judgements and performance transparent to the public. While this is a legitimate aspiration, there is also a risk that too much focus on efficiency, flexibility and transparency reduces accountability to a set of managerial requirements at the expense of a holistic professional responsibility (Bovens, 2005). There is evidence from a variety of professions that the mechanisms of accountability imposed by versions of new public management have led to 'technicisation' or 'instrumentalism' and the reduction or elimination of professional discretion and judgement (Svensson, 2008).

Autonomy and professional judgement, however, lie at the core of professionalism and professionals are still expected to 'freely' exercise discretion (Eriksen, Grimen, & Molander, 2008). Consequently, professionals increasingly find themselves living in a maelstrom created in the workplace between competing and often conflicting discourses of professional responsibility as defined by professional bodies and externally defined accounting systems. While this may represent competing ideologies, they also mirror the moral complexity embedded in professional work. Our concern, therefore, is with how professionals as individuals are constituted and

[2] Traditionally there has been a well known distinction between occupations envisaged as 'real' professions, requiring graduate higher academic education (i.e. 6 years in Norway from which the data in this chapter is collected), and those which have been defined as 'semi-professions', building on undergraduate higher education (i.e. 3–4 years) (Torgersen, 1972). These traditional boundaries have been eroded considerably in more fluid contemporary conditions. Current use of the term 'profession' includes a rich variety of occupations performed by specially trained people. Teaching, nursing and engineering are as much defined as professions as the classical occupations such as law, medicine and religion (Eraut, 1994; Evetts, 2003). Moreover, it is increasingly accepted that the identity patterns of professions, senses of professional responsibility and performance of professional work are understood as social constructions and situated practices influenced by the respective professional sphere(s) in which they occur (Brint, 1994; Wenger, 1998). Consequently, features of professions and conceptions of professional responsibility are seen as influenced by structural conditions, motives and ideologies of the discourses of historical time. Despite cultural differences however, some normative characteristics persist that are shared by most occupations defined as professions in the western world (Freidson, 2001).

regulated and how this dynamic influences conceptions of professional responsibility and identity.

One responsibility of professional schools in higher education is to prepare their students for this new and emergent environment. Consequently, issues concerning professional responsibility have become more important, though the extent to which they are handled comprehensively and adequately varies significantly within professional schools (Solbrekke & Jensen, 2006). This chapter focuses on *professional responsibility* and how it is conceptualised and mediated within two professional schools (psychology and law) in a Norwegian university. How is it enacted and embodied by novice professionals and embedded within their respective workplace cultures? It is not possible to provide a thorough analysis of all these aspects, but the examples we elaborate provide important glimpses into the real-world challenges of professional responsibility.

10.2 Theoretical Framework

10.2.1 Current Claims of Professionals

At the beginning of the 20th century, it was possible to speak of professionals as being a more coherent group with distinctive social and moral values. In contemporary society, however, professionals are more varied and perform more diversified and specialized expertise and roles (Brint, 1994; Evetts, 2006). Not surprisingly, therefore, notions of professional expertise and institutionalised role patterns, values and 'heroic' role models are more 'fluid' and contested (Stronach et al., 2002; Bauman, 2000/2006). Additionally, in the flow of rapidly expanding information technology and distribution of knowledge, boundaries between expert and novice have become less distinct and lay people are encouraged to put individual professional's actions under private as well as public 'scrutiny' (Castells, 2000). What is considered 'best practice' is increasingly influenced by the interests and desires of 'customers', clients and patients. Contemporary realities of pluralism and relativism render moral positions contested and contestable. Recent empirical studies indicate that professionals' capacity to carry out work that is both excellent in quality and socially responsible has been challenged (Gardner, Csikszentmihalyi, & Damon, 2001, Gardner, 2008). Some claim that 'flexible capitalism' thrusts professionals towards more individual 'self-realisation' and an instrumental effectiveness of specialised work, at the expense of ethical standards, or service in the public interest (Sennett, 1998). On a normative level, the ideal of 'collectivity-orientation', as defined in the classical notion of professionalism (Durkheim, 1957/2001; Parsons, 1951, 1968), is challenged by the rise of marketable expertise and new forms of accountability embedded within the more recent liberal ideology that strongly influences today's working life (Brint, 1994).

While recognising the legitimacy of holding professionals to account in both public and private sectors (Coghlan & Desurmont, 2007), the consequences and essence of a neo-liberal conceived externally imposed version of accountability have been brilliantly captured by Gross Stein when she states: '*My ear has caught more and more public talk about efficiency, accountability, and choice, and less and less about equity and justice*' (2001, p. xi). By way of response, some professionals have sought to assert 'self-evaluation' as a means of re-claiming greater autonomy in the interest of being able to exercise more autonomous professional judgement (MacBeath, 1999, 2006; MacBeath & McGlynn, 2002).

However, no professional agent is free from multiple commitments, the influence of varied interests of other colleagues, leaders or employers, or from the challenges of differing professional identities and even incompatible epistemic traditions and moral priorities (Abbott, 1988). As previously indicated, while an individual professional is expected to make autonomous choices based on professional discretion, he or she is simultaneously obliged to answer to manifold requirements expressed in terms of political and/or economic priorities (Sinclair, 1995). Goals are often defined by politicians or the bureaucracy at a distance from the professional's workplace, yet public institutions and professions are expected to take responsibility for prioritizing and 'delivering' results in accordance with predefined standards, which still leave individual professionals responsible for the total quality of their work (Lian, 2008; Nerland & Jensen, 2007). Consequently, from time to time, professionals feel 'personally squeezed' between conflicting interests and obligations, because 'Professional responsibility involves regarding oneself as personally accountable for the effects of one's professional judgments and actions' (May, 1996, pp. 109, 110) even when they are constrained within frameworks determined by others.

While focusing on the professional, it is necessary also to be cognisant of the private sphere with its domestic and family commitments that may conflict with one's sense of professional responsibility. Collectively these multiple expectations of professionals result in a rather complex and 'messy' concept of professional responsibility, where dilemmas and conflicts are embedded in the inescapable tensions between responsibilities to clients, professional domain/discipline, society, employer, colleagues, family and/or friends, and one's own professional self and personal integrity. Although these dimensions of professional responsibility are not equally pressing for all, and at all stages in a professional's life and career (Fishman et al., 2004), having to cope with them in daily work is demanding, and may result in professionals establishing priorities that do not necessarily correspond with their ideals of 'good work'.

10.2.2 Professional Responsibility: A Symbiosis with Professional Identity Construction?

While articulating contemporary understandings of professional responsibility, May (1996, p. 27) posits a communitarian or group-oriented approach. Such a method integrates personal, professional and wider societal norms and situates the individual professional in the contexts in which he or she operates (May, 1996, p. 109). It is possible, therefore, to regard individual conceptions of professional responsibility as part of the collective and individual professional identities that are constructed and influenced by dominant social attitudes and norms and the respective profession's position and status in society. Furthermore, May emphasises the necessity to understand individual professional orientations, such as development of conceptions of professional responsibility, in the light of a whole life context. Acknowledging the consequences of living in a 'web of commitments' makes it necessary to understand professional responsibility as *legitimate negotiated compromises* 'that must be reached between personal and professional roles' (May, 1996, p. 107). Moreover, formation of conceptions of professional responsibility is inevitably intertwined with the process of learning and socialisation, the process of becoming a professional (Wenger, 1998). This dynamic process is understood as evolving from both *reflexive awareness* (Giddens, 1991) and *participation* in *communities of practice* (Wenger, 1998). Consequently, personal conceptions are subject to continuous reinterpretation and reconstruction in the light of information that informs professional decision-making at any one time. Consistent with this reasoning, conceptions of different phenomena, such as professional responsibility, are understood as constructed in the interplay between reflexive self-examination, action and dialogue with others in the multiple communities in which they live – a result of the dynamic consequences of the reciprocal interaction of personal and cultural factors in both their potentiating and constraining influences (Giddens, 1991; Shotter, 1984; Wertsch, 1991; Wenger, 1998). Central to this process is *negotiations of meaning*.

The idea of active participation, negotiation as well as reflection, strongly suggests that internalisation of societal norms is a result of a dynamic process whereby the individual gradually comes to identify with the (possibly negotiated) enterprise of a community of practice (Wenger, 1998, p. 295). Such an approach does not neglect the influential force of social norms, values and discourses (Gee, 1999), nor the importance of 'significant others' (Berger & Luckmann, 1966/1991) as role models, but it stresses the dimension of intersubjectivity, social action and negotiation of meaning in social communities (Shotter, 1984; Taylor, 1989). It is through this interactive engagement, the articulation and negotiation of the multiple values, rules and norms of the cultural framework(s), that each individual constructs a personal stance and a conscious awareness, a base to rely on in the immediate decision-making of professional practice. By putting the values, norms and traditions of the communities in which we live to the fore, both Taylor and May stress the need to understand personal integrity as intertwined dimensions of identity and responsibility. However, it is reasonable to argue that the strength of influence from the different socialisation arenas on conceptions of professional responsibility is contingent on the extent to which they provide access to participation in practice and negotiations about the theories, values and practices of the respective professional field (Wenger, 1998). Hence, the culture of a community of practice, its distinct symbols and concepts representing the language, norms, values and enterprise of the particular community, is significant to the individual's interpretation of what is at stake in that community: to whom is one accountable and for whom is one responsible in such circumstances? If public accountability is reduced to 'what is measurable', professional values of *respect, personal regard, competence and professional integrity* (indispensable to the exercise of professional judgement and renewal of a professional identity) can very quickly become compliance, conformity and passivity rather than proactive professional agency (MacBeath & McGlynn, 2002, p. 14).

In professional formation, therefore, the traditions, norms and values of a profession and how concepts of professional responsibility are mediated to students are crucial to their individual conceptions. They constitute the primary touchstone from which students' and novice workers' behaviour and achievements are assessed, while simultaneously providing compass readings whereby students and novice workers can navigate (Ylijoki, 2000). Yet this should not be understood as a one-way influence. Personal orientations, local and private discourses, interact with global orientations and public discourses to contribute to an ongoing change of both individual conceptions and collective norms (Gee, 1999). It is assumed, therefore, that a change of contexts, as in the case of students moving from higher education to working life, normally represents a significant cultural shift and new commitments. It may provide affirmation of one's (pre)conceptions, or it may challenge the conceptions of professional responsibility a novice worker brings from the contexts of education to the contexts of work. The meaning of knowledge and conceptions of professional responsibility developed in the context of professional education have to be re-negotiated in the new communities of work practice. There is a period of 'transition' where a new 'settlement' is sought, and an identity dissonance is re-settled and re-negotiated, thus seeking to find more stability and continuity despite destabilising tendencies. It is necessary to paint dominant aspects of the policy context in which the empirical evidence presented later in this chapter is generated.

10.3 The National Policy Context of Higher Education in Norway

Study participants belong to two professional fields with clear normative and professional mandates: psychology and law in Norway (Bahus, 2001; Baklien, 1976; Heiret, 2003). Both professional programmes are prestigious in the Norwegian context located in a traditional research university, the University of Oslo. The Faculty of Law has been offering a professional programme since the foundation of the university in 1811. Within the Faculty of Social Sciences, psychology has a shorter history. Emanating from the discipline of philosophy, it was established as an independent discipline in 1909. The professional programme was formalised in 1956; thus, psychology is considered a young programme (Baklien, 1976).

Being situated in a university context creates a tension for these two professional schools between the dual influences of the professions and the academy. Professions directly and indirectly influence formal education and its curriculum and assessment systems through requirements of licensing and certification of graduate students (Squires, 2005). At the same time, professional programmes are subject to the standards and requirements of the academy. In this sense, professional education is a bridging institution with one foot in the academy and one foot in the world of practice. Professional education programmes, therefore, are expected to arbitrate and reach an acceptable compromise between these two influencing powers and fields of interest. Moreover, higher education has experienced dramatic changes in recent history. During the past 2–3 decades, expansion has altered higher education from an elite system to one of universal and multicultural access. Students recruited to higher education no longer automatically represent the elite of society (Barnett, 1997; Robertson, 2000; Delanty, 2001). Additionally, the role of higher education has come under increasing pressure from society's interest in providing an adequate number of professionals to sustain the economy. The increasing impact of market forces on the academy has altered the traditional idea of higher education to remain publicly committed (Biggs, 2008; Gumport, 2002; Slaughter & Leslie, 1997). The mission of higher education for public good has traditionally distinguished the enterprise of higher education from profit-making enterprises. However, Gumport (2002) argues that an 'industry logic' has gained momentum at the macro-level as an alternative to the traditional logic of the university as a 'social institution'. Consequently, the university's relative autonomy in determining the significance of different forms of knowledge and defining the content of its normative project of 'bildung' has been reduced and challenged (Brint, 2002; Solbrekke, 2008b). In a European context, the object of the Bologna Process challenges the traditional curriculum discourses of higher education through the discourses of competencies, credit accumulation and transfer, and the new curriculum frameworks enhance mobility, employability and competitiveness (Karseth, 2008).

10.4 Data Sources, Methods and Procedures

As part of a larger international research project,[3] 10 law students and 12 psychology students at the University of Oslo were randomly selected from the senior student population of their respective programmes in 2002, and then interviewed towards the end of the final term of their studies and again after approximately one year at work.

As novice workers, the psychologists were in relevant permanent jobs corresponding to their formal psychology degree qualifications. Two worked as clinical psychologists in child and youth psychiatry, four in adult psychiatry and four in school psychology. One worked in an administrative job in social services for children, and one worked as an organisational psychologist in a private consultancy firm. The law students found it more difficult to secure legal work. Two of them

[3] Data in this chapter are from an international comparative EU project (2001–2004) Students as Journeymen between Communities of Higher Education and Work including research teams from Poland, Sweden, Germany and Norway (Dahlgren et al., 2005). The project was supported by the European Union (HPSE-CT2001-00068) and the involved universities. The data used in this chapter were collected and analysed by Tone Dyrdal Solbrekke in collaboration with colleagues in the Norwegian team: Berit Karseth, Gunnar Handal and Kirsten Hofgaard Lycke.

were still unemployed, and one worked in a non-law-related job in a public service organisation. However, the other seven had jobs in which legal competence was either directly or indirectly of relevance for their daily tasks. Two worked in law firms, one worked in the legal department of a large bank and four worked in public administration: three in executive work related to taxation and one in a job related to immigration.

The research approach adopted was phenomenography, which seeks to describe the qualitatively different ways in which people understand a phenomenon. The main aim was to grasp *what* aspects of the phenomenon, 'professional responsibility', were in the foreground (Marton & Booth, 1997) among students and novice workers and how these conceptions were influenced by their experiences of transferring from education to work (Dahlgren et al., 2005). Elements from discourse analysis have been applied (Gee, 1999) for the purpose of identifying the relationship between the informants' conceptions and issues of professional responsibility in curricular documents and ethical guidelines. However, the interview data constitute the main basis for the analysis. A more thorough description of the method and results of the analyses may be found in reports to the EU Commission in the Final Report of the Journeymen project (Dahlgren et al., 2005).

Interviews with final-year students took place between March and June 2002 and with novice workers between June and November 2003. Among a variety of themes, participants were asked to reflect upon their own intentions as well as the varying dimensions of professional responsibility and to consider how the study programme prepared them for professional work and responsibility. The interviews lasted for 60–90 min, and all were audio-recorded and transcribed verbatim.

Analysis was carried out in two steps. First a raw interpretation of individual students' conceptions and experiences was prepared. This was discussed with research colleagues and led to an overall interpretation of patterns typical for the group in question. In order to avoid determining the descriptions too early, the categories were negotiated and refined throughout all phases of the analysis.

Although aware of different approaches and orientations adopted with other students in other contexts, we were confident that this methodological and analytical approach provided a basis for interpreting reconstructed experiences from the different, but specific, communities of practice in which these students negotiated membership, identity and a sense of professionalism. Some features of the educational contexts characteristic for the groups studied here, and which may have had an impact on their formation of conceptions of professional responsibility, are briefly described below.

10.4.1 The Educational Context of the Law and Psychology Students

The programmes of psychology and law both require six years of academic training which are divided into introductory courses and a professional degree programme where the students choose different courses. While psychology requires much compulsory attendance and collaborative work, law relies heavily on independent study. Psychology requires compulsory attendance at a relatively large number of lectures and group activities as well as some practicals. The mandatory internship period of six months in an external institution in the latter part of the programme is seen by students as particularly important. In some cases the internship period offers practical training in real-world settings, yet there is no uniformity. In contrast, law does not offer any external practice. Although it is possible to include a term of practice as an optional element of the professional segment, only a minority of students avail of this opportunity. Some students gain some familiarity with working life through part-time work in law firms or other organisations. Others participate in voluntary work in 'Juss-Buss', a free legal assistance service. However, the main introduction to legal practice is offered by professional practitioners working as part-time teachers, and not providing any direct and personal experiences.

Psychology includes a 28-h mandatory course in professional ethics in its penultimate semester. However, ethical issues are on the agenda throughout most of the programme, e.g. in colloquium groups and especially when training in practice. The law programme offers a two-day mandatory course in professional ethics.[4] Recommended to be taken in the second or third semester of the professional programme, there is no monitoring of student participation. Hence, the extent to which dilemmas of professional responsibility occur in the cases dealt with in lectures and seminars depends on the actual cases and what is initiated by the lecturers. According to the law students, the moral and societal dimensions of professional responsibility are mainly left to be discussed in more informal ad hoc groups (cf. Karseth & Solbrekke, 2006, for further details about the programmes).

10.5 Professional Responsibility: Academic Preparation?

By the end of their studies, on the threshold of working life, the students in both groups articulate a general desire to dedicate their competence to the needs of others. Vibeke, a law student, illustrates this:

> . . . It essentially means that you should apply your competence in the best interest of others, and that you must never act against moral, ethics and societal interests. . . .

Moreover, they are convinced that their professional trustworthiness relies on their ability to live up to the expectations of being 'specialised experts'. Psychology student Alf exemplifies this:

> As psychologists we enjoy much confidence from society related to solving a good deal of problems that other professional groups so to speak are not meant to cope with.

[4] Currently, the Faculty of Law is revising its pedagogy to integrate more ethics into the programme, to arrange alternative assessment methods and more collaboration between students.

Both student groups foreground the claim to dedicate their expertise to meeting the needs of individual clients, while the law students also include the balance of responsibility between individual client *and* public interest. They rely heavily on formal regulations as their primary 'guide' to responsible performance. The law students refer to 'justice according to the law', and the psychology students point to national health regulations and formalised guidelines, as Guri illustrates:

> All the ethical guidelines are of immense importance. And much is fixed by law, as well – actually most of it.

These comments suggest a more technicist, conformist understanding of a profession's requirements/responsibilities, but this is not the entire picture.

Alongside the moral responsibility for clients, the students acknowledge a *societal responsibility* that is implicit in their emerging professional identity as *academically* trained 'experts'. Having developed a scientifically based competence, they are obliged to make their knowledge available in pursuit of a more humane society. Arne, a psychology student, states:

> With the knowledge we possess and which we no doubt shall gain in the course of our work, we have, as I see it, a certain responsibility to disseminate what we know and write in the newspapers or even better write a book.

Law student Anne promotes a similar conception of the link between academic knowledge and societal responsibility:

> ... because one is a well-educated individual with comprehensive training in how a system works and has to work for society to function.

There is a strong reliance on scientific or academic knowledge as the 'hallmark' of responsible performance. While they all underline personal engagement and empathy as important 'qualifications', the need to be scientifically and analytically trustworthy seems to dominate their horizon. Their immediate responses to professional responsibility reflect what is highlighted in their study plans. In psychology this is articulated as

> the capacity for critical judgment and the ability to see the possibilities and limitations in the application of different theories, methods and research results (Faculty of Social Sciences, 2001, p. 8; see also Solbrekke & Jensen, 2006).

In law the main responsibility is synonymous with being rational and able to *'resolve legal questions according to the law'* (Faculty of Law, 2001, p. 15). As stated in their professional oath as legal practitioners, their primary duty is to *'promote justice and combat injustice'* (Føllesdal, 2005). According to these students, this is achieved by applying the 'legal method'. Clearly, for these students, the basis of professionalism is intellectual capacity, the codified knowledge and universal norms, which are to be applied in practice. It was apparent from the manner in which students spoke about the intellectual 'capital' they had gained through their studies that it was a source of pride and confidence.

Although these conceptions emphasise an intellectual analytical attitude, the students are also 'idealistic' in their desire to help other people and 'to do good' for society. Lisa, a law student, illustrates an attitude common to both groups:

> You have to see the client as a very important person, not because you get money from them, (. . .) but because it is your primary duty to help the person.

What happens, then, to conceptions of professional responsibility when moving from the theory-oriented training in communities of higher education to communities of work – when responsibility is to be lived out in practice?

10.5.1 'Real'-World Encounters: 'Forging' Professional Responsibility?

When comparing the data from the interviews at the end of their studies with similar data after a year at work, there are no *profound* transformations of conceptions of professional responsibility, but there is a notable change in what they now foreground when talking about professional responsibility. There is still a strong confidence in science as the most important hallmark of responsibility. Clinical psychologist Susanne typically demonstrates this when immediately linking professional responsibility to being scientifically trustworthy: *'You must never come up with a sloppy diagnosis'*. Yet the language and terms they use when talking about professional responsibility are somewhat changed. As students they spoke in relatively abstract and theoretical terms. As novice workers, their responsibility becomes 'real'. Their descriptions are more nuanced and flavoured with more personal engagement linked to concrete experiences. This evidence suggests that experiential learning adds a missing dimension to more abstract 'book' learning that alters or encourages the individual to re-negotiate earlier understandings.

Another emergent issue is that the *complexity* of professional responsibility is more evident after a year at work. At the end of their studies, the participants primarily spoke of responsibility in terms of being professionally competent in order to serve the individual clients and/or society. As novice workers they include accountability to their employer, obligations to other colleagues as well as how these have to be balanced with private interests and family concerns. The multiple expectations and commitments that come to the fore also mirror compound conflicts of interest. However, the data show that the intensity of conflicts varies contingent on contextual factors, on the kind of tasks the novice workers are expected to complete and on their commitments in private life. The moral quandaries seem most pressing for those who have personal responsibility for individual clients. Susanne, the clinical psychologist, says:

> I think of the responsibility towards patients, first and foremost. (. . .) I have really ill patients. A couple of months ago I had the feeling that all of them planned to commit suicide. (. . .) It is a heavy responsibility – to make the right decisions.

Even though the great responsibility they were assigned from day one at work was perceived as rather overwhelming, for most of them it also had an empowering effect. For example, the realisation that their clients' destiny depends on their professional competencies and efforts to find the best solutions in each case is experienced as both demanding and an energising force encouraging them to handle scary situations. Assistant attorney Lisa says:

> I can never deceive my client, irrespective of how nervous I am. You have the responsibility for that deprived client sitting next to you [in court]. I cannot back out. I cannot have a nervous breakdown or not be able to talk; it will not work out – for the client.

As the above quotations indicate, most of the novice professionals have encountered demanding aspects of professional responsibility. Yet, and although the learning curve has been steep, the challenges have not been insurmountable. According to them, the theoretical knowledge acquired at university has been invaluable and helped them to cope rather well with most of the challenges at work. Nevertheless, a few speak more negatively regarding what was expected of them. Clinical psychologist Elna illustrates:

> The responsibility was rather overwhelming: Now you are a psychologist and you are expected to know this, that and the other and be able to do various things, and it was rather difficult.

Diverging views on 'quality of good work' were defined as a problem by all novice workers, particularly when superiors promoted solutions and priorities that collided with their own personal values and evaluation. In such situations they are pushed towards a revision of their 'idealistic' conceptions. Assistant attorney Lisa exemplifies how her conception of professional responsibility is challenged when she encounters tensions between the financial interests of the firm and what she defines as her primary responsibility to a client. While she struggles to adhere to standards that she finds morally defensible, simultaneously she begins to (re)negotiate her (pre)conception of professional responsibility. As a senior student, as shown above, she declared how a client's interest must always prevail over financial interest. However, as a consequence of participation in work practice, and as a result of discussions with significant colleagues about economic interests, concrete work tasks and moral quandaries, she apparently moves towards a compromise of her ideals. She even begins to wonder whether her values as a senior were too idealistic:

> I think about the responsibility for the client of course, which is not always easy to attend to. And maybe you don't always understand what is 'best' for your client morally speaking. (...) At the same time I think that maybe my moral code was too high, I mean in a way unrealistic ... I have to face the fact that the world is not such an ideal place and that you can't expect it to be one either.

However, perhaps it is necessary to distinguish between compromise and renegotiation; the former suggests sacrificing some higher commitment in the interest of practice or expediency, while the latter suggests more agency on the part of the individual towards reaching a new synthesis.

10.5.2 Professional Responsibility: Re-configuring Ideals and Embedded Norms at Work

Lisa illustrates the vulnerability of the novice worker's legitimate but peripheral position in the community of practice (Wenger, 1998). She enjoys her job, appreciates her colleagues and aspires to become a full member of her work community. To achieve such a position, she has to negotiate her personal stance in light of the norms of the community. Although confident that she is acknowledged, her position as a newcomer puts restrictions on her own performance. This is illuminated when she has to negotiate with her boss about the amount of payment to be covered by a client and how she strives to keep a 'personal space' for acting in accordance with her own professional values:

> Sometimes I want to tell him to stop nagging about the income. (. . .) But I cannot do that all the time, because then I may loose my position in relation to him (. . .) as a person he actually listens to. I don't want to loose that position, but I will not be compelled to do things I find immoral.

The moral quandary experienced by Lisa, the conflict that may arise between the interests of a client and the claim of efficiency in a private law firm that depends on its income, comes as no surprise. However, the data in this study show that the novice workers employed in public administration or even in the public health sphere also experience conflicts between the claim of efficiency and the ability to provide the best possible treatment for each individual patient or client. The extent to which the experiences of these publicly employed novice workers are the result of neo-liberalism and the system of new public management (Barnett, 2003; Komulainen, 2006) is not possible to determine on the basis of the data of this study. Yet it seems quite evident that professionals in the public sphere are increasingly exposed to dilemmas between being accountable to the 'demands of efficiency' and to what they perceive to be the best standards of good work – a tendency also confirmed by other researchers (Benner, Sutphen, Leonard, & Day, 2010; Brint, 1994; Gardner et al., 2001; Hoshmand, 1998; May, 1996). Even the clinical psychologists responsible for the treatment of seriously ill patients highlight such conflicts between responsible treatment and the demands for increased instrumental efficiency. Elise demonstrates this by saying,

> I think there is too much focus on quantity – in spite of the fact that as a clinic actually we have relatively high production. I think quality gets pushed into the background.

Others point to how administrative priorities and structural constraints have influenced their own expectations of what they would be able to do for their clients. The consequences of such experiences are often 'loss of energy' and reduction of one's own ambitions. Hanne, a clinical psychologist working in a public organisation, illustrates such an experience:

> I believe I was more idealistic as a student. . . . I saw my role as more omnipotent in terms of what I might be able to get done. Had much more will to fight. . . . But the system does not function, and therefore, . . . you have to protect yourself a little.

These comments suggest very clearly that the responsibilities that come with being a practising professional, as opposed to a student professional, imposes burdens and additional responsibilities that oblige them to re-think earlier perspectives. However, their comments also suggest that since, in Wenger's terms, they are on an 'inbound trajectory' into their professional community, power relations are uneven; thus it is more challenging to assert and espouse positions held in the less-praxis-oriented context of university classrooms. Regardless of the outcomes of such unevenly matched professional dialectics, it may be that tutorial dialogues on professional responsibility in higher education need to be more frequent. As the above and other research indicate (Shulman, 2009), most professional schools deal inadequately with issues of professional responsibility. Deliberating on implications of professional responsibility in authentic cases may encourage students to develop 'critical and practical reasoning', thus enabling them to consider what is distinct and unique in each situation (Benner et al., 2010), while also becoming more self-conscious regarding the importance of seeking synthesis rather than asserting positions and perspectives.

10.5.3 Professional Responsibility; Re-negotiated and (re-)Enacted as Legitimate Compromise?

As described above, a hallmark of professional responsibility is a level of specialised theoretical knowledge. Hence, acting responsibly necessitates keeping theoretical knowledge up to date in order to offer clients the best advice or treatment. However, most of the novice workers describe intensive work-days that provide little room for developing their theory base. Alf, a school-psychologist, says: '*I have become a "worker" to a larger extent than I have developed as a psychologist*'. While this represents a potential problem – because they know that their competence as well as societal status and trust depend on the ability to stay updated on theoretical knowledge – at this stage of their careers, they have to reduce their ambitions. They do not find much time to read literature other than what is needed to address an immediate issue.

Another discernible change in conceptions of professional responsibility found among most of the novice workers is that the societal dimension of professional responsibility is 'pushed' aside. Some continue to highlight the need to engage in societal issues, such as the clinical psychologist Elise when she says; '... *dare to challenge the established societal norms and structures*'. But although they still maintain a moral engagement towards their individual clients, they seem to have been 'caught' in the business of their local communities of work practice and responsibility to the extent that concern for the larger society tends to be occluded or to 'vanish' entirely. However, this dilemma is not explicitly identified as a problem by the participants. Nevertheless, perhaps they have lurched from being comfortable in theoretical abstract knowledge to finding a 'home' within a practical epistemic. This existential sense is rendered more intense by their neophyte status and inbound trajectory, while continuing to negotiate their way into reconfiguring their identities for handling some ambiguity within their new community. It may be the case therefore that they are not consciously aware of their changed orientation, or that they do not want to acknowledge such change. The assistant attorney, Lisa, illustrates such a 'reorientation'. As a student, Lisa was indeed concerned with societal responsibility and underlined the need to engage in public debate and seek to influence policies in order to combat injustice or inhumanity in society. She said then:

> You cannot just accept that the rules are as they are, if they are unjust. (. . .) I think you should always take the responsibility if you see something wrong.

However, after a year at work, in the role of assistant attorney, a discernible renegotiation of her concept of professional responsibility is taking place. It appears as though her loyalty to the individual client is given such high priority that her societal engagement has been diminished. She legitimates her changed orientation by explaining that this is what is expected of the professional role:

> Sometimes it is a conflict between the interest of society and the client. Then it is the client who is my responsibility, and the rest must be left to others. We have different roles.

This shift in orientation observed in Lisa's interview appears to move towards Brint's (1994) thesis that current professionals are exhibiting a lack of social or civic engagement while this tendency may also resonate with neo-liberal policy rhetoric where volunteerism, public commitment and participation are on the wane, that cross-nationally more and more people are 'Bowling Alone' while simultaneously hankering after a lost (collective cultural) truth that we are 'Better Together' (Putnam, 2000; Putnam, Feldstein, & Cohen, 2004). However, it may also illustrate a reasonable division of tasks and responsibilities in working life. Professionals have to rely on pragmatic considerations and apparent results when making immediate decisions (Freidson, 1988). Without doubt, all professionals, and particularly novice workers (Fishman et al., 2004), have to concentrate on the tasks that are most pressing. As May reminds us, it may represent a 'legitimate compromise' and a way of 'surviving' in the complexity of challenging daily tasks at work (May, 1996).

Many of the participants in the study are at the stage of having children. Hence, due to family commitments, they balance the interests of family and work. After six years of study, the chance to define boundaries between their work and private spheres appears to be as important to them as the immediate pursuit of ongoing professional development. The possibility to work regular hours and not be compelled to study in the evenings propels them towards what they see as a legitimate negotiated compromise of the 'quality' of work. Most of them do their jobs as well as possible, time permitting, while balancing this commitment with responsibilities to families and/or friends. Psychologist Alf illustrates the balance between doing something meaningful while also living a regulated life:

> It is good to be able to practice what I've studied, to be allowed to go out and do something. Contribute, work and earn money. Live a normal life. . . . I work from eight to four.

Tore, a lawyer working in public administration, decided that although he aspires to becoming an attorney in the future, his first years at work would be in a regulated work situation, because

> I have a daughter who is 8 ½ years old and I want to spend a lot of time with her . . . I have friends who have started to work as assistant attorneys and they work their heads off. They do of course have a good salary, but I am not tempted . . . I work regular hours from eight to four and then I go home.

Such priorities do not necessarily mean that these novice professionals do not take their professional responsibilities seriously. Rather, it suggests that it is necessary to understand professional responsibility in light of all the relationships that exist for a person, '. . . based on reasonable expectations for individual behaviour' (May, 1996, p. 120).

10.6 Professional Integrity: An Ongoing Search for Synthesis?

The foregoing analysis indicates that professional responsibility is not easy to pin down. Rather within the 'global' (Beck, 2000) interdependent world that is increasingly characteristic of our milieu, it is an ongoing struggle to find an appropriate epistemic fulcrum sufficiently secure to form the basis of professional decision-making. The data also suggests that these law and psychology students have every intention of living up to their societal mandate. Although they do not see their future work as a self-sacrificial calling, they want to dedicate their expertise to the needs of others, and the service of society. However, it appears that the shift from the context of education to contexts of work, where the subjects encounter the realities of 'multiple responsibilities' and conflicts of interest in daily situations at work, causes them to renegotiate their (pre)conceptions of professional responsibility. While such re-negotiations might be anticipated, deemed necessary and apposite, the evidence suggests a tendency at this career stage to lurch from a broader notion of professional responsibility to a professional horizon that is overly narrowed to the local and confining contours of the actual community of practice. Nevertheless, it is important to acknowledge that the participants in this study were at a delicate stage of negotiating community membership of a particular professional group and, in so doing, had to re-negotiate newly created understandings of professional responsibility, all of which simultaneously shape the creation of a professional identity – a tall order and a steep learning curve.

In recognition of the complexities and stresses of these re-negotiations, induction programmes in some professions have been created, but there is ample evidence, in teaching for example, that such provision may be overly 'scripted', thus becoming part of an instrumental accountability apparatus rather than being supportive of developing a moral base of professional responsibility (Gronn, 2009). Compliance and conformity to imposed regulations is anathema to professional responsibility and is ultimately disempowering if not critically considered by professionals. Nevertheless, lest this recognition of a moral dimension to the exercise of professional judgement be seen as naive, recent fiscal global implosions are belated reminders of the importance of public regulations and rules. However, while public accountability legitimately require efficiency and transparency, it must accord appropriate importance simultaneously to the voices of professionals and competence embedded in professional judgement.

The evidence in this chapter indicates that novice workers strive to deliver what is expected of them in terms of responsibility for their clients as well as accountability to their employer, while also protecting their personal lives. Living in such a web of commitments makes it necessary to reach 'negotiated compromises'. We are in agreement with May that compromising one's moral stances or principles does not necessarily mean that a professional acts irresponsibly (May, 1996, p. 120). Rather, compromises are most likely necessary in the context of plurality, insecurity and the need for flexibility, because making *legitimate* compromises implies taking into consideration the multiple conflicts of interest a professional is obliged to handle, a requirement to deal with complexity, rather than a more reductionist approach that ignores too many factors.

We are also aware of the significance of language in relation to seeking a more satisfactory resolution to the tensions and dilemmas in the rhetoric and practice of professional responsibility and accountability. Professionally responsible behaviour is contingent on the professional's integrity and a profound understanding of the moral implications of professional work. Thus, there is a critical limit to how far personal stances, professional values and commitments may be (re)negotiated before they 'tip' towards 'illegitimate' compromises. Without a moral awareness of the normative professional mandate, there is a risk that what remains is 'compromised' compromises – and not what results from *legitimate negotiations*. In order to avoid a language which is technicist and confining the meanings of 'legitimate' and 'compromise' to be either legitimate (lawful) or illegitimate (unlawful or against the law) compromises, we have to revive a language of professional integrity (wholeness, soundness, uprightness, honesty). This would not merely seek to barter in the workplace in anticipating a legitimate outcome, but seek to use such tensions productively to generate alternative syntheses, thus maintaining professional integrity that requires both an ongoing community conversation and an 'internal conversation' (Archer, 2003).

Particularly in times of rapid change and the influence of powerful market forces, prospective professionals should be trained – in education as well as in ongoing professional learning – to evaluate continuously and negotiate the core values of their professions and the implications of the unwritten contract with society. It is unrealistic to expect that graduate professional education alone can instil a sense of sustained commitment to a larger purpose. Nevertheless, it is assumed that the context and priorities of professional education and initiation into work are of great importance to the formative experience of prospective professionals. Therefore, professional education should aim at integrating theoretical competence and generic skills with ethical comportment and reflective competence to enable prospective professionals to evaluate critically the implications of their future role (Benner et al., 2010; Morgan, 1994; Sullivan & Rosin, 2008). Perhaps professional preparation programmes need to promote a kind of anticipatory learning through scenarios and role play, whereby prior to entering the workplace, some of the challenges may be rehearsed and the manner in which professional integrity may be maintained, particularly in situations of unequal power. Students need to learn about the price of professional autonomy in order to exercise professional judgement that may run counter to a prevailing 'scientific' epistemic of technical efficiency and accuracy.

In an increasingly interdependent world, part of the challenge to professional schools is to understand and communicate how local actions may not just compromise the individuals concerned; their consequences are often imperceptibly global (Sachs, 2008; Stiglitz, 2006). Perhaps, in combining the local lessons from the analysis here with more global lessons from 'the market', there is a growing realisation that professional responsibility rather than regulation is key. A particular aspect of this responsibility is the ongoing necessity to keep a critical dialogue on professional responsibility going (Barnett, 1997). This presupposes a learning community that provides a shared repertoire and a space for articulation and negotiation of the norms and implications of professional work, while also critically evaluating professional responsibility in practice. Even though full articulacy is unachievable, and self-reflexiveness can never be fully explicit (Wenger, 1998), it is possible to improve one's understanding of what is implicit in personal moral and evaluative languages through social action and dialogue (Taylor, 1989). In May's (1996, p. 20) terms,

> The mechanism for moral growth is this confrontation process, which causes us to doubt our values and beliefs and then to affirm certain values and beliefs that have stood the test of critical reflection.

The realities of contemporary professional lives demonstrate the necessity for professional programmes to encourage deliberations, not to create harmony and consistency but as a way of representing pluralistic attitudes and conflicts of interest that prospective professionals will encounter in working life (Barnett, 1997; Delanty, 2001; Solbrekke, 2008a). In order to avoid capitulation to a 'slide-rule approach', both higher education and the workplace may need to create learning spaces where the dilemmas of professional responsibility can be revisited on a regular basis. Without such provisions, the retreat from being socially responsible may well be precipitous, creating a situation in which legitimate compromises are replaced by self-interested, exclusively client focused professional behaviours that erode and undermine notions of collective-orientation and civic engagement. We suggest that keeping the notion of professional integrity at the centre of such reflective dialogues from the outset is important in keeping the conversation going, but in an open manner, while also signalling the necessity for individuals and their communities to take (ongoing) responsibility for contributing to and participating in the re-shaping of the conversation. We anticipate that a more open, sustained and robust dialectic has the attraction of promoting and sustaining a more vital and vibrant professionalism, as well as richer and more rewarding conceptualisations of accountability that are perceived more as collective responsibility rather than an external imposition or requirement.

References

Abbott, A. (1988). *The system of professions: An essay on the divison of expert labor.* Chicago: University of Chicago Press.

Archer, M. S. (2003). *Structure, agency and the internal conversation*. Cambridge: Cambridge University Press.

Bahus, K. (2001). *Advokatstanden I Norge. En rettssosiologisk studie av advokatene i Norge, med vekt på faglig og sosial bakgrunn, yrkesvalg, arbeidserfaring, inntekt og likestillingsproblematikk.* (The profession of lawyers in Norway. A sociological study of lawyers in Norway, with emphasis on professional and social backgrounds, professional choice, work experience, income and the problem of equal opportunities.) Oslo: University of Oslo, Department of Criminology and Sociology of Law, 71/2001.

Baklien, B. (1976). Psykologprofesjonen og dens omgivelse. (The profession of psychology and its environments.) *Utredninger om forskning og høyere utdanning,* (Studies on research and higher education) *1976:6*. NAVF's Utredningsintitutt Norges Almenvitenskapelige Forskningsråd.

Barnett, R. (1997). *Higher education: A critical business*. Buckingham: SRHE & Open University Press.

Barnett, R. (2003). *Beyond all reason. Living with ideology in the University.* Buckingham: SRHE & Open University Press.

Bauman, Z. (2000/2006). *Liquid modernity*. Cambridge: Polity Press.

Beck, U. (2000). *What is globalization?* Cambridge: Polity Press.

Benner, P., Sutphen, M. Leonard, V., & Day, L. (2010). *Educating nurses: A call for radical transformation*. San Francisco: Jossey-Bass.

Berger, P., & Luckmann, T. (1966/1991). *The social construction of reality. A treatise in the sociology of knowledge*. London: Penguin Books.

Biggs, P. (2008, December 9–11). *The implementation of ethical education marketing*. Paper presented at the SRHE Annual Conference Valuing Higher Education, Liverpool.

Bovens, M. (2005). Public Accountability. In E. Ferlie, L. E. Lynn, & C. Pollitt (Eds.), *The Oxford handbook of public management* (pp. 182–208) .Oxford: Oxford University Press.

Brint, S. (1994). *In an age of experts*. Princeton: Princeton University Press.

Brint, S. (2002). The rise of the "Practical Arts." In S. Brint (Ed.), *The future of the city of intellect* (pp. 231–259). Stanford: Stanford University Press.

Castells, M. (2000). *The information age: Economy, society and culture volume III end of millennium* (2nd edn., Vol. III). Oxford: Blackwell Publishers.

Castells, M. (2004). *The information age economy, society and culture volume II the power of identity* (2nd edn.). Oxford: Blackwell Publishers.

Coghlan, M., & Desurmont, A. (2007). *School autonomy in Europe policies and measures*. Brussels: Eurydice.

Dahlgren, L. O., Dahlgren, M. A., Hult, H., Segerstad, H. H., Johansson, J., Handal, G., et al. (2005). *Students as journeymen between communities of higher education and work,* HPSE CT-2001-00068. Final report. Submitted to the European Commission, Fifth Framework Programme 1998–2002.

Delanty, G. (2001). *Challenging knowledge. The University in the Knowledge Society*. Buckingham: SRHEducation & Open University Press.

Dubnick, M. (2006, May 1). Promises, pervasions and perversions in the age of accountability. *Magazines Business,* 35–38.

Durkheim, E. (1957/2001). *Professional ethics and civic morals*. London: Routledge.

Eraut, M. (1994). *Developing professional knowledge and competence*. London: Falmer Press.

Eriksen, E. O., Grimen, H., & Molander, A. (2008). Making welfare state professionals accountable: The problem of discretion. Paper presented at the 5th Interim Conference of the International Sociological Association: Sociology of Professional Groups. Challenges to professionalism. Limits and benefits of the professional model. Centre for the Study of Professions, Oslo University College, 12th–13th September 2008.

Evetts, J. (2003). Reinterpreting professionalism: as discourse of social control and occupational change. In L. Svensson & J. Evetts (Eds.), *Conceptual and comparative studies of continental and Anglo-American professions*. Research report no. 129 from the department of Sociology. Göteborg: Gothenborg University.

Evetts, J. (2006). The sociology of professional groups. New Directions. *Current Sociology, 54*(1), 133–143.

Faculty of Law (2001). *Law study program*. Faculty of Law. Oslo: University of Oslo.

Faculty of Social Sciences. (2001). *Psychology study programme. Programme of study for the profession oriented degree in psychology*. Oslo: The Institute of Psychology, Faculty of Social Sciences, University of Oslo.

Fishman, W., Solomon, B., Greenspan, D., & Gardner, H. (2004). *Making good: How young people cope with moral dilemmas at work*. Cambridge, MA: Harvard University Press.

Freidson, E. (1988). *Profession of medicine. A study of the sociology of applied knowledge*. Chicago: The University of Chicago Press.

Freidson, E. (2001). *Professionalism: The third logic*. Cambridge: Polity Press.

Føllesdal, A. (2005). *Å fremme rett og hindre urett* (draft). Retrieved January 12, 2007, from http://folk.uio.no/andreasf/ms/Follesdal-juristetikk.rtf. (To be published 2007 as: *Å fremme rett og hindre urett: juristetikkens begrunnelse og grenser,* Oslo, Andreas Føllesdals forlag).

Gardner, H. (Ed.) (2008). *Responsibility at work – how leading professionals act (or don't act) responsibly*. San Fransisco: Jossey-Bass.

Gardner, H., Csikszentmihalyi, M., & Damon, W. (2001). *Good work – when excellence and ethics meet*. New York: Basic Books.

Gee, J. P. (1999). *An introduction to Discourse Analysis. Theory and method*. London: Routledge.

Giddens, A. (1991). *Modernity and Self-Identity*. Cambridge: Polity Press.

Gronn, P. (2009). Hybrid Leadership. In K. Leithwood, B. Mascall, & T. Strauss (Eds.), *Distributed leadership according to the evidence* (pp. 17–40). New York: Routledge.

Gross Stein, J. (2001). *The cult of efficiency*. Toronto: Anansi Press.

Gumport, P. (2002). Universities and knowledge: Restructuring the city of intellect. In S. Brint (Ed.), *The future of the city of intellect* (pp. 47–81). Stanford: Stanford University Press.

Heiret, J. (2003). Profesjoner og profesjonsbegreper i norsk historieforskning. (Professions and concepts of professions in Norwegian historical research) *Historisk tidsskrift, 3*, 201–228.

Hoshmand, L. T. (1998). *Creativity and moral vision in psychology. Narratives on identity and commitment in a postmodern age*. London: Sage Publications.

Hoyle, E., & Wallace, M. (2009). Leadership for professional practice. In S. Gewirtz, P. Mahony, I. Hextall, & A. Cribb (Eds.), *Changing teacher professionalism* (pp. 204–214). New York: Routledge.

Karseth, B. (2008). Qualifications frameworks for the European higher education area – a new instrumentalism or "much ado about nothing"? *Education & Democracy – Journal of Didactics and Educational Policy, (Utbildning & Demokrati – tidskrift för didaktik och utbildningspolitik), 17*(2), 51–72.

Karseth, B., & Solbrekke, T. D. (2006). Characteristics of graduate professional education: expectations and experiences in psychology and law. *London Review of Education, 4*(2), 149–167.

Komulainen, K. J. (2006). Neoliberal educational policy. A case study of Finnish textbooks of entrepreneurial education. *Nordisk Pedagogik, 26*(3), 212–228.

Lian, O. S. (2008) Pasienten som kunde. [The patient as customer]. In A. Tjora (Ed.), *Den moderne pasienten*. [*The modern patient*]. Oslo: Gyldendal Akademisk.

MacBeath, J. (1999). *Schools must speak for Themselves: The case of school self-evaluation*. London: Routledge.

MacBeath, J. (2006). *School inspection and self-evaluation working with the new relationship*. New York: Routledge.

MacBeath, J., & McGlynn, A. (2002). *Self-evaluation what's in it for schools?* New York: Routledge.

Marton, F., & Booth, S. (1997). *Learning and awareness*. Mahwah: Lawrence Erlbaum Associates.
May, L. (1996). *The socially responsive self. Social theory and professional ethics*. Chicago: The University of Chicago press.
Morgan, D. F. (1994). The role of liberal arts in professional education. In C. Brody & J. Wallace (Eds.), *Ethical and social issues in professional education* (pp. 13–28). Albany: State University of New York Press.
Nerland, M., & Jensen, K. (2007). Insourcing the management of knowledge and occupational control: an analysis of computer engineers in Norway. *International Journal of Lifelong Education, 26*(3), 263–278.
Parsons, T. (1951). *The social system*. New York: The Free Press.
Parsons, T. (1968). *Professions*. International encyclopedia of the social sciences (Vol. 12. pp. 536–547). New York: The Free Press and Macmillian.
Putnam, R. (2000). *Bowling alone: The collapse and revival of American community*. New York: Simon & Schuster.
Putnam, R., Feldstein, L. M., & Cohen, D. (2004). *Better together restoring the American community*. New York: Simon and Schuster Chapterbacks.
Robertson, D. (2000). Students as consumers: The individalization of competitive advantage. In P. Scott (Ed.), *Higher education re-formed* (pp. 78–94). London: Falmer Press.
Sachs, J. (2008). *Common wealth economics for a crowded planet*. London: London Penguin Books.
Sennett, R. (1998). *The corrosion of character. The personal consequences of work in the New Capitalism*. New York: W.E Norton & Company.
Shotter, J. (1984). *Social accountability & selfhood*. Oxford: Basil Blackwell.
Shulman, L. (2009). Foreword. In S. Sheppard, K. Macatangay, A. Colby, & W. B. Sullivan (Eds.), *Educating engineers. Designing for the future of the field* (pp. vii–xi). San Fransisco: Jossey-Bass, The Carnegie Foundation for the Advancement of Teaching.
Sinclair, A. (1995). The chameleon of accountability: Forms and discourses. *Accounting Organisations and Society, 20*(2–3), 219–237.
Slaughter, S., & Leslie, L. (1997). *Academic capitalism*. Baltimore: John Hopkins University Press.
Solbrekke, T. D. (2007). *Understanding conceptions of professional responsibility*. Doctoral Dissertation, Series of dissertations submitted to the Faculty of Education, University of Oslo, No. 88.
Solbrekke, T. D. (2008a). Professional responsibility as legitimate compromises – from communities of education to communities of work. *Studies in Higher Education 33*(4), 485–500.
Solbrekke, T. D. (2008b). Educating for professional responsibility – a normative dimension of higher education. *Educating towards civic and professional responsibility – The future of higher education? Utbildning & Demokrati (Education & Democracy), 2*, 73–96.
Solbrekke, T. D., & Jensen, K. (2006). Learning the moral order of professions; the contrasting approaches of nursing and clinical psychology. *Learning in Health and Social Care, 5*(4), 181–193.
Squires, G. (2005). Art science and the professions. *Studies in Higher Education, 30*(2), 127–136.
Stiglitz, J. (2006). *Making globalization work*. London: Penguin.
Stronach, I., Corbin, B., McNamara, O., Stark, S., & Warne, T. (2002). Towards an uncertain politics of professionalism: teachers and nurse identities in flux. *Journal of Educational Policy, 17*(1), 109–138.
Sullivan, W. (2005). *Work and integrity. The crisis and promise of professionalism in America*. San Fransisco: Jossey-Bass.
Sullivan, W., & Rosin, M.S. (Eds.). (2008). *A new agenda for higher education. shaping a life of the mind for practice*. San Fransisco: Jossey-Bass, The Carnegie Foundation for the Advancement of Teaching.
Svensson, L. (2008). *Professions and accountability. Challenges to professional control and collegiality*. Paper presentert på den 5th Interim Conference of the International Sociological

Association: Sociology of Professional Groups. Challenges to professionalism. Limits and benefits of the professional model. Centre for the Study of Professions, Oslo University College, Oslo, 12th–13th September 2008.

Taylor, C. (1989). *Sources of the self: The making of modern identity,* Cambridge: Cambridge University Press.

Torgersen, U. (1972). *Profesjonssosiologi. (The sociology of professions)* Oslo: Universitetsforlaget.

Wenger, E. (1998). *Communities of practice. Learning, meaning, and identity*. Cambridge: Cambridge University Press.

Wertsch. J. V. (1991). *Voices of the mind. A sociocultural approach to mediated action*. Cambridge: Harvard University Press.

Ylijoki, O-H. (2000). Disciplinary cultures and the morals order of studying – A case-study of four Finnish university departments. *Higher Education, 39*, 339–362.

Chapter 11
Learning Communities of Surgeons in Mid-Career Transformation

Jan Armstrong

11.1 Qualitative Approaches to the Study of Professional Communities and the Challenges of "Studying-Up"

Adult development involves growth, change, gains, and losses throughout the life span. As individuals develop, they do so in contexts characterized by relationships to people, places, objects, and culturally defined practices and symbolic systems. This has important implications for the study of professional learning through the life span. Identity, learning, adaptation, and transformation reside not only within individual bodies and brains but also within the settings and relational networks that constrain and direct our modes of thought and action (Chaiklin & Lave, 1993; Epstein, 1990; Lave & Wenger, 1991). Naturalistic and qualitative research methods are well suited to the study of professional lives-in-context, providing well-established strategies for understanding the social world. The study described in this chapter used a qualitative approach to study general surgeons as they experienced a sweeping transformation of their core professional skills. It employed a qualitative, field-based approach for understanding an elite and relatively inaccessible professional community undergoing rapid technological change.

11.1.1 Qualitative Research Methods: A Brief Overview

Qualitative researchers observe, describe, and interpret human experiences and activities, placing these phenomena within a wider cultural and societal context. They employ a number of different methods: direct observation, participant observation, case studies, grounded theory, unobtrusive methods, ethnography, documentary analysis, and field research methods. Typically, researchers draw upon observations, interviews, and other sources of descriptive data as well as their own

J. Armstrong (✉)
College of Education, University of New Mexico, Albuquerque, NM 87131, USA
e-mail: jka@unm.edu

A. Mc Kee, M. Eraut (eds.), *Learning Trajectories, Innovation and Identity for Professional Development*, Innovation and Change in Professional Education 7,
DOI 10.1007/978-94-007-1724-4_11, © Springer Science+Business Media B.V. 2012

personal ("subjective") experiences and reflections, to create engaging descriptions of the human experience. Qualitative research methods are useful when there are no pertinent theories or theoretical frameworks available and when limited information is available about the people, groups, or social phenomena of interest. Such designs produce insights that might eventually lead to the creation of new theories, particularly local theories pertinent to specific groups and settings. Those of us who work in this tradition *deploy* theories as they interpret and describe findings, often articulating multiple interpretations of the same data set. Qualitative researchers collect and analyze data concurrently in a process that is *iterative* rather than sequential, using a variety of verification strategies to ensure that data are trustworthy and conclusions are warranted. We are generally less concerned with objectivity in the traditional sense than with achieving rigor through deep and prolonged engagement with the people and settings investigated (Armstrong, 2010; Dowling, 2006; Macbeth, 2001). Most importantly, qualitative researchers have made significant contributions to the study of postmodern identities (Gergen, 1991, 2001; Hoffman, 1998; Strauss, 1997) and professional life.

11.1.2 Qualitative Research on Professional Communities

Sociologists have produced rich descriptions of professional socialization in medicine (Bosk, 1979; Zetka, 2003), law (Guinier, Fine, & Balin, 1997; see also Seron & Sibley, 2004), finance (Blair-Loy, 2003), business (Kanter, 1977), education and social work. Anthropologists of education have focused primarily on professionals in school and university settings. For example, Harry Wolcott (1984) wrote a classic ethnography about a school principal; Hugh Mehan (1993) examined the social construction of learning disabilities, providing a detailed micro-ethnographic description of a multidisciplinary professional team. And many anthropologists have written about school teachers (e.g., Eddy, 1969; Jackson, 1968; Rogers, 2002; Spindler & Spindler, 2000). Though anthropologists of education remain tied to traditional school contexts, there are exceptions to this general rule. For example, Mike Rose (1999) studied physical therapists; Priyadharshini (2003) investigated an Indian MBA program, and Susan Urston Philips (1982) examined how law students acquired "the cant" in law school.

Cultural anthropologists have cast a wider net, studying professionals in diverse fields. Many of these studies have been conducted within the "science, technology and society (STS) studies" tradition. Sharon Traweek (1988) investigated the lives of high-energy particle physicists in the United States and Japan. Gary Downey (1998) and Diana Forsythe (2001) studied computer engineers. Anthropologists and sociologists of medicine have produced another large body of literature on professional communities. Illustrative studies include works on medical students (Becker, 1976; Konner, 1988), surgeons (Bosk, 1979; Cassell, 1990, 1996; Katz, 1998; Zetka, 2003), nurses (Chambliss, 1996; Maeve, 1998), and psychiatrists (Luhrman, 2001).

11.1.3 The Hazards of Studying-Up

Although there is a rich tradition of qualitative research on professional communities, there are special challenges faced by those who pursue this pathway. Laura Nader (1969) coined the term "studying-up" to refer to projects directed at understanding those at the top of the status hierarchy, whose daily activities and decision making exert a powerful effect on those below. In the United States, ethnographic and field-based studies have typically focused on people who are of lower status and less powerful than the researchers who study them. It is likely that *studying-down* will remain the dominant focus for anthropologists and sociologists of education. This may be linked to the identity issues encountered by researchers engaging with elite groups. Priyadharshini (2003) provided a rigorous and insightful "reflexive" analysis of identity issues for researchers who set out to study professional communities. Her analysis links discipline-wide resistance to studying elite groups to the unsettling impact such work may have on the researcher's self-image. Priyadharshini's reflexive self-critique mirrored methodological strategies now widely used by educational anthropologists, but less often employed by researchers who study education in the professions. She inferred that research on high-status individuals can be unsettling for researchers. My own experiences as a researcher support her claims (Gamradt, 1998). The weaknesses of "those below" can be explained (and forgiven?) by virtue of participants' lack of access to power (education, money, political influence). It is more difficult for researchers to grasp, and come to terms with (and accept) the failings of those above us—those to whom we entrust our own health and welfare. Given the complexity of such work, the problem of distinguishing between learning from mistakes and denying responsibility for foreseeable disasters can be difficult to discern. Such awareness might, indeed, make us more aware of the inescapability and pervasiveness of risk in contemporary life (Beck, 1992), lowering our personal self-confidence and raising anxiety. On the other hand, the political economy of academic work in the United States may simply provide more incentives for investigating institutional settings from the point of view of students, clients, and patients (rather than focusing on the professionals who care for them). It is noteworthy that there is a stronger tradition of studying elite and managerial groups in Europe (e.g., Eraut, Alderton, Cole, & Senker, 2000; Chapter 2, this volume).

Summing up, understanding professional communities from the ground up through field-based research, and placing those we study "in context," is an enterprise that is both technically and psychologically demanding. Those who study professional communities need to consider how the privileging of research on "those below" and the challenges of "studying-up" impact our own work and developmental growth as individuals and members of a nascent field. The next section provides some historical background pertinent to my study, followed by sections describing research methods and findings.

11.2 The Rise of Minimally Invasive Surgery: A Brief History

With the introduction of minimally invasive surgical techniques in the early 1990s, some basic principles of surgical practice were challenged and revised, and the culture of surgeons entered into a new, technology-intensive era (Zetka, 2003). The day of the cyborg-surgeon, operating at a distance through small incisions in the patient's abdomen, had arrived. Although medical professionals often need to learn new things, the advent of minimally invasive (laparoscopic) abdominal and pelvic surgery created an unprecedented situation for the surgical community. In 1987, Philip Mouret performed the first video-assisted, minimally invasive gallbladder removal (laparoscopic cholecystectomy) in Lyons, France. Mouret was a community physician and not affiliated with a university medical center. The significance of his work was not immediately recognized. Francois Dubois, a proponent for the "mini-cholecystectomy" (open, small incision) procedure, trained with Mouret, and performed his first laparoscopic cholecystectomy operation in 1988. His group subsequently published an early report on a series of 36 cases (Dubois, Icard, Berthelot, & Levard, 1990). In North America, the pioneers of laparoscopic cholecystectomy were community surgeons in private practice: J. Barry McKernan and William Saye of Marietta, Georgia; Eddie Reddick and Douglas Olsen of Nashville, Tennessee; and Leonard Schultz and Jack Graber of Minneapolis, Minnesota. As a consequence, in North America, the first centers of knowledge production and transmission for this new operation were located outside academic (research university) medical institutions.

In the beginning, there were no journal articles to read, no "prospective randomized studies," no data collected by disinterested parties. All that was available was clinical information compiled by the community surgeons who had invented the technique. These inventive physicians, with the assistance of industry, created temporary educational institutions that marketed hands-on training in the new procedure. For example, Eddie Reddick, who published the first series of laparoscopic cholecystectomies in the United States (Reddick & Olsen, 1989; Reddick et al., 1989), was active on the laser surgery teaching circuit when he began using laparoscopic techniques to remove gallbladders in human patients. With Bill Saye, he established the Advanced Laparoscopic Training Center (ALTC) in Marietta, Georgia, which offered basic and advanced training workshops for gynecologists and general surgeons. In the early 1990s, he divided his time between his surgical practice in Nashville, the ALTC, and collaborative work with industry. Schultz, Graber, and colleague Joseph Pietrafitta conducted monthly laparoscopic training workshops in Minneapolis and Phoenix. Schultz, like Reddick, was involved in the laser surgery teaching circuit, teaching other general surgeons how to use surgical lasers.

In the early 1990s, the cost of a two- or three-day laparoscopic abdominal surgery workshop was just under $3,000, excluding hotel and air fare. These workshops were places in which new knowledge and technical skills were transmitted to mid-career trainees who had relinquished their customary roles as expert practitioners and become novices again for two or three days. Separated from the demands of everyday surgical practice, the trainees became "liminaries" (Turner, 1977), participants in a ritual process that transformed them from one professional status to another, from low-tech to hi-tech surgeon.

11.3 Methods

In this ethnographic study, I attended 35 two- or three-day surgical training workshops offered across six independent training program sites in various regions of the United States.[1] The majority of workshop participants were community surgeons in mid-adult life (ages 40–60) with established practices. Other study participants included operating room nurses, medical technicians, and surgical instrument manufacturer representatives. During the course of the study, I conducted 42 interviews with participants, recording additional field-based narratives in my fieldnotes. As part of this work, I observed surgeons performing surgery outside the operating room, temporarily removed from the social context normally supporting their professional autonomy—a quality that is a basic element of surgical practice (Katz, 1981; Zetka, 2003, p. 25). Workshops began with a didactic day of slide-enhanced lectures in an amphitheater or large conference room. Then on the following day, surgeons worked in groups, assisted by nurses, in simulated operating rooms in a nearby training facility. I attended lectures from beginning to end and observed the hands-on training sessions in which surgeons operated on live animal models (usually pigs, sometimes dogs). I recorded my observations in a field journal, writing notes during the didactic (lecture) portions of the workshops and recording other observations after leaving the field site at the end of the day. In addition to observing workshop training activities, as a participant observer, I tried to find ways to be helpful: answering the phone, helping trainees find their way around the training facility, fetching medical supplies, dimming lights, and helping wash instruments at the end of the day. At the end of the first year of my field observations, a nurse encouraged me to gain hands-on experience by "scrubbing in" as an assistant (Gamradt, 1998).

I captured the perspectives of trainees and other participants (nurses, operating room assistants, business representatives) through a "field-based narrative" approach. This strategy began with a focus on a particular point in the interviewee's educational or professional life history. For example, I asked surgeons attending an "advanced" workshop to tell the story of how they learned to perform laparoscopic surgery and to describe the circumstances that led up to and occurred after their first case. Researchers who collect field-based narratives are not usually able to arrange for multiple interviews and may not be able to capture their informants' words on audiotape. This is because the interviewee is a temporary visitor to the field site, which in this case was a temporary educational institution. As in most ethnographic

[1] See Gamradt [Armstrong] (1998) for a description of the methodological challenges I encountered as an anthropologist of education during the course of "studying-up" (e.g., studying general surgeons).

field interviewing, conversations occurred at odd moments: during breaks, at receptions and meals, by the pool at the conference hotel, on the bus ride to the laboratory or the airport, at airline terminals, and only rarely, in doctor's offices. Using this strategy, I was able to collect a large number of stories from a diverse sample of practitioners.

I conducted traditional, tape-recorded interviews with workshop directors and selected community surgeons, usually outside the workshop setting. Adopting a lifenet view, I tried to visualize the surgeons' places within wider networks of connections to people, places, and objects. In particular, I tried to visualize the flow of ideas among all those whose lives were touched by the rise of laparoscopic abdominal surgery. I wanted to understand where new ideas originated, how they were communicated, and by what means. Which ideas caught on, and which were abandoned? I imagined the flow of ideas as though these were tangible, fluid, multiple, and capable of rapid amplification or attenuation.

By way of verification, I cross-checked facts with workshop participants and interviewees. I read relevant newspaper reports, magazine articles, medical journals, and workshop syllabi. Over time, I identified themes that captured repeated and congruent narratives expressed in workshop lectures, interview transcripts, documents, and fieldnotes. I asked directors and other knowledgeable participants to read and provide feedback on drafts of the conference papers through which I shared findings with professional colleagues ("member checking"). Participants who read these papers said that my depictions were accurate. One observed that my interpretations offered new ways of thinking about his work as a surgeon. Further, I had the good fortune to meet, interview, and eventually collaborate with Dr. Susan Graham, a gynecologist who is also a Ph.D. anthropologist. She was a trainee at one of the workshops I observed during the course of the study and provided a sounding board for my interpretations as they evolved during the course of the project. As a researcher, I was deeply engaged with the people, settings, and events that are the focus of this chapter for an extended period of time (four years). Years later, I am still engaged intellectually with this work. Given the concrete limitations of field research for assistant professors, I had only a few days each month to devote to this effort. Yet the training workshops provided critical access to the knowledge production and transmission process. Most importantly, they afforded opportunities to hear what surgeons had to say about their teaching and learning experiences.

11.4 Findings

11.4.1 Liminality and Communitas at a Surgical Training Workshop

Perceived market demand forced members of the tribe of general surgeons to acquire a new set of technical, perceptual, kinesthetic, and interpretive skills, and to do so as quickly as possible. Surgeons felt they had to learn laparoscopic surgery rapidly because failure to do so would mean losing gallbladder cases to other community surgeons, and hence "going out of business." Many of the surgeons I met in 1990 and 1991 doubted the benefits of the new procedure for patients. A general surgeon, KT, described initial reactions to the procedure.

> [In 1989], we came back from a meeting and we had heard, already, through the grapevine—there were some doctors who talked about being able to take out gall bladders with a laparoscope. But when we heard that, without seeing it, it sounded crazy. You know, everybody was sceptical, including myself. (KT-19, 8/19/91)

Another general surgeon, TS, had been performing laparoscopic cholecystectomy for about 18 months at the time of the interview. She recalled surgeons' first reactions to hearing about laparoscopic cholecystectomy.

JA: As I said, I'm interested in learning about anything at all that you would like to tell me about how you learned to do lap chole.

TS: Funny thing is, the first time I ever heard anything about it, I was at a meeting in New York of the Bronx chapter of the American College of Surgeons. . .[in January of 1990]. . . .and someone brought a video of a lap chole that either he or someone else did, and we were all shocked and amazed and really sceptical and in some ways—I don't know—angry, that someone had done this gimmicky kind of thing that we felt might jeopardize patients, and we didn't really understand it, but we thought there was something about it that was not quite the way surgeons do things, and I think probably every surgeon there felt that this was a gimmick of some sort, and the guy who brought the tape along just looking for attention and notoriety and all that. [TS laughs]

JA: You don't remember who this was now that—

TS: I think it was a urologist. [oh really?] Who had—I can imagine that he did the surgery, because they are all just going into gall bladder surgery—but I don't know. It wasn't clear to me. I just wasn't ready to hear the whole story. I was just so shocked. And obviously, we all knew it wasn't going to last, and it was just this crazy guy. (TS-43, 1/9/93)

Surgeons viewed conventional gallbladder surgery as a safe, benign procedure—"the gold standard." They saw the new procedure as a more dangerous one for patients—and they were right (Cameron & Gadacz, 1991). They remained doubtful that the new operation was really that much less painful for patients and doubted that the postoperative recovery period had actually been reduced from six weeks to a few days. They came to the workshops full of doubts, worried, in some cases angry, and in many cases resistant. The directors and faculty of the workshops had two or three days to persuade their trainees that the operation could be done safely, and to transform these surgical liminaries from low-tech to high-tech surgeons. A workshop director's introductory lecture captures important aspects of the context in September 1990. (These are direct quotes recorded in my fieldnotes.)

> You are nervous, paranoid—the other guy across town is taking away your patients. [But] if you cut someone's common duct in half, everyone will know. We *want* you to be a little paranoid about this operation. . .this is a dangerous operation. If you are not sceptical

> about laparoscopic cholecystectomy, you really should be. And you really missed the boat if you're not sceptical about lap hernia repair.

For an anthropologist of education, this represented an unprecedented opportunity to watch a powerful professional community adapt to a rapid transformation of its technical knowledge base. The new procedure was invented and taught by community practitioners—but the pace of the revolution was greatly accelerated by external forces: the corporate sector, the media, patient demand, and cost-conscious insurance companies. The training workshops were practitioner-initiated, entrepreneurial responses to an external challenge to their own technically conservative, high stakes professional community. Community surgeons who set out to learn the technique early on were mindful of the potential financial benefits. KT, who practiced in Arizona, explained how he and his partners decided to learn the new procedure from a surgeon who worked in Pennsylvania. His comments illustrate the persuasive power of media (video-tapes of the operation) and the complex interaction of new surgical technologies and pragmatic (business) considerations in the decision-making process.

> It was about December of 1989 or so. He [a partner] came back from this meeting, and he said, "you wouldn't believe what I just saw. You know that laparoscopic cholecystectomy you've heard people talking of? Well, I saw videos of it. And it looks fantastic. And I don't care what people say, this is the wave of the future. I know it. And we got to be the ones"—(We've always prided ourselves on being very progressive, kind of state-of-the-art—we have a very busy practice. And I think largely because we enjoy the reputation of being very up-to-date.)—and he said, "we got to do this before anybody else does."
>
> Okay, and this is the business part now. And he showed us, he brought home videos that he got there, and he showed it to us. His point was, sooner or later, this is going to be the norm. When it catches on, if we're the first in our community to do this, it'll be a year or two before anybody else comes close to having our experience in this. We could become the authorities for [city name] in this operation. Think of all the extra work it will bring us. Okay. [uh-hmm] I'm being honest with you. Financial compensation. And from there, (we were having dinner over this, and we started brainstorming), from there we're thinking about how, boy, from this we could end up becoming—we can write articles, we can give courses on it. We can make all sorts of —all these extra spin-offs. We were thinking. What an opportunity. (KT-19, 8/19/91)

Ironically, as noted earlier, university medical schools initially played a relatively small part in the laparoscopic revolution (see, however, Flowers, Bailey, Scovill, & Zucker, 1991; Zucker, Bailey, Gadacz, & Imbembo, 1991; Soper, 1991.). The practitioner/educators who invented the new technique were pedagogically and institutionally isolated. The workshops they developed were temporary educational institutions that, in my view, brought surgeons together in a ritual performance that deserves careful study and analysis.

In the next part of the chapter, I introduce, and then employ, anthropological theories of ritual as an interpretive framework. It is important to note that the study was not designed to investigate ritual, or to test specific hypotheses drawn from ritual theory. Theories of ritual provided one of many possible vantage points from which to view and articulate findings.[2] Working inductively, I recorded what I observed in my fieldnotes. Over time, I noted that surgical training workshops shared structural similarities. In other words, there were repeated patterns in observational data across workshop sites. My interest in ritual and its relevance emerged through the iterative process of data collection, analysis, and interpretation that characterizes qualitative research.

11.4.1.1 Interlude: On Ritual

Rituals create human experiences that foster cultural continuity and change. Early theories of ritual emphasized the role they play in reaffirming values and maintaining the status quo (Durkheim, 1965, pp. 52–57). Rituals involve the performance of deeply held cultural values. They allow people to culturally construct and reconstruct social realities. However, they are "not only naturally occurring units of meaning but are also periods of heightened activity when a society's presuppositions are most exposed, when core values are expressed, and when symbolism is most apparent" (Bruner, 1986, pp. 9, 10). Focusing on non-industrial societies, Turner presented evidence that

> . . .where transition in space-time is ritualized, *how* it is ritualized, the nature and properties of the ritual symbols and of their interrelations, give us clues not only to the cherished values of the society that performs the rituals, but also to the nature of human sociality itself transcending particular cultural forms. (Turner, 1977, p. 38)

In other words, rituals reveal a group's core values and share common structural characteristics that afford insight into transcendent (trans-cultural) human cultural patterns.

All rituals share some similar structural features. When people participate in rituals, they enter into a realm that is set apart from ordinary, everyday life. Emile Durkheim (1965) spoke of the "sacred" and the "profane." Victor Turner (1969) used the terms "structure" and "anti-structure" to indicate the distinction between everyday life (structure) and a realm outside or beyond this sphere. Van Gennep (1960) noted that ritual events (rites of passage) have stage-like (processual) characteristics. Turner (1977) elaborated on this observation, arguing that secular rituals are characterized by the following elements:

(1) Separation of participants from normal life activities (liminality)
(2) Transition to a state of spontaneous (anti-structural) marginality
(3) The creation of communitas (equality, authenticity, shared identities)
(4) Reintegration into the social order and revitalization

The first stage (separation) involves crossing a threshold or "limen" and entering into a state of liminality (betwixt and between-ness). The second stage (anti-structure) is associated with experiences that turn the normal everyday world upside

---

[2] Chapter (10, this volume) uses ritual theory in her study of professional life in higher education.

down. For example, depending on the type of ritual, those in high-status positions might adopt subservient roles; the powerless assert authority; competitors might cooperate; workers play, the playful work. Customary status distinctions and hierarchies dissolve and a new sense of group solidarity arises during the ritual process, a phenomenon Turner (ibid.) called "communitas." Communitas is "the individual's subjective sense of connectedness to, and unity with a social group, experienced in association with collective participation in rituals unique to that group" (Armstrong, 2001, p. 9; see also, Turner, 1977, pp. 125–133). It emerges within a sacred realm where aesthetics might, for example, take precedence over pragmatics (or efficiency). Social structure is associated with cognitive schemas that make life predictable and orderly, but also constrain imagination, foster conformity, and enforce hierarchies. In contrast, communitas embodies "the essence of interrelatedness" (Fernandez, 1986, p. 179) wherein normal status distinctions are replaced by a shared sense of community, authenticity, and equality among group members.

Ritual activities are flexible and easily adapted to changing cultural conditions. Once linked to social order maintenance, rituals are now believed to provide a mechanism for enacting social change as well. As Dirks observed,

> To the extent that categories of "high" and "low" are constructed anew in any given ritual setting, we must be attentive as well to the contests over authority and power that take place around and through ritual means and idioms...Not only are caste identities and relations deeply politicized, they are contested throughout the field of ritual practice; all symbolic correlations within the ritual domain and between it and the social are opened to doubt, question, contest and appropriation. Because of the open and disorderly character of the ritual process, ritual is one of the primary arenas in which politics takes place (Dirks, 1994, pp. 500, 501).

Thus, ritual performances involve a dynamic interaction between cultural polarities—structure versus anti-structure; hierarchy versus equality; individuation versus group belonging. Rituals provide a venue for reaffirming professional values and identities while simultaneously challenging and disrupting accepted practices and assumptions. The link between ritual and cultural transformation has important implications for the study of professional groups in industrialized nations. Professionals foster societal change. How do professionals maintain stable identities and shared commitment to core values while adapting to changing social, political, and material conditions? What role might rituals play within professional communities, with what effects?

11.4.2 Surgical Training Workshops as Ritual Performances

In the interest of brevity, I will highlight features that seem to be particularly relevant to the topic at hand—the interaction of professional identity and mid-career transformation in response to technological change in the workplace.

11.4.2.1 Separation

The trainees came to the workshops from all over the country. Community surgeons rarely attended workshops held in their own towns. Most came by air, a few drove. As a rule, successful surgeons worked long hours and followed demanding schedules that were largely controlled by others: office administrators, hospital personnel, and wives. (Almost all of the surgeons I saw at the workshops were men. I don't know whether husbands and administrators manage the time of female general surgeons in a similar manner.) Like most professionals, they were deeply enmeshed in the social order. Given the intensity of the surgeon's everyday life, a two or three-day sojourn to another town, isolated from patients, staff, and (with some exceptions) family, was a significant break from routine. One workshop director told attendees, in advance, to wear casual clothing to the event. He felt his trainees needed to learn to see their work (and their lives) in a new way, and that dressing informally would help this process. Some workshop directors wore suits and ties to the first day of the course, dressing less formally or in 'scrubs' the second day. Others wore plaid or checked shirts and casual pants from the start. We associate casual attire with the *liminoid* sphere—with leisure, play, and re-creation, as opposed to work. Thus, workshop directors and faculty members who wore casual clothing while giving formal lectures (what we would call "scientific papers") may have contributed to the liminal atmosphere of the occasion. Symbolically, and as innovative professionals, they were "betwixt-and-between."

11.4.2.2 The Creation of Community

One of the striking features of the workshops was the way in which the directors and other speakers generated *community-building rhetoric*. This discourse emphasized qualities that set apart surgeons from other professional groups. Opening talks were sometimes punctuated with such messages. For example,

> You are here because you are interested in less invasiveness. . . . We all know that surgeons are resistant to change; surgeons are anal retentive [audience laughs]. We have gotten so much *grief* about this operation from other surgeons! . . . You must take a side on this operation. It is not possible to be a surgeon and not decide.

Speakers created a sense of community by identifying and highlighting shared experiences, personality traits, and points of view, cultivating a sense of "WE-ness" and (I suspect) reaffirming professional identities. Sometimes such statements appeared to have explanatory power. For example, in the workshop context, "live operations" were actual operations performed on patients in a nearby hospital. The operation was videotaped and broadcast onto a large screen in the lecture hall. Because the operation was laparoscopic, the audience saw the same view of the operation as the one displayed on the operating surgeon's video monitor. A surgeon who had encountered numerous technical problems while performing a "live operation" for the audience commented: "You know, surgeons are a little mad. We're not going to deviate from our routine, so we're just going to wait until we have our shop in order."

Some community-building rhetorical efforts inspired audience laughter. For example, one director routinely embedded the following comment in his narration of a "live" operation being performed by another surgeon: "Now, you are all surgeons, and you know that behind every fetish, there's a screw-up." His comment almost always produced laughter. It was an inside joke, one that tapped into the shared experiences of the audience. Their shared identities as masters of the operating room were highlighted and perhaps magnified in a moment of shared appreciation. Another way presenters built a sense of professional camaraderie was simply by identifying those who were *not* members of the tribe. The director of a workshop for gynecological surgeons regularly included the following comment in his introductory overview of the course: "You are gynecologists, so you will probably start to relax and enjoy yourselves after a few hours in the lab tomorrow. I also direct workshops for general surgeons, and you know, they have a lot better *sphincter tone* than we do. It takes them a lot longer to loosen up." Again, the audience always responded with laughter. Speakers often made pointed comments about members of other specialty areas and, occasionally, lawyers. The general surgeons joked about gynecologists, and the gynecologists joked about general surgeons.

11.4.2.3 Anti-Structure

Laughter is inherently social and "anti-structural." Workshop presenters who employed humor not only helped to build a sense of community, but also, in Turner's terms, were creating anti-structure. From this perspective, group laughter can be seen as an expression of professional communitas. Although a great deal could be said about anti-structure in laparoscopic training workshops, I will limit my remarks to a few key observations. First, the work that surgeons do is in many ways itself anti-structural. This may be one of the reasons sociologists and the general public has shown such an intense interest in surgeons and surgery. However, my sense is that the surgeon's work is carried out in a context of intense social and bureaucratic pressure and that surgeons themselves feel that the intensity of this enmeshment in the social order is increasing (Cassell, 1990). Although the professional autonomy of surgeons has been seriously undermined in recent years, the surgeon's responsibility for medical outcomes has remained the same. They are, in their own eyes, responsible for just about *everything*. The fact that surgeons tend to think of themselves as self-reliant captains of their own ships had important educational implications. As noted earlier, in order to learn to do the new surgery every surgeon had to become a novice again: to "get liminal." My second point, then, is that for workshop participants, taking on the role of novice represented an inversion of the normal social order.

Third, laparoscopic surgery itself, being new, represented a disruption of the social order because new methods are inherently anti-structural. The new approach required surgeons to violate—or at least compromise—some basic surgical precepts. To make matters worse, the new approach lacked any formal benediction from the university medical establishment; there were no "prospective randomized studies" by trained university medical researchers to shed any light on the matter.

Those who gave talks during the didactic portion of the course employed all of the usual symbolic devices associated with scientific medical presentations. They identified their historical forebears; they displayed charts and graphs; they wielded laser pointers; they showed slides and videos, and some even critiqued the design and/or interpretation of relevant studies. The presenters invested large amounts of time and money in order to conform to the customary standards for transmitting knowledge within the medical community. However, the lecturers whom I thought to be the best *teachers* were those who were most likely to violate the implicit rules that guide presentations at academic medical conferences. This is my fourth point.

An examination of the discourse taking place in the didactic part of these training programs indicated that most of the content of lectures was technical in nature. However, woven into the structure of the surgical training workshop experience, there appeared to be distinct teaching moments that may have, in turn, produced professional communitas. Lecturers sometimes seemed to step out of their own technical discourse in order to engage in various kinds of anti-structural pedagogical tactics. My theory is that these teaching moments were associated with the speaker's willingness to reveal the human aspects of surgical practice. They arose in response to the humorous, the deeply ironic, or even the tragic aspects of the lecturer's "case." After describing in detail a particularly difficult case to his workshop audience, a director warned, "Stay away from the medial side of the cystic artery. We have knabbed the cystic duct. We have learned from that experience, which was harrowing to say the least.... .It is a difficult case to talk about, but we want you to remember." These gestures may have been *anti-structural* because *public* displays of authenticity and self-revelation are not a part of surgeons' normal stance toward the world or toward each other. Alternatively, they may illustrate the phenomenon of "putting on the hair shirt" (Bosk, 1979).

Surgeons are "men of action" working in a highly competitive technical field (Goffman, 1967; Zetka, 2003, p. 25). My conversations with them suggest that some feel very much alone in their communities. For example, one interviewee, describing his isolation from other surgeons in the city in which he practiced medicine, observed, "Everyone is either a critic or a competitor. You can't really talk to other surgeons." It is significant, then, that program directors often invited trainees to call them with questions or concerns after the end of the program. In so doing, they expressed willingness to extend their teaching activities into the next phase of the learner's development. A director told his audience, "Call our 800 numbers if you need information about procedures, courses, or credentialing. Don't feel that you are bothering us. We want to help any way we can in all that you do in the future." Referring to the probable futures of his trainees, one program director assured me, in a *grim* tone of voice: "things are going to come up."

11.4.2.4 Reintegration: Going Home

After two days of intensive learning activity, it was time for the workshop participants to return home to their practices. The trainees had participated in at least two simulated laparoscopic operations. They were (presumably) now ready to employ the newest tools of their trade, to participate in an emerging world of surgical practice. In this new realm, contact between surgeons and patients would be mediated by complex technologies, technologies that enhanced anatomical visibility and minimized pain, but which also robbed the surgeon of tactile sensations and forced him or her to work in two dimensions rather than the customary three.

A few of the trainees appeared to be "born laparoscopists," adjusting quickly to the constraints imposed by cyborg surgery. They learned to manipulate tissue, identify anatomy, cut, staple, and sew without the tactile cues upon which they had long relied. They entered into this novel universe with an impressive degree of determination, concentration, and eye–hand coordination. If they mourned the loss of tactile sensation they did so quietly, focusing their energies on mastering skills needed for working in the laparoscopic surgical environment.

Others—and there were many—seemed to have a very long way to go on the "learning curve"—the period of time needed for mastery of the new techniques. It would be months, perhaps longer, before they would begin to use the new tools and techniques effectively. For most, the laparoscopic revolution brought about higher levels of stress in the operating room. But at the end of the workshop, even the most resistant trainees appeared to be convinced that laparoscopic gallbladder removal could be done, and would be done by surgeons in the future (if not by them, then by their competitors). The "learning curve" would require practice with other operating room team members, on human patients, in hospital settings back home. Workshop directors addressed the learning curve issue in various ways. Some were explicit: "You won't feel comfortable with all of this until you've done 25, maybe 50 cases." Some displayed tables showing operative time for laparoscopic cases decreasing as a function of the number of cases performed. Others used historical data from other medical fields. For example, one presenter focused on the introduction of tubal ligation in the field of gynecology, an innovation that resulted in a rapid rise and gradual decline in complications and fatalities for patients.

Regarding the reintegration process, two issues seem especially critical. First, workshop directors dealt with the reintegration process in different ways. In some workshops, all the trainees were brought together for a final "wrap-up" session at the conclusion of the course. The purpose of the wrap-up was twofold: to answer any remaining questions and to obtain evaluative feedback from the trainees for use in planning future training sessions. My field data do not permit me to make claims about the benefits of these wrap-up sessions for participants. However, it seems to me that the nature and value of wrap-up sessions is an issue that deserves careful consideration by medical educators.

The logic behind my argument goes like this: The nature of the questions asked during wrap-up sessions reflected the transformation of those who posed these questions. Questioners pointed to areas of particular concern regarding the next steps in their evolution as practitioners. Some of these questions reflected anxieties directly tied to the local context to which the practitioner was about to return. Others were both practical and ethical in nature: "What should I tell my first patient?" These kinds of questions could emerge only after the trainees had attained enough hands-on experience with the technique to begin to think about the problem of implementation. In a sense, questions posed at the end of the course could not have been asked at the beginning. This was a last chance for faculty members to explore issues, offer strategies, and discover topics requiring additional clarification. Wrap-up sessions gave course instructors an opportunity to reaffirm various core values of the profession and to remind the audience that surgery (like teaching) is a moral enterprise. During one such session, a program director asked faculty members whether they had any final words of advice for trainees. One instructor, getting right to the heart of the matter, put it this way: "Yes. Here is my advice: if you have scheduled your first laparoscopic case for next week, cancel it!"

The second issue is that little is known about what happened between the time the average surgeon completed formal training and the time they performed their first "lap chole." However, it is clear that after the close of the workshop, surgeons needed to organize their own learning process before performing laparoscopic cholecystectomy on their first human patients. Community surgeon KT and his partners first learned the procedure by working one-on-one with a community surgeon in Pittsburgh. KT offered this account of how his group prepared for their first case.

> So the hospital was very enthusiastic, and said 'fine, pick a team from the volunteers in the operating room.' And everybody was very enthusiastic to be part of something new. We assembled a team, and on their own, after hours, about three or four nights a week, when we were all done, about 7 o'clock at night we'd go over there, to the hospital, and following [their teacher's] suggestion, what we did was, we got a carton from the supermarket. We bought some chickens in the meat department. Okay. Put them under the carton, poked holes in the carton—the carton was about the size of a torso—and placed these instruments through holes in the carton, pretty much the same place they would be if they were on the body. Okay. Hooked them up to the equipment, just like it was going to be the real thing, and looking at the TV monitor, while a person who was learning how to be the scope technician was working the scope. We practiced things like peeling the skin off of a chicken, putting clips on the tendons, cauterizing little veins in the chicken. The main thing was, we were trying to learn how to get familiar with the instruments, and how they feel, and to develop the hand-eye coordination, which is the learning curve. And our other colleagues, who thought we were crazy even trying this laparoscopic cholecystectomy 'cause they thought it was a bunch of garbage anyway, they would say, what are those guys doing, playing with chickens? And they were making jokes about us. But we knew what we were doing, and we were crazy like a fox. So sure enough, we had our first one scheduled for April 6, 1990, it was [done] April 7, 1990, and that patient actually was booked in February.

KT and his partners scheduled their first cases on weekends, in part to protect their reputations. He continued,

> And the next day we did our next one, purposely scheduled for a Saturday. And the next one was scheduled for Sunday. Again, we're in a competitive world now. We're talking, giving you this whole background. A lot of our—first of all, we have a lot of professional jealousy from other surgeons, because we're busy and of the reputation we enjoy. They would have loved to see this blow up in our faces. So we thought that we would much rather have it blow up in our faces on a Saturday, when there is nobody else around, to know what's blowing up in our faces. . .Because if we did it on a regular day, and something didn't work out well, all the other operating rooms are going, there are surgeons all over the place, it'll be all over town in five minutes. (KT-19, 8/19/91)

KT and his group went to great lengths to ensure success. Each interviewee had a different story to tell. Some surgeons scrubbed in with more experienced peers after attending training workshops. Some teamed up with gynecological surgeons (who knew laparoscopy) for their first cases. Many attended more than one laparoscopic surgical training workshop. And there were anecdotes about those who attended one workshop and scheduled their first patient the next week.

In summary, the teachers of minimally invasive abdominal surgery constructed roles for themselves that resulted in dissolution of customary status distinctions and the creation of "professional communitas." They used humor and anecdotes to generate an atmosphere of collegiality and to build solidarity by highlighting the shared realities of members of the tribe of surgeons. They presented themselves as practitioners—just like the members of their audience. This may have helped them establish the authenticity of their claims and the credibility of their arguments (which at first had to be made in the absence of authoritative, scientific information). My work with surgeons has persuaded me that the study of how knowledge and expertise are transmitted in professional communities can lead to new ways of thinking about teaching and learning.

11.5 Discussion

11.5.1 Multiple Functions of the Workshops

Viewed anthropologically, the training workshops served many purposes. They facilitated the transmission of a rapidly evolving technical and conceptual knowledge base to practitioners, including the development of both hands-on and decision-making skills among trainees. Surgeons not only had to acquire a difficult new set of fine-motor and perceptual skills, but also needed to be taught to use good judgment concerning patient selection, when to abandon endoscopy and "open" the patient, "team-building" and staff training, whether to begin doing specific procedures (hernia repair, appendectomy, bowel resection, etc.), dealing with expensive and complex technologies, billing and reimbursement tactics, and so on. The design of the study does not illuminate how specific workshops impacted the practices of attendees. What can be concluded is that the workshops I observed conveyed a rich array of detailed information in multiple formats. With respect to the political economy of surgical practice, the workshops mediated between changing technological and material contexts and market demand for minimally invasive surgery. Further, the content of the curriculum changed as new knowledge emerged.

As temporary educational institutions, training workshops supported the periodic (monthly), informal compilation and synthesis of the experiences of faculty members. This process was a significant feature of workshops taught by faculty from across the United States and abroad. Workshop faculty members engaged in laparoscopic "shop talk" at every opportunity. This may have provided an important mechanism for the dissemination of clinical information and new technical innovations in a period of time in which the surgical knowledge base was expanding very rapidly. And since at this time the center of knowledge production and technical innovation was located in the community and the corporate sector, rather than in academia, the customary channels of medical knowledge transmission (journals, conferences, universities) may have been either inaccessible or inadequate venues for conveying new discoveries, warnings, and advice.

Workshops provided an ideal setting for test marketing by instrument manufacturers; they also provided important selling and customer bonding opportunities for industry. Directing and participating in such workshops enhanced the visibility of directors and faculty members within their own institutions. Such activities afforded directors access to surgical instrument and technology manufacturing corporations. This had several potential benefits. Directors could get special instruments made for them, make money as consultants; have instruments named for them, travel around the world as lecturers, and, perhaps most importantly, could locate themselves at the front end of the knowledge production process. Being among the first surgeons in the world to try out prototypes of future instrumentation might have been one of the most appealing benefits received by those who chose to work with industry. Clearly, workshops served many purposes, with training surgeons to operate safely using new procedures a central concern. The educational history of laparoscopic surgery, as represented in the structure and content of laparoscopic training workshops, may contain valuable lessons for the members of other professional communities.

11.5.2 Context, Risk, and the Intensification of Professional Work

Surgeons in the late 20th century encountered threats to their core skill set and work domains as laparoscopic techniques and other medical (pharmaceutical and endoscopic) treatments for gallbladder disease expanded beyond traditional disciplinary boundaries (Zetka, 2003). In U.S. medical institutions, pressure to generate revenue was increased by the rise of managed care, declining reimbursement rates, the perceived need to acquire high-tech surgical devices (lasers), and competition between hospitals for patients and prestige. All of these conditions contributed to the rapid mid-career transformation of thousands of general surgeons. Through collaboration with the corporate sector, general surgeons reclaimed exclusive rights to treat gallbladder disease by surgical means. Surgical removal of the gallbladder remains the definitive treatment for gallstones.

From the vantage point of the political economy of medicine, early adopters of the new surgical technologies gained patients, and therefore maintained and generally increased their market share. This required an increase in risk exposure for them and their patients. For patients, risks involved serious complications resulting from surgical accidents (Altman, 1992a, 1992b; Cameron & Gadacz, 1991; Zetka, 2003, p. 28; Zucker et al., 1991). For surgeons, risks included increased work-related stress resulting not only from the need to acquire and use new technical skills but also from a changing operating room and hospital environment that demanded a new kind of collaboration with coworkers (see Zetka, 2003, pp. 39–44). In the operating room, surgical actions not previously visible to others became visible to a wider audience of coworkers on a large video monitor. Early on, surgeons videotaped procedures, viewing the tapes on their own with an eye to improving their performance in the future. By the end of the first year of my study, surgeons videotaped procedures less often, perhaps due to litigation concerns.

It seems clear that the emergence of new technologies has contributed to the intensification of work (Larson, 1977) for medical professionals. In the early 1990s, surgeons struggled to acquire a new set of technical skills as well as the knowledge required to exercise good judgment concerning their application. They sought, and rapidly acquired the explicit and personal knowledge (Eraut, 2000, 2002) needed to carry out their roles and responsibilities as surgeons. Although the new procedure, in experienced hands, was advantageous for patients, it seems clear that the nature of work in the operating room became more difficult and demanding for all. The 'learning curve' raises risks for patients and stress levels for surgical teams whose outcomes are monitored and made visible by outsiders (government bureaucracies, insurance companies, hospital management, patient advocacy groups). Surgeons continue to work under pressure today as new surgical devices and techniques make possible operative procedures that must be evaluated, learned and integrated into the surgical repertoire.

Acknowledgments I would like to express appreciation and gratitude to Anne Mc Kee, Michael Eraut, and Ilene Harris for their astute insights and practical suggestions for improving this write-up. Thanks are also due to the many medical professionals who allowed me to watch them as they worked and learned *in context* during the course of this study.

References

Altman, L. (1992a, June 14). Surgical injuries lead to new rule. *New York Times*. Retrieved March 9, 2009 from "http://nytimes.com".

Altman, K. (1992b, June 23). When a patient's life is the price of learning a new kind of surgery, *New York Times*, A-3.

Armstrong, J. (2010). Naturalistic inquiry. In N. J. Salkind (Ed.), *Encyclopedia of research design, Vol. 2* (pp. 880–885). Thousand Oaks, CA: Sage.

Armstrong, J. (2001). Knowledge transmission and professional community in higher education: An anthropological view. *Educational Foundations, 15*, 5–25.

Beck, U. (1992). *Risk society: Towards a new modernity* (M. Ritter, Trans.). London & Newbury Park, CA: Sage.

Becker, H. (1976). *Boys in white: Student culture in medical school*. New Brunswick, NJ: Transaction Books.

Blair-Loy, M. (2003). *Competing devotions: Career and family among women executives*. Cambridge, MA: Harvard.

Bosk, C. (1979). *Forgive and remember: Managing medical failures*. Chicago, IL: University of Chicago.

Bruner, E. (1986). Experience and its expressions In V. Turner & E. Bruner (Eds.), *The anthropology of experience* (pp. 3–30). Urbana and Chicago: University of Illinois.

Cameron, J., & Gadacz, T. (1991). Laparoscopic cholecystectomy (Editorial). *Annals of Surgery, 213*(1), 1–2.

Cassell, J. (1990). *Expected miracles: Surgeons at work*. Philadelphia, PA: Temple University.

Cassell, J. (1996). The woman in the surgeon's body: Understanding difference. *American Anthropologist, 98*, 41–53.

Chaiklin, S., & Lave, J. (Eds.). (1993). *Understanding practice: Perspectives on activity and context*. New York: Cambridge University Press.

Chambliss, D. (1996). Beyond caring: Hospitals, nurses, and the social organization of ethics. Chicago: University of Chicago Press.

Dirks, N. (1994). Ritual and resistance: Subversion as social fact. In N. Dirks, G. Eley, & S. Ortner (Eds.), *Culture/power/history* (pp. 481–503). Princeton, NJ: Princeton University.

Dowling, M. (2006). Approaches to reflexivity in qualitative research. *Nurse Researcher, 13*(3), 7–21.

Downey, G. L. (1998). The machine in me: An anthropologist sits among computer engineers. New York: Routledge.

Dubois, F., Icard, P., Berthelot, G., & Levard, H. (1990). Coelioscopic cholecystectomy. Preliminary report of 36 cases. *Annals of Surgery, 211*, 60–62.

Durkheim, E. (1965). *The elementary forms of religious life* (Originally published in 1915, J. W. Swain, Trans.). New York: Free Press.

Eddy, E. M. (1969). *Becoming a teacher: The passage to professional status*. New York: Teachers College Press.

Epstein, C. F. (1990). The cultural perspective and the study of work. In K. Erikson & S. P. Vallas (Eds.), *The nature of work: Sociological perspectives* (pp. 88–98). London: ASA Presidential Series & Yale University.

Eraut, M. (2000). Non-formal learning and tacit knowledge in professional work. *British Journal of Educational Psychology, 70*, 113–136.

Eraut, M. (2002). Menus for choosy diners. *Teachers and Teaching: Theory and Practice, 8*(3/4), 371–379.

Eraut, M. Alderton, J., Cole, G., & Senker, P. (2000). Development of knowledge and skills at work. In F. Coffield (Ed.) *Differing visions of a learning society, Vol. 1* (pp. 231–262). Bristol: The Policy Press.

Fernandez, J. W. (1986). The argument of images and the experience of returning to the whole. In V. Turner & E. Bruner (Eds.), *The anthropology of experience* (pp. 159–187). Urbana & Chicago, IL: University of Illinois.

Flowers, J., Bailey, R., Scovill, W., & Zucker, K. (1991). The Baltimore experience with laparoscopic management of acute cholecystitis. *American Journal of Surgery, 161*, 388–392.

Forsythe, D. (2001). Studying those who study us: An anthropologist in the world of artificial intelligence. Stanford, CA: Stanford University.

Gamradt [Armstrong], J. (1998). 'Studying up' in educational anthropology. In K.B. deMarrais (Ed.), *Inside stories: Reflections on qualitative research* (pp. 67–78). Mahwah, NJ: Lawrence Erlbaum Associates.

Gergen, K. J. (1991). *The saturated self: Dilemmas of identity in contemporary life*. New York: Basic Books.

Gergen, K. J. (2001). Psychological science in a postmodern context. *American Psychologist, 56*, 808–813.

Goffman, I. (1967). *Interaction ritual: Essays on face-to-face behavior* (pp. 149–270). New York: Pantheon.

Guinier, L., Fine, M., & Balin, J. (Eds.). (1997). *Becoming gentlemen: Women, law school and institutional change*. Boston: Beacon.

Hoffman, D. (1998). A therapeutic moment? Identity, self and culture in the anthropology of education. *Anthropology and Education Quarterly, 29*, 324–346.

Jackson, P. W. (1968). *Life in classrooms*. New York: Holt, Rinehart, and Winston.

Kanter, R. (1977). *Men and women of the corporation*. New York: Basic Books.

Katz, P. (1981). Ritual in the operating room. *Ethnology, 20*, 335–350.

Katz, P. (1998). The scapel's edge: The culture of surgeons. Boston: Allyn & Bacon.

Konner, M. (1988). Becoming a doctor: The journey of initiation in medical school. New York: Penguin.

Larson, M. (1977). *The rise of professionalism: A sociological analysis*. Berkeley, CA: University of California.

Lave, J., & Wenger, E. (1991). *Situated learning: Legitimate peripheral participation*. Cambridge: Cambridge University Press.

Luhrman, T. M. (2001). *Of two minds: An anthropologist looks at American psychiatry*. New York: Vintage.

Macbeth, D. (2001). On "reflexivity" in qualitative research: Two readings, and a third. *Qualitative Inquiry, 7*, 35–68.

Maeve, M. (1998). Weaving a fabric of moral meaning: How nurses live with suffering and death. *Journal of Advanced Nursing, 27*, 1136–1142.

Mehan, H. (1993). Beneath the skin and between the ears: A case study in the politics of representation. In S. Chaklin & J. Lave (Eds.), *Understanding practice* (pp. 241–267). New York: Cambridge University.

Nader, L. (1969). *Up the anthropologist: Perspectives from studying up*. In D. Hymes (Ed.), *Reinventing Anthropology* (pp. 284–311). New York: Random House.

Philips, S. (1982). The language socialization of lawyers: Acquiring the cant. In G. Spinder (Ed.), *Doing the ethnography of schooling: Educational anthropology in action* (pp. 176–209). Prospect Heights, IL: Waveland Press.

Priyadharshini, E. (2003). Coming unstuck: Thinking otherwise about "studying up". *Anthropology and Education Quarterly, 34*, 420–437.

Reddick, E., & Olsen, D. (1989). Laparoscopic cholecystectomy: A comparison with mini-lap cholecystectomy. *Surgical Endoscopy, 3*, 131–133.

Reddick, E., Olsen, D., Daniell, J., Saye, S., McKernan, B., Miller, W., et al. (1989). Laparoscopic laser cholecystectomy. *Laser Medicine & Surgery News and Advances* (February), 38–40.

Rogers, P. (2002). Through the eyes of the institution: A critical discourse analysis of decision making in two special education meetings. *Anthropology & Education Quarterly, 33*(2), 213–237.

Rose, M. (1999). "Our hands will know": The development of tactile diagnostic skill—Teaching, learning , and situated cognition in a physical therapy program. *Anthropology and Education Quarterly, 30*, 133–160.

Seron, C., & Sibley, S. S. (2004). Profession, Science and culture: An emergent canon of law and society. In A. Sarat (Ed.), *The blackwell companion to law and society* (pp. 30–59). Maiden, MA: Blackwell.

Soper, N. (1991). Laparoscopic cholecystectomy: A promising new "branch" in the algorithm of gallstone management. *Surgery, 3*(1), 342–344.

Spindler, G., & Spindler, L. (2000, 1982). Roger Harker and Schoenhausen: From faciliar to stratnge and back again. In G. Spindler (Ed.), *Fifty years of anthropology and education: 1950–2000* (pp. 201–216). Mahwah, NJ: Lawrence Erlbaum Associates.

Strauss, C. (1997). Partly fragmented, partly integrated: An anthropological examination of "postmodern fragmented subjects." *Cultural Anthropology, 12*, 362–404.

Traweek, S. (1988). *Beamtimes and lifetimes: The world of high energy physicists*. Cambridge, MA: Harvard University Press.

Turner, V. (1969). *The ritual process: Structure and anti-structure*. Chicago: Aldine.

Turner, V. (1977). Variations on a theme of liminality. In S. M. Moore & B. Meyerhoff (Eds.), *Secular ritual* (pp. 36–52). Amsterdam: VanGorcum.

VanGennep, A. (1960, 1909). *The rites of passage* (Originally published in 1909, M. B. Vizedom & G. I. Cafee, Trans.). Chicago, IL: University of Illinois.

Wolcott, H. (1984, 1973). *The man in the principal's office: An ethnography*. Prospect Heights, IL: Waveland.

Zetka, J. R. (2003). *Surgeons and the scope*. Ithica & London: Cornell University.

Zucker, K. A., Bailey, R. W., Gadacz, T. R., & Imbembo, A. L. (1991). Laparoscopic guided cholecystectomy. *The American Journal of Surgery, 161*(January), 36–44.

Chapter 12
Academic Identities and Research-Informed Learning and Teaching: Issues in Higher Education in the United Kingdom

Anne Mc Kee

12.1 Introduction

Teaching and research are core functions of universities, and academics are expected to engage in both activities. In practice, both the function of universities and the roles of academics are more complex, diverse and emergent than this simple 'teaching and research' characterisation implies. In the United Kingdom, what universities do, how and for whom is now the focus of policy makers, academic professionals and a range of stakeholders. The latter include not only traditional users of higher education such as students, commissioners and users of research but also parents, employers, entrepreneurs and other partnerships. Consider these extracts from *Higher Education in England: Achievements, Challenges and Prospects* (O'Leary, 2009):

(1) A growing number of universities now describe themselves as 'business-facing' institutions. Hertfordshire is one example, where teaching and research are geared to the needs of the local economy. Two-thirds of undergraduates undertake work experience, and staff are encouraged to run businesses relevant to their subject. The university places a high priority on applied research, and its commercial turnover is bigger than its grant from the Higher Education Funding Council for England (HEFCE, p. 38).
(2) Higher Education Institutions have extended their sphere of influence into activities far beyond teaching and research. Among other public amenities, universities have run museums, galleries and sports centres, bus companies, health and legal clinics. Universities are by far the most influential public institutions in their area not just as the largest employer but also as drivers of innovation, centres of cultural life, and business activity. (ibid., p. 44).
(3) The value of UK Higher Education resides in the international excellence in teaching and research, in discovery and in learning. Universities are cosmopolitan organisations, which are tolerant of different race, religion and views. But while we have much to celebrate, more work is needed before the less privileged groups in society can talk with pride of 'their university' and what it does for them. (ibid., p. 51).

A. Mc Kee (✉)
Faculty of Education, Anglia Ruskin University, Chelmsford CM1 1SQ, UK
e-mail: anne.mckee@anglia.ac.uk

A. Mc Kee, M. Eraut (eds.), *Learning Trajectories, Innovation and Identity for Professional Development*, Innovation and Change in Professional Education 7,
DOI 10.1007/978-94-007-1724-4_12,

Extracts 1 and 2 illustrate ways in which the contemporary role of higher education is being re-shaped and re-interpreted. The emphasis has shifted to focus upon an expectation that universities *should contribute* to local and regional economies, social and cultural amenities. Extract 3 begins with a more traditional view of the role for universities in terms of establishing or maintaining international excellence in teaching and research. However, a significant caveat remains. More learners need to benefit from those activities, particularly those from *social groups who have not previously thought of universities as serving their needs.*

These shifts reflect government-led policies in higher education. Recent Higher Education Funding Council for England (HEFCE) initiatives in these areas are evident in policy documents which prioritize higher education activity on *employability*[1] and *widening participation.*[2]

These policies are attributed to global trends, associated with the emergence of what has been described as a knowledge-based society (Garnham, 2002). Although debated widely in academe, there is a broad consensus that a knowledge-based society requires that students should be prepared for a world in which change is rapid, frequent and radical. This kind of challenge is familiar to educators in professions, who have developed many pedagogic approaches to prepare practitioners for complex and quickly changing demands in practice settings. These include evidence-based practices, self-directed learning and required continual professional development. However, staff in the disciplines in higher education often find that the need to focus on working practices is a new challenge. They and their universities are experiencing a gathering momentum to reconsider what they do, for whom and how they do it.

Dr Nick Hammond, senior adviser at the Higher Education Academy (HEA), describes the implications for learning and teaching in particular:

> The changing world to be faced by today's students will demand unprecedented skills of intellectual flexibility, analysis and enquiry. Teaching students to be enquiring or research based in their approach is central to the hard–nosed skills required of the future graduate workforce. (Hammond, 2007, p. 3)

Hammond focuses on student need: I will consider the implications for academic roles, practices and individual and institutional identities. I argue that academic practice, particularly in the area of learning and teaching, is a site for innovation and change. Key catalysts for change include contemporary higher education policies and professional views about the relationships between teaching and research. In this chapter I draw implications for how learning and teaching are evolving and consider how this development is supported and valued at individual, institutional and sector levels.

As an example, I refer to the evaluation of a national programme in the United Kingdom called Centres of Excellence in Teaching and Learning (CETLs), one of

---

[1] Higher Education Funding Council For England: For employability: http://www.hefce.ac.uk/econsoc/employer/, accessed June 2009

[2] Ibid. For Widening participation: http://www.hefce.ac.uk/widen/, accessed June 2009

a series of UK initiatives to improve the status and quality of learning and teaching. Leaders of the CETL initiative support national and international trends pertinent to contemporary changes in higher education. These trends provide a vital context for locating the evaluation of the CETL initiative and relating that to the wider contexts and audiences of this book. Two trends are particularly relevant: the international emphasis upon the linking of teaching and research and pressures to recognise and promote scholarship within learning and teaching.

12.2 Centres of Excellence in Teaching and Learning: Policy Instrument and Theory of Change

The government white paper, 'The Future of Higher Education' (2003), announced the intention to '*better (understand) where and how good teaching and learning take place and to take steps to ensure that standards are high and continually improved, and that best practice is effectively shared*'. To this end, the White Paper outlined a series of strategies to

- fund 'strength in teaching',
- promote human resource strategies that explicitly value teaching and reward and promote good teachers,
- develop professional standards for teaching in higher education which could become the established basis for accredited training,
- establish a 'teaching quality academy' to develop and promote best practice in teaching,
- establish Centres of Excellence in teaching to reward good teaching, with each centre getting £500,000 a year for five years and the opportunity to bid for capital funding.[3]

Through dedicated funding for excellence in teaching, this White Paper aimed to create

(a) a *regulatory* framework through professional standards,
(b) *institutional financial reward* through funding 'strength in teaching',
(c) *individual reward through* the development of human resource strategies that *recognise good teaching*,
(d) a focus for the *development and dissemination of good practice within CETLs and beyond to the whole HE sector* and
(e) a *national body* to oversee these processes, later called the Higher Education Academy (HEA).

---

[3] The Department for Innovation, Universities and Skills: The Future of Higher Education: http://www.dcsf.gov.uk/hegateway/strategy/hestrategy/teaching.shtml, accessed August 2009

The White Paper described a plan to put in place mechanisms, infrastructures, initiatives and incentives at individual, institutional and sector levels to enhance the quality and status of teaching in higher education.

In 2003, when the UK government funding council launched these proposals, the higher education sector greatly valued its autonomy because it formed a critical part of academic professional identity. Voluntary collaboration with the sector was essential, and it needed to address some powerful obstacles. In particular, there was great disparity between the status of research and the status of teaching, and it was embedded in the organisational structures and practices of reward and recognition. This disparity had to be challenged especially because students with rising debts were clamouring for greater attention. Even so, research contributions remained the more reliable and prestigious indicator of quality at both institutional and individual levels, and established funding patterns prevailed as separate and distinctive functions within higher education. In short, financial, institutional and professional areas all resisted improving the status and quality of teaching.

The Higher Education Funding Council (HEFC) and the Department for Education in Northern Ireland (DENI) jointly commissioned the CETL initiative. These funding councils began with a collaborative approach which was highly valued by universities that were invited to submit proposals to establish Centres of Excellence. Funding was loosely targeted to enable creative and academically driven conceptualisations of 'Beacons of Excellence'. Funding councils encouraged universities to form partnerships with other universities and to plan for the development, promotion and dissemination of good practice. Thus, universities submitting proposals for CETLs were expected to provide leadership through defining and implementing change within and beyond their own institutions.

Eighty-one Centres of Excellence were established across England, Wales and Northern Ireland from 2005 to 2010 at a total cost of £350 million pounds. Seventy-four where based in England and Wales, and seven in Northern Ireland.[4] These covered a variety of disciplinary and cross-disciplinary groupings and a variety of teaching and learning foci. Each CETL produced its own interim evaluation, and an independent national evaluation was also conducted, which included a meta-analysis of the 74 self-evaluation reports from England and Wales. I draw upon this national evaluation to examine how CETLs sought to enhance learning and teaching, and with what success, both within their institution and across the higher education sector. The national evaluation was commissioned by HEFCE, the main funding council.

Leaders in the funding councils who sponsored the CETL programme took the view that academics needed to lead and implement the change process themselves in order to improve the status and quality of teaching. However, they also brought

---

[4] The seven CETLs in Northern Ireland did participate in the national evaluation of the CETLs. However, the Northern Ireland office separately managed them and their self-evaluation reports did not form part of the meta-evaluation of these.

a theory of change to the programme and embedded it in the call for proposals for CETLs. This theory of change, noted by the evaluation team, assumed that

- reward and recognition would enable and promote good teaching at individual, institutional and sector levels,
- excellent teaching would produce excellent learning and
- recognising individual and institutional excellence in teaching would promote excellence across the sector.[5]

Were these assumptions sound? Was the theory of change embedded in the CETL programme broad enough to address the more fundamental challenges involved in developing and repositioning teaching practice?

12.2.1 The Design of the National CETL Evaluation

A formative evaluation of the CETL programme was conducted between 2007 and 2008. Its brief was to determine the extent to which the CETL strategy of rewarding and enhancing excellence was achieving its intended effects 'of encouraging and inspiring positive changes in teaching and learning *in the HE sector as a whole'*. Both HEFC and DENI, who jointly commissioned the CETL initiative, described its purpose to be

> To reward excellent teaching practice and to invest in that practice further in order to increase and deepen its impact across a wider teaching and learning community.[6]

However, this purpose and its progress within the timescale and structure of the programme was to prove challenging for all except a small minority of CETLs, as the national evaluation team reported.[7]

Three evaluation approaches informed the design of the national evaluation. The first is *utilization-focussed evaluation* (Quinn-Patton, 1996) with its emphasis upon providing stakeholders with analysis, data and feedback that they can use for policy development and improvement of practices. The second is *theory-based evaluation,* which focuses upon the intentions of a policy and programme and what actually

[5] The National Evaluation report may be found at Higher Education Funding Council: http://www.hefce.ac.uk/pubs/rdreports/2008/rd08_08/, accessed August 2009

[6] HEFCE; Centres for Excellence in Teaching and Learning, Invitation to bid, http://www.hefce.ac.uk/pubs/hefce/2004/04_05/ , Executive Summary Key Point 2, accessed August 2009.

[7] The national evaluation of the CETLs was co-ordinated from the Centre for the Study of Education and Training (CSET) at the University of Lancaster. CSET has a team of educationalists with extensive national and international experience, who specialize in programme and policy evaluation. These included several recent initiatives in higher education funded by HEFCE to enhance learning and teaching in the sector. I joined the team in the later stages of this evaluation. The following discussion draws upon the research design they outlined in the original proposal.

happens, that is the activities and realities situated within particular contexts (Weiss, 1995; Connell & Kubisch, 1996; Hughes & Traynor, 2000). The third is *appreciative inquiry* (Cooperrider & Srivastva, 1987), which approaches critique by examining what is working well and moves from that to an appraisal of what would enhance and improve what is being evaluated. This approach seeks to encourage disclosure as its strategy for developing open, positive and purposeful conversations.

These theoretical orientations reflect the formative intentions of the evaluation. The evaluation worked closely with and within the programme. A detailed methodological discussion of the methodology is beyond the remit of this chapter, but it is worth noting that a distinctive feature of the national evaluation was the relationship between it and the local CETL self-evaluations. Three critical dimensions to that relationship were as follows:

- Dialogues about the nature, purpose, focus and practices of evaluation
- Dialogue and debate about the framework for the meta-evaluation of the self-evaluations
- A brokering role between all the stakeholders around the framework for the meta-evaluation of the CETLs

These forms of engagement enabled the national evaluation team to get 'inside' the programme on a number of different levels. For example, discussions about evaluation provided insight into how individual CETLs were interpreting the commissioning brief and developing expectations about how they were undertaking their work and how it should be reviewed and reported. However, such access to 'insider' perspectives was challenging to achieve in a programme that was both high profile and high risk. CETLs had been charged with immense ambitions but were operating on short timescales with time-limited funding. This created a politically sensitive evaluation context which required sophisticated strategies for access, engagement and reporting.

The evaluation team did not typically formulate research questions. Rather, the team anticipated effects of the innovation and sought to determine whether and how they took form, as described in the following extract from the original proposal for the evaluation:

> Multiplier effects can be expected when innovations progress from the CETLs, as the original enclaves of good practice, to the formation of bridgeheads, and then enclaves in other contexts and thence, in the most successful cases, to more systemic effects and the promise of a step change in routine practices. We look for effects in:
>
> - The practices of those immediately involved in the CETLs (teachers, practitioners, departments and wider partners engaged in specific courses or programmes). Examples of innovative practice that directly effect what students are learning will form the basis of this database.
> - Wider departmental, school or faculty practices and systems (focus on T&L strategies and how CETLs fit in).
> - Sector wide influences and external partnerships (focus on strategies for active engagements). (Personal Communication from Saunders, August 2009)

The evaluation team created nine aims and five objectives. While I draw on all the evidence collected from the national evaluation, I give in-depth consideration to only some of the aims and objectives because this particular evidence concentrates on what was actually happening to learning and teaching practices on-the-ground, why and with what effects. This includes changes in the practices of individuals, groups within CETL partnerships and their attempts to disseminate these practices more widely, both within their institutions and across the sector. This also brings into focus what was happening within organisational structures and how they either enabled and responded to change or acted as obstacles to innovation. These aims include the following:

1. Provide formative independent evidence of the overall effects of the strategy to HEFCE and its partners.
2. Offer an analytical account of the experience of the programme from the perspective of all the key stakeholders.
3. Be responsive and flexible enough to capture unintended outcomes and unanticipated effects.
4. Test and extend understanding of the CETLs theory of change.

Related objectives include the following:

A. Provide objective formative input on the overall effectiveness of the programme at the different levels of sector, institution, teacher, student and external stakeholders.
B. Provide objective formative input on the effectiveness of the strategy as viewed from particular perspectives, including those in senior management within the institutions, academics, students and communities of practice.

The evaluation team used both quantitative and qualitative methods as follows:

- Twenty-two semi-structured interviews were conducted with key informants both within and outside the English and Northern Irish higher education systems. The sample included CETL managers (not included in the case studies), pro-vice chancellors, non-English informants (those holding relevant higher education roles outside England who might see taken-for-granted assumptions in the English system), HEFCE, the HEA, the Leadership Foundation, Action on Access and CETL directors.
- Visits were made to 36 sites, over 50% of the CETLs in order to develop case study data. The case study visits included observations of practice and interviews from 693 participants.
- A survey of a sample of CETL directors achieved an 86% response rate and collected data about their perceived effects of the CETLs, how the CETLs were developing and issues identified as significant.
- An overview analysis of the 74 CETL self-evaluation reports completed by June 2007.

- Examination of pertinent documents and other literature (for example data that emerged during CETL conferences, workshops, Web sites and wikis).
- Participation in CETL activities (for example two national events and invitations to work with CETLs).
- Ten interviews with vice-chancellors from institutions hosting CETLs and 10 vice-chancellors from institutions not hosting CETLs.
- Ten interviews with Higher Education Partners who were not the lead CETL. (CETLs usually have two or more partner institutions)

The evaluation provided an analysis of data from the following sources:

- Key informant interviews (22),
- Interviews with senior managers of Higher Education Institutions (vice chancellors, pro-vice chancellors and other senior managers) (22),
- Interviews with partners[8] of lead CETL institutions (10),
- Visits to CETLs undertaken since the beginning of the evaluation (36 CETL visits and 698 respondents),
- Survey of CETL directors (86% response rate),
- A meta-analysis of the CETL self-evaluation reports submitted at the end of July 2007 (74 CETL evaluation reports)
- (Saunders et al., 2008, p. 7)

This covered a broad range of aspects of the programme, which included the following:

- unanticipated or unintended effects of the programme,
- outcomes of HEFCE capital funding investment,
- promising and effective practices,
- institutional and sector presence of CETLs,
- HEFCE's 'light touch' management approach of the CETLs
- effectiveness of the programme in supporting and improving teaching and learning. (Saunders et al., 2008, p. 7)

12.2.2 Illuminative Findings

Evidence from surveys, interviews and case studies shows that CETLs help to create a positive focus on teaching and learning. Overwhelmingly, qualitative data from interviews of nearly 700 informants, taken during case study visits, supported the view that CETLs were innovating in learning and teaching practice. Those informants from CETLs which had received capital funding were typically much

[8] Many CETLs included two or more universities who had formed partnerships for the specific purpose of creating a CETL. Usually, one university was the lead university for this period.

more positive about the CETL initiative than those from CETLs with modest or no capital funding. The following quotes illustrate the claims made:

> (CETLs provide) an opportunity to develop and try out new things in UK higher education.
> (CETLs are) bringing some of the most inspirational people in learning and teaching together.
> (Risk taking and creativity) 'I see that everywhere (in CETLs)'.

CETLs supported innovation and development in pedagogic practice, course content and assessment. Examples of this included piloting the use of new technologies, or new approaches to supporting students, in order to meet diverse student needs. CETLs have provided workshops and supported student projects. They have also established either student networks or mechanisms for consulting and engaging students with curriculum provision, curriculum development and assessment. A rich range of initiatives have sought to enhance practice, extend expertise and encourage an enthusiastic and vibrant teaching and learning climate for both practitioners and students.

The overview analysis of the 74 English and Welsh CETL interim self-evaluation reports describes 1,181 activities undertaken to enhance learning and teaching. These indicate the range of activities used by CETLs to achieve the eight programme objectives:

1. Leading and embedding change
2. Addressing diverse needs in diverse contexts
3. Institutions developing understanding about and ways of supporting students' learning
4. Raising the profile of teaching excellence – institutionally
5. Raising the profile of teaching excellence – across the sector
6. Informing student choice and maximising student performance
7. Reward and recognition of excellent practice
8. Encouraging debate, sharing ideas and practices about learning teaching and assessment across the sector

Methodological issues relating to these interim self-evaluations are discussed in the national evaluation final report (Saunders et al., 2008, pp. 107, 108). These issues include the reporting of the same kind of activity in different categories. For example, nearly half of the CETLs argued that leading and embedding change characterised all their activities, so this was not treated as a separate objective and not reported upon as a separate category. There were other instances where the same activity was regarded by different CETLs as addressing different objectives.

Table 12.1 is a selection of CETL self-reported activities from the meta-evaluation. They relate to the descriptions of innovative pedagogic practices which CETLs identified as enhancing teaching and learning, and therefore shifting practice.

Table 12.1 Extracts from meta-analysis of 71 CETL self-evaluations

Objective	Activity	Number of CETLs
Addressing diverse needs in diverse contexts	New programme modules	28
	Use of new technologies	18
	Creation of learning labs	5
	Projects with employers	8
	Outreach events	11
	Development of new material	8
	Student-led projects	10
Institutions developing understanding ways of supporting student learning	Funding fellowships	20
	Small-scale development projects	23
	Pedagogic research projects	20
	Pedagogic research network	4
	Evaluation of current provision	9
	Collaboration with teaching teams from different institutions	6
	New approaches to teaching and learning	14
	Curriculum development	10
Encouraging debate, sharing ideas and practices about teaching, learning and assessment	Collaboration with other CETLs	17
	Collaboration with other institutions	14
	Collaboration with Subject Centres	13
	Cross-disciplinary work and discussion	8
Raising the profile of teaching excellence across the sector	Development of institutional processes	22
	Networks/communities of practice	16
	Links with other CETLs	3
	Advising other institutions	6

The data offered is reported within the conditions of the funding contract. The evaluation was an evaluation of the programme, not individual CETLs. A methodological decision was taken to analyse self-evaluation reports on the basis of activities not attributable to individual CETLs (personal communication, Saunders, August 2009).

Establishing a link between these innovations and sustained shifts in pedagogic approaches or more effective teaching practices is very difficult. A few CETLs offered proxy indicators of positive effects, such as improved student recruitment, observations made in external examiner reports and increases in successful course completion. Other CETLs viewed new activities as successes in themselves without seeking to collect further evidence of their quality or impact on students, whether these activities were workshops, seminars or other professional development events. Continuing demand for events and faculty engagement (uptake) were cited as evidence of developing teaching practice.

Survey results showed that 83% of CETLs funded pedagogic research and small-scale development projects. This adoption of pedagogic research was reflected in CETL self-evaluation reports. (See Table 12.1, Group 2: Institutions developing understanding ways of supporting student learning.) Indeed a CETL network, 'Internal Pedagogic Research and Evaluation Network' (IPREN), was formed to develop and share understanding and practices in this area. Though many IPREN members were new to pedagogic research and evaluation, they linked with more experienced researchers and evaluators with the intention of building capacity across the CETL programme and sector. IPREN is one example of some of the unintended consequences of CETLs. The development and ongoing evaluation of teaching and learning practice often led to the recognition of new needs. In the case of pedagogic research and evaluation, those developing capacity in this area sought out established expertise in the field. They recognised that while pedagogic research and evaluation was new to them, it was not new to other higher education teachers. They did not need to re-invent the wheel. However, some CETLs embarked on innovations that were only new within their own discipline or cognate group. So a CETL keen to develop inter-disciplinary learning seemed unaware of the knowledge, skills and experience that medical and health sciences education had to offer. Networking knowledge and practice was not always easy when disciplinary barriers or differences were involved.

This more purposeful engagement with pedagogic research and evaluation was not unproblematic. *What research 'is'* and *how different forms of research are valued* are still contentious issues that threaten to disrupt re-conceptualisations of teaching and learning practice. Thus, claims that pedagogic research has its own knowledge base and valid research methodologies and traditions were often challenged on epistemological grounds. These challenges reflect what the national evaluation team described as:

> the uneasy relationship between three dimensions of (academic) practice;
>
> (1) active research within a discipline or cluster of disciplines (traditional research based practice),
> (2) how that research based knowledge is reproduced through teaching and learning programmes (teaching and learning practices embedded in courses), and
> (3) the pedagogic knowledge (produced through research or experientially), which may or may not have a disciplinary boundary. (Saunders et al., 2008)

These concerns about the warrant and validity of pedagogic research often occur when there are doubts about the efficacy of academics teaching particular disciplines, when they are developing expertise in pedagogic research but *are no longer active* in their own discipline-based research. For some academics, the core purpose of higher education is to engage in disciplinary-based research and then to disseminate that research through teaching. Though this critical view of pedagogic research can be strongly held, most interviewees thought that academics should be supported to develop their own pedagogic expertise and that this could involve pedagogic research.

In my view, conceptions about what academic practice involves appear to be changing. For the more research-intensive universities, CETLs appeared to enable a shift towards developing teaching and learning practice and valuing teaching with reward and recognition at individual and institutional levels. In post-1992 universities (new universities, usually without many established research profiles), CETLs seemed to enable a shift towards pedagogical research through providing opportunities to engage with it. How much re-balancing could be achieved depended upon resources supporting engagement in new activities. For example, not all teaching staff were given time by their departments to engage in 'extra' CETL commitments, so efforts to move in new directions were sometimes additional to established workloads. Survey and interview data both indicate that the relationship with the host institution was key to how CETLs could function. Forty-two percent of CETL directors considered they had little or no support from senior managers. This could create challenges around the extent to which CETLs could engage people both within institutions and beyond that to the sector.

Senior managers and key informants talked of missed opportunities to co-ordinate and capitalise on CETL activities. The autonomous and loosely managed nature of the CETL programme limited how knowledge and practice could be shared and disseminated. Within some CETLs, and among some senior managers, there was a view that a central engagement strategy to network and disseminate knowledge and practice would have been useful. While CETLs sought to disseminate through established mechanisms such as journal publications, conferences and seminars, this did not facilitate a coherent programme-wide dissemination.

Sharing within the CETL programme and beyond it could have been more co-ordinated. The annual HEA CETL conference tended to facilitate CETLs sharing with each other, rather than the sector at large. In Table 12.1 under 'Encouraging debate, sharing ideas and practices about Teaching, Learning and Assessment', CETLs report on their efforts to network with other CETLs and institutions. While some CETLs were much more active in this outward-looking engagement, activity levels in this area were generally low. That said, CETLs argued that half-way into the five-year programme, most energy had been spent in setting up CETLs and developing new buildings and/or office spaces. Towards the end of the programme, they argued that it was too early to expect substantial signs of impact. In other words, they felt the timescale for achieving impact was inappropriate.

The national evaluation identified nine factors that enabled the 'deepening effects' of CETLs (Saunders et al., 2008, p. 9). Several enabling factors such as pre-existing infrastructures, practice reward and recognition systems and networking structures were identified. Examples of enabling factors include the following:

> A pre-existing framework for reward and status within the institution that is favourable towards teaching.
>
> A relatively sophisticated approach to strategies of external engagement with the work and outputs of the CETL. (Saunders et al., 2008, p. 9).

Capital funding enabled the provision of new and better physical locations, and resources created visible shifts in the valuing of teaching. Space dedicated to teaching helped foster a sense of identity, shared purpose and enthusiasm. However, while new builds and refurbishments were often regarded as intrinsically beneficial, their development was a more complex and time-consuming endeavour than anticipated. There is little evidence that capital investment and new designs have encouraged similar building improvements in other universities. Indeed, these are unlikely to be affordable in the current recession. As the current funding period for CETLs drew to an end, continuing funding from either host institutions or HEFCE was uncertain.

12.2.3 Difficulties Encountered by CETLs

The assumptions and processes of many university financial systems illuminated the 'newness' of the CETL programme. What CETLs wanted to do and the speed with which they needed to do it created some organisational challenges. Internal university financial processes could take a long time, and this became critical when funding had to be spent by a specified time. For example, the building and refurbishment of physical learning environments were vulnerable to delays caused by the financial procedures of some universities, and one university's financial management system could not fully meet the needs of CETL directors for project financial information. The CETL wanted to allocate funding to categories, which did not exist on the current university system, such as 'dissemination' and 'development'. So this university had to establish a project team, to accommodate the new demands of CETL activities within its financial reporting systems.

Another example of a mismatch between financial procedures and proposed CETL activity was the need to create a system to transfer funds from one university to its associated colleges. Thus, capital spending and accounting illuminated aspects of the 'new-ness' of CETL approaches within the sector and the organisational changes that were required to accommodate them. These practical organisational shifts in the institutional re-positioning of teaching and learning were demonstrated by changes in institutional career paths, teaching fellowships and the representation of teaching perspectives within decision-making structures. (See Table 12.1, Group 4: Raising the profile of teaching excellence across the sector).

A minority of CETLs have had substantial effects on institutional policy and practice: particularly in cross-disciplinary areas such as work-based learning, assessment, student learning and student support. Some have begun to influence the wider teaching community. It would appear that these broader, more generic teaching foci avoided some of the disciplinary boundaries that can create barriers to change. However, most CETLs appeared to have had little or no effect on institutional practices outside their immediate partnership

12.2.4 Personal Reflections and Discussion

Middle and senior managers of CETLs spoke of the 'climate change' in approaches to rewarding and recognising excellence in teaching. CETLs were one of a number of initiatives contributing to this 'climate change'. Since 1997 a series of initiatives within UK higher education were established to enhance learning and teaching and recognise good practice. Subject Centres are a notable example of this,[9] and they are now part of the HEA.

When discussing the implications of the evaluation for academic practice, the role of universities and trajectories of change, I will draw upon theories of identity, organisational management and culture and relate them to the grounded theories captured by the evaluation (Glaser & Strauss, 1967).

> Theories generate issues for experimental investigation (and raise) questions in a sequential way so that each answer elaborates a continuous and developing line of argument (Bannister & Fransella, 1993.)

My intention is to open and unravel the analysis, rather than close and seal it within boundaries of certainty or limitation.

12.3 Self and Identity

One way to characterise the experience of the CETL programme is to view it as a case of interpreting and implementing policy. Interactions between the assumptions of policy makers, institutional realities and hierarchies of academic practices affected how the task of enhancing teaching and learning was understood and approached.

Underpinning social forces, such as differences between the relatively autonomous cultures of academics and those of policy makers and managers with sector performance and accountability responsibilities, helped to shape those interactions. Understanding those forces could strengthen personal and collective agency and inform how stakeholders in the task of enhancing learning and teaching in higher education might better understand both each other and the complexity of the task they face.

Elliott has explored the relationship between identity and social structure by examining a number of major theories of the self. He describes how Giddens's account of 'self' is tied to institutional and social forces and argues that at the core of Giddens's theory is the concept of reflexivity:

> a self-defining process that depends upon monitoring of, and reflection upon, psychological and social information about trajectories of life. (Elliott, 2008)

For Giddens, this construction of self is an ongoing process and the *"relationship between self and society is a highly fluid one, involving negotiation, change and development"* (Elliott, 2008).

---

[9] Subject Centres were established around the year 2001 with a brief to provide subject-specific support to enhance learning and teaching in the UK. There are 24 subject centres, housed within the universities, which successfully bid to establish them. Each has a specific disciplinary or cognate group focus. Details may be found at the Higher Education Academy: http://www.heacademy.ac.uk/ourwork/networks/subjectcentres

Elliott continues:

> To emphasise the impact of social forms and cultural traditions on the self is not to imply that the individual is merely the product of external forces. On the contrary, personal experience and identity (are continually transforming) (Elliott, 2008)

How can these concepts inform our thinking about the CETL programme?

CETLs were a means of re-shaping individual and institutional identities, at least potentially. To be awarded a CETL signalled institutional excellence in teaching. This was a new kind of label for universities within a higher education system where research-intensive universities are held in higher esteem than others. For most CETL universities, embracing the identity of excellence in teaching required organisational shifts in academic career pathways, financial accounting processes and decision-making structures. Teaching gained a different kind of institutional presence in those universities that had CETLs. In some, the shifts were more radical than others, but about 90% of self-evaluation reports perceived significant improvements in the visibility and status of teaching. These shifts created openings that had consequences for individuals as well as systems. New promotion opportunities, influence in decision making and the implementation of a range of reward and recognition devices created new possibilities for academic careers and life trajectories. Expectations that teaching was a dead-end academic option were being eroded. More than this, the development and recognition of expertise in teaching and learning were energising and motivating. While the aims and tasks of CETLs were sometimes experienced as ambitious and daunting, there was a growing sense of personal and team agency, which the national evaluation report described in the following terms:

> Notwithstanding the tendency for newly formed entities like CETLs to have a strong sense of emerging identity, internal culture and excitement, the data points to a range of positive effects that the existence of the programme has enabled. (Saunders et al., 2008, p. 7)

There were other kinds of openings. Capital funding resourced improvements in the physical presence for teaching. About 60% of CETLs talked with pride about the visibility and quality of their new teaching spaces. I have been in some CETL centres that are light, airy, well equipped and comfortable. These centres as physical spaces are a form of 'goods' or socio-symbolic materials, which potentially enhance the status of teaching. For many who work within them, they provide improvements in working conditions. This kind of valuing influences the day-to-day experience of being in a CETL and engaging in teaching or learning development. Potentially, learning spaces improve not just the status of teaching but also the dignity of those who work within them. Being in a CETL primarily involves CETL staff, but it also includes those who engage with it as teachers and students.

However, not all CETLs benefited equally from capital spending. Among those who did not, accommodation could be both modest and dreary. As some CETLs pointed out, their relationship with the host institution was critical. Issues of accommodation reflect how relationships between institutions and CETLs were fluid, not fixed, negotiated and not pre-determined by the aims of the programme or intentions within CETL proposals. On the ground, the experience of being within a CETL could vary considerably.

The fluid and negotiated dimensions of identity are also apparent in the reach of CETLs within their own institutions and beyond that to the sector as a whole. A critical component of HEFCE's strategy in commissioning CETLs was to have institutional and sector-wide impact. In practice, the extent to which CETLs engaged with the sector and prioritised those activities differed significantly. Those CETLs which actively disseminated across the sector tended to have strong pre-existing networks with the HEA Subject Centres and/or their own disciplinary-orientated networks. These CETLs had been, and continued to be, outward looking in their approach. Other CETLs were predominantly inward looking. They were concerned with 'getting it right at home' and saw this priority as being weakened by any wider sector engagements. These stances reflect diversity in academic cultures and may also reflect different levels of pedagogic expertise, experience and awareness. Some CETLs viewed engagement across the sector as a necessary dimension of developing innovative pedagogy and informing institutional change. Others felt external conversations and engagements drained energy from internal initiatives. This meant that for some CETLs, having institutional impact was a priority, which competed for attention with engagement with the wider sector. Neither CETLs nor universities are heterogeneous groups, and CETLs' character, orientation and domain of activities were quite different.

12.4 Academic Practice and Culture

The national CETL evaluation examined the tensions around three aspects of academic practice. These were discipline-based research, disseminating that research through teaching and pedagogic knowledge (research based or student focussed). These elements of academic practice have fuzzy boundaries. Thus Scott, the vice-chancellor of a new university and well-known scholar of higher education, argued that

> (The) boundary between 'teaching' and 'research' is getting fuzzier rather than clearer. Indeed there are some forms of teaching which have less in common with other forms of teaching than they have with some types of research. (Scott, 2004)

What are the implications of the tensions and overlaps between teaching and research practices, and how do they relate to this chapter's assumption that the role of universities and academic practices are related?

Boyer approached the purpose of universities and the implications for their academic practices through an elaborated view of scholarship.

> Given current tensions, is it possible to bring a new sense of vitality and purpose to higher education? Is it possible to strengthen public confidence, and to create for the twenty-first century, institutions of confidence and social influence? If so, how is this to

Table 12.2 Boyer's definition of scholarship

(1) The scholarship of discovery	Discovery is research broadly defined as systematic investigation.
(2) The scholarship of integration	This is an inter-disciplinary approach urging scholars to make connections with other bodies of knowledge, research methodologies and teaching pedagogies (approaches). It requires synthesis.
(3) The scholarship of application	This dimension of scholarship is about the relationship of knowledge to the needs of society, cast in terms of reciprocity. Society and higher education are seen as having mutual obligations and responsibilities. Boyer describes this in terms of a flow from theory to practice and practice to theory.
(4) The scholarship of teaching	Described as the heart of the scholarly endeavour, teaching requires engagement in researching teaching practice as part of a process for making the sometimes very 'private act' of teaching public. The purpose of doing this is to enable both accountability and curriculum development (Boyer 1990).

> be accomplished? (The Carnegie Foundation suggest) the time has come to move beyond the tired old teaching-versus-research debate, and begin to explore the more essential issue: **what is it to be a scholar?** (Boyer, 1990, p. 116)

Scholarship provides a rubric of practice that is aligned to a refreshed view of the role of universities. Boyer described scholarship as a 'four part paradigm' (see Table 12.2).

Taking this theory of scholarship and putting it into practice requires more than simply learning and developing new practices. It requires shifts in organisational and professional culture for these practices to be recognised, supported and embedded.

Boyer's definition of scholarship acknowledges different aspects of academic practice and offers a framework within which research and teaching can be linked. Note the second category, the scholarship of integration. If the CETLs had been conceived as a scholarly endeavour, what implications would this have had for how the programme learned from itself, and how that learning related to other learning in the sector?

Both the Carnegie Academy for the Scholarship of Teaching and Learning (CASTL) programme in the United States[10] and the CETL programme in the United Kingdom[11] treat developing teaching and learning practice as a *substantial and*

[10] The Carnegie Web site may be found at the Carnegie Foundation *for the* Advancement *of* Teaching: http://www.carnegiefoundation.org/programs/index.asp?key=21, accessed July 2009

[11] Links to CETLs may be found at Higher Education Funding Council: http://www.hefce.ac.uk/learning/tinits/cetl/, accessed July 2009

long-term endeavour. This is appropriate not just because of the scale and complexity of the task but also because academic cultures of practice and professional identities are at stake.

What counts as teaching or research is changing as professional practice in these areas evolves. Boundaries between research and teaching can be blurred when research emphasises participatory and user-focused approaches and teaching emphasises research-informed approaches. Thus, the three dimensions of academic practice described by the evaluation team imply different relationships between teaching and learning, as depicted in Table 12.3.

Table 12.3 relates dimensions of academic practice, to pedagogic approaches, forms of scholarship and associated links between research and teaching. These relationships have implications for teaching practices and the learning processes they facilitate. Dimension 1 of academic practice, 'Active research within a discipline', is associated with knowledge transmission. This involves the learning and understanding of facts. In its basic form, this does not include an exploration of the nature of knowledge that the 'facts' assume, their boundaries or limitations. Dimension 2 of academic practice, 'Research-based knowledge reproduced through teaching and learning', is associated with constructivist approaches to learning and teaching. Learners are encouraged to question and determine what kind of information is required, how it might be found, what it means and how it might be used. For example, learners might have to decide what kind of judgements or actions the information would support. The learning process this facilitates engages learners in the selection, classification and critique of information. Dimension 3 of academic practice, 'Pedagogic knowledge produced research or experientially', is associated with systematic investigation and research-orientated or research-based approaches to learning. This involves the learner focusing upon an area for investigation, planning how the investigation will be conducted, undertaking the investigation and classifying, analysing and critiquing findings.

Debates about linking teaching and research encourage a shift from teaching as a means of 'telling' research or transmitting facts to research-informed and research-based teaching. In these teaching approaches, the processes of teaching mirror, or embed, the processes of research. So the kind of teaching that supports post-graduate research is similar to that being applied to other 'levels' of curricula.

In the United Kingdom there are a growing number of diverse examples of research-informed teaching approaches. Some early work in the area can be found on the 'The Linking Teaching and Research' Web site.[12] This Web site is an outcome of work undertaken by Professor Alan Jenkins working collaboratively with the HEA and higher education sector, to develop, support and research possible links

[12] Linking Teaching and Research Web site: http://www.brookes.ac.uk/genericlink/index.htm!, accessed July 2009

Table 12.3 Academic practice and links between research and teaching

Dimension of academic practice	Pedagogical approach, or form of scholarship (see Table 12.2)	Link between research and teaching	Examples of teaching practice
(1) Active research within a discipline or cluster of disciplines (traditional research-based practice)	(1) Pedagogy of knowledge transmission No obvious link to Boyer's definition of scholarship	(1) The link between teaching and research is the dissemination of research through 'telling'.	(1) Providing information to be learned Testing acquisition and comprehension of facts
(2) Research-based knowledge is reproduced through teaching and learning programmes	(2) Pedagogy of knowledge construction (a) The scholarship of discovery (b) Possibly the scholarship of integration	(2) The link between teaching and research is embedded in the design and practice of the course. Teaching becomes inquiry oriented. Examples of this would be problem-based learning approaches and evidence-based project work.	(2) Requiring students to gather information and critique it Setting a problem to be solved which requires gathering and critiquing information; the formulation of a feasible solution(s) to the problem Review and reflection on the process of problem solving and suggested solution
(3) Pedagogic knowledge (produced through research or experientially), which may or may not have a disciplinary boundary	(3) Research-based pedagogy; the fundamental integration of knowledge and inquiry (a) The scholarship of integration (b) The scholarship of application (c) The scholarship of teaching	(3) Teaching involves the conduct of research. This may involve practitioners, such as higher education teachers, examining their own practice within particular courses or modules. There are overlaps between 2 and 3.	(3) Identifying an area for inquiry within a topic or course of study Defining what needs to be known or understood Designing a process for the inquiry Conducting the inquiry Analysing evidence/data Writing a report which includes reflection and critique of what has been discovered

Practice lies along a continuum and the table characterises positions within the continuum. The examples of teaching practices are not mutually exclusive between teaching and research. The site contains examples of institutional strategies for research-led teaching[13] and practical examples of research-informed teaching.[14]

Though these examples are from health sciences, the Web site includes others from Geography, Earth and Environmental Sciences (GEES),[15] Hospitality Leisure and Sport,[16] and Bioscience and Law.[17] More recent examples of emerging approaches and support material can be found at EvidenceNet.[18] The front page of this Web site describes the rational for linking teaching and research in the following way:

> All undergraduate students in all higher education institutions should experience learning through, and about, research and inquiry. There should be a move away from students as audience to individual academics' research toward students becoming stakeholders in a research community in which their experience of research mirrors that of their lecturers. (EvidenceNet: see Web site link)

Linking teaching and research has become an international issue in higher education (Brew A, 2003). Educational rationales emphasise the improvement in learning experiences offered to students and the importance of the research–teaching nexus to the purpose of higher education. However, care is taken to acknowledge 'disciplinary variations in teaching–research relations'. The nexus is neither naturally occurring nor uniform (Jenkins, Healy, & Zetter, 2007, p. 2). As Jenkins et al. argue,

> We are convinced that re-shaping or 're-inventing' our disciplines and departments in a way that focuses more on the teaching-research nexus can aid student's learning, their pride in their discipline and department, staff morale, and the overall effectiveness of the department and the institution. To repeat earlier cautions, we are convinced from the research evidence and our own experience that these links have to be created. The nexus does not necessarily occur naturally; indeed much of current practice and policy in the UK and internationally threatens the nexus. In creating the link, or rather links, departments and disciplinary groups within them have key roles to play. (ibid., p. 78)

The relationship between research and teaching is indeed *'fluid, involving negotiation, change and development'*, and this has impacts on academic identities. These new-ish forms of practice also involve issues of culture. Armstrong, in Chapter 11, describes the role of ritual in fostering cultural continuity and change. This involves

---

[13] Institutional strategies to link teaching and research may be found at Linking Teaching and Research in the Disciplines: http://www.health.ltsn.ac.uk/projects/collaborative project/kholland, accessed July 2009

[14] Practical examples of research-informed teaching Health Sciences and Practice: http://www.health.ltsn.ac.uk/projects/collaborative projectgdunlop, accessed July 2009 (trouble with access on October 25, 2009)

[15] Geography, Earth and Environmental Sciences (GEES), The GEES Subject Centre http://www.gees.ac.uk/linktr/linktr.htm#projplan, accessed July 2009

[16] The Hospitality Leisure, Sport and Tourism Network: http://www.heacademy.ac.uk/hlst/ourwork, accessed July 2009

[17] The UK Centre for Bioscience: http://www.bioscience.heacademy.ac.uk/resources/ltr/ and law, accessed July 2009

[18] EvidenceNet may be found at the Higher Education Academy: http://www.heacademy.ac.uk/ourwork/research/evidencenet, accessed July 2009

people constructing and reconstructing social realities, examining and expressing core values. Using Turner's (1977) identification of four elements of rituals, Armstrong analyses the adoption of minimally invasive surgery while it was in the early stages of development by community-based surgeons. In doing so, she illuminated the processes of change in professional practice and culture. How might Turner's elements of rituals extend our understanding of how academic practice is, or may be, changing?

1. *Liminality: separation from normal life*. Both the creation of CETLs and strategies to develop a research–teaching nexus linking teaching and research separate these initiatives from the normal activities of the university. In each case the approaches to teaching being developed and promoted are innovatory. They are in a state of liminality; as Armstrong describes, they are betwixt and between.
2. *Transition to a state of spontaneous (anti-structural) marginality*. Once those in CETLs began to contribute to decision-making processes, change career pathways and establish structures to reward and recognise good teaching, they were turning custom and practice upside down. Linking teaching and research in new forms of teaching practice also turned the 'world' upside down by challenging some of the separation of these activities. Time will tell how permanent these shifts will be.
3. *The creation of communitas: equality, authenticity, shared identities*. CETLs have been developing their own sense of team and group identity in the activities they engage in to enhance and develop teaching. In traditional academic fashion, they have represented these in seminars, workshops and conference presentations and located them in the academic community. Similarly, those involved with linking teaching and research have engaged in research, published books, hosted conferences and carved out space in which their practice can be credentialised and become part of academic discourse.
4. *Reintegration into the social order and revitalisation*. Part of the criteria for funding CETLs was the requirement to become embedded in the host university. However, funding for CETLs comes to an end in 2010 and alternative sources of income must be found to sustain them. Some of the people within CETLs are on short-term contracts. A number of these have sought permanent positions in other universities. Currently the extent to which CETLs may become embedded is uncertain. It may be limited to people seeking alternative academic employment, rather than CETLs continuing as distinct entities. These people will bring with them approaches and values from their CETL experiences. Also, those who have been part of the CETL initiative (rather than employed directly within it) might use their CETL experiences to revitalise teaching practice and improve attitudes towards it. Those involved with linking teaching and research may continue to engage in this form of pedagogic practice. While CETLs supported this form of pedagogic practice, support and encouragement for it is independent of CETLs. Though higher education policies may foster a separation of teaching and research through funding and accountability structures, this makes engagement in linking teaching and research challenging rather than impossible.

Following the submission of the national evaluation report, HEFCE decided not to continue funding for the CETL programme. It had been generously funded, and perhaps those who commissioned it had hoped for more. In their self-evaluation reports, many CETLs commented that it was too soon to be able to identify impacts. Their experience of implementing change showed that achieving it involved a more complex process than that which is implicit in the theory of change assumed by the HEFCE design and implementation of the CETL initiative. Structures of reward and recognition, the promotion of excellence in teaching and learning and the assumption that excellent teaching would deliver excellent learning did not sufficiently take into account the issues of context, identity and culture described in this chapter. CETL pleas that more time was needed to determine their success reflect the lived experience of the systemic and cultural dimensions of changing practice.

Though the future of individual CETLs is uncertain, they have shown the potential to shape academic identities, extend practices and seed a culture of teaching and learning that is aspirational and self-confident. The scope and long-term influence of the initiative is difficult to judge at this point. In Chapter 11, Armstrong describes the early stages of sharing innovative practice in minimally invasive surgery. At the time of the study, the extent to which that form of surgical practice would be adopted was unknown. Years later, these practices are now embedded in normal professional work. The innovative learning and teaching practices being shared and developed by CETLs are at a similar early point when the extent to which particular practices are adopted is uncertain. However, trends for particular forms of practice and the re-positioning and enhanced valuing of learning and teaching are apparent.

If CETLs, as vehicles for driving and supporting these practice trends and re-positioning survive, they will need to move from the assumption that teaching is the preserve of academics. Within universities, student learning is supported by a range of people including librarians and learning technologists. It is no longer the preserve of academics. A common way of describing this inter-disciplinary involvement in teaching and learning is '*those who teach or otherwise support learning*'. Enhancing teaching and learning will necessitate understanding this shift and attending to the distributed nature of those with a role to play in student learning. Valuing all those who teach or otherwise support learning would be an appropriate extension of CETL aims. It would also open the possibilities of different kinds of practice, some of which could be more team orientated. This may have further consequences for academic identities and cultures.

Perhaps inevitably, attempts to create change whether in practices or systems involve issues of power. The dominance of research over teaching in higher education has power implications. Views about what counts as research can be understood in Foucault's terms as contestations around power. Claims that some research is 'real research' and questions over the legitimacy of other forms of research are also assertions of the dominance of a particular form of knowledge (Foucault, 1972, 1977). Attempts to link teaching and research involve questioning a status quo, in terms of practice, culture, values and systems. Social forces are contributing to the momentum of rethinking the current relationship between research and practice. In the marketplace of education, student loans create a more discerning client base that includes not just students but also their parents and/or partners. The Internet creates an alternative access to information and knowledge that shakes the authority of individual and institutional expertise. Globally, governments are championing a view that the economy requires 'knowledge workers' and skilled technicians. The challenge for universities is to ensure not only the employability of students but also their satisfaction, not just with their university experience but also with the longer term benefits of their education. How will these aspects of the social contract between universities and society be re-cast? How will these judgements be made and whose view will get to count and count most?

References

Bannister, D., & Fransella, F. (1993). *Inquiring man: The psychology of personal constructs*. London: Routledge

Boyer, E. (1990). Scholarship reconsidered: Priorities for a new century. In G. Rigby (Ed.), *Universities in the twenty-first century: A lecture series*. London: National Commission on Education.

Brew, A. (2003). The future of research and scholarship in academic development. In H. Eggins & R. MacDonald (Eds.), *The scholarship of academic development*. Buckingham: Buckingham SHRE and The Open University Press.

Connell, J. P., & Kubisch, A. C. (1996). *Applying a theories of change approach to the evaluation of comprehensive community initiatives*. New York: The Aspen Institute.

Cooperrider, D. L., & Srivastva, S. (1987). Appreciative inquiry in organisational life. *Research in Organisational Change and Development, 1*, 129–169

Elliott, A. (2008). *Concepts of the self, polity* (pp. 45–50). Cambridge.

Foucault, M. (1972). *The archaeology of knowledge: Power of discourse and discipline*. London: Tavistock

Foucault, M. (1977). *Discipline and punish*. London: Allen Lane

Glaser, B. G., & Strauss, A. L. (1967). *The discovery of grounded theory*. London: Weidenfeld & Nicholas

Garnham, N. (2002). 'Information Society's theory or ideology: A critical perspective on technology, education and employment in the Information Age. In W. H. Dutton & B. D. Loader (Eds.), *Digital academe. The new media and institutions of higher education and learning*. London: Routledge.

Hammond, N. (2007) Preface. In A. Jenkins & M. Healy (Eds.), *Linking teaching and research in disciplines and departments* (p. 3). Retrieved September 10, 2008, from http://www.heacademy.ac.uk/resources

Hughes, M., & Traynor, T. (2000). Reconciling process and outcome in evaluating community initiatives. *Evaluation, 6*(1), 37–49

Jenkins, A., Healy, M., & Zetter, R. (2007). *Linking teaching and research in the disciplines and departments*. Higher Education Academy. Retrieved September 12, 2008, from http://www.heacademy.ac.uk/ourwork/research/teaching

O'Leary, J. (2009). *Higher education in England: Achievements, challenges and prospects, higher education funding council*. Retrieved March 9, 2009, from http://www.hefce.ac.uk/news/hefce/2009/heineng.htm

Quinn-Patton, M. (1996). *Utilization-focussed evaluation*. London: Sage

Saunders, M., Machell, J., Willaims S., Allaway, D., Spencer, A., Ashwin, P., Trowler, P., et al. (2008). *The national formative evaluation of the 2005–2010 CETL programme, Final Report*. http://www.hefce.ac.uk/pubs/rdreports/2008/rd08_08/

Scott, P. (2004). *Knowledge work in a knowledge society: Rethinking the links between university teaching and research.* The Higher Education Academy Learning and Teaching Conference, University of Hertfordshire, July, unpublished paper.

The Future of Higher Education. (2003). cm 5735, HMSO, Norwich. Retrieved accessed March 9, 2009 from http://www.dcsf.gov.uk/hegateway/strategy/hestrategy/teaching.shtml

Turner, V. (1977). Variations on a theme of liminality. In S. Moore & B. Meyerhoff (Eds.) *Secular ritual*. Amsterdam: Van Gorcum

Weiss, C. (1995). Nothing as practical as a good theory: Exploring theory-based evaluation for comprehensive community initiatives. In J. Connell, et al. (Eds.), *New approaches to evaluating community initiatives: Concepts, methods and contexts*. Washington: The Aspen Institute.

Chapter 13
Review and Reflections of Chapters

Anne Mc Kee and Michael Eraut

The link between identity and the lifespan learning of practitioners, professional groups and organisations has provided a lens with which to understand the mutual interactions between the contexts and conditions within which learning takes place, what is being learned and how it is being learned. The external contexts examined include policy, technological innovation, economic factors and a range of national and global trends. Each of these contexts helps shape what the nineteenth-century English essayist William Hazlitt (2008) and twentieth-century historian Asa Briggs (1999) have called 'The Spirit of the Age'. This essentially historical concept offers a way of thinking about the 'time' or period in which we live, what characterises that time and the kind of changes it fosters. Identity and shifts in identity help us understand 'The Spirit of the Age' from a learning perspective. The formation and transformation of identity over the professional lifespan help us explore the relationship between a complex set of changes and their implications for professional practice and professional learning.

13.1 Formal Learning

Part of 'The Spirit of the Age' has involved the valuing and extension of formal learning through higher education and educational accreditation processes. On the one hand the weave of knowledge, understanding, judgement and performance has been subjected to intense scrutiny while demands for accountability seek to assure public confidence about practice and service provision. Then on the other hand economic contexts, evolving practice, client expectations and needs challenge established expectations about what should and could be provided.

A. Mc Kee (✉)
Faculty of Education, Anglia Ruskin University, Chelmsford CM1 1SQ, UK
e-mail: anne.mckee@anglia.ac.uk

A. Mc Kee, M. Eraut (eds.), *Learning Trajectories, Innovation and Identity for Professional Development*, Innovation and Change in Professional Education 7,
DOI 10.1007/978-94-007-1724-4_13, © Springer Science+Business Media B.V. 2012

13.1.1 University Degrees and Their Teachers

The very existence of the professions depends on their qualifications and the quality of their work. Although initial qualifications are not the main focus of this book, the connections between university degrees and professional practice are more complex than university professors and professional bodies are prepared to investigate. The usefulness of formal learning is strongly agreed, but other forms of professional learning are more dependent on broad competencies or local agreements about what we do here. We have used three chapters to describe some of the issues involved.

Solbrekke and Sugrue in Chapter 10 were concerned with the complexity of professional responsibility, its implications for how professionals learn and contemporary approaches to how public accountability is exercised. They offered suggestions for how to reconceptualise professional responsibility and then outlined the implications for universities preparing professionals for practice. Professional ethics and professional responsibility were delegated to the relevant departments, where the knowledge of professional requirements was best known, but other factors also influenced departmental strategies. The psychology students engaged in practical work in laboratories, group work, a six-month internship and a 28-hour mandatory course on professional ethics. The law students were offered a two-day 'mandatory course' in professional ethics, where their attendance was not monitored. Examination of ethical dilemmas took place mainly in the higher education context, where the issues raised depended on the cases lecturers used during teaching. The curriculum was strongly theoretical rather than practice based.

However, within a year after graduation, the authors reported that

> Although they still maintain a moral engagement towards their individual clients, they seem to have been 'caught' in the business of their local communities of work practice and responsibility, to the extent that concern for the larger society tends to be occluded or to 'vanish' entirely. However, this dilemma is not explicitly identified as a problem by the participants. Nevertheless, perhaps they have lurched from being comfortable in theoretical abstract knowledge to finding a 'home' within a practical epistemic. This existential sense is rendered more intense by their neophyte status and inbound trajectory while continuing to negotiate their way into and to reconfigure their identities and comfort with ambiguity within their new community. It may be the case therefore that they are not consciously aware of their changed orientation, or that they do not want to acknowledge such change.

Bebeau and Monson in Chapter 7 explored the relationship between moral reasoning, identity formation and ethical practice aligned to the moral purposes of a profession. In doing so, they explored challenges to the formation of professional identity and the implications of this for how decisions about practice came to be made. They brought evidence from multiple sources to support the proposition that ethically responsible professional practice is linked to the development of a professional identity that 'proceeds along a continuum from self-interest and concreteness of thought to more "other" oriented and abstract ways of reasoning'. The 'other oriented' part of the continuum represents service focused, rather than business focused, approaches to practice. Bebeau and Monson argue that there is an urgent need to examine the foundational elements of professional identity formation, to help professional practitioners and their professions align with societal expectations of the moral purposes of each profession. For example, one key challenge to the formation of an ethically based professional identity was the question "How do professional school students understand professional and societal expectations, and is their conception aligned with their profession's values and expectations?"

Their answer was that, in order to achieve a position where moral reasoning in shaping practice is clearly and persuasively made, one needs a well-designed curriculum and a significant period of time, thus providing a new focus for thinking about the role of identity formation within professional curricula and its implications for professional development over the lifespan. This led to a number of strategies to develop moral reasoning and professional identity. These included

- Engaging students in formative assessments of their identity.
- Providing frequent opportunities for students to articulate and reflect upon who they are and who they are becoming. The context in which such a curriculum is delivered is critical. The alignment of values, content and organisation all contribute to the appropriateness and quality of the learning experiences.
- Providing opportunities for students to learn from and value those professionals who embody other-centred moral maturity. These 'exemplars', however, are more likely to explain than argue, because their professional and moral perspectives are so intertwined that they form part of the same identity. Moral responsibility goes with the job.
- Providing examples of disciplined professionals for students to learn from. This group of mid-career professionals had been referred for ethics instruction by a licensing board. It soon became evident that conceptions of professional responsibility were not part of self-understanding and did not guide decision-making. But 38 of the 41 referrals who completed a specially designed ethics course said that the instruction on professional values was the most inspiring dimension of instruction, and contributed a renewed sense of professionalism. (Bebeau, 2009b)

Mc Kee's chapter, *Academic Identities and Research – Informed Learning and Teaching,* explored how the interpretation and implementation of policy is re-shaping professional and institutional practices in higher education in the UK. This has implications for the relationship between teaching and research. While the more prestigious universities argue that teaching and research are closely related activities, these dimensions of academic practice are commonly treated as separate activities. This makes it more difficult for those who want to do both, because more focused research strategies and larger research teams make it increasingly difficult to link research and teaching activities. Over time, members of university faculties may have to choose between full-time research and full-time teaching, and those who will suffer most will be those in professional schools, whose current professional identities will be very difficult to sustain.

She reports on a recent initiative to enhance learning and teaching in the UK, funded by the government-based Higher Education Academy. Eighty-one Centres of Excellence in Teaching and Learning (CETLs) were established over a five-year period. The theory of change underpinning the initiative assumed that

- Reward and recognition would enable and promote good teaching at individual, institutional and sector levels.
- Excellent teaching would produce excellent learning.
- Recognising individual and institutional excellence in teaching would promote excellence across the sector.

The CETL activities ranged across eight programme objectives, including that of *Raising the profile of teaching excellence across the sector.* The majority were developing new learning and teaching practices and helping to create a positive focus on learning and teaching. A key shift in learning and teaching practice was the widespread encouragement and promotion of pedagogic research and small-scale development projects as a means of enhancing learning and teaching. However, despite a growing acceptance for and uptake in the use of pedagogic research, there was an enduring unease with this form of practice. Underpinning this unease was a tension between pedagogic research and established views about what academic practice should involve, particularly around the relationship between research and teaching and how these activities met in the learning and teaching process. Continuing unease regarding pedagogic research centred round concerns that academics engaged with it might reduce their engagement with research in their own subject.

13.1.2 Continuing Professional Education and Human Resources Development

Formal training also plays an important role in keeping professionals up-to-date or enhancing their repertoires. Eraut in Chapter 2 discusses the two main resources of further training, universities and employers. Continuing Professional Education (CPE), mainly provided by universities and professional bodies, is compulsory for many professions, and Human Resources Development (HRD) provides employer training. Both sources include learning modes other than training; for example keeping up with journals may contribute to CPE requirements and HRD may be valuated by its impact on performance. Their roles and differences are compared through a *learning focus* (including transfer to other contexts), a *performance focus* and a *strategic focus* (for senior managers).

The University of New Mexico's (UNM) ECHO programme is large and still growing. Having started with Hepatitis C Virus (HCV), it is now expanding its range of clinics for other conditions. Its particular strength is the combination of several key innovations:

- The recruitment and training of local healthcare workers
- Specialist visits to community clinics, followed by formal video training and distant communication between local HCV workers and UNM specialists
- The co-management of patients by local practitioners and distant specialists on line
- An expanding number of patients and local providers

Although these innovations were considered from the outset, none of those involved had participated in that kind of work on such a large scale. Thus, project participants learned how to make their ideas work in practice through deliberate practice and shared knowledge construction among UNM experts and local practitioners.

The summative evaluation used a range of methods to gather a wide range of important outcome data from patients, local providers and clinical sites. These included clinical data, patient satisfaction data, weekly observation of clinics; clinical site interviews on the co-management of patients, provider outcomes and self-efficacy; and questionnaires and qualitative comments on self-efficacy, achievement in specific clinical activities, benefits of participation in the ECHO Project and overcoming barriers to care.

The implications of this are that the project learned the following from this experience:

- How specialists can develop expertise in supporting impoverished environments
- How to develop local networks for mutual support and learning
- How primary care professionals can independently screen, manage and treat HCV patients
- How to develop co-management practices at a distance
- How to increase the self-efficacy of new providers

This growth in their collective expertise goes well beyond the project's initial objectives and provides a wealth of potential support for other organisations wanting to develop a similar approach to improving rural healthcare. At a deeper level, the enhanced observation of the local health carers enables them to develop a finer sense of patient variation than is normally available. Transfer of knowledge is not just a matter of recognition, but it also involves the expertise of understanding individual variations.

Armstrong's study of the early years of laparoscopy was a very different innovation. She observed workshops across different regions of the United States, each directed by surgeons who pioneered minimally invasive abdominal surgery. She explains how the surgical workshops helped to build confidence in the potential of laparoscopic surgery. However, the need for scepticism and moral concern about the extent to which laparoscopic surgical practice was trialled and tested was acknowledged. The learning process involved the learning of new skills and a form of ritual socialisation that encouraged shifts in identity from sceptic to early adopter of the new technology. All the trainees saw and discussed videos of community surgeons using the new method, and then did two laparoscopic procedures on animals, and these sessions initiated a great deal of mutual discussion at the cutting edge. However, this was not deemed sufficient preparation for future practice by workshop organisers who encouraged participants to continue to practise with the new technology. Thus, advocacy for the new approach was built alongside the realisation that further development of the skills of individuals and practices in the use of the technology was required. Those who attended the workshops could call upon workshop leaders and other participants for help and support when they returned to practice, sharing and disseminating practice-based learning. Some workshop participants went on to develop their own local networks of early adopters.

Finally, Sharu's research into the training provision for Advanced Nurse Practitioners (ANPs) showed that changing role and professional identity within small organisations requires high levels of personal agency. Most ANPs are in an isolated professional situation with few peers within their clinical settings in primary care and little voice within the nursing profession in general. Such isolation and the relative newness of the role have implications for understanding what the role involves and how learning in the workplace may be supported. Sharu found that individual ANPs played significant roles in managing and pursuing their own learning within the workplace. This usually involved negotiating sufficient facilitator support, clarifying the scope and boundaries of their new role and developing new knowledge and skills. The ability to engage in self-directed learning and to be professionally resilient is much needed by these emerging specialist nurses. Hence, their lack of further support from CPE was eventually improved by the author founding a small company to provide the specific needs of isolated ANPs.

13.2 Informal Learning

Eraut's abstract for Chapter 2 starts with his research on informal learning and the factors that affect it, in particular,

1. The roles of informal learning, personal agency and teamwork in most workplaces
2. The decisions, processes and activities that encourage or ignore learning
3. The roles of supervisors and managers in supporting learning through creating affordances for both personal and collective learning

His evidence on the early and mid-career learning in business/accountancy, engineering and nursing showed that, with appropriate methodology, the proportion of informal learning events was at least 80%, but not much of this was recognised because (1) it was seen as a taken-for-granted aspect of their work and (2) learning was closely linked to formal experiences. However, describing examples from a range of eight specific learning contexts enabled participants to recognise these learning events. Four of these involved working with other people: *participation in group processes, working alongside others, consultation and working with client.* The other four could include working with others, but did not necessarily require it: *tackling challenging tasks and roles, problem solving, trying things out and consolidating, extending and refining skills.* Most participants saw themselves as working with other people, but did not describe themselves as members of teams.

The learning factors were summarised by one triangle: *challenge and value of the work, feedback and support* and *confidence and commitment (personal agency).*

Then contextual factors were summarised by a second triangle: *allocation and structuring of work*, *encounters and relationships with people at work* and *individual participation and expectations of their performance and progress*. Changing these factors can significantly increase or decrease the quality and quantity of informal learning. So the work processes and activities that lead to learning are strongly influenced by the immediate supervisors' and/or managers' own interpretations of appropriate working practices. Personal agency and good relationships with seniors and colleagues also provide the confidence to take the initiative.

Support and feedback are critically important for learning, retention and commitment. *Feedback* is most effective within the context of good working relationships, and the rapid feedback essential for short-term learning is best provided by people on the spot. Hence, it is important for managers to develop a positive learning culture of mutual support both among individuals and within and across work groups. More feedback on *progress*, *strengths and weaknesses*, and *meeting organisational expectations* is also needed, and appraisal needs to be carefully prepared both for these performance issues and for discussing future learning trajectories and aspirations. Good short-term feedback on performance was often accompanied by an almost total absence of strategic feedback, giving even the most confident workers an unnecessary sense of uncertainty and lowering their commitment to their current employers. Once again there seems to be a formal pattern that ignores the significance of informal knowledge, and Eraut suggests how the situation might be improved through the development and appraisal of managers.

Saggers and Saroyan are specialists in management learning, who also argue that managers should be giving more attention to the learning of those they manage. Their study is more tightly designed than the others in order to test three related hypotheses about employees preferring managers who give time to enhancing their employees' learning. The sample covered eight organisations and included many different sectors, so they chose to use an intervention study to provide a common reference for all the employees in the sample. Their one-day workshop for the managers of this sample was a very novel way of emphasising the managers' teaching role and giving them a situational leadership model that they could pass on to their employees, and they provided some evidence for their hypothesis that managers who taught their employees would (1) be viewed relatively more productive than those who did not teach and (2) generate higher levels of satisfaction in those that reported to them, and this was reassuring. However, their very broad definition of managerial teaching made it difficult to treat it as a single variable.

People who work together in difficult circumstances tend to develop a sense of mutual responsibility, and this is particularly true of the military. Leadership development in combat requires self-awareness and resilience, as well as decision-making, judgement and willingness to innovate. Allen and Kayes (Chapter 5) have summarised as much they can, using both Kolb's approach to reflection and Klein's and Weick's understanding of rapidly changing circumstances. They also acknowledge how powerfully emotions are felt and held in these situations and the role of this in developing *compassionate leadership* and *ethical practice* when it could be so easy to slide into an abuse of power. Allen and Kayes also found that experienced company commanders acquired a *profound sense of responsibility*, but can this learning process be accelerated? This may depend on how these respondents develop their subordinates and brief their own leaders, as well as those with formal responsibility for training them. Beyond that, this vivid account would be welcomed by civilians who work in the aftermath of natural disasters or the threat of infectious diseases.

Most ANPs (Chapter 9) have a very different problem to address: their role and qualification are new to most doctors, so they have to be proactive when approaching doctors for support and access to patients. The success of ANPs' learning trajectories depends on getting doctors to help them. First, they need to learn from willing doctors, and second, they have to be accepted by them as fit to undertake jobs previously only done by doctors. Although most doctors are over-stretched, they may still be reluctant to take advantage of the ANP's contribution to their group. The culture of primary care doctors is far from managerial, so engagement with some doctors can be difficult, even though finding opportunities to help reduce a doctor's load is important. Those doctors, who give some priority to developing this new support role, may be prepared to mediate ANP support to their colleagues. Managers are not very strong in primary care contexts. But some have given a leading role to a colleague, or appointed a higher level administrator. These people have a good overview of the practice, and, when trusted by their colleagues, they can foster the development of ANPs. Otherwise, the new ANPs have to explain themselves to patients and to tell the receptionists what patients to send to them, once a new level of competence has been informally agreed. Progress from starting to become an ANP to being settled in that role can be seen as a series of mini-learning trajectories, and this concept is embedded in many models of ANP development.

13.3 Errors, Mistakes and Reflective Practices

The issue of errors or mistakes was prominent in three chapters, each providing a very different perspective. The University of Washington project on disclosing errors was comparatively small, but involved a significant aspect of management development. Its use of simulation did not remove the emotions, but helped to make them easier for the participants to gradually accept. The project brought three innovative practices to the difficult and delicate problem of disclosing clinical errors to patients, a responsibility which many professionals try to avoid in spite of the disadvantages for all those concerned of failing to disclose. These were as follows:

- Treating such errors and their disclosure as a team responsibility was intended to avoid scapegoats by sharing this difficult 'burden', but it also brought in a wider range of expertise by including nurses, whose experience of patient communication might lead to improved cross-professional communication and practices that might reduce the risk of the error being repeated.

- Using *actors* rather than clinicians encouraged straight talking and appropriate attention to the patients' voice.
- Training *risk managers* as coaches for disclosure teams helped to connect clinicians with managers in a common purpose, but they needed to teach the managers to perform differently from their accustomed managerial roles because lecturing would not have been appropriate in this context. Targeted feedback in realistic settings enhances the communication skills needed for team disclosure.

Given the low occurrence of errors for any one doctor and the advantages of being prepared before doctors got involved in a major error, this combination of treating errors as team events, simulations with actor patients and using trained coaches for disclosure teams made good sense. It appears to be an important innovation, albeit at an early stage.

This project also brings ethical principles to the fore. In addition to the honesty, mutual trust and responsibility between individuals, these new practices include the need

- To support others and be supported by others
- To recognise the emotional feelings of all those concerned
- To sustain a blame-free approach to the disclosure of errors

Mamede, Rikers and Schmidt argue that medical errors constitute a significant problem that should not be ignored. They critique aspects of medical decision-making that are currently understood, identifying their limitations. For example, medical heuristics draw upon personal theories and medical traditions which may not always be helpful. They use both a literature review on reflection and reflective practice, and their own empirical work, to challenge views that clinical decision-making involves only the objective application of established medical knowledge. Their exploration of the diversity and complexity of reflective practice led them to challenge a tendency among some practitioners to adopt oversimplified views of what reflective practice is and how it might be used to improve other work in this area. This led to an empirical study that identified five reflective practice behaviours, attitudes and reasoning processes which, they suggest, should be incorporated into the diagnostic practices of new and experienced clinicians:

(1) *Deliberative induction*: a tendency to search for alternative explanations
(2) *Deliberative deduction*: a tendency to explore consequences of alternative explanations
(3) *Synthesize*: a willingness to test predictions
(4) *Openness*: an attitude to reflection that enables individuals to better tolerate uncertainty
(5) *Meta-reasoning*: a capability to think about one's personal thinking processes and critically review conclusions, assumptions and beliefs.

In conclusion, they call for further exploration of educational strategies to enhance reflective approaches in clinical reasoning.

Throughout this book, self-reflection, case-based learning, communities of practice and pedagogic research are deployed to learn from experience and inform future practice. Reflective practices, particularly when they are based on systematic investigation and review, offer the possibility of supporting and reasserting professional agency. They provide approaches to learning that enable professionals to identify and articulate their learning in evidence-based ways. In so doing, learning shifts from the opinion of individual practitioners to reflective learning with an evidence base. Amid centralised systems of accountability and stakeholder views of practice, research-oriented reflective practices articulate, legitimate and reward professional learning in ways that are publicly accountable.

13.4 The Emotional Dimension

Careful reading shows that all our chapters have an emotional dimension, and many different kinds of emotion are portrayed. Chapter 2 gives considerable space to *learning contexts* and the factors that affect them, showing how both personal approaches and complex structures can interact. At one level it discusses *individual experiences*; at another level those who *share, lead* and/or *manage*. People are involved in their own work and have *relationships with significant other workers*. Both are likely to have some emotional effect, whether it comes from common daily activities, difficult clients or other professional colleagues. The chapter starts with groups of professional workers, what they do, how they learn, where they meet and for what purpose. This then raises questions about where their work comes from, the balance between their clients, colleagues and managers and how often they meet. The *allocation of work* is also critical for most professional workers. Is their normal workload too much, too simple or too difficult? Is there sufficient variety? Are they given sufficient support to tackle new problems? Three critical factors that are given far too little attention are as follows:

- Clear communications that respect their audiences
- Appropriately challenging work and learning trajectories that give workers a sense of ongoing progress
- Feedback that is both honest and forward looking, and covers relationships with other workers (see Section 13.2 above)

The second part of Chapter 2 discusses practices used to support learning at higher levels and helps to show how much the formal practices and the emotional dimension are always intertwined. To save space, a reduced version of the right column of Table 2.1 is presented in Table 13.1, which focuses on examples that hinder workplace learning.

Table 13.1 What hinders workplace learning?

Individual-level factors	**Team level factors**
Unnecessarily restrictive job design	Work issues not discussed with others
Excessive work pressure and stress	Unsupportive or threatening relationships, or social isolation at work
Line management	**Approach to learning and development**
Line managers who are defensive or unwilling to resolve work issues in a constructive way	Seeing on-the-job learning as not needing any resource or time
Lack of time and attention on giving employees meta-skills and confidence in learning	'Courses' seen as the main or only means of learning
Line managers unwilling to delegate	Learning interventions unrelated to current or future work needs
Leaving managers to develop their staff even if they lack the skills or motivation to do it	Overly mechanistic or bureaucratic approaches to competence, assessment and documentation of learning
Organisational context, processes and leadership behaviour	
Promotion and reward mechanisms which emphasise the short-term and individual performance at the expense of investing in medium-term or collective performance	
Political and senior management context in which people avoid change to protect their job security and/or power	

Chapters 3 and 5 all show very positive approaches to helping people learn in difficult contexts, and this enables the positive half of Chapter 2, Table 2.1, to be used (Table 13.2). Project ECHO (Chapter 3) is one of the largest single ventures in this book and is still expanding its medical work in the least supported parts of New Mexico. Their team upgrades many keen but less-qualified healthcare workers by a combination of formal training sessions, distance learning and supported deliberative practice with patients. The key message is that these ECHO pathways can develop excellent heath workers nearer to their patients, without getting standard higher education training separated from their additional new work. This is done by the enthusiasm of the new workers, the quality of those that train them and the communal commitment to the project. The emotive dimension is very strong indeed.

Allen and Kayes's research (Chapter 5) on the leadership of company commanders in the Iraq War opens up crucial aspects of their practice that are rarely discussed in leadership research. This time it is the professionals who are, literally, in danger of death during their work in Iraq, and their company commanders were the informants of visiting researchers. Handling the emotional dimension in a war zone is a huge challenge, and the military have to think on their feet in situations of very high uncertainty and unpredictability about their enemy and what

Table 13.2 What helps workplace learning?

Individual-level factors	**Team-level factors**
Appropriate degree of challenge in work Frequent and constructive feedback on job performance Time to learn at work, especially through talking to others	Supportive relationships with others, based on mutual respect Frequent informal discussions of work with colleagues Formal team processes (e.g. team meetings, project reviews) which include discussion of skills and learning Attention to learning opportunities when allocating and designing work processes
Line management	**Approach to learning and development**
Clear role for managers and experienced workers in supporting learning of others Attention by managers to emotional aspects of work Tolerance of diversity and willingness to consider alternative suggestions Selecting line managers with an interest in, and aptitude for, developing others	Employees motivated and supported to take responsibility for their own learning Accessible learning advisers for both managers and employees and a flexible capacity to design bespoke learning interventions and work with teams Learning interventions linked closely to the work context
Organisational context, processes and leadership	
Performance systems which pay attention to knowledge sharing Clear organisational values underpinning work and personal behaviour Behaviour at the top which discusses problems and issues and develops other people Encouragement of networking and development of social capital outside the immediate workplace	

they might do next. What cannot be avoided is the strong emotions of both leader and led, and one consequence is that *errors* are often attributed to a failure to reflect before reacting to bad news. However, this combination of uncertainty and danger prompted most commanders to become more reflective. Thus, the dominant themes in Allen and Kayes's research are the need for *reflection* on chaotic, complex, volatile and ambiguous experiences and the willingness to confront one's deeply held assumptions when almost overcome by intense affect, embodied feedback and compassion.

Robins et al.'s (Chapter 4) project at the University of Washington also engages with possibly dangerous problems when dealing with medical errors. Hospitals now stand to lose high damages and gain bad reputations when failing to disclose errors. Disclosure is necessary and can no longer be ignored. Robins's team has been both careful and thoughtful in their approach, and it is becoming a promising innovation. We return to it here because the emotional aspects of the problem are significant for all those involved and must be supported and understood. Their training approach insisted on (1) making the problem team based rather than person based, (2) asking all team members to give their view and (3) allowing time for all team members to gradually come to terms with disclosure. Thus,

> *The actors judged how truthful, forthright, apologetic, or empathetic they perceived the team's communication to be and adjusted their reactions accordingly to simulate more realistic interactions.* For example, if during a disclosure a team failed to explicitly state that they had made an error, the actor/standardized patient would repeatedly ask 'how could this have happened' until the team explicitly stated that they had made an error and provided a truthful accounting of how it occurred (based on the facts of the simulation scenario). Or, if the team didn't offer an early explicit apology the standardized patient was instructed to 'turn up the emotional heat' until the team offered an apology. Conversely, when a team was forthright about having made an error and then effectively offered an upfront, explicit apology, the actor was instructed to demonstrate more understanding towards the team.

Bebeau and Monson (Chapter 7) discuss changes in the social reasoning of college students that suggest an increase in personal interest reasoning at the expense of moral judgement and ethical outcomes. Their analysis of Minnesota senior dental students' reflective essays found that

> 44 percent of the 91 students perceived professional self-regulation and professional monitoring to be the hardest responsibilities to fulfil, whereas achieving the knowledge of the profession and meeting responsibilities for lifelong learning were considered easiest. Putting patients' interests before the self and serving the underserved were considered difficult, but not as difficult as questioning a superior about a judgment that seemed questionable or admitting an error in one's own judgment. Our curriculum studies (Bebeau & Monson, 2008; You, 2007), reveal that even when professional expectations about self-regulation are well understood, reluctance to report instances of misconduct comes both from uncertainty about how to do so and from the negative reactions of colleagues that often follow such actions.

When ethical options are opposed by socialisation, the professions and universities need to develop a strong response. The current emotional response of peer groups should not be taken for granted. However, some professions give significant time to ethical issues, while others hardly mention it. Although psychology gives more time than law, its ethical perspectives relate to idealised practices where psychologists have time to follow the book and rarely meet incompatible rules or clients. Solbrekke and Sugrue (Chapter 10 and Section 13.6 below) have written the only chapter in which the non-professional world of families and friends are discussed, in spite of their importance for understanding clients and dealing more holistically with their own emotional world.

Sharu's description of the UK beginning of ANPs in Chapter 9 can be usefully compared and contrasted with the upgrading of healthcare workers in the ECHO Project (Chapter 3). Both groups were created to strengthen the available healthcare workforce but started in very different ways. The ANPs started as excellent nurses with good reputations and were seen as capable of doing more complex and independent work. The ECHO workers were less qualified and less confident, but were encouraged by the UNM group to include the addition of Hepatitis C to their current loads and learn on the job with the support of visits and distant training. The ECHO Project helped and encouraged them and gave them a great deal of support, whereas many ANPs had to struggle to get any support beyond the formal university teaching for their advanced degree. Both groups needed emotional support, but only the ECHO group and some of the UK primary care doctors provided it. The other ANPs had to rely on their own capabilities. Another interesting question is whether this same kind of transition could help with the decreasing number of community doctors in most wealthy countries.

There is also an interesting parallel with the community surgeons in the United States taking on laparoscopic work.[1] This change was also very challenging, and they had very little local support, only the training and continuing contact of the early pioneers. Many of them felt that they had to make this change or go out of business, and their eventual success showed once again the potential of people to upgrade their work above their wildest dreams. These very challenging transitions require a strong emotional resilience, which helps them to mould their new identities.

13.5 Identity, Transition and the Management of Change

This book concludes with a complex discussion that cannot easily be separated. People's identities go well beyond their working life, but their work is still a significant part of it. Changes in people who work with you can be as important as changes in your work, and this is often most apparent when new changes are required. The management of change is often the least effective of all working practices, for several reasons: insufficient consultation and preparation, failure to consider the emotional impact, over-planning the change being introduced and under-planning the need for adjustments or revisions to the original plan, and an inappropriate balance between formal information and learning new practices.

The innovations described in this book can be explored in terms of new knowledge, new practices and new roles. These words carry separate meanings but also overlap. Knowledge gives stronger attention to reading, discussing and talking; new practices give more attention to doing, sharing and checking; new roles give more attention to interacting, supporting and managing. Eraut (in Chapter 2) argues that the way people think about knowledge is a critical feature in any change, even though it may not be recognised by those present.

> Given these difficulties, many people have recognized that it is more appropriate to treat knowledge management as a process for sharing knowledge rather then codifying it. These will be easier to develop if the groups are small, and someone with training in knowledge elicitation is present. Improving communication also depends on good relationships, and may be improved by using mediating artefacts as foci for conversations. The knowledge

[1] This work was started in the US by community surgeons, not by hospitals

to be shared is not only in the text and/or pictures but in the conversations around them; and that is where a facilitator, familiar with the artefacts, can be most helpful. The artefacts themselves can be narrative accounts of cases, customers and critical incidents or prototype diagrams or knowledge maps that invite detailed additions from practical experience and adaptation to fit them.

Another source of new practice is the *transfer of new knowledge* from one context to another. This may either come with a newcomer or be imported as an innovation. In either case being accepted and resituated in a new context will be greatly helped by the support of a team or network, which can bring several minds to bear on the transition problem as well as providing those involved with emotional support during the more difficult problem-solving activities. To adopt an innovation is not just a decision but a significant learning process for all concerned, in which the mutual interaction of the knowledge accompanying and embedded in the innovation and the explicit and tacit knowledge embedded in the context of adoption creates yet newer knowledge The failure to recognise the need for innovations to be resituated by creating new local knowledge, and the learning and time this requires, is responsible for the failure of the majority of potentially beneficial innovations and the late detection of inappropriate innovations.

Project ECHO's local healthcare workers were able to learn from visiting experts, distance learning and guided on-the-job practice, and then gradually acquired expertise in working with Hepatitis C. Then they began to contribute their own understandings about the patients they looked after, got to know their patients and their background, and were able to take on a new role as a co-manager with distant staff at UNM. The Washington group involved less people but engaged with equally challenging work in a very private setting. Their novel approach to the problem of medical errors not being disclosed was to use actor patients and train risk managers as coaches, but the key was in their ability to enable doctors and nurses who worked together to see themselves as teams and to brief the actors and coaches to focus on doctors' and nurses' gradual entry into seeing how they could manage this threatening problem together.

Chapters 5 and 6 were located in very different contexts. Allen and Kayes had to handle an unavoidably messy context, while Saggers and Saroyan were more orderly. Both were researchers from outside the organisation under study. Allen's careful interviewing and strong attention to theories of reflective practice enabled him to develop a picture that described his sample of company commanders in Iraq. Three of his respondents were used for member checking when they returned to the United States and felt that the analysis reflected their experiences. 'Two of the commanders (unsolicited) expressed the sense that as they were reading they were reading a language to describe their experiences—a language that they did not have before. Concepts that were previously implicit were made explicit for them in the text. Furthermore, all three communicated that this study should be made available to the profession as a means to prepare the next generation of leaders for the rigors of combat'.

Saggers and Saroyan argue that leadership and management are two overlapping, interdependent and complementary processes. They succeeded in finding a large and representative group of 20 managers and 43 employees and showed that 'both employees' satisfaction with their managers, and their perceptions of their manager's relative productivity, were positively correlated with the time managers devoted to teaching' their subordinates. 'Moreover those managers, whose employees said they had been "taught" the lessons of the leadership workshop by their managers, were seen by their employees to be more effective'. This supported the theory of situational leadership, even though the managers' study day of lessons was very dense.

Bebeau and Monson see leadership as linked with identity formation and note that advanced levels of leadership can develop only after sufficient experience has been understood. Hence this crucial stage, if reached, will develop in practice settings where few, if any, moral exemplars may be available to give ethical support to new arrivals.

Mamede, Rikers and Schmidt present evidence that much professional work is developed holistically through recognition of previous experiences. But, while their approach works quickly and effectively in simple cases, it can lead to serious mistakes in more complex cases, which practitioners do not necessarily recognise. The practical problem is that of convincing all doctors that they need to reflect on their diagnosis before they assume that they have got it right. It is also likely that, as the average age grows older, the diagnosis is more likely to have further conditions but you do have more time to check it out. When dealing with complexity, both using reflective practices and getting second opinions from appropriate colleagues should become standard practice.

Sharu (an ANP) and Armstrong (an anthropologist) both researched how new practices in community healthcare involved the creation of new professional identities within the workplace and the profession. A key difference was that Armstrong was studying community surgeons who were self-employed, while Sharu's mid-career nurses, now qualified to do more challenging, independent work, were dependent on their employer doctors giving them more challenging work and supporting them in learning to become fully competent in their new role. Thus, Armstrong described where and how learning associated with new medical practices was provided and the social processes at work that created space for change to take root, and later become embedded. Another key difference was that the surgeons felt forced to adopt the new technology in order to stay in business, while the nurses felt that the new ANP role would give them the more independent and challenging role they had always wanted.

Sharu's examination of the development of an expanded nursing role, the ANP, shows that nurses were learning an increasing range of skills and extending their knowledge base. These practitioners were self-directed and autonomous learners, recognising and responding to urgent cases, conducting independent diagnosis, developing sound management plans, referring and becoming more time efficient. They were developing these skills at a time when there was little understanding of what the role involved and when there was only a cautious valuing of that role. There were few established professional support networks within which to share practice and offer professional encouragement. These pioneering ANPs were beginning to form support networks for themselves and to promote their role. Sharu explained why ANPs were needed to meet the patient demand for services and a wider range of providers in primary care settings. Thus, their role was clearly aligned to societal expectations, thus responding to the moral purposes of their own profession.

However, not all community doctors wanted more independent nurses, and some found it difficult to give them the support they needed in their first year after qualification in their new role. Currently, high levels of personal agency are necessary for ANPs in the UK to define and negotiate changes in their practice, so Sharu also identifies a need for better recognition from the medical and nursing professions to value and support these fledglings.

Solbrekke and Sugrue report that the law and psychology students saw themselves as being academically trained experts within particular knowledge bases. The undergraduate courses they followed had less emphasis upon the ethical and moral dimensions of practice than knowledge expertise, particularly for the law students. The psychologists tended to see themselves as academically trained experts, the lawyers as experts resolving legal questions according to the law. In the first year of practice, the complexity of professional responsibility becomes evident for both groups. Many felt overwhelmed as they tried to balance the competing demands of their clients, their professional businesses and their personal needs. Each group had to reach negotiated compromises between their personal and professional ethics, values and commitments, for which they felt unprepared.

Their chapter also made a very important point.

> *Many of the participants in the study are at the stage of having children. Hence, due to family commitments, they balance the interests of family and work. After six years of study, the chance to define boundaries between their work and private spheres appears to be as important to them as the immediate pursuit of ongoing professional development. The possibility to work regular hours and not be compelled to study in the evenings propels them towards what they see as a legitimate negotiated compromise of the 'quality' of work. Most of them do their jobs as well as the time available permits while also attending to families and/or friends... Such priorities do not necessarily mean that these novice professionals do not take their professional responsibilities seriously. Rather, it suggests that it is necessary to understand professional responsibility in light of all the relationships that exist for a person, ...* based on reasonable expectations for individual behaviour. (May in Chapter 10)

In summary, professional identity, formation and change are central to professional learning over the lifespan. Changes in practice evoke changes in identity and visa versa. Bebeau and Monson argue that 'The professional and the moral are so intertwined that they form part of the same identity. Moral exemplars are incapable of seeing their work in any other way'.

Designing and implementing change in professional practice is a highly complex endeavour. This book has addressed dimensions of that process that are either not sufficiently examined or not taken into account.

As Mc Kee's chapter illustrates, realising sector-wide changes in professional practice involves a sophisticated programmatic approach that takes into account national and international policy directions, the dynamics of organisational change, professional and organisational identities and contested views of feasible timescales for complex change. The longer term impact of the CETL programme is uncertain. It may have catalysed change or provided learning about how to design and implement wide-scale change. Learning how to change is an enduring challenge that is context sensitive, as this book has explored.

Index

A. Mc Kee, M. Eraut (eds.), *Learning Trajectories, Innovation and Identity for Professional Development*, Innovation and Change in Professional Education 7,
DOI 10.1007/978-94-007-1724-4, © Springer Science+Business Media B.V. 2012

MIX
Papier aus verantwortungsvollen Quellen
Paper from responsible sources
FSC® C105338

If you have any concerns about our products,
you can contact us on
ProductSafety@springernature.com

In case Publisher is established outside the EU,
the EU authorized representative is:
Springer Nature Customer Service Center GmbH
Europaplatz 3, 69115 Heidelberg, Germany

Printed by Libri Plureos GmbH
in Hamburg, Germany